On the Way to Self

On the Way to Self

EGO AND EARLY OEDIPAL DEVELOPMENT

Johanna Krout Tabin

COLUMBIA UNIVERSITY PRESS   New York   1985

Columbia University Press
New York   Guildford, Surrey
Copyright © 1985 Johanna Krout Tabin
All rights reserved
Printed in the United States of America

Clothbound editions of Columbia University Press Books are
Smyth-sewn and printed on permanent and durable acid-free paper.

Library of Congress Cataloging in Publication Data

Tabin, Johanna Krout.
   On the way to self.

   Bibliography: p.
   Includes indexes.
   1. Anorexia nervosa—Etiology.   2. Personality in
children.   3. Psychoanalysis.   4. Ego (Psychology)
5. Oedipus complex.   6. Electra complex.   7. Self.
I. Title.   [DNLM: 1. Anorexia Nervosa—etiology.
2. Anorexia Nervosa—psychology.   3. Ego—in infancy
& childhood.   4. Personality Development.   5. Psychoanalytic Theory—in infancy & childhood.
WS 105.5.S3.T113o]
RC552.A5T33   1984   150.19′5   84-15558
ISBN 0-231-05944-2 (alk. paper)

47,838

To My Father
Maurice H. Krout
Mentor and Friend

Contents

Acknowledgments

Most authors express thanks to several colleagues and friends whose thought, judgment, and skills contributed to the completion of a book. I, too, am grateful for great help, as I mention on these pages. However, I must make particularly clear the extraordinary collaboration that my son, biologist Clifford James Tabin, brought to the development of the theory that is this book's subject and to its form as it is presented here. From the time when I first had a glimmer of the theory, his probing questions pushed my thinking. His own insights substantially furthered the growing theory. Indeed, when I thought only in terms of a set of conditions that might be universal among toddler girls, it was he who recognized that there must be a counterpart set that affects the development of toddler boys. He further conceived of the diagrams which make the theory explicit. The eventual book would not have taken shape if he had not several times stopped his own work to help to bring it about. Whatever satisfaction the reader may have from thought stimulated by this book will be derived in a large measure from his efforts.

I am very grateful to several others who gave of their valuable time to reading the manuscript at various stages of its development, always with useful suggestions for its improvement. Foremost was Bruno Bettelheim, whose encouragement was sustaining. Dale Stern, Albert Boxerman, Marjorie Flarsheim, Monna Lighte, Konstanz Robertson-Rose, Myril Landsman, Irving Leiden, Jean Anderson, Lawrence Knobel and Annabelle Levitan contributed much, each in a special way. I am also indebted to Anna Freud for general comment. Editorial assistance came from Lance Knobel at an early stage and later with particularly helpful ideas, from Edward Hundert.

In turn, Marlys Jejorian, Yamima Osher, and Elissa Freud by application of their research skills gave me access to libraries I could not otherwise have reached in so adequate a way. The preparation of this manuscript was safe in the hands of Fern Erickson, whose patience, flexibility, and thoughtfulness matched her amazing ability to follow my handwritten mazes.

I am obviously fortunate in family and friends. My mother, Sara Krout, has given me unfailing support and enthusiasm for this project, as in any other I have undertaken. I recall with deep appreciation how my son, Geoffrey Craig Tabin, managed to give me precious emotional backing even from faraway places. I could always count on him for it throughout the years.

To my husband, Julius Tabin, my gratitude is incalculable. His tolerance for household clutter of paper, books, and journals over so many years is symbolic of his constant wish for me to do what is important to me. His love and understanding have been as necessary to this book as to my happiness in all else in my life.

Introduction

This book attempts a single, coherent model of the many complex aspects of early child development, clarifying the process of healthy ego development and explaining certain gender-related pathologies such as anorexia nervosa. Such understanding comes only from fresh recognition of the interrelationships between the many tasks and conflicts a young child faces. I invite the reader to explore with me the reasons why this should be so.

Before embarking on our journey in earnest, I offer a brief summary of the ideas to be presented. These are given without justification to give some indication of where we are going and the general plan as we proceed.

Our focus will be on a child's second year of life. By that age many new capacities develop, each of which facilitates a greater exploration and understanding of the world and therefore the child's own place in it. Some of these newly acquired capabilities are neurologically based: the development of language and with it the ability for categorical thought (e.g., good and bad), the ability to hold constructs in the mind (object permanence), and a sense of time. Other simultaneously developing capabilities are of muscular origin: growth of locomotor potential and sphincter control. The psychological growth of the child reaches a stage (affected in timing by the above-mentioned physical developments) when it begins identifying itself as an individual. As part of its self-identification, the infant is becoming aware of genital sensations, enabling it to develop a gender identity. These processes occur in conjunction with a key shift in emphasis from oral to anal concerns.

From the standpoint of adults trying to understand personality development, one or another of these factors might at various times be considered of primary importance. Indeed, each one's effect on personality development is so profound that it has been treated in some psychological theory as a basic organizing principle for defining developmental stages and for understanding pathologies. Yet these factors occur together, forcing upon the toddler a tremendous psychological challenge. The child must create an integrated self-concept while dealing with the interpersonal significance of becoming autonomous.

The array of factors facing the infant are not independent entities in its great task. The infant does not arrange priorities among the many factors that confront it. They exist, rather, as parts of a whole that the child must sort out and from which it must make sense. Only by following this process do we gain real understanding of the personality traits arising during the second year of life, enabling us to understand both normal development and disorders that result from unsettled conflicts and arrested development at that stage.

Concentration on a single key element, even one as basic as separation/individuation, neglects the full magnitude of the task the child at this age faces. Cataloging all of the elements is not enough either. There is need for a unified theoretical framework encompassing the full set of major elements the child must put together for itself. This book is an attempt to work toward such a framework by adding to previous such efforts a recognition of the "primary oedipal phase."

The primary oedipal phase refers to a period of ego organization when gender identity, the process of separation/individuation, and the advent of categorical thinking (via development of language) all occur at one time. This simultaneity leads to anxieties comparable to those of the later "classical" oedipal complex, but on a more primitive level, at which such anxieties are incorporated into the newly developing sense of self-identity.

In terms of the developmental timetable of an individual child, the primary oedipal phase begins during the earliest days of separation/individuation, as the child shifts from the oral phase into the anal phase. It continues until the first ego-organization is consolidated, usually by the age of three years. Typically the child then enters a relatively comfortable period for about a year until the storminess of the classical oedipal phase becomes paramount.

In the course of this book I refer to gender identity as the core of the developing ego. I do not mean to imply that gender identification is the most basic part of ego development for, as stated above, all of the tasks the two-year-old faces in self-determination are interrelated at the most fundamental level. Rather, I use the word *core* to convey two ideas. First, the concept of gender is an important organizing principle for the child in the process of self-identification; and second, gender identity is a key aspect of ego, which is formulated in relation to the intense conflicts arising at this stage. Thus gender identity is involved, too, in resolution of psychological conflicts that arise later in personality development. Moreover, pathologies resulting from failure to deal adequately with any of the two-year-old's challenges (and the conflicts they entail) carry with them a range of interrelated symptoms invariably including gender or sexually related problems.

Until now I have merely stated that conflicts arise in the process of ego formation. Figure 1 shows how these naturally occur. In this simplified diagram the dynamic process of ego formation comes from three accomplishments: (1) awareness of sexual feelings as part of the body; (2) gender-based self-patterning; and (3) separation/individuation and autonomy/dependency. As the sense of self develops in this way, the child's ability to work increases on each of these tasks. At the same time, the development of the ego means, in part, the growth of the concept of gender identity. This in turn is critical for gender-based self-patterning and for the further handling of awareness of sexual feelings.

As can be seen in figure 1, conflicts arise for the child in three interconnected ways. This complex of conflicts is of two different forms depending on the sex of the child. The little girl finds conflict in the fact that ego formation is much based on both patterning by gender and separation from mother. With ego growth, identification with her mother is in direct contradiction to her need for individuality. Second, the little girl's awareness of her sexual excitement with her father makes her feel a rival of the mother, from whom she is still attempting to separate. The more she gains autonomy, the clearer her ego formation and her gender identity and, therefore, also the greater her ability to sense her sexual feelings for father. The girl, sensitive to her mother, has a final source of conflict within the separation/individuation process itself: the comforts of dependency versus the self-actualization of autonomy.

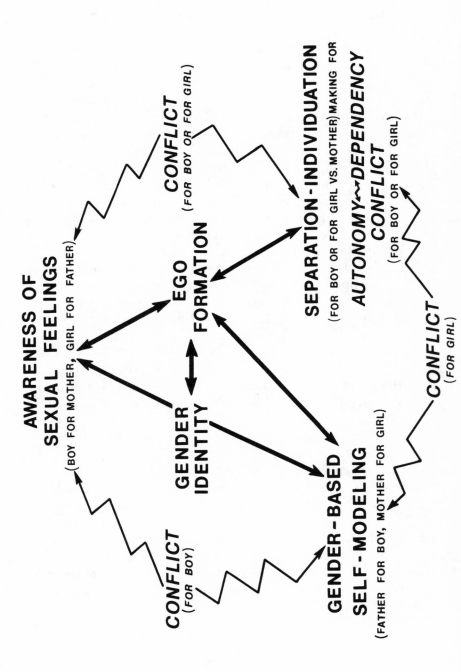

Figure 1. Interrelationships between various tasks and conflicts faced simultaneously by a young child.

The little boy also has three interrelated areas of conflict in ego formation. The boy experiences sexual feelings toward his mother at the same time as he is attempting to separate himself from her. His excitement is increased in close contact with her, which supports his sense of self in gender-identity. Yet closeness to mother, at his age, psychologically threatens engulfment. Genital feelings and "closeness" seem at odds as one is tied to more and the other to less sense of self. A second conflict for the little boy is that the growing sexual awareness he feels with the mother makes him a rival of the father, on whom he simultaneously needs to model himself in establishing a sense of gender. Both sexual awareness and gender modeling continue to grow with ego formation. Finally, the little boy also feels the conflicting desires for autonomy and dependency.

As separation/individuation is involved in creating most of the other conflicts that occur within the child at the same time, the separation/individuation struggle is often used as the focal point for understanding psychological development at the two-year-old stage. The problem with this approach is that it is incomplete. By concentrating on only a single aspect of ego formation, one loses the dynamic nature of the total process. To find an organizing principle that encompasses the full extent of the process, I have developed the above model, which is a synthesis of all the various psychological challenges of the period. The nature of the conflicts that arise within the infant as it responds to these challenges suggests the terminology of a primary oedipal complex.

As has been discussed, the form of the primary oedipal complex differs for the little boy and little girl. Therefore, psychopathologies that derive from this period of life have gender-related components associated with them. The vulnerability to such pathological development comes from the imposing set of psychological changes, which occur all at once. It is worth noting, however, that while this situation produces conflicts, it also offers the possibility to achieve a strong, integrated ego.

Research on memory shows that when a "complex" of tasks such as those involved in ego formation is worked through in development, an *associative network* is formed wherein emotions serve as memory units. Therefore, in later life the activation of any one of the elements of the complex can produce behavior associated with the entire emotional complex. Conversely, a therapeutic analysis can be based on one aspect of the complex, with resultant alleviation of an array of symptoms without ever directly touching on other issues that make up the complex. Thus it is that clinical success has not required the synthesis considered in this book.

The theory of the primary oedipal phase provides an integrated model of the various developmental processes a human infant simultaneously goes through during the earliest time of ego organization.[1] Emphatically, the theory to be presented is not an attempt to draw wide-ranging consequences from a single postulated (early oedipal) conflict. Rather, an interrelated set of conflicts, collectively referred to in this book as the primary oedipal complex, are used as a handle to understand the large number of processes that take place in early life.

It is tempting to try to discuss, to the fullest extent possible, all the complexities of human experience that contribute to a child's development in the time of first ego-formation. Such an encyclopedic effort is beyond the scope of this book. Therefore, I shall not try to speculate about why a given child resolves its primary oedipal conflict in a particular way directing the organization and functioning of its nascent ego. I shall be content if these pages adequately state the case for the existence of the primary oedipal phase and point to some of its consequences for the development of a human personality.

In constructing the model, two special contributions to our knowledge of early development aided my thinking. The first was Mahler's careful working out of the process by which a child senses itself apart from its mother (1965). She established that this occurs roughly in a child's second year of life. Then Stoller (1968b) and Money and Ehrhardt (1972) found that gender identity is established during the same period of time. This background prepared me to appreciate evidence for the primary oedipal phase, which was particularly accessible in the treatment of one case. It became increasingly clear to me over a span of years how important the experience of the primary oedipal complex is in personality development.

The thinking here is the product of a gradual development of ideas brought about by a succession of clinical cases. Increasingly, I was able to see how the events in the stormy life of a two-year-old are interrelated and how these interrelationships are the basis for future personality formation.

The pivotal first case was Patty. For immediate purposes, a synopsis will tell the dramatic way I came to consider the possibility of a primary oedipal phase and to see some of its ramifications. Patty was a nineteen-year-old who came to see me in a suicidal panic. During the session, Patty alternated between two ego states. One was a terrified small child curled up in her chair, fending off someone or something with her arm in front of her face. The other was present-day Patty crying out for understanding and help. Patty and I proceeded on the basis that the small-child scene and her suicidal panic were somehow related.

Consistency within her material and corroboration with significant facts such as dates convinced us both that the small-child mode was a reenactment of scenes she went through long ago. Her present-day suicidal feelings linked up with the feelings from the early episode in terms of her mother's leaving her. The original incident turned out to have occurred when Patty was two. Patty's mother was away to give birth to Patty's younger brother, leaving Patty in her father's care.

Earlier in our analytic work, Patty used to refer to feeling as if she were only two. I took that then as an expression of feeling very young without any more specific meaning. When recovery and processing or working through of what I have come to call primary oedipal material resulted in dissipation of Patty's suicidal urges, I was glad, but I did not understand it.

Unexpectedly, Patty made other gains, too, without directly addressing them in therapy. There was a cluster of changes, all of which related to a two-year-old's major developmental issues. These issues included (1) separation/individuation; (2) categorical thinking, e.g., good versus bad; (3) symbolic use of food in terms of the relationship with mother in handling sexual feelings; (4) splitting as a defense. In Patty's case, at age nineteen, these issues could be seen in the following changes, all opposites of her previous behavior: separating from her mother and managing on her own; seeing herself as good though imperfect; feeling free to be attractive rather than obese; forming a meaningful love relationship rather than being promiscuous with strangers; a sense of freedom to think with permission within herself to understand connections rather than to operate intellectually on the basis of rote. I had made no interpretation of her behavior in any of these matters, nor were there extra-analytic circumstances to explain her gains. It is clear now that Patty progressed because she integrated feelings left over from her primary oedipal phase.

Thus it was that in pondering the clinical significance of Patty's experience I came to see that there had been a syndrome of primitive behaviors that did not seem to be logically interconnected and yet dissipated together in favor of more constructive, mature behavior as Patty processed primary oedipal material. At last I appreciated that all these behaviors were *theoretically* traceable to the mental life of a two-year-old child.

Both the power and the test of a new theoretical framework come from its ability to explain psychological phenomena other than those from which it was derived. After the experience with Patty, I began to see how some old puzzles about behavior could indeed be understood by recognizing the primary oedipal phase.

One instance of such a puzzle is the fact that anorexia nervosa is primarily a pathology of women and girls. The literature contains some partial explanations. For example, J. F. Masterson (1977) viewed anorexic patients in terms of separation/individuation and problems in gaining autonomy from their mothers. Bruch (1973) considered the anorexics' plight in cultural terms, such as our culture's emphasis upon slimness. Palazzoli (1974) saw her cases in terms of family dynamics in which the girls developed as spoiled beings. Anna Freud (1958) looked at the anorexics' condition as deriving from troubled oral phase experience with their mothers. Yet none of the models is complete enough to account for the gender specificity of such a drastic condition. Why some 90 percent of all cases are female can, however, be explained in terms of an intense primary oedipal conflict, including the problem of separation/individuation, as we shall see later. Similarly, other conditions that tend to be gender-specific, such as transsexualism in males, become understandable as the aftermath of a poorly resolved primary oedipal phase.

The gender-related aspects of psychopathologies traceable to toddlerhood are explainable because of the very different forms the problems of toddlerhood take depending on whether the child is a boy or a girl. Gradually this realization enabled me to see other manifestations of an emerging model of development. My understanding continued to expand over a seven-year period as other cases unfolded in addition to Patty's.

Excerpts from these cases will illustrate various aspects of the theory. Some of the examples occurred before I had any notion of a primary oedipal phase. Subsequently I thought about the material in the light of a primary oedipal conflict and the framework it provides for understanding personality development. I found that I then understood these early cases more clearly.

Throughout the book, I am mindful that a theory is valueless without evidence to show that it is true. As a psychologist I am also mindful that my expectations might guide my perceptions. The persons involved have confirmed the accuracy of all case material taken from my own practice. In addition, whenever possible I draw the evidence for the primary oedipal phase from published case material of others, quoted as completely as is possible. I also try to present more than one example to illustrate points to show that the kind of clinical material presented is not particular to a single case. In the quoted material I take occasional liberty to emphasize a point, and so, except where otherwise noted, all italics are mine.

Part I provides background for identifying the primary oedipal phase, starting with the history of the idea in chapter 1. We see here that some psychoanalytic pioneers such as Horney and Jones were aware of the possibility of a primary oedipal phase. That more work was not done on it then is an interesting story involving Freud's relationship to his followers. A later factor that delayed recognition of the primary oedipal phase was the extreme nature of Melanie Klein's ideas on the subject. Those who disagreed with her were many, and the tendency was to dismiss the idea of a primary oedipal phase along with other things she stated. However, the later findings of Mahler and Jacobson on the timing of ego differentiation, of Stoller and Ehrhardt and Money on the timing of gender identity, and of Lamb and others on the early importance of the father in a child's life all were necessary in order for a true understanding of the primary oedipal phase to occur. Chapter 1 establishes that the idea of the primary oedipal phase is one whose time has come.

The argument opens in chapter 2 with a review of the main developmental issues that a child encounters during its second year of life, showing that the earliest organization of a child's ego is based upon the interrelated tasks in the resolving of these issues. Chapter 2 mentions the use of gender identity as the core of the ego in this effort. Chapter 3 details why this fact is natural, gives evidence that it is true, and explores some of its implications.

Part II is an exploration of the theory of the primary oedipal phase. It begins with a chapter showing how all the developments of the child's second year described in chapters 2 and 3 combine into an emotional complex with gender identity at its core. In chapter 4, I consider the way in which an emotional complex works in a personality and show how much this relates to the primary oedipal complex, shedding light on the use of characteristic defense mechanisms.

Why and how the primary oedipal emerges can now be examined closely. What it means to see oneself as of one gender or another—a male or a female human being—takes up chapters 5 and 6, dealing, respectively, with the pattern of the primary oedipal phase as it occurs in each sex.

With these patterns delineated, we can examine evidence for the existence of the primary oedipal phase from direct observation of two-year-olds (chapter 7), from treatment cases of boys and girls in this period of life (chapter 8), and finally from the study of the treatment of adults (chapter 9), including in all chapters examples of both males and females.

Concluding the theory, chapter 10 is a comparison between development at the primary oedipal level and at the classical oedipal level, illustrated fully with case material. It shows that the differences between them are not in degree of oedipal conflict but in the child's level of ego organization.

Part III applies a rigorous test to the theory of the primary oedipal phase. If the theory is valid, it must contribute fresh understanding of psychopathologies that may derive from a putative primary oedipal phase. These chapters first examine existent theories of anorexia and assess them and their deficiencies in terms of the primary oedipal phase. They next include a detailed review of each of the symptoms making up the anorexic syndrome. Excerpts from treatment of a two-year-old anorexic reveal the anorexic syndrome as an extension of the normal behavior of a two-year-old. The relationship of these data to the primary oedipal origins of anorexia will be clear. This relationship is clear also when explored in case material from work with older anorexics of both sexes. Part III can be seen, too, as a model for the study of other severe psychological disturbances that may emanate from early childhood.

In the summary and conclusions, the basis of the theory of the primary oedipal phase is just briefly reviewed. Under "Reflections Through Life" I place the primary oedipal phase into the greater context of personality development. I then suggest factors that lead to individual differences in the resolution of the primary oedipal phase. Finally, I present a sampling of theoretical issues, such as guilt and shame, penis envy, and castration anxiety, that could be reexplored in the light of the primary oedipal phase.

As a last note, I offer seven tests of the truth of the theory as a reminder to myself and to the reader that one must approach the theory of the primary oedipal phase as any new idea, with open-mindedness. In this spirit, then, I wish to introduce the primary oedipal phase as a unifying principle in understanding the paths one takes "on the way to self."

Part I Background

1 History of the Idea of a Primary Oedipal Phase

Neither the importance of sexuality at the two-year-old stage nor its interdigitating nature with the multiple tasks a two-year-old faces has been generally recognized. These omissions have been left standing for so long largely due to historical reasons.

Freud's original idea of a child's early psychosexual development did not differentiate between boys and girls in their first three years of life. He referred to the girl as "a little man" (1917).

In 1924 Horney described the unique qualities of feminine development in the very young girl, postulating a primary femininity. Jones (1925) quickly added a description of the early oedipus. Both drew upon their clinical experiences for their theories.

Freud, strongly supported by Fenichel and Lampl-de-Groot, opposed the idea that girls recognize their femininity without first being bitterly disappointed to learn that they are different from boys. Intense debate followed because Freud felt keenly that any digression from his fundamental ideas would weaken the very cause of psychoanalysis. Fliegel explains:

Freud, threatened in his survival, shaken in his trust in his closest collaborators, worried about the cohesion of the psychoanalytic movement and the survival of his life's work, responded to the "alien thoughts" emanating from Horney and then Jones as a threat to the integrity of his theory. He reacted with what was perhaps the most dogmatic stand of his career, despite an often reiterated awareness of limited insight and understanding in this area. . . . The debate was essentially closed with Freud's 1931 paper. The issues were not re-examined for some decades. (1973:406)

Strangely, Freud himself did in *Civilization and its Discontents* (1931) refer to oedipal feelings in boys at the age of two. He did not develop the idea, though, or even then refer to comparable feelings in girls.

There is one more factor that affected the situation. Klein described the early oedipus in 1929, citing its existence and taking into account the significance of at least the oral and anal aspects of a child's development in the two-year-old period. She linked these to super-ego formation. She was aware of the effect in sexual masochism and sadism produced by convergence of anal concerns with the early oedipus. Although Klein did not take account of such aspects of ego formation as language development, she saw how fateful early oedipal conflict is for future personality development.

Unfortunately, Klein went on to concentrate on her reconstructions of still earlier infantile mental life, placing the oedipal conflict as early as three months. Her speculations about part-object images and introjects based upon the child's intimacy with its mother inspired an offshoot psychoanalytic movement. However, as summarized in a devastating treatise by Glover (1949), the extremeness of her views on the timing of the oedipal conflict stimulated a counter-reinforcement of the orthodox Freudian position that everything before the fourth year of life is preoedipal.

An occasional voice still suggests that significant oedipal development starts earlier. Clinical material cited by two of these, Behn-Eschenburg and Sachs, is quoted in chapters 7 and 8, giving evidence of the primary oedipal phase. Behn-Eschenburg recognized in at least some cases the occurrence of an early oedipal phase. In referring to the idea of someone "not reaching" the (classical) oedipal stage, he states, "The less sign there is of the oedipus complex the earlier it may be assumed to have occurred" (1932:85). Lorand (1943) presents a successful treatment of a case of anorexia nervosa matter-of-factly in terms of early oedipal conflict. However, neither of these investigators generalized their discussions. Nor were their observations incorporated in the mainstream of psychoanalytic thought.

There are a number of directions of theoretical thought that might have led to a theory of a primary oedipal phase but for various reasons have not done so. One such avenue is the study of bodily sensations in the very young child in relation to ego formation. Bell (1964) describes in neurological terms the combined sensations from the genital, urethral, and anal systems that affect the child's feelings and its ideation about its body in the two-year-old period. Bell takes note of fantasies about anatomical relationships, which, of course, affect the child's sense of itself. Greenacre (1958a), Jacobson (1964), and Mahler (1965) chiefly, among many others, concerned themselves with the varieties of bodily sensation that contribute to the self-concept: feelings about castration, penis envy, and toilet training. However, they considered these in relation only to the mother in interpersonal relationships. When they confronted the issue of the existence of the early oedipal phase, their criteria for its existence were based upon the form the oedipal conflict takes in children of the (later) classical oedipal period. They did not consider the strength and significance of oedipal feelings before the child is capable of the obviously triadic formulations of the four-year-old. Therefore, their conclusions fit into the orthodox position so energetically defended by others when Horney and Jones first reported what they saw. (This is an important distinction to draw. What is being referred to as the primary oedipal phase is oedipal in the sense of its overall form, but the elements of which it is made are different from and not totally analogous to those of the classical oedipal phase, as will be discussed later.)

The concept of the primary oedipal phase could have been arrived at by efforts to understand the interrelationships of various aspects of the two-year-old's experience. Bleich (1976), for example, investigated the relationship between anality, object relations with the mother, and the onset of linguistic ability as interrelated phenomena facilitating human development. The origin of splitting as a defense is clear when Bleich contrasts the child's inner experiences of old and new affects with its growing linguistic ability. Galenson (1979a) and Edgcumbe (1981) also show the development of symbolic processes in terms of object relations and other contributors to ability. Hendrick (1970) refers to the sexuality of the toddler, but does not expand his thoughts about it in his focused discussion of cognitive development. Galenson (1979) and Edgcumbe (1981) also show the development of ego formation. These studies are among many in the literature that try to integrate various elements of ego development in the earliest period. Unfortunately, none of these studies to date develop a primary oedipal conflict as a central developmental theme, incorporating separation/individuation.

Another approach to discovery of the primary oedipal phase might have been the direct observation of it in early childhood behavior. Galenson and Roiphe (1980a,b) charted the development of young children by observation in a nursery school setting and interviews with their mothers. These authors concluded that oedipal behavior was transient and without deep significance. Using Glover's term (1949), they believed that in the "early genital phase" the child is chiefly occupied by the genital difference between the sexes without "any oedipal resonance."

Also from direct study of two-year-old children, Parens and his colleagues (1976) identified what they called the "first genital phase." Oedipal behavior did not seem definitive to them because they used criteria suitable to study of viewing children who are four years old. As will be clear in chapter 10, in comparing the primary with the classical oedipal phase, the level of ego development of the two-year-old must be taken into account. Appropriate criteria that permit identification of both oedipal stages in both sexes are (1) genitally derived, contrasting behavior patterns in relation to the two parents; and (2) use of these patterns as the basis for the organization of the ego (including the core self-concept, fantasy systems, and development of characteristic mechanisms of defense against anxiety aroused by the child's oedipal conflicts, with distribution of energy into various activities in consequence of the oedipal conflict). It is in this perspective that the emotional complexes of the primary and of the classical oedipal phases can be clearly seen. Until now, however, Freud's strong defense of his original conceptual framework still constrained the search for the primary oedipal phase.

Study of the role of the father in early child development would have been still another way to discover the primary oedipal phase. Instead, for a long time the father was left out of serious study of very young children in another aspect of that constraint of psychoanalytic thinking. In this there were two consequences. First, the role of the father could not be understood. Second, there was an emphasis upon the vicissitudes of early psychosexual development in the female without reference to the father. This delayed full understanding of psychosexual development in children of both sexes.

In keeping with Freud's view (1926) of adult female sexuality as a "dark continent," most writers on the subject of psychosexual development shed light on this darkness by continually exploring what happens in the human female. They seemed to assume that the details of psychosexual development of the human male were clear. Perhaps this was because his original love-object is his mother and therefore his heterosexuality seemed easy to come by, or perhaps because of the comfortable notion that having a penis should mean no problem in gender identity. The statistics on the subject show how simplistic such views are. As primary oedipal theory helps to explain (chapter 6), males make up most of the population with severe problems of gender identity. For example, Stoller (1964) found that men comprised nearly three-quarters of those wishing sex-change operations. Pauly (1965) and Benjamin (1966) report even more lopsided statistics.

The magnitude of the father's importance to the very young child needed to be recognized. We can be grateful to academic psychologists like Lamb (1976a,b) for redressing the balance, as their work started the accumulation of evidence that fathers are as important to children emotionally as are their mothers by at least the beginning of the second year of life. Among psychoanalysts, Abelin described "a boy's discovery of himself, including his gender, through his observation of his father in relation to his mother" (1977:23). Abelin sees this "'early triangulation' as helpful in forming a self-concept in the late second year of life" (1977:23). He does not, however, examine fully the affective consequences in each sex of this early triangulation.

Greenson (1968) and Parens (1979), too, recognize that the implications, in Greenson's term, of "dis-identifying with the mother" on the part of the boy make for a different course in development between boys and girls. Parens notes oedipal conflict but only after separation/individuation is largely accomplished. This line of work left at the brink the discovery of the primary oedipal phase.

Another path of exploration could have taken us earlier to this discovery. Evidence for the primary oedipal phase might have been demonstrated through study of the transference, for early development is gauged by its recapitulation in the transference. The trouble with this basis for constructing theory is that preconceptions can govern our reading of patients' material.

If we assume that triadic relationships involve a patient's child-self with both parents only after the age of three and a half, as is traditionally proposed, then we may not look beyond dyadic replays of the early mother–child relationship in analyzing a transference. However, dyadic transferences that seem to occur during therapy, when more completely explored, turn out in fact to exist within triadic fantasies. In chapter 2, I substantiate this point with case material. Kramer (1980) approaches but never quite spells out this conclusion in her sensitive description of her patients' triadic transferences coexisting with dyadic ones, rapprochement and practicing subphase material coexisting with primitive oedipal concern.

One more way that a primary oedipal phase could have been discovered is through studies of longitudinal development. Coltrera looked at oedipal development in such a context and saw it not as distinct stages but as a continuum from the beginning:

To offer preoedipal conflict as a fair developmental exchange for a later and more classical oedipal one in narcissistic disorders faults the very biological premises that join preoedipal and oedipal events in a developmental dialectic wherein each is the holistic condition of the other. For where there can be little doubt that severe preoedipal trauma distorts the shape and force of the organizing oedipal conflict and the resolution in the phallic-oedipal phase, it does not displace it in the developmental continuum of psychosexual epigenesis. (1977:300–301)

Although Coltrera speaks of preoedipal events and reminds us of the holistic coexistence of the oedipal, he does not zero in on the implications of what he says. A further reason that none of the above-mentioned studies led to an earlier appreciation of the significance of the primary oedipal complex is that complexities of the psychosexual development of children of both sexes are so embedded in the details of general development that three further landmark contributions (discussed in chapter 2) were first necessary.

First Mahler and cognitive psychologists such as Piaget and Kagan proved that the initial clear organization of the ego occurs during the second year of life. Second, Mahler, Greenacre,

McDevitt, Parens, and Galenson and Roiphe all found that intentional genitality appears then, too. It is not surprising to find that in studying hermaphrodites Stoller and Money and Ehrhardt learned that gender identity is fixed during the same period as ego organization becomes manifest. Finally Lamb, Abelin, and others established the importance of fathers in the libidinal lives of their infants. The way is now open to reviewing the situation.

Kernberg (1978) states that he is newly impressed by the importance of oedipal factors when he deals with patients, but he does not yet refer to the early oedipal complex in the borderline adult. Stewart (1981) acknowledges the existence of a "second dyad" that develops between babies and their fathers. However, being committed to the idea of oedipal feelings only during the classical period, he is unable to make sense of how relationship to the father becomes such an important factor in the child's personality. Chodorow (1978) also explores the special relationships of very young children with their fathers, stopping short of recognizing the primary oedipal phase.

Loewald (1970) saw a fresh appreciation of the oedipus complex coming from new knowledge of the origins of psychic substructures. He, along with Serge Lebovici, Samuel Ritvo, and Margaret Mahler in the Paris 1973 Panel, agreed that the early developmental situation "determines the fashion in which the sexual drives interact with the state of self and object differentiation and with self—and object relationship reached by the child." This wording comes from Kramer continuing further with quotation of Shapiro, who says that the "oedipus complex is as much a result of the ego as of the drives" (1980:246–247).[1] Fast (1979) also comes very close to tying it all together when she describes gender differentiation, but she reports the process as purely cognitive even though she recognizes that it may include such an obviously emotional aspect as the giving up of all genital pleasure. Abelin (1980) surveys the literature and his own research and presents a theory of personality development based upon what he calls "the tripartite model of early triangulation." He, too, cites many cognitive effects of the toddler's recognition of the existence of the two sexes although without taking into account the affective significance of oedipal feelings at that stage. Little (1981) even links an early oedipal phase with the process of self-differentiation and calls the later oedipal phase the "classic" one.

In other words, recognition of the primary oedipal phase requires only a shift in emphasis from the thinking we have generally developed in the field. Clearly at this point in the study of personality development we are ready to examine thoroughly the theory of the primary oedipal phase.

2 Assessment of a Two-Year-Old's Psychological Challenges

Toward the age of two years, a child's ego busily forms an idea of place in the family and begins to take charge of impulses in a satisfying way. To achieve such an ego, the child masters many oncoming psychological challenges. Some of these stem from unique qualities of a particular child's family, and some are determined by the child's heredity and individual biological state. There are also formative processes occurring in every two-year-old's development. These involve changes within the child and so present a challenge to the development of a cohesive sense of self. Of these challenges, the most important are separation/individuation and issues of autonomy and dependence; the shift of emphasis from oral concerns to anal concerns, engendering problems in inner and outer control and violent fantasies; the inner and outer experiences in regard to sphincter maturation and locomotion; language development, in its contrast to affective experience, producing splitting as a defense; categorical thinking, e.g., good versus bad; the conceptualization of time; and last but hardly least, awareness of gender identity with its concomitant, primary oedipal conflict.

Each one of these changes engages the child's passions and energies and somehow must become integrated within a single sense of self. Each of these processes adds to the complexity of the initial organization of the ego.

The child's experience in these processes forms the foundation of its personality. Not simply an accumulation of experience, *personality organization* implies an ordering of experience. The child's way of ordering its experience is what determines the shape and style and (to push the foundation analogy a bit) the structural strength of subsequent personality development.

The Beginning of an Organized Ego

For Freud, the (classical) oedipal phase was the time of major personality organization. Acceptance of this idea did not come easily. When Freud (1905b) recognized the oedipal conflict, thinking on infantile sexuality was strongly resisted.[1] The existence of oedipal conflict is still questioned, even in psychoanalytic literature (Lester 1976).

Increasingly, interest has shifted away from oedipal concerns to infants' very early experience, with an emphasis upon its preoedipal quality. The significance of the classical oedipal phase gets buried in a stream of concepts about seemingly preoedipal factors including early maternal identification, oral fixation, separation/individuation, anal concerns, and penis envy.

For Freud, however, the oedipal phase was not simply another guide to development. He saw in the oedipal phase the organizing core of the personality, identification based upon gender. That is why Freud (1909) considered this phase so critical for the achievement of either a successful adult personality or one filled with neurotic compromise, pain, and confusion.

Still, the work since Freud has traced so many major personality traits and problems to earlier stages, the classical oedipal stage cannot be the time of primary ego organization. For example, destructive, hostile fantasies are leftover responses from the earlier anal stage (Anna Freud 1965); defects in the quality of emotional relationships later on in life can find their origin in the separation/individuation process (Mahler 1975).

To find the earliest critical periods of personality development, some, including Klein (1932), Winnicott (1965), Kernberg (1968a) and Balint (1968) have gone much further back in the developmental sequence, to stages preceding the point at which we know an infant has the ability to retain images (and thus build permanent memories). These theories are based chiefly upon reconstructions that come from analysis of older children and adults.

Others have started their theories of critical periods of personality development with studies of infants that do not support the idea of definitive personality formation in the first months of a child's life. Kagan (1978) leads the way in viewing the earliest months of a child's life as a time of "shifting sand."[2] He found that older babies do not register in their behavior what might be expected from their earliest experience. For example, children with undeniably traumatic long-lasting mechanical feeding problems, such as constriction of the esophagus in infancy, do not necessarily grow up with severe psychological oral disorders to plague them (Engel 1967 and Viedemar 1979). Chisholm (1983) analyzed the effects upon behavior of infants of their being carried in cradleboards many hours each day. He made cross-cultural comparisons in an elegant way. His findings were that cradleboarding inhibited infants, but the effects tended to be reversed during the second year of life.

We can surmise that the effects of experience upon later behavior of an infant are related to the age of the infant at the time of the original experience. Well-designed experiments demonstrate that nine-month-old infants, unlike five-month-old ones, retain images creating anticipatory behavior (Meicler and Gratch 1980). Piaget (1954) also found that a capacity for longterm memory was demonstrable by age nine months. He called the achievement of lasting memory for forms *object permanence.*

Piaget (1962) describes the essential step for lasting memory as development from mere recognition memory to evocative memory. Holding onto impressions permits adding to them and organizing them. With this capacity the child can begin to crystallize a true sense of self.

The idea of self immediately produces the idea of nonself. One cannot think of one without the other. We therefore consider (in the same way as the child must experience it) how important the capacity for permanent evocative memory is to the development of a sense of relationship to another person or object. Fraiberg (1969) pointed out that the traditional psychoanalytic concept of *object constancy,* as stability of object cathexis, is consistent with Piaget on object permanence. Achieving this underwrites the child's ability to maintain a constant libidinal attachment to a temporarily absent mother despite any ambivalent feelings toward her: object constancy in the psychoanalytic sense. Mahler (1965) applied the term *object constancy* to the same capacity, referring additionally to its use in enabling the child to retain an impression of good treatment by the mother against any discouraging treatment the mother might provide. Stable memory of good treatment by the mother facilitates the development of interpersonal relations and sustains the child during periods of a mother's absence.

Bemporad (1980) shows that both object permanence and object constancy are uses of the same neurological capacity, starting at about the same age, nine months, with rapid development from sixteen months to twenty-four months. He makes the further crucial point that organizing and retaining a mental construct of *self* is another use of that same capacity. Referring to the question of internal objects as significant early structures in differentiating the self from the nonself, he questions whether the construct of inner objects fits observed developmental data. Also, there are logical difficulties, which he examines in the light of the history of these ideas.

[The alleged] internalization of objects . . . is said to occur *before* eighteen to twenty-four months, that is, before the stage of object representation, which would be quite a feat in the annals of epistemology. . . . Freud postulated that the infant built a sense of self by incorporating pleasant experiences as his own and projecting out the unpleasant as the not-self. Klein (1948) added that both good and bad objects are incorporated. Fairbairn (1952) reversed Freud's position by postulating that only the bad are internalized as a means of defensive control, there being no reason to internalize good experiences. However, there is a significant difference between what was intended by Freud and what was intended by the object relations theorists. Freud spoke of primitive experiences; the latter speak of objects being internalized. *Now how an object can be internalized before there is a cognitive concept of an object is beyond my comprehension.* The formation of the concept of breast or mother, good or bad, may seem to imply a greater sophistication than the differentiation of self from nonself. (Bemporad 1980:63–65)

Bemporad helps us to recognize that theories of early development must be tied to evidence of infant capacities. On this basis we know that the earliest sense of self and sense of others must coexist.

In keeping with Mahler's observations that most toddlers are in full swing of forming an interpersonal relationship with their mothers by the middle of the second year of life, we see parallel growth in the child's self-concept. For example, Amsterdam (1968) discovered that at eighteen months 65 percent of toddlers recognize themselves in the mirror. That this means the development of a self-concept is confirmed on the verbal level by such studies as Lewis' (1963). Words like *me*, *I*, and *self*, all frequently uttered in exclamation, appear in the latter part of the second year. By evidence as well as by logic, we see that self-awareness and awareness of others proceed apace.

The process of developing these awarenesses (separation/individuation) is generally considered to be dyadic, that is, involving only the mother and child. Yet the child organizes its ego in relationship to both parents while classifying itself as to gender. Jacobson (1964) has described how the process of separation/individuation *requires* the idea of both parents so that the child can crystallize a sense of itself in terms of one gender category in contrast to the existence of another.

This truth has not as yet been generally applied to the triadic aspect of seemingly dyadic transferences of patients. However, if our understanding of early development is to extend our understanding of normal and abnormal adult personalities, we need evidence that triangulation provides the context of dyadic transferences. I can provide an example of this from work with a patient before I appreciated the significance of the primary oedipal phase. The evidence was forced on me. I present it in detail so that the reader can review it.

> Barbara, a recent college graduate, held a job, but was devoid of even shallow interpersonal relationships. Her inner state was chaotic. During therapy sessions she could not remember one emotionally charged statement she made when she next uttered a contradictory one. Mostly her sessions were spent in quiet tears. Typical material concerned feelings about seeing someone and being seen, with panic about forgetting an absent person. She also experienced confusion about who was really disappearing, herself or the other.
>
> This symbiotic material appeared in the transference around our seating arrangements.
>
> Barbara had occasionally made reference to the couch, but in practice preferred to use a chair facing me.
>
> One day Barbara told me her reason: she wished to be close to me. However, my chair was actually very much closer to the

couch than to Barbara's chair. I said so. She appeared distressed. As with a very young child getting a fix on reality through its eyes (White 1975), she needed to see me. Yet, greater closeness to me was not all that she wanted.

    I thought of Barbara's panic and confusion about people disappearing. "Out of sight, out of mind" was a very scary thing, as if someone were destroyed. Knowing of her own existence, she would have to believe that the one "destroyed" would be me.

    The real issue turned out to be Barbara's panic that she had "forgotten" me by thinking of men. That was why she needed the reassurance of being able to see me: to know that I still existed.

    I learned that Barbara fled into the symbiotic relationship with me as a mother figure whenever she felt aware of men and her own sexuality. A further point that became clear eventually was that keeping an eye on me enabled Barbara to make sure I did not attack her by surprise because "Mother/I" was so angry that Barbara had sexual thoughts. In Barbara's mind, the symbiotic pattern protected her from this danger.

The theoretical question here is why Barbara had to regress so far in handling her sexual feelings. Subsequent work proved that separation/individuation was for Barbara invariably connected with sexual implications. Achievement of separation/individuation requires an individual's sense of readiness and self-permission for whatever autonomy implies; and in Barbara's case, autonomy seemed dangerous because it meant availability for sexual relationships. Feelings toward men (of a sexual nature) dating to the time of separation/individuation can only be interpreted as relating to father concerns. Barbara frequently provided evidence for the oedipal nature of her feelings toward men with such statements as, "I don't want anything to do with men. They are all alike . . . all like my father." Her statement also reflects the primary oedipal time frame by the use of the all-or-none, splitting categorization that is characteristic of that early age. *For Barbara, the symbiotic transference was protection against recognizing her sexual feelings and her inner conflict over them.* It was not that she was trapped in a symbiosis but rather that she was using symbiotic behavior to mask her sexually based conflicts.

    Barbara demonstrates separation/individuation as a triadic phenomenon. Jacobson's view is supported: in organizing its ego, the child is aware of both parents. These triadic perceptions during separation/individuation combined with the earlier discussed capacity for object constancy and the child's developing awareness of genital sensations set the stage for the formation of a strong gender identity and cohesive sense of self.

We can see the complexity of the child's situation as it struggles to form a cohesive sense of self, using its capacity for object constancy to hold on to a sense of self as well as the sense of another, its sense of personal existence achieved to an important degree through uniqueness of its genital sensations. These form a basis for gender identity, a vital factor in the child's first organization of its ego. [3]

Gender Identity and Its Implications

Its sex is one of the most significant aspects of physical being that the child takes into account in establishing a sense of self. Amsterdam and Levitt note: "The intense interest in looking at and touching the genitals is an integral part of establishing a sense of self, separated and differentiated from others" (1980:73).

As Stoller (1975) established, interest in the genitals also leads to the child's sense of gender identity. [4] Interest in its genitals thus helps the child to specify and also to categorize itself. Conversely, in the fluid early ego, possessing gender identity helps the child to deal with its genital feelings. As gender identity crystallizes, the sexual feelings that existed from earliest infancy (Kestenberg 1975) become focused. The child can place them in context, knowing itself as a being with gender.

All this was once considered to be later development, part of the phallic phase, when the child was at least three (Abraham 1927; Gesell et al. 1940). The studies of Money and Ehrhardt (1965) and Stoller (1975) prove that gender identity is already being established in the second year, during the same period as is the sense of self. The child is guided by its sexual reactions to use its gender as the great organizing principle of its personality.

Gender identity, including feelings of the genitalia, is integral to being a self and gaining psychological ownership of inner feelings. The sorting out of personal gender by a child must logically proceed in conjunction with an awareness of adult gender. Kleeman (1966) and Galenson, Miller and Roiphe (1976) describe children under two masturbating while at the same time acting in a way to show perception of their mothers' gender. In this we see that a child establishes its sense of gender in relation to its parent. Conversely, sorting out different feelings toward its two parents has meaning for the child in terms of gender. Guided by genital interest, the child learns it is like one or the other parent, enabling it to identify with the parent of the same sex. For the girl this means rivaling the mother, on whom she is still very much dependent, complicating her wish to become more independent. The little boy finds himself in conflict in moving away from the object of his sexual feeling (as part of individuation), and he finds himself the rival of the one with whom he is starting to identify. Roiphe (1979b) calls gender identity "fallout" from the process of separation/individuation. However, that is compartmentalizing into distinct processes what is a single effort for the child. We have now seen how, as a single process, separation/individuation/gender identification leads in a natural way to conflicts we would label as oedipal.

In their recognition of early oedipal feelings, Jones (1925) and Klein (1928) believed that the oedipal process for the girl begins with moving away from the mother in response to frustration at the breast and consequent mother-directed rage. They did not explain why the same inevitable frustration would not equally push the boy away from the mother, in his case thus precluding oedipal feelings. Jones and Klein were in any case limited at the time of their explorations because they did not know how and when the sense of self develops.

On the other hand, I believe Mahler (1972) and Greenacre (1978), as well as Galenson and Roiphe (1980), did not appreciate the oedipal consequences of gender psychodevelopment because they were distracted by the drama of a child showing recognition of "genital difference." These authors do record observations of what happened after a toddler demonstrated such awareness: the child's behavior was different in relation to each parent, and the child adopted behavioral characteristics of his or her gender. They do not consider this pattern significantly oedipal. I believe this is appreciated as true, significant oedipal behavior when it is looked at in the total context of the two-year-old's life. Galenson and Roiphe in ascribing profound changes in behavior to the shock of discovery of the anatomical facts insufficiently consider the context of each child's reactions. The timing of the "discovery" is determined by the combination of a developing sense of self and others with intense interest in the genital area due to the intensity of the child's sexual feelings. Apparent perception of the anatomical differences between the sexes is not always based upon a child's first chances to observe that these differences exist. The child makes the "discovery" when emotionally prompted by its recognition of that center of strongly pleasurable sensations helping it to distinguish its own body. What the child makes of its perceptions of others' genitals is related to all the other significant factors that affect the formation of its ego.

Kohut (1971) recognized the relationship between self-cohesion and gender identity. The way "Who am I?" is answered forms the core of the child's personality organization. The crucial role of gender identity lies in the answer "Boy!" or "Girl!" Identifying itself by gender, the child thus places itself in a social context.

As gender identity depends upon a child's identification of adult gender (of both sexes), it is important to demonstrate that awareness of the father develops simultaneously with the child's capacity for object constancy and awareness of the genital sensations. We must, therefore, examine the new evidence concerning a child's feelings about its father by at least nine months of age and into its second year.

The Role of the Father and the Plausibility of the Primary Oedipal Phase

Mächtlinger's review of the subject (1976) shows that psychoanalytic literature abounds in explorations of infant–mother relationships as if there were no feelings about fathers. Now much new work shows that fathers are the objects of positive attachment early in infancy and that they engender different responses from their babies than do mothers.[5]

Brown (1979) proved that at as early as four months infants discriminate and respond differently to their mothers', their fathers', and strangers' voices. An interesting sidelight is that, of the three, the father's voice stimulated the greatest attentiveness on the part of the infants.

Abelin (1971) followed the development of awareness of their fathers in a group of infants. By the age of six months, thirteen out of fourteen infants had recognized their fathers with happy smiles. The same number were strongly attached to their fathers by nine months.

We note that nine months is also when object permanance develops and thus self/other determinations by the child can be internalized. The child is then capable of discerning the triangular configuration Jacobson said the child must use to establish an independent ego. This also suggests an emotional richness that must make us think further about infant personality.

Lamb (1980) pioneered longitudinal studies in the home. In this natural setting he could observe that fathers interact with their infants in a unique and differentiable way. He found that infants are attached from the earliest age to both parents, and the two relationships differ qualitatively.[6]

The whole interpersonal situation of the infant is even more complicated than most traditional theorizing would have it. Pedersen (1980) denotes this in his summary of research in father–infant relationships:

The ongoing relationship between parents influences the child's experiences. The child responds selectively to each parent, determined, in part, by how each behaves and by the child's own sensitivities and temperamental characteristics. Parents jointly influence different spheres of development, effects that are the product of complex patterns of experience, and each is responsive to the child's emerging social and cognitive competence. (1980:162–163)

The evidence is considerable, therefore, that both sexual feelings of the child and differentiated, strong feelings toward both parents exist by the time a child enters its second year. In this light the existence of a primary oedipal complex becomes a possibility, and we can take seriously references in the literature to oedipal feelings in very young children.

One such reference is Sachs' treatment (1977) of a two-year-old who displayed castration anxiety beginning at eighteen months.

Sachs states, "Certain aspects of the case support the possibility of an oedipal conflict." Again, Kleeman (1966) gives very detailed observations of a boy's apparent genital self-discovery with comments as to the oedipal nature of much sexual activity beginning at fifteen months. Further such evidence will appear in chapter 7.

Some investigators have previously accepted this early existence of oedipal conflict. Klein (1928), in recognizing the child's need to deal with oedipal issues at the same time as anal ones, was led to the discovery of some of the consequences of the primary oedipal phase, including the formation of the primitive super-ego. Jones also foreshadowed the concept of the primary oedipal phase, referring to the girl:

In the second half of the first year, and regularly by the end of it, the personality of the father plays an increasingly important part. True feminine love for him, together with the desire for access to his sexual organ, begins to conflict with his evident relationship to the mother. In the second year we can definitely speak of an oedipal complex. *It differs from the later more familiar form in being more deeply repressed and unconscious* (1935:487–488).

This last point may have contributed to the slow acceptance of these ideas. In any event they did not gain wide support at the time, as we saw in chapter 1.

The primary oedipal child cannot express its feeling as clearly as it can during the classical oedipal phase. The extent of the triadic mode is limited by the amount of ego differentiation that has so far taken place. A four-year-old is able to organize its sense of role and to maintain a sophisticated assortment of behaviors that make its oedipal conflicts more obvious. Nonetheless, the primary oedipal conflict does explain behavior in a two-year-old and certain further developments in the personality.

The emerging self needs a framework for its interpersonal relations in order to obtain social self-definition. The primary oedipal phase is when the child forms a cohesive ego with a self-concept that is consonant with its psychosocial self. The core feelings of both the individuated self and the psychosocial self are based upon the child's genital sensations; body ego is integrated with gender identity. The two-year-old's ego in process of cohesion must, however, also contain many other impulses, emotions, and thoughts, which simultaneously claim a great deal of the child's energy. Some sources are its oral experience and what it takes in by sight and hearing, anal concerns, increasing muscular ability, feelings about autonomy and dependency, and the enormous effects of the rise of language. It is the integration of all of these factors that creates the organized ego, the child's great achievement in the resolution of the primary oedipal conflict. This nascent ego reflects the primary oedipal complex. In order to examine the properties of the primary oedipal complex in a meaningful way in part II, we first consider these concomitant factors of self-definition singly.

Concomitants of Self-Definition

Maturation of Impulse Systems, Sphincters,
and Locomotor Capacities
From birth onward, the child uses its experiences and impulses connected with oral, ocular, and aural capacities for information upon which to base its behavior (Abraham 1934; Emde and Robinson 1979). However, by nine months this information becomes part of the ego building that object permanence begins to make possible. Intentional interest in the genitals also appears at this point (Kleeman 1966). Thus as the child enters the primary oedipal phase, oral, ocular, and aural experiences are available to contribute to the primary oedipal complex. This allows the fusion of sexuality and oral/ocular fantasies that are found, for example, in such syndromes as voyeurism and anorexia. We shall see in later chapters that these syndromes can be traced to the primary oedipal phase.

To return to the normal course of development, the materials for ego building are greatly enriched by maturational factors. Great changes happen in the child during its second year of life. Maturation of the sphincters and of the large muscle system introduces new powers of control, both within the child and in its effectiveness outside itself. Abraham (1927) and Erikson (1959a) detail the ramifications of this development in the young personality. Oral and sensory processes were the child's main sources of information, but maturation of the large muscle system and the sphincters enables a more forcefully interactive order of experience. So pivotal are these developments that the two-year-old stage is classically referred to as the anal phase.

There is a shift of emphasis from oral/perceptual competence (the earliest ways in which the child is active and can feel mastery) to anal/muscular competence, which brings with it a power struggle. For the first time the child has conscious control of a completely inner process (in contrast to the subjective experience of food intake, which combined inner and outer forces). The question of who controls its sphincters—the mother or the child—is a serious one in establishing individuality. Glover describes the situation: "[In the second year] . . . as the oral phase closes the primacy of impulse is taken over by the urethral and anal group . . . at the cost, however, of considerable hatred against the persons responsible for interference with these functions" (1949:102). Anna Freud extends these observations of hostility: "Above all, the peak period of aggressiveness was found to coincide with the anal stage of sexuality. On this level of instinctual development the wishes to harm or to destroy things or people, and to make sadistic attacks on loved persons were shown to assume equal importance with the anal interests themselves. The preponderance of aggressive tendencies on the anal level led to the description of the stage as the *anal-sadistic* phase" (1968:66). The violent fantasies deriving from anal issues are tribute to the conflict caused by this new ability to control an inner process and by the newly augmented control of movement. These provoke such tortuous response rather than a purely positive feeling of greater competence because of interpersonal issues in the fundamental process of developing a sense of self.

Other aspects of ego derive from maturational events. For example, anality is associated with orderliness, as Abraham (1927) believed, from the reaction-formation of cleanliness. Rhythmicity in anal functioning furthers the concept of order. Additionally, increased sense of order accompanies the simultaneous integration of the ego. The reason that anally fixated personalities can seem very strong is not only that the intensities and angers of the anal stage are integrated into the ego at that time. The self-disciplinary aspect of a positive anal fixation reflects the integrative activity of the ego during the primary oedipal phase.

Attitudes toward punctuality similarly are traceable to the anal period (Abraham 1927) because maturation of the sense of time coincides with the great emotional significance of anal matters (see discussion below). These attributes are assimilated into the ego according to the ways in which the child experiences separation/individuation and its primary oedipal feelings.

Less obviously conflicted for the child is the achievement of locomotor maturity, which occurs during the primary oedipal phase. A priori one would expect the conflicts stemming from separation/individuation to be as great with the new-found locomotor skills as with anality. The much greater intensity of the anal concerns derive from the intensity of the urges and from the inner struggle for physical control, neither of which is present in the process of learning to move independently. However, there are enormous contributions to the nascent ego that come from the new locomotor capacities. First is the sense of personal wholeness that occurs in overcoming gravity. To become upright, the child coordinates its muscles in a new way and feels its own strength as it stands alongside the large persons in the family. Second, the child's freedom to explore and to participate in its world is vastly greater when its range of activity increases.

How the child pictures itself in terms of activity and passivity is affected by its locomotor capacities. Conversely, its use of these capacities is affected by its attitudes about itself in terms of separation/individuation, primary oedipal conflict, and whether it feels itself to be good or bad.

Ambivalence, Autonomy, and Dependence

Demonstrably, the toddler is ambivalent. One source of mixed feelings is the balancing of the comfort of dependence against the fulfillment of mastery (Erikson 1959b).

This is the *behavioral aspect* of intrapsychic separation/individuation. The process is burdened by the child's conflicts over what it perceives as its own badness and its wish to be good. The sense of responsibility derived from its sense of self means it can feel guilt and shame. Being connected to mother feels like protection against being independent in some bad way. For an example of how far reaching in the personality this maneuver can be, again I recall Barbara, who in order to feel safe in enjoying any experience mentally included her mother. Trust in its own goodness must be strong for a child to enjoy its increasing autonomy. This issue affects whether the child can allow a sense of independent existence to develop out of the mother–child matrix of its initial perceptions. While this has not been explicitly stated, it has been implied in the writings of many today. Kernberg for example, says: "The structural characteristics of narcissistic personalities . . . are a consequence of the development of (faulty) differentiation and integration of ego and superego structures, deriving from pathological (in contrast to normal) object relationships" (1975:271).

Successful achievement of personal autonomy is one of the requirements for ego integration. This is the conclusion shared by various authors who otherwise disagree on how that autonomy is developed. Jacobson accepts the idea of a "symbiotic mother–child relationship as the beginning of human identity formation." However, she adds that "separation from the mother and the resulting process of individuation seem at least as essential" (1964:30). Kohut (1977) argues against this model of self evolving from a previous psychological merger with the mother.

It is interesting whether a child feels itself connected with its mother in a primitive sense of unity at the beginning, as Jacobson and Mahler state, or whether, as Kohut and Kagan say, infants from the beginning react to experience with degrees of self/nonself-discrimination. Either way, however, *at the time of ego organization, the monumental conflicts that stir both boys and girls require that they establish clear ego boundaries.* Their wishes then to feel connected with mother are reasons enough to create the symbiotic behavior of small children and severely regressed patients.[7]

Regardless of whether there is a previous sense of connectedness with the mother, at the point of object constancy, the establishment of ego boundaries is a requirement for a complete sense of self. The degree of comfort a child feels in taking responsibility for its own behavior affects the child's ease in establishing such boundaries. A child's feelings in the process are glimpsed in a symbiotic-psychotic girl who undergoes a delayed rapprochement phase (at five and a half) while in treatment. Bergman (1971) discusses her and the "delusion of omnipotence" evident in the child's desperate attempts to control the mother and her insistence/desire that the mother be able to "read her thoughts."

This child struggles over who she is and who her mother is. We can speculate that, while she tries to control her mother, she also is panicky because of danger in her thoughts. Anxiety about power and privacy of thought rather than ambiguity of physical facts causes the child's efforts to eliminate separation between herself and her mother. Regardless of whether the child earlier felt a clear unity with her mother, she denies separation when she has too much anxiety about the possibilities and consequences of individuation.

Implied in this already complicated picture is another factor in ego formation: self-awareness means ownership of one's own feelings and thoughts. Perforce, this includes angry feelings, well known to be a major problem for the two-year-old. Kestenbaum in a thorough description of the first years of the child presents typical two-year-old behavior: "The wise physician should probably prescribe two aspirin with the admonition, 'Yes, madam, there is indeed something wrong. Your child is two. Take a vacation and come back when he's three.' Not for nothing the expression 'terrible twos'" (1980:99).

As Erikson (1963), Anna Freud (1965), Mahler (1965), and Parens (1979) point out, these feelings stem from both the process of psychological individuation and the pressures connected with being in the anal phase. As discussed above, feelings of guilt and shame become possible in this time period, doubtless adding to the two-year-old's storminess. Guilt and shame become part of the personality to the degree that the child takes ownership of its own thoughts, feelings, and behavior. Intense feelings in relation to anality, along with capacity to conceptualize good and bad, can intensify feelings of guilt and shame.

In the same developmental period, the child's sexual feelings are wrapped into the process of self-individuation, especially because genital sensations contribute so much to the process of defining the self. We remember that sexual feeling is present just about from birth (Kestenberg 1975); but great interest in genital feeling is evident only by the child's second year (Galenson and Roiphe 1980b). Attitudes about the genitalia are linked then just to body-ego and anal fantasies and sex-role behavior. Primitive, harsh feelings of guilt and shame can attach to body-pleasure and genital sensation during the anal/separation/individuation/primary oedipal phase.

The nascent ego must take account of its angers and its genital feelings and what it assumes to be counterpart feelings in its parents or other caretakers. Thus, ambivalence as to dependency and autonomy is more than merely a choice between the comforts of being taken care of versus the joys of self-actualization. The intensity of this conflict is complicated by the child's sense of anger and sexually based feelings in caretakers and in itself.

The Experience of Personal Change
How the child handles the autonomy versus dependency issue relates to its concept of being a baby or a nonbaby. This is another concomitant of self-recognition during toddlerhood. The child's perception of personal change coincides with its need for inner permission for independence, demonstrated by whether or not it considers itself a baby. Ahrens (1954) conducted research establishing that by nine months a child can distinguish between babies and adults, a perception that augments the beginning process of identifying self and nonself as autonomous persons.

Knowing it is a "Me!" means that a child integrates a tremendous number of perceptions of inner and outer reality, differentiating degrees of selfness in all of them. For example, in early feeding, food intrudes into the mouth, where it is received with voluntary control shifting to reflexive swallowing. By contrast, toddlers can reach for food, bite off appropriately sized pieces, and manage the entire voluntary process, including awareness of swallowing. This one example provides some insight into the complexity that rapid personal change brings to learning one's own boundaries in defining the self. It is an obvious example in a constant stream of experience. Furthermore, the infant rapidly changes in its capacities. Improvement makes a sense of personal continuity more feasible neurologically, but confusing as well. Also, as in learning to walk, one may take a step only to find that the next time one tries it one does not succeed. Through it all, the crux of the matter is that one's very dimensions keep changing and yet one remains oneself. This was perceived by Langer, who said:

Identity formation is the child's growing capacity for simultaneous perception, awareness and belief that he is continuous in time, . . . that although he has changed he remains identical with himself in his previous state and that others have the same view of him. . . . The subjective feeling of personal identity lies precisely in the child's awareness of his continuous "self-sameness," or conservation in which the ego capacities master experience. (1969:32)

The observer of the infant often fails to account adequately for this "self-sameness" as the child develops. As Greenacre says: "[It] may be that we do not adequately take into account that the continually changing actual size of the infant (due to the rapidity of the early growth) is an important factor in the subjective situation . . . This complicates the central registration of the infant's perceptions of the outer world" (1969:157). What the child feels about further change is not simply a choice between comfort (dependency) and mastery (autonomy). Other, interrelated, issues are involved.

The young child distinguishes three classes of beings: boys, girls, and babies (see chapters 3 and 7). *Babyhood* is in the toddler's mind, an undifferentiated, genderless state. By contrast, a developing sense of *selfness* involves gender identity as part of its structure. Thus, the issue of moving ahead from babyhood to greater autonomy is tied to a developing gender identity. While the child is developing its sense of gender, it is also coming to know future time, but *perceived* connection with the past comes later. Therefore the first integration of the ego makes a break with the infantile state. The issue of gender and thus the primary oedipal conflict comes to bear on how the child feels about its progressive changes.

The handling of oedipal feelings, angers, and other sources of primitive guilt and shame profoundly affects the formation of the ego. Implicit in this is the child's awareness of the dichotomy of good versus bad. Such awareness comes from one other fundamental concomitant of formation of an organized ego, the rise of language.

The Significance of Language
There are several aspects of language development that contribute to ego formation. *Prelinguistic thought contrasts with the use of language* in several important ways (Levin 1938). It is imagistic, relatively unorganized, and utilizes *pars pro toto* symbolization. The last reflects the fact that the child has not yet organized a complete sense of itself or others. Thus early inner representations of outer reality are in part-objects and concrete symbols for them. Also, as Freud (1905a, 1909) pointed out, words themselves seem to be objects to the child at first.

The prelinguistic child, reacting globally, makes sense of things by association. Analysis of cause and effect forms the major basis of logic only after the rise of language when concept formation develops. Without language, feelings cannot be identified except in terms of the time and place in which they occur. Piaget (1946) found that young children do not separate time and space in early stages of thinking. Events and feelings are remembered through their original context in time/place.

This aspect of prelinguistic thinking explained in a case of mine why an early adolescent called Milton was drawn to amusement parks. Milton felt both high excitement and contentment there as nowhere else. We learned that when he was a toddler his pretty teenage babysitter very often took him to an amusement park. Now on the brink of adolescence, he yearned for a safe time of experiencing libidinal urges *and* separation from his mother. These feelings remained connected in his mind with the kind of place where he first experienced them. Being in that kind of place was therefore evocative of old feelings. This is an example of how early nonlinguistic thought can continue to play a role in later development.

Thought involving language is by contrast analytical, making sense of cause and effect, and involves concept formation so that abstract ideas such as what is good or bad can be dealt with. Descartes' dictum, "I think, therefore I am," brings to mind how linguistic thought means being able to be aware of oneself. The great role of language in self-awareness makes it part of the separation/individuation process. Kramer demonstrates that "my thoughts are me" in a poignant vignette in which she traces this connection of self and thought to experience during the time of language acquisition:

Slowly [the therapist] focused on the patient's need to maintain autonomy at any cost, including her need to reassure herself that he would not know too much about her or make her do things his way. The patient responded by recalling the past (and the current) intrusiveness of her mother, [whose most common expression] "Tell me, Tell me," caused the patient to feel trapped, "as if all of what is mine, no, I mean all of what is *me*, is taken away." [The analyst felt that the patient's picture was similar to an ambivalent rapprochement subphase (15–22-month-old) child who had to attract and yet elude the swooping and shadowing mother.] (1980:250–251)

We see that for this patient, in dealing with issues from the age we are discussing, the ownership of linguistic thought was equated with ownership of self.

Another example comes from an adult, my patient, Elisabeth. This case shows how various issues of toddlerhood appear together and the importance of language in the process: After some acknowledgment of an interest in men, Elisabeth struggled with feelings of merger/separation in regard to her mother. "I never realized how much I was a part of her craziness. If I had bad feelings, somehow that *was* me—*I* was bad."

In Elisabeth's very next session, she used transference material and direct material to deal with the question of how much her mother knew of her feelings. It seemed crucial for her mother to ignore the extent of their involvement with each other and not to know how difficult this was for Elisabeth. Because of this, Elisabeth felt that knowing was dangerous and that her own "brain did not work." In increasing psychological separation from her mother, she began to feel free to think and to know. For the first time, she spontaneously integrated new things she learned, taking delight in seeing their implications, recognizing she had ideas of her own that were worthwhile. Linguistic thought was integral in Elisabeth's experience of being herself.

Another aspect to the role of language in the separation/individuation process is the question of *privacy of thought*. For the child it can be a grave matter to find out to what extent mother has power over the child's own thoughts.

As patients work through material relating to this early stage of life, a recurrent theme is secrecy. I have come to understand this to reflect the fearful feeling, "Mother knows everything." In the child's mind Mother just knows when it is hungry, wet, cold or hot, happy or sad, ready to run, or feeling tired. Mother seems so powerful and all-knowing, it is not surprising that a very young child will feel Mother can even know unspoken thought. This feeling also occurs in someone who shows symbiotic defenses in adulthood.

I referred previously to Barbara in an example of seemingly symbiotic behavior. She could not permit herself to be aware of her own thoughts lest they prove to have a sexy content, in which case she felt she would die. She felt safe to have thoughts that were someone else's—as in memorizing things for school. Otherwise, she had to be sure she was thinking what her mother wanted her to think. When she dared to have sexy thoughts, she immediately began to eat compulsively, feeling that only so could she prevent annihilation. Her belief in her mother's omniscience made her desperate. Barbara could have secrets only by immediately befogging her thoughts and forgetting them. She truly believed that whatever she allowed herself to know would automatically be known to her mother as well. Living two thousand miles away from her mother did not matter. Space/time was of no help to Barbara in securing a sense of separation from her mother while Barbara maintained her acute conflict over sexuality. Barbara thus not only demonstrates how language affects the ego in relation to privacy of thought. Her case also directs attention to the child's concept of space/time while first organizing its ego.

The concept of time is a special linguistic tool that affects the handling of experience. The child in its second year of life can at first conceptualize only the immediate moment. By twenty-one months it begins to speak spontaneously in terms of the present (Ames 1946). This coincides with the child's growing sense of its own existence. By two years of age, the future appears in such words as "gonna" and "in a minute." Only by two and a half is an expression of recent past added. Then it takes another two years to refine these understandings. In terms of overall development, the issues of the primary oedipal phase are first confronted when a sense of urgency, the apperception only of "now," characterizes the child's behavior. This places a limitation on its resources to cope with the developmental challenges that emerge in the second year. The feeling that there is only "now" can remain attached to other elements in the child's mental life.

Colarusso spells out in terms of separation/individuation and anal concerns some of the consequences of the limited time sense of the two-year-old child. Taking into account previous work on the subject, he shows the deep significance of their connection:

Freud (1909), Abraham (1921), and Jones (1923) noted the relationship between time and anality as they described the psychopathology of the anal period, particularly the obsessional neurosis with its compulsive rhythms and unconscious equations between castration anxiety, death, and time. In so doing they laid the groundwork for the exploration of the normal developmental factors of the anal phase which expand time sense.

Because I view the emergence of time sense as a developmental continuum, I see the events of the anal period influencing the moulding of the ego's experience of time in relation to both the previous experiences of the oral period and the events of future developmental stages.

Kolansky pointed out the toddler's tendency to treat words concretely, as faeces, making them in effect another body product. Since temporal words appear for the first time during the anal phase, the sense of manipulation and control of time, now through the powerful new tool of language, is greatly heightened. (1979:246, 249)

Colarusso then quotes Solnit on noting a definite connection between children's limited time sense and poor tolerance for separation. We see here that the well-known anal and separation/individuation issues of the toddler are affected by its sense of time. Indeed, the level of time perception that guides behavior reflects a person's achievements in separation/individuation. We shall see many instances in the clinical material in this book that will show interrelationship between ego organization, separation/individuation, and maturity of sense of time.

There are further specific connections between language development and the child's efforts at separation/individuation. Part of the problem of tolerating separation is that *early linguistic thought operates in terms of dichotomous categories.*[8] That means the child is capable of comprehending only allness or noneness. Omnipresence is opposed by nonexistence. Separation/individuation can seem to threaten annihilation of mother or of self.

Strong guilt feelings greatly heighten the danger of annihilation. As we have seen, guilt feelings are possible only as a child achieves some degree of separation/individuation and hence a level of ego formation capable of assuming responsibility. If the child has overly strong guilt feelings about wishes that seem unacceptable to mother, then further separation/individuation becomes more difficult. The child might even back away from the degree of separation/individuation it has already achieved. To be autonomous threatens being capable of carrying out the forbidden.

The question of good versus bad is another categorical dichotomy that besets the child when language first develops. This is a change from infancy. An infant can have tropic feelings toward what is good or bad, but that is different from the capacity to conceptualize the dichotomy. In his study of vocabularies of the very young, Lewis (1963) documents the new mental process. Just as the child's language indicates emergence of a sense of self during the latter part of the second year of life, language usage reflects emergence of categorical thinking and the capacity for guilt. Ethical values show up in language of approval and disapproval, leading to rules and assigning responsibility. The availability of a new process of logical thought (Kestenbaum 1980) helps the child to structuralize these events.

Noy describes the process of structuralizing an ethical system, demonstrating its importance to the way the ego is organized:

The nature of reflective thought to separate itself into observing and observed parts gives the individual the experience of possessing a divisible self. This is expressed in the various experiences such as the cleavage between emotions and reason, fantasy and reality, wishes and constraints. The ability to pit the observing part against the observed one in order to control it gives the experience (or illusion, depending on one's philosophical attitude) of possessing a "free will" and of being responsible for one's own actions.

The experience of self-control and responsibility serves as the basis for the development of human ethics, a socially shared system of moral rules, partly internalized and partly imposed by society, which guides the individual in his thoughts, feelings, and behavior. (1979:207)

Noy seems to take for granted what is fundamental in this process, so I wish to underscore it. A sense of responsibility develops simultaneously with the idea of the good/bad dichotomy. This combination produces a capacity for painful shame and guilt, inspiring the need for a moral code. The child must be able to govern inevitable conflict between wishes and feelings adjudged within the self to be "bad" on the first side and on the second, the child's precious self-esteem as someone who is "good." To be happy with oneself, "I am 'Me!'" must mean "I am good."

There are further significant consequences to organizing the sense of self while conscious thought develops. One has options to label or not to label feelings and experiences: guilt-tinged secrets, violent fantasies, and the child's sense of power in self-mastery of its sphincters, for example. In other words, what is too painful or unacceptable can simply be left unlabeled and not be part of consciousness. Or, made-up language can tag something unacceptable in a secret way only the child itself can understand. Language can of course be used to hold on to experience and gain a sense of mastery over it. These may be important reasons why two-year-olds are observed to develop ritualistic and obsessional behavior.

Obsessional behavior in adults is often associated with anal-sadistic materials. Blum, finding this always to be true states, "The analysis of a case of obsessional neurosis will eventually deal with symptoms and character traits related to anal phase conflicts" (1977:781).

Finally, the rise of language during the second year shapes the defensive system of the ego. The statement quoted above from Noy refers to this. Conscious thought contrasts to the earlier and continuing mode of nonverbal mentation, making for a dichotomy of thought versus feeling. This allows the possibility for splitting and repression as defense mechanisms.

Bleich used phylogenetic evidence to gain understanding of this contrast, which gives us an idea of the constructive importance it has for human functioning:

Consciousness of objectivity and consciousness of self . . . seem to mark the beginning of characteristically human reasoning. . . . Language learned by the chimpanzee, Washoe, . . . falls short of the structure exhibited by even the youngest of human speakers, and . . . remains dependent on sensorimotor behavior. This means that in animals and in preverbal children the capacity to think independently is still not differentiated from associationist modes of emotion and behavior. It seems likely, therefore, that the *capacity for representational thought, because it is independent of affective sensorimotor behavior, affects the human being's species-specific differentiation between the affective and the cognitive.* (1976:53)

The young human's experience of contrast within itself between the cognitive and the affective is useful for handling anxiety. We have seen that intense concerns about being good or bad, safe or endangered, can be eased by not naming the unacceptable. What one does not know is excluded from the sense of self. This is generalized in setting up defensive systems for the ego. As Brenner explains, "The mechanism of repression consists in the establishment of a countercathexis by the ego" (1957:43).

Simple repression is a special, passive form of splitting as a defense. In active forms, splitting allows for acknowledgment of two sides of a conflict, one good, one bad. Then the child can disavow the "bad" without ignoring it. Considering the amount of anxiety engendered by the highly polarized conflicts of toddlerhood, it is not surprising that splitting is the characteristic defense mechanism of the period. Paradoxically, splitting provides a means for a primitive degree of ego organization. With growing powers, the child evolves more sophisticated defenses, which enable it to integrate its ego more solidly. In the meantime, the toddler seeks strength for its ego through affirmation of its core, its gender identity. Evidence for this occupies the next chapter.

3 The Formation of Gender Identity

The formation of gender identity is a recent subject of study. Money (1970) spoke of imprinting gender identity at the end of the first year of life, i.e., as ego differentiation begins. Kohlberg (1966) traced gender identity to a cognitive maturity that enabled a child to recognize its sexual qualities. From his research, Stoller (1968b) concluded that gender identity, once formed in either sex very early in childhood, remained fixed. Parens (1973), interested in primary heterosexuality as a biologically determined phenomenon, saw gender identity as arising from innate properties of the brain at around two and a half years and catapulting children of both sexes into the oedipus. Lewis (1979) considered the larger social context as crucial in forming gender identity. The number of different theories speaks to the complexity of the subject. However, except for Parens' thought, all are based on fact and supplement each other.

This work provides a basis for examining the nature of gender identity and its central role in the formation of the ego.

Several factors contribute to ego formation. Observers variously list overcoming gravity in being upright, large muscle coordination, perception of one's face, and representational thinking, which enables the experiencing of self as an object and resolving conflict.[1] Genital sensation is included on all lists, sometimes with only one other factor that seems important enough to explain how the sense of self forms.

Greenacre, after pointing out first that "establishment of the body image . . . is the core both of the incipient ego and the later self-image" and that the "sense of the self-image is maintained and perhaps vitalized [through] comparison and contrast with others," notes that "the body areas which are the most significant in comparing and contrasting and establishing individual recognition of the body self, and that of others, are the *face* and the *genitals*" (italics Greenacre's) (1968:616).

Galenson and Roiphe, in a typical reprise of the role of genital sensations in ego formation, recall Roiphe's 1968 description of "the occurrence of a normal and regularly emerging early genital phase in both sexes beginning sometime between fifteen and twenty-four months of age" (1980a:805). Genital arousal was taken as an indication of genital maturation "enough to provide a channel for tension discharge and pleasure possibilities. *All major experiences would have a genital reflection thenceforth.* . . . The normal increase in endogenous genital sensations at this time would contribute to the establishment of genital schematization and to the sense of self with which the sense of genital identity appears to be coextensive" (1980a:805). I came to appreciate this general judgment in a session with my patient, Alison, who confided, "When I masturbate, then I know I'm really me."

This still begs the question of whether sexual feelings and gender identity provide the ego core.[2] That a core is necessary is easy to agree. The organization of ego-nuclei (Glover 1968) requires a stable core to which to attach an enormous number of impressions of self, a flux of inner and outer experience.[3] Genital sensations provide an opportunity for arriving at such a stable core. Amsterdam and Levitt describe the essential dynamic: "The genitalia provide the child with a unique opportunity for directly pleasuring himself. Perhaps for the first time the child treats part of his body as a distinct object, or takes an objective view of that which produces intensive subjective feelings" (1980:81).

Genital sensations are integral to self-definition, but they alone do not produce gender identity. Biological factors such as hormones in the brain, perceptions of forms of genitalia, as well as psychosocial factors such as parental cueing, all may be involved.

There is help in assessing the relative roles of these factors because of a "natural experiment," hermaphroditism. Due to either a genetic or prenatal endocrinal anomaly, hermaphroditic children have sex parts that are poorly differentiated and/or combine the morphologies of the two kinds of genitalia (Greenson 1968). Their condition enables learning about gender identity formation when self-observation is ambiguous and the endocrinology of the brain is at variance with assigned gender.

The first yield for our purposes from study of hermaphrodites is knowing when gender identity is achieved. Stoller (1975) investigated hermaphroditic children's reactions to efforts to change their original sex assignments. He discovered that by roughly the age of two intrapsychic gender identity is fixed. He then confirmed that this timing is true for normal children as well, in keeping with Galenson and Roiphe's observation that gender identity formation coexists with forming identity of self. All children need to categorize themselves psychosocially and to make meaning out of their intense genital sensations. That hermaphrodites develop gender identity at the same age as other children supports Kohlberg's finding that cognitive development is fundamental to this achievement.

Money and Ogunro (1974), Ehrhardt (1970), Greenson (1968), Stoller (1979), and Lev-Ran (1974) are foremost in publishing studies of gender identity in hermaphrodites. Some hermaphroditic children followed the sex assignment they were given at birth, usually by a doctor. In these cases the sex assignment was accepted by their parents. The determination of gender identity was, therefore, for these youngsters, strictly a product of social patterning. This was true when children of "opposite sex" were compared whose external genitalia were similarly and completely ambiguous. Considering themselves to belong to the chosen sex, they lived normal lives, including growing up to marry. They resisted any possibility of sex change, even upon learning in certain cases that the original assignment was wrong according to more sophisticated tests than were first used. Greenson and Money report cases in which parents' certainty of the initial sex assignment was safeguarded by corrective surgical and hormonal treatment of the children. Lev-Ran's cases lived in a culture (Russia) in which the authority of the physician was unquestioned in the making of sex assignment at birth. Accordingly the hermaphrodites in his sample had the benefit of being raised unambiguously.[4] Lev-Ran cited several cases of adults whose mature bodies displayed blatant characteristics contradicting the original sex assignment, but the patients were interested in possible treatment only to conform with their assigned genders. We can see in this how strong gender identity develops from parental cueing alone. We can also see how gender identity becomes intertwined with the self-concept.

The question arises to what extent biochemical, particularly neurophysiological, factors play a part in the gender identity of hermaphrodites. Ehrhardt and Meyer-Bahlburg (1980) carefully review the research in this area. Although most studies were conducted without controls, Ehrhardt and Meyer-Bahlburg are able to form a reasonable conclusion. From the weight of the evidence, the degree of ambiguity or clarity of gender assignment by the parents is the determining factor in a hermaphroditic child's formation of gender identity. This evidence refutes Parens' suggestion that innate brain chemistry triggers and directs gender identity sometime after the age of two.

Looking to the inner life of hermaphrodites, Lev-Ran (1974) Ehrhardt, Evers and Money (1968), and Ehrhardt and Meyer-Bahlburg (1981) studied the erotic childhood dreams and fantasies of various groups of such children. Here again they confirmed that intrapsychic gender identity rather than stereotypical external genitalia determines sexual behavior. The erotic inner life of the hermaphrodites corresponds with their gender assignments, as did their outer behavior.

We have sparse material from childhood observation or reconstruction through treatment of adults tracing the vicissitudes of early psychosexual development in these cases. Still, it is reasonable to consider that primary and classical oedipal behavior develops in such children since hermaphroditic adults practice effective heterosexual behavior in terms of their assigned gender, including getting married. We do have information about the fantasies of hermaphrodites, and these confirm the intrapsychic importance of gender identity. The most startling data about hermaphrodites concern their mental health. *They present no more mental disturbance than the general population, including disorders of gender identity.*[5] This is difficult to believe, but it is the finding independently of Money, Lev-Ran, Stoller, and Greenson among cases raised unambiguously. We may speculate that ambiguity of external genitalia inspires the parents of hermaphroditic children to be particularly clear in cueing about gender. Such treatment would reinforce the child's development of a strong ego, a sense of knowing "who I am!" We see that strong egos are associated with clear gender identity, supporting the idea of gender identity as the ego's core.

Although cultural patterning and natural interest in its genital sensations suffice for a hermaphroditic child's development of gender identity, in building its ego, the question remains how being born a normal boy or girl enhances the process. What sort of primary masculinity and/or primary femininity might there be? Curiously enough, primary femininity is the only one that has been seriously questioned, at least in psychoanalytic writing. Primary masculinity has been taken for granted.

The idea of primary masculinity was easy to accept in parallel with the thought about femininity. If we assumed that every little girl wished to be a boy, then it was believable that boys had no conflicts about gender. Yet, as Rado (1933) points out, as does Greenson (1968), if this were valid, we should expect that gender identity problems in adults, and the wish to change sex, would be a common serious problem for human females. The statistics run dramatically in the other direction: gender identity problems are seen much more commonly among males compared with their incidence among females (Green 1974). We remember also that among hermaphrodites who are offered the opportunity to change gender in adulthood, they reject equally absolutely the possibility of turning from female into male as of turning from male into female.

There is another interesting sidelight to this question of whether primary femininity exists in human females or whether they turn to femininity only because masculine strivings are frustrated. Biologically, femininity could be primary. Each human organism (and lower mammals) starts development closer to female morphology.[6] It is only by superimposition of androgens later in an embryo's development that males are created (Ede 1978). I do not argue in any way that this is evidence for feminine primacy. However, if there were a single predisposition, the logic of the biology of development would suggest that it be primary femininity. This would be true at least to the extent that gender identity depended upon biological prompting rather than cultural patterning. There is, therefore, no sound basis for thinking that a primary masculinity exists in all children, from which the feminine personality emerges much as woman from Adam's rib.

Research to date is inadequate to tell us how much innate qualities operate to confirm a normal child in its gender identity. We are still collecting facts. Erikson (1965) and Kestenberg (1968) emphasize the different sense of inner and outer space that genital sensations inspire in girls and boys, respectively. Parents seek out gender-appropriate behavior in their offspring and reinforce it (Seavey, Katz and Zalk 1975). The fact that hermaphrodites can be so clear about gender identity is an extreme case of independence of gender identity from innate factors.

To the degree that we learn anything from the hermaphroditic experience, it is that *there is not necessarily either primary masculinity nor primary femininity but a tremendous need to organize, to build an inner psychic structure.*

The last fact does not diminish the value of normal structures in confirming gender identity for a child. There is an analogy in studies of children who are blind from birth and their problems in forming an overall sense of identity. They are able to form a strong sense of self, but they are disadvantaged in the task. Stoller (1968a) reports a young woman who had no vagina until the lack was discovered and corrected surgically when she was fourteen. This young woman was secure in her identity. However, as she grew up, she was puzzled by references to internal structures, and her dreams reflected an absence of the usual container-type feminine symbolism. The little girl with a vagina from birth is stimulated to associate her inner structures with her gender identity.

Again a pioneer, Horney (1926) was aware of primary femininity in this sense of meaningful perceptions. Rado and Greenson more recently made an important point of it. Parents commonly believe they see signs of it in their girl babies along with a perception of primary masculinity in their boy babies.

Nonetheless, psychoanalysts followed Freud in presuming primary masculinity. This led to a model of early development in which all babies identify *with the mother,* after which all feel like boys or wish to be boys, until out of frustration little girls accommodate to being girls. One reason this confusing picture has been acceptable to so many earlier investigators, including women such as Deutsch, Lampl-de-Groot, and Greenacre, is the observation of penis envy. Horney (1926) placed penis envy in the context of the other (oedipal) feelings of a little girl. However, this interpretation of hers was set aside.

Penis envy continues to divert many present-day workers such as Roiphe and Galenson, Mahler, and McDevitt. As Rado makes clear, however, penis envy requires more explanation than is usually given it. We cannot assume that adoption of feminine behavior patterns occurs coincident with apparent notice of the genital difference because toddler girls automatically perceive male equipment as more intriguing than their own or something they sorely miss having.[7] Can visual perception of the genitalia of the two sexes compare in subjective experience to the strength of a girl's personal pleasure in her genital sensations?[8] We must investigate further.

Chasseguet-Schmirgel (1976) notes that daughters of strongly controlling mothers (and passive fathers) demonstrate the strongest penis envy reactions. This seems surprising. Logically, a two-year-old might feel that the equipment of the stronger parent is the better. Yet Chasseguet-Schmirgel points out in her clinical evidence that *fear of the mother is the correlative of penis envy.* As the idea of the primary oedipal phase is accepted, penis envy becomes truly understandable. A girl with penis envy wishes to have a penis because then she would not be her mother's rival and could safely move closer to her father. This wish can be developed to a greater extent in little girls who have less ego integration (which would carry with it the gender-modeling "I am like mother"). A lack of such strong individuation is seen in children with dominant mothers where there is a fear of the consequences of separation/individuation. The little girl thus chooses not to identify with her mother/aggressor *because it is identification with her father— though he is weak—that is the safest way in which to permit herself closeness to him.* Elisabeth expressed this idea to me when she said in relation to her feelings for her father, "Liking is the same as being like."[9]

Satow offers another version of such dynamics in a case of hers. It is particularly interesting because, for the patient she describes, "penis envy, even penis worship is part of the . . . cultural reality." Yet this patient responded only in part to

the manifest privileges of Puerto Rican boys, but she was also responding to conflicts that were uniquely her own. She was trying to cope with an abrupt separation from her mother that she was not developmentally prepared for as a child, and a consistent sexual overstimulation by the women in her house. She was also attempting to hold on to her mother by identifying with her father as a defense against oedipal wishes toward him which the mother clearly forbade, yet separate from her mother by refusing to identify with her. Thus, the extreme intensity of Maria's penis envy can only be fully understood as the result of the convergence of both cultural and individual intrapsychic factors. She was socialized in a culture which idealizes penises and brought up in a family, within that culture, that is the type which is most prone to producing penis envy—a family in which the mother is experienced as dominant and controlling while the father is experienced as weak and passive." (1983:555)

Just as this is true of penis envy among girls, castration anxiety among toddler boys becomes understandable in light of the primary oedipal complex. A boy who has such fantasies during the primary oedipal phase develops them out of his own struggle between desiring closeness to mother (due to genital urges) and his fear of closeness to her with its concomitant loss of sense of self. In being close to mother, he is afraid he will cease being a "Me!"— which, since gender is the core of self-definition, means ceasing to be a boy. The castration anxiety comes from the faulty resolution in reversal, "It is not 'Me!' desiring closeness and with it risking the loss of my boyhood, it is mother who wishes for closeness and to take away my penis." In this we see the reason castration anxiety is greater in boys who have what they perceive to be seductive mothers (Kramer 1954). A further way of handling these anxieties is to dissipate them by moving them into less frightful realms via metaphor. Thus, the boy may move his castration anxiety into the framework of anal concerns where the struggle with mother for control and possession involves not his penis but his feces. Such cases are seen in the work of Bell (1964), who showed in her careful studies of anal concern that, at the age of two, loss of "stool-penises" can seem as a threatening sign of mother's power.

The classical oedipal boy's fear of his father's retaliation is not necessarily involved in a boy's castration anxieties at the primary oedipal stage. Sharing his father's differentness from mother helps the primary oedipal boy to crystallize his sense of self. Herzog's cases (see chapter 8) are examples of how this works in two-year-olds. These little boys with sleep disturbances show how they do battle against their genital impulses toward their mothers in striving for personal identity.

Penis envy and castration anxiety dramatize the link between achieving gender identity and separation/individuation. They point to the fact that vicissitudes of separation/individuation, including the practicing and rapprochement subphases, can be understood only in relation to the powerful emotions accompanying the formation of gender identity. However the child interprets them, masculine and feminine behavior become part of the ego along with gender identity, giving character to the child's self-concept.

In the same automatic way, gender identity links the nascent ego with a psychosocial identity. The roles of both parents are vital in the process of achieving gender identity. Jacobson (1971) calls attention to the primal scene as a significant provocation to the child to help it understand that one person can be different from another. Abelin (1980) refers to a *primal constellation* by which the child develops a sense of relationship between the parents as well as between itself and each of them. These formulations, the process of intrapsychic triangulation, help the child to think of itself as being yet another person rather than something fused with the mother. Triangulation gives the child a social scheme. The primal scene dramatizes for the child that genital sensations accurately guide recognition of both sexes, that the child belongs to one of them, and that feelings of intimacy with another are connected with these facts.

The sense of triangulation does not require actual primal scene experience, common though such experience is. Sirota presents a well-documented case of a basically healthy twenty-four-month-old boy who did not have opportunity to witness his parents' lovemaking. Nonetheless, the boy, Samuel,

would often say to his father, "Daddy you stay at work all night and I'll take care of Mommy." He enjoyed climbing upon his mother's lap, straddling her legs while facing her, and tried to push her down onto the couch. When such behavior was curtailed he would turn to some dolls, particularly a teddy bear, upon which he would climb, rock up and down, and say how much he loved it. Periodic masturbatory activity with his hands increased at that time. It should be noted that Samuel was never exposed to parental intercourse and from birth slept in a separate bedroom. (1969:257)

This behavior occurred when Samuel was at age twenty to twenty-four months.

Freud's case, the Wolf Man, provided primal scene material in dreams he had at age four, based on experiences that occurred at eighteen months. The idea that the primal scene can be observed when a child is eighteen months old and held in memory for reactivation during the classical oedipal period makes sense only if this child was emotionally geared to respond intensely to the experience when it happened. Fear is not the only emotion likely to be involved. Although much is made of the frightening specter of the primal scene, we know that much laughter and cooing and affirmatively passionate behavior also accompanies sexual embrace. The child's acknowledged jealousy does not stem from just negative impressions. The frightening form primal scene fantasy can take derives from the experience of jealousy in the context of the primary oedipal/anal period. Whatever the form of a child's primal scene fantasy, by exemplifying the triangular situation it aids in formation of gender identity—the linchpin of an independent ego.

A profound significance of gender identity lies in the meaning it gives to bodily experiences, welding body ego to the sense of self. Early sexual fantasies are full of oral and anal elements. Movement is eroticized.

By the same token, because gender identity emerges from intense, self-initiated pleasure, attitudes toward genitally based pleasure are applied to the ego. We can see what this means to the developing personality in terms of the "good versus bad" dichotomy in an illustrative Amsterdam and Levitt study. They investigated genital sensation as a foundation for the sense of self when genital pleasure is reproved by parents. The resulting inhibition of pleasure can spread "from sexual expression to other body-related activity" and "in extreme cases, the child may become alienated from his body" (1980:78), (sex being "bad" extended to body being "bad"). This underscores how gender identity, based on genital sensations, links with the formation of body ego in the earliest organization of the personality. We see the integrative quality of gender identity at work.

During the primary oedipal phase, we have seen, gender identity forms the essence of self-awareness. For the child, this means being a boy or a girl as opposed to being a baby.

Kleeman's William (1966) at twenty-two months was playing with his mother while she diapered him. Responding to the fact that there was to be a new baby soon, William told his mother, "I am not a boy; I am a baby." In a similar fashion, Jenny, aged two, was observed by Dunn (1981). Jenny informed everyone that she was no longer "Jenny."[10] She would not respond to that name. She had been to nursery school in training pants and insisted from then on that she was "Girl." Jenny spoke of "Girl go now," "Girl spoon," etc. In her mind, her newly autonomous state required naming herself by gender. This thinking is an accomplishment of the newly forming ego, but it persists in two common myths of babyhood.

Adults often romanticize infancy as a state of perfection (Josselyn 1953). Another romantic notion is baby innocence. Both contain the idea of being a baby as nonsexual and therefore a happier state of being. The truth about infancy is that there is much frustration in it that is inevitable and therefore much angry feeling. It is not possible for the most vigilant caretaker to prevent every hunger pang or sign of gum tension during teething. What is absent in the youngest infant's life is the kind of *inner conflict* that besets the child in the process of separation/individuation and oedipal conflict, as it becomes capable of inner thought and aware of its feelings.

Both fantasies about infancy—perfection and innocence—reflect the transition from babyhood to gender identity, which carries with it the primary oedipal conflict. Thus, the contrast is between a time of sexual innocence and the time when fantasy accompanies sexual feelings, making for oedipally derived feelings and a "loss of innocence."

An associated myth is that everything was once perfect between mother and child. Obviously, nothing is ever perfect, yet some people idealize to that extent how it was to be with mother during babyhood. We can explain this in light of the primary oedipal phase. During the era of the nascent ego, we have seen how "unity with mother" obviates feelings of rivalry on the part of girls or obviates the need to safeguard a sense of differentness on the part of boys. The intensity of the child's ambivalence toward its mother during the primary oedipal phase fosters regression as a solution to the conflict. Idealization of babyhood in fantasies of previous perfection and innocence makes one seem to prefer that time to the independence and sexual awareness that distinguish the nonbaby, reducing the toddler's sense of guilt over its sexual feelings.

Nonetheless, each child must deal with the fact of gender. Its genital sensations lead to a gender-based recognition of its uniqueness, including all of its impulses. Gender identity links sexuality with autonomy. Providing a core sense of self that will not change, gender identity is a source of the ego's strength, giving focus to self-awareness so that the child feels it is not a baby. A psychosocial organizing principle, gender identity helps the child to place itself in relation to others, making sense of genital excitement in the organization of self–other perceptions. Thus it takes the child into the primary oedipal phase.

Part II A Theory of Interrelated Tasks in Early Development

4 Interrelated Tasks in Relation to Personality Structure

The interrelationships of a child's thoughts and feelings during the second year of life make up a network, an emotional complex. This complex includes the primary oedipal feelings as the child sorts out its social position in its primitive world. The nature of emotional complexes is that they remain associated in the human mind and can be reactivated to have impact and meaning at any later stage in life, long after the complex was first formed. Therefore, that network of thoughts and feelings making up the primary oedipal complex can seriously affect later behavior. Hence is derived the ultimate significance of the primary oedipal complex, beyond its importance as a foundation on which later development is structured.

The idea of an emotional complex, a network of thoughts and feelings that operate dynamically in the personality, is well known in psychoanalytic thought. Freud began to use the concept very early, in 1892. Jung (1910) and Adler (1925) also applied the term *complex* to refer to all the feelings engendered by a certain condition, as in "oedipus complex" or "inferiority complex," respectively. Jung spelled out the fact that an emotional complex is dynamically effective because diverse elements of feeling and experience are bound together. He explained, "The constellating power of a complex consists of the number of groups of items that are brought into association by the nuclear element of the complex" (1910:93). It makes sense that the more elaborate an emotional complex is, the more pervasive will be its power.

The primary oedipal complex could not be more elaborate, encompassing all the elements of a two-year-old's life (the toddler's categorical patterns of thought [e.g., good versus bad, omnipresence versus nonexistence], ambivalence and intensity of emotion, concrete symbolization, secrecy and thought control, splitting as a defense, use of part-object fantasy, immediacy in the sense of time, oral and anal concerns, and the emergence of guilt and shame), all related through separation/individuation to the—in Jung's terminology—"nuclear elements" of ego formation and gender identity. Moreover, most of these issues, due to reasons of maturation, are being dealt with and fitted into a context for the first time. Thus, the primary oedipal complex not only includes a vast array of factors but also is the first complex into which most of those factors are fitted and therefore is the complex that defines them at the most basic level. *In other words, the constellating power of the primary oedipal complex lies in the reconstitution of the two-year-old experience.*

How the primary oedipal complex or any emotional complex works to affect behavior is illuminated by recent research into memory and cognitive psychology. For example, Rovee-Collier and her colleagues (1980) studied memory in three-month-old infants. They proved that retrieval of memories and new learning based upon memories are primed by contextual cueing. We learn in a context, and parts of that context are operationally involved in our use of a memory. It corresponds to much psychoanalytic observation that even very young infants learn in relationship to a context and that this manner of learning continues to be in evidence in the learning patterns of adults.

In keeping with psychoanalytic theory that emotions are a powerful factor in establishing the contexts of memories, there is specific evidence for the impact of emotion on the formation of memory complexes. In a series of experiments using hypnotic induction of sad or happy moods, Bower investigated the influence of emotions on memory and thinking in adults. He proved the significance of emotional context in learning. Accordingly, he proposed an associative network theory, which explains the mechanism by which an emotional complex is formed and operates. It corroborates psychoanalytic belief. He states: "An emotion serves as a memory unit that can enter into associations with coincident events.

Activation of this emotion unit aids retrieval of events associated with it; it also primes emotional themata for use in free association, fantasies, and perceptual categorization" (1980:129).

Thus we can appreciate the dynamic quality of the first ego-synthesis of the child in its second year of life, the complex of all the elements several times listed in this book. The experiments of Rovee-Collier et al. and of Bower show that activation of any of the elements of such a complex can produce behavior associated with any of its other elements. So it is with the primary oedipal complex, explaining why various manifestations of two-year-old behavior appear together as a complex in older individuals. Memory theory explains why successful analysis of some manifestations of this complex causes a diminution of other derivatives of the primary oedipal phase in the same person. Successful treatment of a patient can be based upon some aspects of the primary oedipal complex without either patient or therapist being aware that other primary oedipal issues exist. This is one reason that a unified theoretical model has been so slow in coming to the field: a partial theory of the dynamics of the primary oedipal phase can be fully successful when applied clinically.

The case of Patty was especially instructive to me because the processing of her primary oedipal feelings resulted in spontaneous changes in other behavior, which I only much later came to realize must have derived from a primary oedipal phase. Obesity, promiscuity, restriction of intellectual activity, and fragmentation of her ego all receded together, without any specific therapeutic work on any of them. We were directly addressing issues from her memories of her early relationship to her father. On the other hand, clinical attention to Patty's feelings about eating might have given her similar relief without recovery of her memories of her early (primary oedipal) situation. It helped me to develop my thinking when I learned that other symptoms that were making her life difficult were intertwined with problems of both separation/individuation and sexuality.

The list of human problems and suffering that derive from relatively unresolved primary oedipal phase issues is long because so much of the later personality is built upon the achievements of the child at the point of first organization of its ego. The more leftovers of the primary oedipal conflict appear in the behavior of someone who is past toddlerhood, the more we are likely to see extensive pathology. Conversely, as a patient in treatment comes to rely less on those old mechanisms developed first during the primary oedipal phase, the more solid the personality will appear to be, the more integrated the ego, and the freer in its capacity for successful love and work.

Behavior deriving from an emotional complex has a global quality. During treatment a person may explore some part of his or her systematic behavior deriving from a complex. As the person's ego is strengthened, through the therapeutic process, the manifestations of the complex recede as a whole.

The different elements of the primary oedipal complex are not just connected as a single unit that comes and goes through therapy. They are also interconnected in such a way that all the other elements can be brought to bear by a two-year-old when dealing with any single element. Thus, in regard to the primary oedipal complex, ego fragmentation might not be the subject of analysis, but as the individual feels clearer about personal identification and confidence in a sense of gender, and feels freer simultaneously to enjoy his or her individuality, the ego appears less fragmented and other aspects of primary oedipal phase behavior recede, such as problems in the capacity to wait for gratification and the ability to make a personal commitment in a sexual relationship.

We can see how the other elements of the primary oedipal complex are utilized by the child in coping with its specifically oedipal conflicts. An illustration here is a report from direct observation of a girl at that age. Galenson, Miller, and Roiphe describe Rose giving background to an incident when she was twenty-three months old:

This avid interest in the sight of her father's penis and urination, and her devotion to him in general, continued unabated. She also pursued and flirted with a number of male observers in the nursery, often insisting upon sitting on their laps and "riding" their crossed ankles. There was no doubt about her clear preference for males. (1976:88)

After emphasizing Rose's anal concerns, the background account continues with signs of primary oedipal conflict:

Her anger at her mother and other females emerged again and again. She bit, defied, and provoked her mother, as well as female nursery observers,

while her "love affair" with her father and other males continued . . .
Whereas she had seemed entirely unself-conscious previously [when she
masturbated] she now seemed aware of her mother's and a female observer's attention, and shifted her own gaze as if to avoid theirs. Some
elements of discomfort seemed to have become connected with her sexual
activity. (1976:91–92)

When she was twenty-three months of age, the key incident was
provoked by her father's absence from home for several days:

Many of her "lost and found" games reflected her feelings of loss during
his absence; they included repetitive toilet flushing, shutting herself into
boxes and rooms, piling blocks into containers, devotion to the old wrist-
watch, and a renewed "kleptomania" as she came and went from home to
nursery. She also "stored" pennies in her mouth and explored every stair-
case. We speculate that once again these openings and enclosures represented the oral and anal routes she had earlier explored in her
investigations of the oral and anal areas, and in search of the hidden stool-
phallus. Now she returned to these sites in the absence of her father.
(1976:92)

We can see Rose gathering primary oedipal elements into a
complex consisting of both directly oedipal matters and other elements that are utilized to help to cope with the oedipal conflicts:
fascination with her father's penis and her preference for males;
resentment of her mother and other females; masturbation in a
guilty manner while avoiding her mother; concrete symbolization
with cigars, crayons, and pens obviously substituting for her father;[1]
oral and anal fantasies to express loss when her father was away;
immediacy of time sense—in contrast to frustration-tolerance born
of a sense of expanded time—in that her father's absence required
concrete symbolization of his existence in order to make his absence
bearable.
      Referring to the process of concrete symbolization, Galen-
son, Miller and Roiphe explain, "[Rose uses] association by structural *pars pro toto* thinking" (1976:99), which gives insight into the
function of part-object fantasy. Concrete symbolization of a part
that serves for a whole is a method of handling anxiety, which is
typical of the primary oedipal complex as it is of the two-year-old
mind. Rose's behavior gives a glimpse of the primary oedipal complex in nascence.

To see resonance of the primary oedipal complex in the behavior of an adult, an excerpt from a case of Stoller's is useful. Stoller writes of Belle, who displayed overt sexual masochism, predominant oral and anal fantasies, splitting as a defense, private language, intense problems of separation/individuation, sterotyped relationships with men: either an uncommitted, cold, but sexual lover or a committed, kindly, but sexually ineffective one. Such a group of symptoms suggests the primary oedipal complex as a dynamic in the patient. It is therefore not surprising that "Belle knows from her masturbatory pleasure that she enjoys mild anal stimulation. She wants her lovers to do this, but if they do so knowing it excites her then she has only intense discomfort; only as long as it is her secret can it be erotic" (1979:101). Belle welds together guilt over sexual pleasure, anality, and secrecy of thought. The combination of Belle's symptoms make sense in an adult if the primitive ego structure of the primary oedipal phase is not adequately reintegrated into a stronger structure during the classical oedipal phase and adolescence.

Like all psychoanalytic constructs, the primary oedipal complex helps to explain aspects of personality beyond childhood. For example, as a consequence of the simultaneity of strong oral and anal drives with the rise of gender identity, sexuality is fused to oral and anal drives. According to primary oedipal theory, consequent symptom patterns should be gender-related. Anorexia is an example of oral-sexual fusion occurring chiefly in females (see part III).

Voyeurism is a condition peculiar to males (Stoller 1976). Alpert and Bernstein, carefully reviewing the literature for theoretical understanding of a case they present, conclude that voyeurism is phallicized expression of the oral drive (1964:29). Edgcumbe and Burgner (1975) trace scotophilia to the late oral phase, which means around nine months, when selfness/gender/identity/oedipal reactions begin. At this point of limited motoric ability, the child's sense of mastery derives greatly from active looking (White 1975). Visual mastery and experience are linked to mother in both sexes, but only the primary oedipal boy also would connect it with sexuality.

Similarly, Stoller describes the importance of sexuality in the sadomasochistic fantasies of his patient, Belle. Anality, which inspires rageful fantasy, is also linked to other strongly emotionalized aspects of the two-year-old's life. At that point in the primary oedipal conflict anality and sexuality are fused. This can be reflected in adult behavior in gender-related different patterns of eroticized cruelty and pain.

Fantasies play a crucial part in the process of integrating the ego at the primary oedipal level. Amalgams of inner and outer experience with its wishes and fears provide the child with views of itself and its world. Their nature comes from prelinguistic thought.[2] Early fantasies are imagistic, concrete, relatively unorganized, utilizing *pars pro toto* thinking and concrete symbolization, and structured by associations of time and place. The early ego has the capacity to fix in memory feelings without verbal content but in terms of the space/time context in which the feelings were experienced. The very young child's sense of things, its logic in this time of life, is chiefly based upon spatial-temporal associations rather than cause and effect. Thus, when contiguity rather than cause and effect seems to govern the logic of someone's behavior, we can expect behavior based on issues from the primary oedipal period and the influence of early fantasies.

The mode of thought reflected in early fantasies are what we customarily call primary process. Such qualities can be useful in the context of adult thought, too, especially in creative effort. However, as a dominant mode of thought, primary process is primitive and characteristic of the ego-state of the very young child. Secondary process just begins during the primary oedipal phase. Thus, the more mired someone is in the emotional condition of that time, the more primary process appears in the person's thought processes along with other characteristics of the primary oedipal complex (e.g., fragmentation of the ego, expression of feelings through concrete symbolization and images, concern about thought control and secrecy, immediacy of need gratification, categorizing the self and others in rigid terms of good or bad and perfect or despicable, with suicidal-homicidal fantasies, orally and anally based behavior such as eating disturbances and/or eliminatory symptoms, and the use of splitting as a defense.)

All of these accompany inner struggle to balance sexual forces with the need for autonomy. Greenspan (1980) and Edgcumbe and Burgner (1975) state that the "true" (classical) oedipal phase includes capacity for a significant degree of commitment. The highly ambivalent toddler does not have that capacity. Therefore relationships formed on the level of the primary oedipal complex are characterized by great intensity without commitment. Sudden crises are characteristic of the primary oedipal phase because the ego-state of the two-year-old is so intensely ambivalent. While the child is in the throes of the primary oedipal phase, switches from one extreme to another are both natural and unstable, producing a volatile situation. Sadomasochism and part-object sexual practices such as fetishes are direct reflections of the fantasies formed during the primary oedipal phase. Early fantasies often retain their influence on behavior without a person's awareness that they are a motivating factor. It follows that the roles of basic unconscious processes, repression and regression, are essential to understanding how we use our emotional complexes. A key to such understanding is Brenner's point, cited in chapter 1, that capacity for repression requires development of an ego. Repression means that an ego is there in charge. A degree of intrapsychic separation/individuation has to have taken place for the child to have ego enough to use repression.

In order to understand why the nascent ego needs to use repression as a mechanism of defense, we recall that the very process of separation/individuation involves genital sensations and oedipal feelings. The child protects itself from being overwhelmed by the intensity and confusion of forbidden impulses by not admitting to them, keeping the secrets even from the self.

What we call unconscious matter remains to varying degrees within reach. Sandler and Nagera show how the adult ego can draw upon the repressed store of material:

In normal mental functioning repressed content may be derived from memory images of all sorts, including those of wish-fulfilling fantasies, "real" experiences, dreams, reality orientated thoughts. . . . Derivatives of the repressed (indicating a "return of the repressed") may be expressed in perceptual images, wishes, acts, reality-orientated thinking, dreams, play, free associations, screen memories, distorted recollection of the past, manifest transference content, symptoms, delusions, scientific theories, hypnagogic phenomena, artistic and literary creations as well as daydream fantasies. (1963:172)

In addition to repression, the ego uses regression and other defenses to maintain its integrity as well as possible. Temporary and partial regressions are sometimes needed by someone under stress and then not required further. On the other hand, the greater the degree of regression, the more entire emotional complexes will likely affect someone's behavior. The greater the number and severity of someone's symptoms, the more complete the regression is likely to be to the primary oedipal stage. That is why in relation to Stoller's case Belle I said that her extensive list of primary oedipal level behaviors and issues made it unsurprising that she also merged sexual and anal feelings with the issue of secrecy of thought.

Through analysis of regression of someone in treatment (as in use of the transference), repressed material becomes manifest. Then patients are able to reintegrate their feelings in a way more appropriate and satisfying to their present lives. Warner (1983) demonstrates that the differences in patients' dreams, comparing those at the start of treatment with those at the end, lies in the integration of the "styles" of the two hemispheres. In a general sense this means integration of thought and feeling. (This is in accordance with the possible model I suggested in chapter 2 of repression as a natural consequence of the rise of language-conscious thought.) When repressed material is worked through, an increase in energy often occurs as well. This upsurge of energy when a repression is released was noted by Freud (1911). He hypothesized that energy itself was bound to repressed material and, on being neutralized, became available for general purposes.

It is more in keeping with what is now known about neurological and endocrinal functioning to think differently about the process: energy is not kept in a pool from which it is shunted to one use or another but is mobilized as needed. We might speculate that massive repression is bound to feelings of badness in the ego and a sense of danger about allowing free behavior. We recognize that the ego is the psychological manifestation of cortical activity. Any emotion or thought has its correlative in the organism's physiological state, and the cortex is in charge of it all. Therefore, the person's neural and endocrinal activity is geared to an ego-need to feel either controlled or free. Increased availability of energy when the ego gains greater ease comes physiologically through neural and endocrinal adjustment under cortical control.

The individual uses physiological resources according to demand. When self-permission is gained for exploring the repressed, the adult ego is relieved of harsh infantile self-judgments; thus, the adult ego feels freer and capable of using more of its physiologic resources for energy.

The glorious feeling of freedom and energy that accompanies self-understanding may come also from increased efficiency of brain functioning in that integration of left brain and right brain impulses (the cognitive and the emotional) is involved in effective insight.[3] A feeling of energy accompanies all experience of self-mastery, smoothness and efficiency of function, and aesthetic integration. We classify our feelings in such experiences as "good," meaning that we are good when we have them, thus having the right to greater confidence and ease. Dealing as an adult with what was originally repressed in one's childhood can be such an experience.

What is not integrated into the self during the primary oedipal phase remains in the nonverbal memory traces of the primary oedipal complex. Kernberg (1966) explains that ongoing expression of aspects of the person's originally "not well-crystallized state of the early ego" reveals what is as yet "nonmetabolized." The two-year-old's powers of psychic metabolism are limited, if by that we mean the ability to develop a well-integrated ego. In Kernberg's term, an "easy oscillation" exists from one loosely integrated part of the child's combined inner and outer experience to another part. This easy oscillation is reflected in the instability of the behavior of those, such as borderline personalities, for whom the leftovers of the primary oedipal phase are particularly prominent. It parallels the instability of children in the second year of life as they struggle with ambivalence.

Questions of what is acceptable within the ego and the early struggles with ambivalence have a centrifugal effect on the nascent ego, making for fragmentation and looseness. A major force for cohesion of the ego is gender identity. The balance of these forces determines for a two-year-old what it means to be "Me!"

As we have seen, the forces that go into balancing the ego— both the fragmenting conflicts and the bonding of gender—derive from interactions between the child and both parents. Yet the two-year-old is often viewed as purely dyadic in its relationship with its mother. The toddler's need to react in terms of its dichotomous mode of thought gives the impression of dyadism to the observer, and this has directed some thinking on the subject; but for the child,

becoming independent means the recognition of different relationships with each of its parents.

We can see evidence for this triadic two-year-old state in a
case that was published in order to prove an opposing (dyadic) view.
Greenspan describes the analysis of a five-and-a-half-year-old girl to
illustrate what he termed a dyadic-phallic phase of development. As
we read the material in his article for content without immediately
focusing on whether the child was displaying so-called preoedipal
material or not, this is what we learn:

Her parents felt S. showed an unusually strong sexual curiosity. This was
evidenced by her running into the bathroom to see her daddy undress and
attempting rather enthusiastically to get under his towels and touch his
genitals. The father seemed to enjoy this and responded seductively and in
a stimulating manner, while mother responded with feeling tense, threatened, and competitive. (1980:577)

Greenspan knows classical oedipal behavior when he sees it.
These presenting symptoms did not impress him because the child's
ego state was so primitive. However, we can readily recognize the
focal importance of S.'s oedipal conflict in terms of the primary
oedipal phase. Continuing with Greenspan's description:

S. appeared as a cute, well-coordinated, extremely alert, somewhat tense,
fearful-looking child. In the initial sessions she readily revealed many
areas that disturbed her, as if to give me a full picture of herself. . . .
There was an impersonal but intense (needy) quality in the way she related. She revealed aggressive themes (animals eating and killing all family
members and the therapist); unfulfilled yearning for dependency gratification . . . heightened sexual curiosity and interest (attempts to jump on the
therapist and touch his genitals, uncontrolled excitement when talking
about body parts such as a penis); a great interest in pregnancy. . . .
Following the development of aggressive themes in her play with
the family dolls, she began to hit herself on the head and exclaimed, "I am
bad." (1980:577–578)

This excerpt includes most of what Greenspan tells of the
beginning phase of treatment. We recognize chaotic ego organization, emphasis upon part-objects, separation/individuation problems, intense but impersonal relating, uncontrollable sexual
excitement toward males, strong oral and anal fantasies, life-and-

death struggle, preoccupation with her own badness. Her sessions make sense in terms of the existence of a primary oedipal complex. Later in Greenspan's account, one sees S.'s transition to the classical oedipal phase. Then S. shows greater organization, sophistication in the handling of oedipal tensions, and a form of triadic involvement that we are accustomed to label oedipal. While not originally of that same form, the oedipal overtones of S.'s case material from the beginning are nonetheless evident.

More material from the case appears in chapter 10 on the contrast between primary and classical oedipal behavior. We can see from this much, however, that the child came into treatment with the tumultuous syndrome characteristic of the primary oedipal phase.

An adult case of mine kept me confused by her supposedly dyadic orientation until her associations led me to understand the true nature of her conflicts. My learning began when Marianne took significant steps in asserting her autonomy and effectiveness at work. For days afterward, her monotheme was her helplessness; she cried about her inability to end sessions or telephone calls. She complained that she had no friends but still felt she must be alone. She woke up during the night compelled to eat. It was all she could do to get to my office because of spells of physical weakness. Finally, she closed one session by telling me how her older sister used to tease her because even when Marianne was a toddler she acted as if she could not do what everyone knew she was capable of. Then she said, as if prompting herself, that she "needn't feel helpless." Having just connected feelings of helplessness with the time she was a toddler, she freed herself for the moment to feel that she need not be helpless.

An interesting postscript followed as Marianne prepared to leave. It dramatically showed how oedipal feelings were intertwined with those around separation/individuation for Marianne in this episode. Putting on her sweater, Marianne told me how angry she was that it was time to go. Then she mentioned that it was a long time since she last wore the particular sweater. Marianne: "It is light and warm; it is my spring tennis sweater." Her brightened tone made me think. The only other reference I recalled her making to tennis was attending a tennis camp years before where she met the only man with whom she ever formed a relationship.

Thereupon she grew thoughtful and said that the connection made sense. The night before she had dreamed of being in a cafe in Tijuana (where she had visited in spring). In the setting of the dream, people were doing sexual things that she felt were forbidden. Marianne giggled. She told me she really did not want to leave the office.

A little while later Marianne telephoned me. She was weeping again about the need to say goodbye to me. Thanks to the associations about the sweater, I was able to sense her ambivalence. I suggested that she was crying so hard because she wanted to be sure we could not hear something else she was feeling inside, namely, a wish to be rid of me so that she could do nice things like playing tennis and going to Tijuana. Marianne replied furiously that it could be as simple as being afraid of being independent and just wanting to be herself. I agreed. Marianne then said that perhaps being independent would mean also "those other things." After a pause, she whispered, "That's why I am so afraid."

This material shows how the seeming dyadic transference of this patient actually covered a hidden agenda. The crisis began with her daring to be self-assertive at work. Her subsequent intensified dependency on me proved to be a cloak for her real but unacceptable wish to be sexual, the vital concomitant of independence. She had effectively split off and repressed her sexual feelings, but a new sense of self threatened the old compromises. Her sexual wishes were dangerously still too tied to the image of her father.

In subsequent sessions I learned that her father had originally taught her to play tennis, although Marianne usually averred that she had not had any relationship with her father and only her mother mattered. In keeping with her primary oedipal complex, she used concrete symbolization of her sweater to approach her real feelings. Only the key words attached to the sweater, "spring, tennis" enabled us to reach the underlying triadic significance of Marianne's painful tie to me.

Marianne's shaky solution to her dilemma is an example of the instability of the primary oedipal complex compared with later integrations of the ego. Even gender identity may be at risk when the primary oedipal conflict is too hard for the child to handle successfully. We learn much from study of the primary oedipal complex in its lingering forms in psychopathology. However, its greatest significance is in providing the first scheme in organization of all personalities.

5 Patterns of the Female

Freud's formulation (1931) of the girl's early object relationships had her first fixate on her mother and then—in frustration and anger over not being a boy (for which she blamed her mother)—turn to her father. This way of looking at the vicissitudes of feminine development persists in the writings of current psychoanalysts (e.g., Mahler and Galenson and Roiphe). However, "turning" to the father is not necessary because he has been important all along. It is the sorting out of her relationships with both her mother and father that is the source of trouble. To understand this we must review the process of ego formation for the little girl and the primary oedipal conflict it entails. This process for the girl is schematically outlined in figure 2.

A girl's ego formation is based upon four simultaneously occurring processes: her increasing separation/individuation; her self-modeling after her mother; her growing awareness of her sexual feelings toward her father; and her developing sense of gender. Her gender identification itself is based in reciprocal fashion on her level of ego formation, again together with her recognition of her sexual feelings and their focusing on father. Gender identity is also a requirement for the girl's ability to model herself after her like-parent (i.e., mother). These interlocking determinants of ego formation hold three powerful sources of conflict for the girl. One conflict is in the direct separation/individuation process, where the price of individuality, gained by distinguishing self from mother, is the threatened loss of the protection and support that mother provides. A second source of conflict for the girl is that the important process of self-modeling on the same-sex parent (i.e., mother) is at odds with the concomitant process of individuation or distinguishing

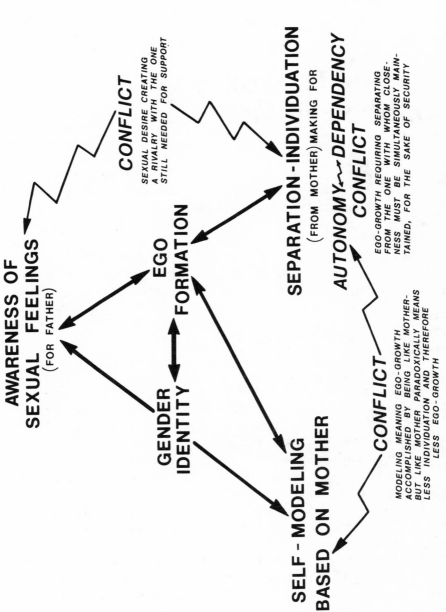

Figure 2. Interrelationships between various tasks and conflicts faced simultaneously by a girl.

herself from mother. The final way in which ego formation produces conflict for the girl is that awareness of her sexual feelings and their direction toward father brings her into a position of being the rival of the mother on whom she still depends. All three of these conflicts bear on the same great problem: who the girl is. In breaking it down into three distinct forms, we are conceptualizing. For the girl they are not separate: they are all aspects of a single, complicated conflict, which we call the primary oedipal conflict.

It is important to reiterate that neither the mother nor the father is of primacy in the sorting out of the young girl's ego. The relationship the girl has with each is tightly intertwined with the other; and it is out of this net that the conflicts and resolutions of the primary oedipal phase arise.

Her mother is a *nonself like herself* upon which she is additionally almost totally dependent for physical survival as well as for a whole range of comforts and satisfactions. Her father's importance is in being a *nonself unlike herself*, in addition to being an exciting person. He also is linked with the larger world in that he is often the parent who more frequently leaves the home. As the girl's individuation from mother (Mahler 1965) and sense of gender continue to develop, her sexual feelings for father become ever more focused (Galenson and Roiphe [1980] and Kleeman [1966] observed change in behavior with parents at this same age.) Modeling based on mother directs the sexual feelings toward father, which in turn increases the sense of rivalry with mother. Thus, deep sexual feelings relating to father and wishes for independence from mother are intertwined.

It is important to keep in mind that while the intertwined relationships with her parents are at the root of the little girl's tensions as she sorts out who she is, it is the large group of other developmental events she simultaneously faces that determine the way in which she deals with those tensions. Thus it is that the advent of categorical thought, splitting, and other two-year-old mentation patterns determine that she will deal with fear of her mother's anger in terms of herself being good or bad and safe or endangered. Similarly, her being in a transition from oral to anal concerns will mean that her fantasies, which are stimulated by her sexual impulses and confusions, will contain oral and anal elements. The earlier in the time frame of the primary oedipal phase she is, the more oral elements relative to anal elements will appear in the fantasies. These two-year-old patterns for handling tensions will reappear as a complex in later life when dealing with primary oedipal issues. We shall, therefore, be able to use such symptoms as splitting as indications that a patient in therapy is working through primary oedipal material.

With this background, we will now be able to examine evidence for the existence of the three conflicts I have described as making up the girl's primary oedipal complex. As I have discussed, these are not really separate conflicts but intricately interlinked with one another. Thus, in most examples, we will see each only in connection with evidence for other aspects of the dynamic. Yet, while all three are always at work, at moments a child may be distracted enough by aspects of a single conflict (as I have defined them) that her behavior will demonstrate that conflict unclouded by the others. In the following vignette we see a primary oedipal girl so caught in the conflict between her attraction for her father and her worry about her mother to whom she is still very attached.

E. Freud (1981) observed a two-year-old girl who sat on a chair cuddling up to her responsive father. She repeatedly alternated between hugging her father and jumping off the chair, anxiously asking when her mother was coming back. One can imagine her worry: "If Mommy leaves the room while I am glad to be with Daddy, will she ever come back? If I am angry at Mommy when she comes into the room while I am with Daddy, will she know it and get back at me?" In the categorical all-or-none thinking of the two-year-old, rivalry with her mother can mean the possibility of only one survivor.

A second conflict that I outlined as part of the girl's primary oedipal phase is the one inherent in the separation/individuation process itself. In the case of Lynn, an adult patient of mine, problems in separation/individuation were very much evident in a mother transference. A number of two-year-old derivatives she displayed date the issue to the primary oedipal phase. In this instance, the conflicts of separation/individuation are clearly tied to sexual implications, as our model would predict.

In one session Lynn demonstrated concrete symbolization (physical objects in my room symbolized my death; recall Galenson showed that such symbolization begins during the second year of life), immediacy of time sense (my being four minutes late was as if I would never appear—here-and-now thinking to the exclusion of past and future), and strong feelings of fusion with me (by transference: fusion with mother), all reminiscent of second-year-level functioning. When I pressed her to explain the intensity of her rage about waiting for me, she responded, "If I need you, then I am not myself." She was in terrible conflict to feel so dependent and at the same time feel unable to tolerate it because the dependency meant fusion with me.

Abruptly her thoughts shifted. On my office wall was a picture of a snowy forest scene. The gradations in tone were like clouds in making it easy for a viewer to find personal images in it. Lynn had an association to this painting. Previously she had felt that the painting expressed uncontrollable sexual feelings. This time she saw a strange figure lurking in it who looked like her father when he was a young man. Her next thought was that she did not feel like a person unless she was connected to somebody else. Reflectively, she explained that "life-and-death" meant that someone had to be destroyed if there were to be only one person present and that she had no right to exist. Separation/individuation in the transference and oedipal reaction in placing the image of her father in a picture she felt depicted rampant sexuality led to Lynn's questioning her right to survive.

To a child too young to understand future time, ordinary separations mean total disappearance. Fearing that mother might never return in combination with ambivalence toward her, the girl feels that she must make it clear to her mother that she will not survive (to triumph with father) if her mother leaves her. The life-and-death quality of this conflict can be retained in some individuals so that sexual impulses in later life remain bound to a sense of mortal conflict.[1]

In addition to the two-year-old's time sense being limited to the present, another feature of the young child's world perception has great implication for the way the separation/individuation conflict is managed. Because a two-year-old identifies physical objects (human and otherwise) in terms of positions and patterns of movement, the idea of "place" becomes a key element in the categorization of the two-year-old's universe. The use of such categorization in processing the separation/individuation conflict can be seen in the case of Patty (again in conjunction with elements of the other conflicts I have outlined).

Patty began a session by telling me that she almost casually decided to see me just before killing herself. The phrase she kept repeating was, "There's no room for me. There's room for only one." Two operative circumstances were (1) her mother was leaving town, and (2) Patty was working to define her ego boundaries.

Patty's panic that day was not simply over separation from her mother, however. Recurrently, pressingly, she insisted there was room for only one, place for only one, and therefore she must kill herself. Patty suddenly curled up in her chair, looked up with a horrified expression, and held her hands as if to protect her face. Patty's associations quickly led to recovery of memory of the time when she was two that her mother went to the hospital for the birth of Patty's brother and Patty was left in her father's care. She recovered a memory or significant fantasy that her alcoholic father stimulated her sexually at that time. As she processed her feelings about being alone with her father in the next sessions, the statement of place for only one and the suicidal impulses were no longer expressed. Apparently associated were oral and thought-use components, for Patty dropped from obesity to normal weight and felt free to think in school without prior mention of them in her therapeutic efforts with me.

In Patty we have thus seen evidence of two of the three sources of conflict we have identified for the primary oedipal girl: separation/individuation and sexual rivalry over father. The third origin of conflict is found in that, in modeling herself on her mother in ego development, the girl paradoxically *keeps* herself from feeling autonomous *because* she is more like mother. This can be observed in the case of Barbara. In her adult behavior, Barbara appeared to others as someone poised and in control. However, within herself she constantly checked that she was thinking only what her mother would think and approve.

This conflict ties in with the other two we have discussed. The girl can feel she cannot allow herself to model herself on her mother's strengths (although they would seem to be the most attractive aspects of her mother to model upon) because to do so would make the girl also strong and thus more of a threat as a rival.

We can see how self-modeling and separation/individuation fit into sexual concerns in such a manner by continuing to examine the case of Barbara. In many respects her scenario paralleled that of Patty. She, too, expressed suicidal agony alternately with expressions of her feeling that there could be only one, that she had no place, no right to exist. As our work progressed, she and I began to understand that these episodes were invariably a consequence of permitting herself sexual thoughts. We could not document the timing of events during her second year of life as Patty was able to do, but in the playing out of Barbara's transference to me and her associations during our sessions, remarkable similarities to Patty's history emerged. Barbara, too, had had an alcoholic father who was extremely seductive with Barbara when she was in her second year. Repetitive patterns in her material led me to recognize how excruciating inner conflict grew out of Barbara's feeling that her father would go out of control in the sexual excitement they shared and make her unable to resist him while she still needed her mother for survival. In addition, her mother's signals to Barbara about sex can be appreciated from the fact that when Barbara's younger brother was born, her mother told her that the stork had brought the baby. Awareness of sexual feelings was taboo.

Growing up, taking steps toward independence, seemed possible only if sexuality were surrendered. This was a significant metaphor because Barbara knew from family stories how as a toddler she contrived to get her mother to carry her. We can conjecture how self-awareness and thus a sense of responsibility affected her age-typical genital interest. The clinical fact is that as sexual material began to surface during the analysis she developed overwhelming fatigue when walking even short distances. This symptom proved to be caused only by her feeling state.

What makes these connections persuasive for this discussion is that Barbara chose to tell me about the early behavior spontaneously in the context of the work reported here. To be independent and sexual meant there was "room for only one," and that had to be the all-powerful and the all-good mother. The only safe course was to remain psychologically fused with mother. Whenever the feeling of fusion was disrupted, tortuous conflict reappeared. Sexual feelings asserted themselves, and Barbara doubted her right to exist. Barbara's agony was controlled only by use of splitting. She felt safe, good, and asexual because she psychically fused with her mother. This compromise fell apart once when Barbara was offered promotion at work in which she would exceed her mother's level in her own career. With the idea of such autonomy, sexual feeling started to break through, and Barbara immediately felt she was bad. The use of splitting, the severity of the individuation/separation problem, the intense good versus bad conflict, and all-or-none thinking with suicidal implications, all bound to the issue of sexuality, are typical of the primary oedipal complex.

Barbara's efforts to find herself reveal the intensity of the intertwining issues to be resolved by a little girl in the process of determining who she is. In the two-year-old mind, this question has a strong physical side to it. Wanting to be like mother is and wanting what mother has both mean to displace her.

The reason that a primary oedipal child thinks in such terms is suggested by our knowing that babies and even toddlers achieve object identification by means of an object's characteristic patterns of movement and by its placement (Piaget 1948; Bower 1982). Therefore, a strong sense of knowing "who I am and who you are" is likely to be connected mentally with occupying a particular space. The little girl is perplexed by the problem of establishing her differentness from her mother even though her "gender-selfness" is the same as her mother's. Separateness with sameness of important desires is hard to safeguard when it leads to feelings of competition. When one simultaneously is learning about the meaning of "all gone," the interconnections can be powerful. How can two coexist in the same position? As often as I have encountered this dilemma, so-stated, in guilt-ridden women, I do not encounter it in men. *The girl is by gender the same as mother and wants to be in her place. The problem is different for the boy, who by gender is different from his mother and expects to occupy another space.*

Occupying the mother's space has several simultaneous positive meanings for the girl: individuation—from no longer *sharing* the space; positive gender modeling—in occupying a mother (female) position; and sexuality—in occupying the mother's space in relation to the father. The first two aspects are nonetheless terrifying in their loss of maternal support and the third even more so in its posturing the girl as a direct rival of her mother; all three aspects are thus strongly desired but also threaten annihilation.

The little girl needs to resolve this conflict over space with her mother. The need for resolution is given immediacy by the tension of her requiring her mother (and also feeling attached to her) while she is ever more aware of her special intense delight in her interaction with her father. Independence from a very controlling mother can especially produce conflict because of the mother's ambivalence. Independence can become a trade-off for sexuality: in allowing herself autonomy, the girl avoids her mother's further wrath by giving up her sexual wishes for her father. Unless she gains confidence in her femininity and her relationship with her mother by the time she resolves the classical oedipal conflict, the primary oedipal level split between sexuality and autonomy persists. She enters adolescence with a strong sense that she can be feminine but dependent (with the man fully responsible for her sexual behavior) *or* that she can be competent in the larger world as a peer of men but without the satisfaction of a permanent, loving, sexual relationship with one man.

Some behaviors call attention to this conflict among toddlers. Girls' coquettishness toward father is frequently described as basically an antagonism to mother, heightened while separation/individuation proceeds. Horney (1933), Abelin (1971) and Galenson and Roiphe (1977) specifically mention such coquettishness, without classifying the behavior as oedipal. Chasseguet-Smirgel (1975), implying that the relationship with the father is a primary matter, points out that when the mother is very strong and controlling, the girl cannot afford to develop her femininity too overtly. Under such circumstances, she must find a way of being close to father without involving her sexual feelings, and thus getting past mother without arousing her ire. Two ways could be intellectual interest in things she and father share or an interest in doing things with father that mother approves of. A tomboy who pleases her father by being like him does not seem to compete with her mother for him. At another extreme is the little girl who becomes a "mama's girl," in which case she may permit herself to enjoy her femininity as an extension of her mother, stopping short of a good relationship with her father. Depending on the messages the child picks up from her parents, she works out her loyalty struggles as best she can.[2]

There is an important difference between boys and girls in the use of incorporative psychic skills during the oral phase to form a beginning identification with mother. A girl's feelings of connection with mother are compatible with the girl's own developing sense of gender (unlike a boy's case where, as described in chapter 6, the connection to mother is in direct opposition to his developing gender sense). This connection reinforces the girl's sense of safety in feeling part of a mother–child matrix. With dependency being linked to her gender identification, a girl may allow herself autonomy only by simultaneously repressing her sexuality. This pattern is epitomized in women by the stereotype of an old maid. The dependency/sexuality fusion dating to the primary oedipal phase is clear in a case of Bychowski. In a paper on frigidity, he describes the following woman whose father had died when she was two years old.

A had been brought up by a psychotic mother and, without being clinically psychotic, presents some symptoms of ego fragmentation. In the morning, after sexual experience with her husband, she sees, upon awakening, my shoes leaving her. This to her means that in reality she was making love with me. Her childhood reminiscences indicate that she used Ɪ expect part of her body to fall off, to stay behind while she would ꞮꞮevitably follow her mother with whom she had a most unusual symbiotic relationship. Since she felt that she was but an appendage to her mother, she could not really envision herself remaining in the same room where she had had a love session with her mother, after the latter left the room. (1963:59)

Such extreme pathology most apparently reflects the primary oedipal phase. This woman could permit herself sexuality only if, in her mind, she remained fused with her mother. Sexual behavior is overcast by her sense of fusion with her mother and feelings that she cannot depend on a man to stay with her. (In her fantasy, lover/therapist's shoes leave her.) The symptoms of ego fragmentation, faulty separation/individuation, concrete symbolization (in her hallucination of the shoes), part-object imagery (of her body), and use of splitting, all in response to sexuality, are characteristic of the way in which the primary oedipal complex can intrude in the life of even an adult woman who never achieved inner permission to separate from her mother. She could let herself have a husband and even have sex with him, but only on the basis of not knowing who was who, confused about who left and who remained.

There are other issues to consider. A part of self-definition in relation to gender has to do with the concept of passivity. Freud (1931)
specifically stated that women are not passive creatures, but the idea
that they are is still attributed to him. The idea that passivity is part
of femininity clearly comes from a confusion of sexual receptivity
with general behavior. A woman's genital response to sexual stimulation, her very anatomy, is geared to receiving the male organ.
However, when she is not being sexually receptive, a woman can be
as active as a man. Feminine passivity does not extend for example
to doing housework, a most physical and active matter. Nor is a
woman passive in taking care of her children, the most important
way in which her children experience her. The "passivity" that is
expected relates to cultural structuring of behavior between adult
males and adult females.

Cultural patterning of activity/passivity in relationship to
men is not the only cause of such behavior. A girl's feelings of
passivity (and perhaps the origins of the cultural patterns themselves) are a consequence of her own sexual feelings as she first sorts
out impressions about separation/individuation and gender. One
clue as to how the passivity arises is found in the nature of her
sexual organs (Kestenberg 1975). Their being less accessible than
those of a boy means that she has less opportunity to control her
own sensations. This could lead to the need a mature woman has
for a man to take the dominant role in enabling her to have a full
sexual response. A second factor that may influence the development of feminine passivity is the style of play the girl has with her
parents (Erikson 1965). The exciting play with the girl is likely to
involve her as a passive partner. This is also true, of course, of the
father's play with the boy; but since the father is not the boy's sexual
interest, this does not affect his role in the same manner. In his play
with the object of his urges, his mother, his active behavior binds
with his genitally based self-concept. To a girl such factors become
critical because her sense of gender, her feelings of sexuality, and
her sense of self (which contains integrated within it how she will
respond to her sexuality) all developed together in the primary oedipal phase. The key is the guilt feelings we have seen that a girl
develops from her sexual urges, making her a rival of the mother on
whom she depends. These guilt feelings are mitigated by the father's

responsibility for the excitement.[3] We shall see that this does not arise for the boy because there is not conflict between his desire and his source of comfort (both being his mother). Passivity thus means a little girl can enjoy her sexuality while continuing to display loyalty to her mother.

We can see how this pattern of feminine passivity develops during the primary oedipal phase by examining the case of Emily. Her conflict had been so intense when she entered treatment, she could only stay at home and fight with her mother rather than get a job, although she was an honors graduate of a fine college. After some years of work on her excruciating problems in separating from her mother, we were at a point of exploring her sexual fantasies.

At the point in her treatment that I wish to tell about, Emily was a junior executive in a large company and living alone. She had a continuing preoccupation with herself as a bad person (using splitting, categorical thought), while she struggled with her tie to her mother (separation/individuation), both of which show that she was still gripped by primary oedipal concerns. She still felt inhibited in beginning assignments at work and felt a need for a man to take the lead in knowing what she required for each project on her job. She had lovers but was unable to have orgasms with them. She complained that they did not take charge and teach her what she needed to know about making love. She wanted them to release her passion. Emily was aware of deep feelings of distrust that kept her from letting go. She spoke of being afraid of being overwhelmed by the man's sexual feelings. Through the transference, however, she expressed fear of her mother, which clearly attached neither to her lovers nor to her father. Her mother was not only the ruling force in Emily's life, she also dominated Emily's father. Her mother's anger turned out to be the real source of Emily's fear.

Emily's emphasis upon the importance of learning from a man about her own sexuality made me wonder out loud about what early situation could have laid the groundwork for her problems. It occurred to me that this must stem from a very early time, because even by age four (during the classical oedipal phase) a little girl would be old enough to have clear ideas about her own body *if* she had emotional freedom to do so. Accordingly, we speculated together about what it might have been like for her as a child just emerging as a "Me!" to contend with complex feelings about her mother and father, including awareness of her own genital sensations. Her present feeling might somehow trace to an original time of need to know from her father what was happening within herself when she felt so excited by him. Emily would just have been learning about her genitals and classifying people in terms of gender.

In keeping with Kestenberg's insistence (1975) that a woman needs her man to be a teacher in sex, Emily repeatedly talked of her basic frustration with her lovers because they did not show her what to do. I mentioned Kestenberg's work to Emily at this point as an example of the naturalness of her feelings. We speculated further together about why this should be. Emily seemed to find it interesting to imagine herself as a tiny girl whose excitement came from daddy swooping her up, therefore expecting him to control what came next. We discussed this in connection with the separation/individuation issue and her mother's domination.

In the succeeding weeks, Emily not only seemed more at ease with her sexual feelings, but after two years on the job, she suddenly began to consider herself part of the team, no longer so anxious about being treated the same as the men and becoming confident about her work. Emily's progress came with linking the power struggle with her mother to a new consciousness of their rivalry. With the connections came a new freedom from passivity in her professional life.

As discussed in chapter 4, when a girl's father is relatively passive and her mother is very controlling, the girl cannot count on her father to take responsibility for her sexual feelings in response to him, nor can she count on her mother's benevolence in rivalry with her. In such a situation, if the toddler girl identifies with her father for closeness to him and safety with her mother, the simultaneous importance of anality may be put to use. My patient, Heidi, illustrated this situation. She confided to me that she could not "believe in her vagina" even though as a physician she was sophisticated about anatomy. She explained that good feelings exist only in a penis. In sexual activity with a man, she felt his penis was hers and his good feelings were really hers.[4] She could have good feelings in her anus, however, because there she made no dangerous choice between father and mother: everybody is the same in having an anus. I did not interpret any of this to Heidi. However, as dream material and the transference gradually revealed her attachment to her father and her difficulties in separation/individuation, Heidi began to experience awareness of her vagina.[5]

The girl resolves her primary oedipal conflict in the context of her other feelings and capacities at the age of two. To the degree that she integrates all of this, her first ego-organization enables her to be a happy, confident three-year-old who enjoys her femininity, her fun with her father, and a good relationship with her mother. She is then well prepared to develop the fuller, richer personality she can achieve through her resolution of the classical oedipal conflict. If the strains of her primary oedipal conflict are too great, the girl will compromise her ability to differentiate herself from her mother and, in doing her best with the resources of a two-year-old, approach the classical oedipal phase with a heavy burden of bad feelings and a relatively fragmented ego.

6 Patterns of the Male

A boy's ego formation is based on the same four simultaneous processes as a girl's: his increasing separation/individuation; self-modeling, in this case after his father; his growing awareness of his sexual feelings, in this instance directed toward his mother; and his developing sense of gender (see figure 3). Again, gender identification is itself based in reciprocal fashion on the level of ego formation that has been attained together with recognition of sexual urges, in this case focused on the mother. Gender identity is also a requirement here for the boy to be able to model himself on his like parent, his father. All these tasks parallel those faced by a girl, as would be expected since the problem is essentially the same: sorting out the identity of a little human being and the relation that child bears to the world around it.

However, the conflicts that arise for the boy as he works on this problem of self-awareness are quite different from those conflicts that develop for the girl. There are again three distinct conflicts as we will break them down, two of which are unique to the male and one of which is paralleled in the female. But then, as the three sources of conflict are all interrelated and not distinct in the real world of the two-year-old boy, both in the interrelations of the conflicts and in their total picture, the pressures of the age will be of a different character for him than for his sister.

As with the girl, one conflict is in the direct separation/individuation process, where the price of individualization gained by distinguishing self from mother is the threatened loss of the protection and support that mother provides. A second source of conflict for the boy is that awareness of his sexual feelings for his mother brings him into a rivalry with the father on whom he is

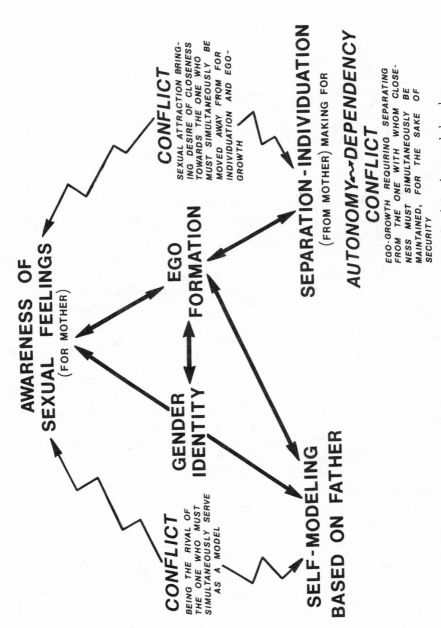

Figure 3. Interrelationships between various tasks and conflicts faced simultaneously by a boy.

simultaneously trying to model himself in sorting out his ego and gender identity. The more successful the modeling process, the greater the ego formation, which leads to greater focus of sexual feelings and hence even greater rivalry. Because of the dual nature of this conflict, the feelings are mitigated by desire for closeness in the modeling/ego-building process. This is very different from the classical oedipal stage (ages four to six), when the core of his ego is more solidly formed and the conflict is therefore less ambiguous: the boy feels the rivalry with his father in full force. The final source of conflict for the boy is in the fact that his sexual attraction is directed at the very person whom he is attempting to move away from in the individuation process. His desire for physical closeness is at odds with his desire for distance and ego growth. Having identified the three sources of conflict a boy in the primary oedipal phase will encounter, we must seek real understanding of them as with the girl in their interrelated forms as they arise and direct the ego-building process. Again it must be emphasized how important the fact is that the child is dealing with these issues on a two-year-old level. Thus, as we now look at each of the three conflicts we have identified for the primary oedipal boy, we must seek to understand them on that same two-year-old level because it is on that level that the connections between different conflicts are made and the real terrors they entail are formed.

One of the conflicts a two-year-old boy faces is between his desire for closeness with his mother (due to his sexual desires) and his need to separate himself from her in establishing his identity as an individual. This conflict gets its force from the concrete conceptualization characteristic of the age. Closeness to mother does not have distinct physical and emotional meanings for the child. Closeness to her in two-year-old thinking means being like her, and if he is like her (a female) then he cannot be a male. Yet it is his very maleness that drives him toward her. There is where the terror lies. Being close to the object of his sexual desire means engulfment: the loss of his self. Conversely, individuation means a loss of sexual comfort because individuation depends on separation; the boy organizes a sense of being different from his mother. Genitality thus is a two-edged blessing for him. It helps him to recognize his individuality, being different in a special way. Yet it impels him to be with his mother. His conflict can only be resolved later, when there is enough individuation that the ego is no longer in danger from the engulfment that closeness means at this early stage.

We can see that this conflict is indeed an issue of the age in a case of Boxerman's (1981). He tells of a session with a young man whose problems included a need to keep himself distant from females. In talking about his sexual wishes, Jim told of wanting a girlfriend who would be there waiting for him, whom he could control. Boxerman queried whether Jim could in part be dealing with early feelings about his mother and himself, when he was first developing a sense of his own autonomy. Jim said nothing to this. His very next statement was, "My dog needed to shit in the middle of the night last night and I had to go take her out." Boxerman noted how anal material immediately related to interpretation about autonomy from mother and early sexual feelings.

For a boy, with the mother, engulfment may become acceptable on the basis of giving up his masculinity. A corollary of such a solution is to feel like a baby (before he had a sense of gender), explaining the babyishness of "mama's boys." Or, if the fear of engulfment is severe enough, this fear may remain bound up with the issue of existence. With this fear of maternal engulfment being a major factor in the primary oedipal boy's emotional complex, the father acts as an ego-stabilizing force through his role as a model. However, the boy also feels conflict in his relation with him because, as his ego is stabilized, his sexual urges become increasingly focused on his mother, which makes him a rival of his father. Loewald (1951) and Herzog (1980) recognize the way in which the toddler boy finds positive identification in his father, although they downplay the role of rivalry at that age. In Loewald's words:

Against this threat of maternal engulfment, the paternal position is not another threat or danger, but a support of powerful force. . . . The father figure, then . . . is not primarily hostile, representing the threat of castration with which the boy copes with massive submission and/or rebellion. Earlier, . . . more essential for the development of the ego (and reality), is his positive stature with whom an active, nonpassive identification is made; . . . lying before and beyond submission as well as rebellion. (1951:160)

Herzog's cases (see chapter 8) show the need that primary oedipal boys have for their fathers as self-models and in addition give evidence for the simultaneous feelings of rivalry the boys feel with their fathers over their mothers. Herzog gives poignant examples of boys younger than two years of age who become deeply distressed when fathers abandon home and mothers are very seductive. These boys slept in the same room as the mother, some actually in her bed. During the day they clung to their mothers, while at night they suffered night terrors for which their mothers were of no help. These night terrors included segments involving both fear of engulfment and fear of retaliation by their fathers for getting possession of their mothers. These dreams are evidence of the feelings of rivalry already present at that early age. (Note also in this regard that their mothers are described as being seductive, which would have intensified the boys' sexual feelings and hence feelings of rivalry.) Yet, they needed their fathers to confirm gender identity and control the sexual impulses that otherwise led to fear of maternal engulfment. Besides the conflicts and the contradictions between being a rival with an ego model and between feeling desire for closeness with one who must be kept at a distance, the little boy has a third source of conflict: that inherent in the separation/individuation process itself. For the boy to achieve ever more autonomy, realizing and acting upon the realization of separateness from the hazy, disorganized sense of self and mother, implies not only taking over some of mother's caretaking functions but also pushing her away and setting out upon the lonelier road of responsibility for himself. Both of these carry the threat of angering mother because her role is being diminished and thus there is a concurrent danger of her withdrawing more of her caretaking function than the toddler desires or can bear. Here is the fear of abandonment, which implies total disappearance to the two-year-old mind.

When the danger is combined with other primary oedipal fears such as engulfment and father retaliation, the two-year-old boy must come to grips with "existence" in an immediate sense. This can lead to a very strong sense of self when the primary oedipal complex is productively integrated. However, when this does not happen, the question of personal existence can remain attached to a shaky ego in later life. In the extreme case this can even lead to suicide.

An example of how gender-related psychopathology reflects the primary oedipal phase, suicide in the male occurs four to six times as frequently as in the female (Shneidman 1976). To understand the gender specificity, we must investigate the origin of the pathology in the form of the primary oedipal complex that is particular to the little boy. We have seen that for the boy the issue of separation/individuation is tied to fears of engulfment. We recall that at the two-year-old stage the child does not possess a sense of time beyond the here and now. Because of this and the categorical mode of thought the child employs, the toddler sees in relation to existence only the possibilities of omnipresence and total nonexistence. Thus the little boy responds to an immediate threat of engulfment with either wishes to disappear or for mother to disappear; in either case, disappearance meaning annihilation. This extreme a response is prompted because engulfment itself means an end to his ego, and thus his end to his existence.

A girl's very existence is not similarly endangered in the parallel situation. Fusion with mother reinforces her gender identity; and while fusion does impinge upon her autonomy and sexuality (and such issues can give rise to intense, guilt-related behaviors), they do not carry the same emotional urgency as the question of existence. When the little boy adds to this urgency the intensity borne in oral/anal fantasies, there is great terror, which is held off only by the integrity of his ego/gender/core, which has in the best of cases been built up as these issues are developing to the extent that they never became a destructive force for him.

A man who has not adequately resolved the classical oedipal or his adolescent conflicts can become seriously suicidal if his bodily integrity, his sexual prowess, or his achievement as an individual is diminished. A crisis about any of these can shake his confidence in his ego core, his gender identity, and reduce him to despair on the primary oedipal level. This means no hope of a future and a mortal choice to resist engulfment by asserting individuality/masculinity through final separation.

A general theory of human behavior must be transcultural. The suicide of a Japanese, Mishima (Abel 1978), is therefore of special interest. His culture accepted suicide as a solution to personal difficulties. Yet Abel's study of Mishima reveals a primary oedipal complex that could characterize a man from any country.

Yukio Mishima, a prominent Japanese writer, committed suicide in 1970 by the traditional samurai method of ripping himself open with a sword. Yamamoto and Igo (1975) cited him to show the cultural aspects of suicide in Japan. Mishima's conscious motivation was to demonstrate and inspire return to worship of the emperor, more self-discipline, and social order in Japan. His samurai identity was a masculine defense against confusion he felt about whether he was a man or a woman. Abel brings out the idiosyncratic factors in his case that reveal Mishima's primary oedipal concerns. Taking material from Mishima's autobiography, *Confessions*, she writes: "Even after he was married he always kept on a sofa in his drawing room a doll and ragged stuffed lion as transitional objects that were still present in what would be considered an inappropriate setting" (1978:409).

Transitional objects are objects the child feels connected to and that help it in establishing a sense of separation from the mother (Winnicott 1968). Thus Abel's observation indicated Mishima's difficulties in feeling complete and autonomous: "Mishima wrote . . . that he was like a person not knowing how to express love, mistakenly killing the person he loves" (1978:410). Extreme ambivalence is apparent. "He felt uncomfortable about his sexual feelings, for it appeared to him that these feelings became an obsession (*Confessions*, p. 89). But he was aware his curiosity was purely intellectual" (1978:411). Here he shows the split between thought and feeling.

"To die at the height of manhood and sexual potency (with no deep desire for women, for this might have meant weakness) was what Mishima saw as sexual ecstasy; dripping blood representing semen was glorious to him" (1978:413). Mishima linked ultimate separation to proving he had no felt need for women (mother) in order to have sexual ecstasy. He confused dripping blood (perhaps menstrual?) with semen and allowed himself sexuality as long as his desire for the woman was not deep, which would have threatened his strength (masculine identity).

Mishima wrote that when he was twelve he went to the seaside with his mother and became afraid because he found her too seductive (or did she arouse sexual feelings in himself?). . . . After his death Shizu, his mother, is reported to have said, "My lover has returned to me." . . . (Shizu, his mother, went along on [his] dates.) The girl eventually married another person. (1978:414)

His mother's pathology was consonant with his difficulty in resolving primary oedipal conflict.

Mishima died under a complicated hierarchy of motives: to become a hero, a male, to die for an ideal father (the ideal emperor of old under the feudal system), to kill his real father introjected into himself, and to experience death as an ecstasy, a fusion of orgastic beauty—sex, violence, and pain. There was a good deal of rationalization in some of these motives, and certain defenses against feelings of femininity and dependency. . . . But apparently, what Mishima hoped for most was seeing blood flowing and his entrails spilling out, as well as believing that excruciating pain would give him the really deep feeling of ecstasy he had always been seeking (a fusion of sex and aggression). (1978:422)

Although Mishima's delusion about the social import of his suicide was associated with Japanese culture, we can plainly see his use of allegiance to the "perfect father" to clarify his confused gender identity, difficulty in separation/individuation, fusion of sexuality and anality (violent fantasies), split between thought and feeling. The act of suicide was in his own description an assertion of self through self-discipline, proof of his gender, expression of violently self-punitive sexuality. Abel's assumption that Mishima was killing a father introject is not substantiated in the material she quotes, although it may have been true. The evidence is clear, however, that his behavior, including his suicide, reflects primary oedipal issues.

Suicide is not the only psychopathology that is more prevalent among males. Greenson (1968) documents the fact that serious confusion over gender identity is overwhelmingly more common among males than females. It flies in the face of this reality to insist that boys come by secure gender identity more easily than do girls, as some theorists have proposed (Mahler 1975; Galenson and Roiphe 1971).

Greenson attributes this incidence partially to male envy of the female. However, such explanation falls short, as we can tell from the number of pages in psychoanalytic literature devoted to female envy of the male. Clearly, each sex can build a good case for envy of its opposite. Greenson (1968) looking deeper, emphasizes the "disidentifying" process of the boy from his mother. Yet this implies too well-crystallized a prior stage of identification with her.

The boy's ego is organized at the start in conjunction with and on the basis of his gender identity—which precludes such a level of identification with his mother.

To understand the boy's difficulties, Greenson (1968) also considers fear of engulfment by the mother, as does Parens (1979). However, as they interpret engulfment strictly on account of the disidentification process, complicated by dependency issues, they cannot explain why the boy's fear of engulfment should be so much greater than the girl's. Granted, by their model, engulfment would still threaten the little boy's gender identity in a way it would not for the little girl. However, that still leaves open the question of why obliteration of gender identity should be so terrifying relative to the general obliteration of the ego and of the physical self that are threatened for both the boy and the girl in engulfment. Recognition of the primary oedipal complex first lets us see how gender identity is at the very core of the ego, giving a partial explanation. Then we observe that the little boy is additionally impelled to closeness to his mother by sexual urges. This exponentially increases the pull toward engulfment. That is why his ambivalence is so much greater than the girl's. Gender identity is crucial for him on both sides of the equation; his sense of maleness impels him toward his mother even though that very closeness threatens him with engulfment and loss of gender/self identity. At the same time, securing his independence/gender identity by distancing himself from his mother means denying the very sexual urges that help him to establish gender/self identity.

It is complicated for the boy to sort out the sexual attraction from the dependency and unity of his relationship to his mother. In this work, the toddler boy needs his father as an ally to support a sense of maleness and differentness and thus individuality. At the same time, the boy's sexual feelings toward his mother put him in a position of rivalry with his father. He thus has the additional confusion to sort through how someone can serve as a model and a rival at the same time. At the two-year-old level of cognition, rivalry cannot be settled in the more controlled ways that are possible in his thoughts by the time of the classical oedipal phase. Unlike the four-year-old's, the two-year-old's thinking is only in the present time frame, and his identification is by fixed positions. Thus the only option to the presence of the rival is the annihilation of the rival.

Yet, that means the destruction of the model the boy simultaneously needs to build his ego and therefore to give him access to the sexual feelings that set up the rivalry in the first place. Only when the boy has consolidated his sense of maleness and personhood can he afford to take his father on fully as a rival in the classical oedipal phase.

The identification he has with his father brings a reinforcement of security about gender identity to the toddler boy's ego core. This might lay the groundwork for the male-male clubbiness that is further developed with ever greater sophistication in the work and resolution of the classical oedipal phase and the later transformation from adolescence into adulthood. Cultist protection of maleness in various cultures may begin with the toddler's need to maintain independence from mother as part of his male identity. Whiting, Kluckholn and Anthony (1958) hypothesized that harsh initiation rites for boys occurred in various societies in order to require the adolescent boy to put final stop to clinging to his mother, preventing open revolt against the father, who replaced the boy in his mother's bed, and ensure identification with the adult male society. They found twenty societies in which two conditions coexisted: (1) a child shared his mother's bed for at least a year after its birth, excluding the father; and (2) the mother's sexuality was restricted for the period. Fourteen such societies proved to have harsh initiation ceremonies. In societies in which only one of these conditions existed during infancy, initiation rites were held but in an attenuated form. Out of twenty-five societies with neither practice, only two had initiation ceremonies. The connection between primary oedipal stress and institutionalized emphasis upon male group identification is illuminating.

Adventuresomeness is another quality that is often attributed to males. In many cultures, including our own, a boy is often reinforced by social approval, which may be the basic source of the behavior. It is grounded, however, in the primary oedipal boy's practicing independent behavior in order to achieve the ability to leave his mother, the source of security (Mahler and Furer 1968). Biologically this process is given a great boost by sphincter control and rapid increase in muscular ability. The universal human need for a sense of personal competence (White 1959) provides added motivation for individuation/separation. This, however, is all true for girls as well as boys. The difference is in the character of the oedipal pressures that accompany the separation/individuation process. Resolution of the boy's autonomy/dependency conflict is augmented by his equating his "nonmother self" with being an exciting member of the world outside of the home. From Lamb's detailed study of infants in their homes comes an observation which is often noted in various studies: "Whereas mothers engaged in more conventional and toy-mediated types of play, fathers initiated more physical (rough-and-tumble type) and idiosyncratic types of play" (1976:7). This characterization is linked with an exciting quality in the father-child relationship that is initiated by the father.

This exciting prototype of nonmother/self behavior can lead to the Don Juan syndrome in men who have never formed a solid gender-ego core. Such a man can be highly romantic as the exciting father type as long as he alone is committed in the relationship with a woman. Such a man presents himself to women as being very exciting—capable of "sweeping them off their feet"—and as being very successful in the outside world, which he prominently displays. However, the Don Juan feels free to be exciting and therefore confident with women only by identification with father on an imitative basis and the gender/ego reinforcement it provides. In real closeness to women the poorly integrated ego loses its identification with father and concomitantly loses its gender/ego support. When the woman responds with a commitment on her part, his terror of engulfment reasserts itself. He must then flee. Eber (1981) demonstrates the use of Don Juanism in striving for self-cohesion, which supports the idea that the primary oedipal conflict underlies the behavior. Klein (1950) refers to Don Juan's fear of his destructiveness toward the woman. As he needs to protect the object of his love, his impulse to destroy when feeling engulfed, in order to protect his masculinity, forces him to leave one relationship with a woman after another. He satisfies his defensive anger toward women just by controlling them through conquest and then leaving them to feel violated and betrayed.

More blatant sadism on the part of a man toward a woman derives from primary oedipal fusion of anal and sexual fantasies. This makes sense if we appreciate the defensive rage of the boy at endangering his masculinity by indulging his intense need for sexual fulfillment in closeness with a woman.[1] Whiting (1965) points out from cross-cultural studies that hostile male aggression is motivated by the need to break an identity with powerful women.

Whiting's insight applies at an extreme to overt sexual sadism. This behavior is significantly more prevalent among men than among women (Stekel 1926). We can understand why in considering the roots of the condition in the boy's primary oedipal phase. In keeping with his barely organized ego-state and the other characteristics of his two-year-old's mental life including anality, the toddler boy copes with his conflicts through the mechanism of splitting. Defying mother—the negativism so typical of two-year-olds—is a way of defining the "bad" self, as opposed to engulfment by the "good" mother. The value of negativism to prove separateness extends to expressing frustration and anger in his ambivalent wish for closeness to his mother. Sexuality thus becomes confused with terror and anger, and at the extreme of negativism, the inflicting of pain and taking complete control over the other. To control seems the opposite of engulfment.

An example from my own practice illustrates how various elements of the primary oedipal complex combine in sadistic behavior. George, a man of thirty, had told me of masturbatory fantasies in which he tied up women. In the material given here, he presented a masochistic version of this basically sadistic orientation, which revealed its primary oedipal origin.

He began this session by telling me that masturbation inhibited his individuality and creative work. In this statement we already see evidence of two-year-old connections: by permitting himself sexual feelings, he moves emotionally closer to the object of these feelings, threatening engulfment. Part of that threat is the lack of possession of his own thoughts and secrets (since to the very young child with an incomplete concept of self, mother, who knows when to feed it, etc., must know his thoughts) and hence the result of loss of individuality in creative thought.

He next said that he had prepared for a fantasy by lying on the floor. He tied himself up in a tight bathing suit with a padlock, making it impossible for the suit to come off, but he further tied himself so that, in his words, he "otherwise is entirely available." This meant that women could taunt him and tease him. The women did this to him to get back at him for his having tied them up in previous fantasies. In the present fantasy, he felt unworthy to touch them. He felt disgust for himself afterward lying there on the floor.

George's next associations were first to an untouchable, lovely girl, whom he had known long ago, and then to how he fought going back to his present girlfriend after a quarrel, feeling it a defeat. The issue was establishing control in degrees of closeness. This tied in with the issues of control of thought he raised in relation to masturbation to open this session about his sexual difficulties.

We can see in this excerpt from George's material hallmarks of the primary oedipal phase. They all contain the use of splitting, the characteristic defense mechanism of the primary oedipal phase. We can observe how splitting is applied to primary oedipal phase issues: (1) the segmenting of his body (padlocking his genital organs); (2) splitting of the female into a sexual (bad) imago and an idealized nonsexual (good) imago; (3) power struggle and cruelty (anal phase derivatives) that include sharp polarizations; (4) fear of closeness literally tied to sexuality and both together split off from his other feelings; and (5) individuality being curtailed as the price of sexual expression, particularly by splitting off and preventing intellectual endeavor (danger in having his own thoughts).

The use of splitting to handle sexual feelings appears in well-documented psychopathology. The Kinsey, Pomeroy, and Martin report says: "There are cases of males who are totally impotent with their wives, although they are successful in extra-marital relations, which they may carry on throughout the whole of their marital histories" (1948:593).

Being dependent can equal being nonsexual because the toddler boy feels danger in continuing his bond with mother if he directs sexual interest toward her. One way of reacting to this threat is by splitting the mother image in accordance with his two-year-old's way of managing his own impulses. If the two halves are not connected during the classical oedipal phase, the pattern can persist in a split mother image: the sexual woman and the caretaker. The sexual woman, in keeping with the primary oedipal complex, may be a "bad woman" (because in the good–bad dichotomization of the toddler mind, what is unacceptable to the ego for any reason is bad), while the asexual, caretaking woman is a "good woman." This use of the splitting mechanism was also seen by Stekel in a closely related syndrome:

Some men are potent only with harlots, or with women of low caste, while their spiritual love is linked to persons with whom they are sexually impotent. Here we find the interplay of those important mechanisms described by Freud as infantile fixation and infantile feeling-attitudes and the split between "tenderness" and "sexuality." (1926:43)

Kernberg (1980) more recently discusses this kind of splitting in his borderline patients. The use of splitting in these syndromes is a clue that the origin of this "prostitute-madonna" complex can be found in the primary oedipal age. We know that for a two-year-old boy being dependent can equal being nonsexual because he feels danger in continuing his bond with mother if he directs sexual interest toward her. His sexual urges could overwhelm him and push him into a degree of closeness that would result in a loss of self. One way of reacting to this threat is by splitting the mother image in accordance with his two-year-old's way of managing his own impulses: a mother-half which he can react to sexually without fear of being pushed into a dependent, pre-ego state, and a mother-half offering support but without the sexuality that could force greater closeness until he is lost. This splitting when it is reflected in impotence involves part-object use of the penis. The man's penis seems independent of his will. Similarly, penis envy in girls requires part-object fantasy and splitting (Chasseguet-Smirgel 1976). These mechanisms enable a primary oedipal child to order its difficult feelings. Frequently a boy gains ease through these mechanisms in a split between sexuality and attachment.

Kinsey, Pomeroy and Martin tried to explain this split as it appears in the male use of prostitution: "Men go to prostitutes because they can pay for the sexual relations and forget other responsibilities, whereas coitus with other girls may involved them socially and legally beyond anything which they care to undertake" (1948:607). We can see, however, that additionally responsibility for sex can be equated with ties to the love-object and that to a man who has not solidified his ego-core such closeness threatens engulfment.

This pattern, of early splitting in relation to mother and sexuality, is very common. One who may have shown it was Sigmund Freud. I would like to beg the indulgence of the reader as I digress briefly to speculate how some of the events in Freud's life and ideas that he is responsible for might be reinterpreted in light of the primary oedipal complex. This speculation gives cognizance and due to the psychoanalytic circle that over the years has tried to explain Freud's life and findings. Once we start to think in terms of the primary oedipal phase, there is an intriguing quality to certain well-established facts about Freud.

Some facts to which we have access[2] about his early life include that Freud remembered sexual arousal at his mother's nudity when he was around two years old; yet it was not to her, his "constant companion," but rather to an "ugly and mean" old woman who was his nursemaid during that age period that he attributed his learning about "sex and life and the worth of living," his consistently benevolent picture of his mother (even though she was known to be tyrannical, violent of temper, and quite vain), his relative ease in expressing ambivalence toward his mild and indulgent father, and that a baby brother died when Freud was eighteen months old. Two more historical facts are relevant. First, when his father died, years later, Freud associated his feelings then with those he had had about the death of his baby brother; second, his discovery of the classical oedipal phase came about when he explored his feelings about both events. Freud concentrated upon his death wishes for those two in his personal analytic explorations and mentioned no ambivalence toward his mother.

I should like to suggest a construction to link and help understand all this material. It seems possible that during his primary oedipal phase Freud experienced an especially intense fear of merging with a powerful mother during the time when he was trying to achieve separation/individuation. Furthermore, if we assume that the pull toward her due to his sexual feelings was particularly great due to her seductiveness, then it makes sense that the two-year-old Freud had to maintain a split between the impact of the sexual strivings for his mother and the organization of his sexual feelings in terms of the nursemaid (who taught him about sex but was herself unattractive). To trade autonomy for closeness with his mother may have seemed most threatening because that powerful person was also associated with a baby's disappearance—annihilated, to his tod-dler's eyes, just as Freud was developing awareness of himself as a male individual.

Freud's primary oedipal resolution could have been as fol-lows, with parenthetical suggestions as to consequences for his later development: "Mother has only good feelings for me." (*Therefore women are good and I can maintain long-term relationships with them.*) "I believe that danger occurs to me if I am rivalrous with my father, although I know he is safer to be with than my mother, and I desperately need his help if I am to affirm my masculinity." (*Men-tally, I maintain two male images, friends like myself and rivalrous enemies.*) "To diminish my anxieties connected with mother, I must believe that it was father—with whom I really feel safe—who is associated with baby brother's death." (*Therefore the question of "The Deed" remains to the end unresolved: "Did memories of childhood events really happen or are they fantasies?"*) "Fear of father, which I can handle, must seem my greatest concern." (*Therefore the father is always responsible for neurosis.*) "I disclaim oedipal feelings be-fore the classical oedipal period because only by then, with my resolution of the primary oedipal conflict, was my sense of gender identity secure from the terror of merger with mother." (*Therefore, although I remember my own attraction to my mother when I was two, I dare not integrate the significance of it.*) "Mother's love for me is based upon my being a boy." (*Therefore she would not have de-stroyed my baby brother.*) "All children want to be boys since mother does *not* destroy boys." (*Therefore girls think of themselves as girls only when they blame mother for having castrated them, which they might well feel the death-dealing mother could do.*) "To understand someone, feels to the two-year-old to be the same as being that person, fused through thought. I as a boy must not understand women, particularly in terms of their sexuality. If I did I would lose my autonomy and be engulfed by my tempestuous mother. Further, I would have to acknowledge her dark side." (*Therefore, sexuality of females is a "dark continent" no man can really understand.*)[3]

The reader will recognize in the parenthetical statements positions that Freud actually took. This not quite tongue-in-cheek suggestion about his primary oedipal phase could explain several ideas of Freud's that run counter to common experience but that have dramatically influenced psychoanalytic thinking until now.

Regardless of how the events of Freud's second year of life actually affected him, this exercise illustrates a developmental process that appears clearly in the case material in chapters 7, 8, and 9. These chapters are devoted to evidence for the existence of the primary oedipal phase in both sexes.

7 Evidence for the Existence of the Primary Oedipal Phase: Direct Observation of Young Children

The literature is notable for providing examples of oedipal behavior in children who are called preoedipal. In presenting it, I lean toward overquotation rather than to make prejudicial selections that would diminish the reader's opportunity to evaluate the evidence independently.

Accounts of Development in Boys

Kleeman (1966) had access to a diary a mother kept of her baby son's genital self-discovery. Kleeman quoted fifty observations covering William W.'s development from just over a year to the age of two. William demonstrated awareness of his penis by age nine months. Increasing attention to his penis, visually and tactily, seemed to be part of his learning about his body. We recall that nine months is approximately the age when object permanence begins, and thus capacity for self-concept. The following excerpts were selected from the notes on William at nearly sixteen months and older.[1] They show the simultaneous development of self-concept and gender identity, accompanied by the rise of the oedipal conflict.

We see here that at nearly sixteen months William's sexual feelings were clearly directed at mother.

Observation 6 (1:3 + 20)
Several times this day when his diapers were changed, William squeezed his legs together and each time he had a 3+ erection. On one occasion . . . [causing] the erection, he squeezed his mother's forearm with his fingers and then took her finger in his mouth and bit it (it appeared more like a "love bite," a discharge of some sexual excitement rather than anger). (1966:361)

Observation 7 (1:3 + 23)
The mother was holding William in her lap. He put his hands on her fully clothed chest and then ran them downward in a way that indicated a consciousness of her form as his hands moved over her breasts. Later in the day William was playing on the floor. Mrs. W. leaned over, and she found William staring down her blouse as an older male might. (1966:361)

Observation 7 is interesting in light of the origins of scotophilia in the early part of the primary oedipal phase.

Observation 8 (1:4 + 5), at sixteen months:
. . . At almost every diaper change he reached for his penis. He seemed to know it was there and to realize it felt good to touch it. . . . William slipped his hand down to his genitalia inside the diaper.
     At one point his mother kissed his foot. Immediately, he patted his genital area (over diapers and rubber pants) and said: "Oooh, ooh." His mother felt this could mean "kiss me here as you did on my foot" or "it feels good here," i.e., kissing his foot makes his genital area feel good.
     At sixteen and a half months William touched his genitals in order to stimulate them, without having to look each time. His self-image had reached the point where he now referred to himself by name.
     There was at this time beginning gender differentiation. Looking at a magazine with his mother, he distinguished a "boy" or "man" from a "durl," usually correctly. (1966:364)

     Mental construct of his genitals (reaching for them without needing to look), referring to himself by name, and gender identity all occurred along with genital response to his mother's display of affection toward him. The diary continues:

Observation 14 (1:5 + 4)
This night his penis became erect (2+) when she [put salve on the area].
He giggled and reached for it. (1966:364)

Observation 15 (1:5 + 9)
During this period his putting his hand to his genitals was more prominent
and frequent during diaper changes than during baths. His tugging on his
penis and saying "off" continued, but was now done as a joke. He did this
in his mother's presence; she would jest back, "Oh, Billy, you know your
penis doesn't come off," and he laughed and repeated the "game." This
behavior coincided in time with his having a few bowel movements on the
toilet; thus he experienced a "body part" becoming separated from him
and being flushed away, an experience which was associated with some
apparent anxiety. (1966:364)

We saw here the importance of anality in the primary oedipal phase
and the timing of the development of castration anxiety.

Observation 19 (1:3 + 28)
William had seen his father urinate and watched the process intently with
great interest. [Next day he] tugged on his penis and muttered "Boken." It
was not clear whether this was related to his recent learning of the word,
which he also applied to door latches, etc., resulted from a comparison
with his father, or was part of the game which then followed: he continued
to tug on his penis, saying, "Off." It was no longer an anxiety-free joke
with his mother as she reassured him that it would not come off. He now
showed mild concern about it, and in addition pursued his anthropomorphizing of his penis, offering it cookies and drinks of water. (1966:365)

It is important to note how William's castration anxiety became a real fear for him after observation of his father. It is also
clear here how anthropomorphizing the penis was used as a way of
handling castration anxiety. Note also the importance of part-object
identification in building body-image.

In summarizing William's progress at age one year and a
half, Kleeman tells us:

At eighteen months . . . bowel and urinary training was still at the beginning stages. He now associated urinating with his penis and the penis with
the presence of his father (when his father came to his changing table,
William would often start to speak about his penis) . . . [showed] greater

absorption in pleasure in his genital self-stimulation . . . but did not use it as a means of comfort or relief from frustration. While William developed much autonomy and individuation, he needed his mother when he suffered from the stomach distress, which still contributed to a sleep problem. (1966:366)

Kleeman continued by describing a delightful, bright child. William practiced autonomy from his mother in a teasing way, integrated oral and anal motifs (e.g., sucking his thumb and sniffing a diaper while going to sleep), and began to organize his world view and to develop cleanliness.

Illustrating the active principle in a boy's experience of his genitals, Kleeman depicts William controlling his erections by sucking in his abdomen, vigorously playing with his penis when his mother scolded him. In the chapter on the primary oedipal phase in females, we considered the significance to little girls that so much of their early genital experience is interior. It seemed to be a source of feeling that sexual stimulation must come from the outside. Here we saw how the externalization of his genital experience encouraged a boy to use his penis in an active reaction to his mother's effort to control him.

By nearly nineteen months, William advanced in integration of his sense of self and his need for a psychosocial place in the family as guided by his gender identity. The primary oedipal conflict then became apparent:

Observation 31 (1:7 + 20)
William discussed his parents' double bed with his mother, checking who slept where. He insisted that the place beside his mother was his place, not his father's.

This incident was characteristic of a variety of behavior indicating early oedipal feelings. He greatly enjoyed "possessing" his mother's body, climbing over her head when she rested, kissing her, running his hands over her clothes. There was a clear-cut increase in these activities when his father was not present. Mrs. W. did not forbid such behavior, but often distracted William to prevent his becoming too excited. (1966:369)

In spite of the detailed observations of William's interest in his penis, to the extent of noting the angle of an erection, his oedipal behavior at around twenty months is but briefly mentioned.

Observation 31 nonetheless tells that William displayed significant oedipal behavior at the age of a year and a half.

In the remaining observations, William explored anal interests, feelings about his mother's new pregnancy, and issues around building his body image and gender identity.

The place of gender identity in the organization of the ego is illustrated in Kleeman's summary of William's progress at two years. Noting that William combined self-awareness and self-assertion:

[At two years] . . . "degree of stubbornness," not previously prominent, was emerging. The burst of autonomy, noted at twenty-three and a half months, was expressed in such behavior as insisting on putting himself to bed at night. . . . The heightened independence coincided with signs of greater separation anxiety at other times. His increased individuation was a source of both pride and some fear. At times it contributed to a tendency to regression. For example, he repeatedly insisted that he be referred to as a baby, not a boy, as if he needed to be cared for, lest he "run away with himself." (1966:378)

The contradiction to William in being both a baby and a boy illustrates the crucial role of gender identity in forming an autonomous organized ego. In his new gender-defined selfness, a baby cannot be a boy, i.e., someone with autonomy, aware of his feelings and gender, *including all the implications for interpersonal relationships.* As Kleeman continues his description of William at two years, we see the related and equally crucial theme of sexual wishes for his mother.

He sucked his thumb when tired. His genital self-stimulation was sporadic; his diapers were off relatively little in the course of a day. . . . At times he could be quite seductive. On several occasions at this age he suggested that his mother squeeze his penis (she responded by distracting him to other pursuits). . . . He was very fond of his mother and would seek *her* [Kleeman's emphasis] at moments of stress. Though less intense and sensuous, his relationship with his father was close and represented fun and activity. [Note: Fun with his penis seems to have been reserved for his mother. JKT] There were various indications of a growing fantasy life. He exhibited some oedipal feelings, at times wishing exclusive possession of his mother and displaying some rivalry with his father. There were also clear-cut identifications with his father. (1966:379)

Discussing the behavior notes, Kleeman next indicates how language development helped in laying down mental representations of a body image. Further exploring William's second year, Kleeman refers to several behavioral derivatives of libidinal drives:

1. Early scotophilia (Observation 7).
2. Exhibitionism and its associated affect, pride (Observations 9, 24).[2]
3. Early signs of oedipal feelings appearing from nineteen and a half months on (Observation 31). These are usually reported as appearing later, although Ruth Mack Brunswick declares, without much further elaboration: "In the boy, the pre-oedipal mother attachment is apparently of much shorter duration than in the girl, merging very early into the Oedipus Complex" (1940:384). [Behn-Eschenburg (1932) states the same idea, except for girls' attachments to fathers—JKT.]

Kleeman's comments about oedipal implications are rather brisk. There seem to be more notes about exhibitionistic, masturbatory, scotophilic, and anal behavior and/or responses to separation. These are all very important elements in the primary oedipal complex. Still, when William is two years old (as described by Kleeman (p. 379), we see the essence of the primary oedipal complex of a boy: his sexualized preference for mother in conflict with separation/individuation and needing his father for confirmation of his gender/personal identity against a background of rivalrous feelings with him.

We note that it was when William was two, long after he had "discovered" the differences between the genitals of the two sexes, but perhaps stimulated by his mother's pregnancy, that he began to show the wholesale patterns of behavior of the primary oedipal phase and distinguish it from an early genital phase. He thus showed conflict between being a "baby" and a "boy," overt sexual oedipal tension, and identification with his father. Oedipal feelings contribute to our comprehension of William's personality organization and his use of scotophilic and exhibitionistic behavior when handling promptings toward his mother. These observations of William are especially valuable because they were collected so carefully without the concept of the primary oedipal phase as a guide.

Therefore, we can have confidence in this evidence that a boy's genital sensations accompany the rise of gender identity and how gender identity in turn supports integration of his body ego, how simultaneous anal concerns affect genitally based anxieties, and how increasing ego differentiation and oedipal feelings appear together.

Galenson and Roiphe, describing the early psychosexual development of another boy, used a single example because they felt he was representative of the many in this age group whom they had studied. I excerpt all pertinent material from direct observation.

At about fourteen months, Jeff showed behavioral evidence of beginning anal-phase organization. He became interested in toilets and garbage pails, pulled at his soiled diaper selectively, smeared his food, and became much more demanding, flaring up in temper tantrums. At about the same time, evidence of urinary organization appeared: he took pleasure in stopping and starting his urinary stream for the first time, a urinary interest that soon extended to his mother as well.[3]

With this upsurge in urinary interest and awareness, a new type of behavior involving the genital area made its first appearance. At fifteen months, Jeff began to regularly and rather frequently point to, look at, and pull at his penis, playing a hide-and-seek visual game with it by pulling in and relaxing his somewhat protuberant abdomen. This new level of genital cathexis was accompanied by a parallel development in that he began to imitate many of his father's activities for the first time: he tried to walk in his shoes, draped himself in his father's ties and belts, and initiated a number of games which he now played only with his father.

During the next two months—that is, between his fifteenth and seventeenth month—Jeff's genital play took on a distinctly masturbatory character in that genital self-stimulation was now frequent, more definitely pleasurable, and often culminated in the production of an erection. By seventeen and a half months, *he rubbed his penis during each diapering, giggling as he did so, and invited his mother to share in this pleasure and excitement by glancing up at her with an inviting smile.* That there was an element of doing to himself what had previously been done to him was evident from the careful and tender way in which he powdered his own penis on several occasions.

With the intensification of his masturbation came several episodes of prolonged and intent inspection of his father's penis itself, in contrast to his previous interest in the father's urinary process.[4]

The two-month period of intense masturbation began to decline by about eighteen months. Jeff now became interested in his own umbilicus as well as those of others about him, and he and his mother developed a mutual umbilical tickling play. The balance of interest in his parents also began to shift at about this time in that he now preferred to kiss his father, whom he eagerly awaited each evening, and he acted differently over the weekend when his father was home. He continued to show a very active interest in his father's urination. His father responded by initiating a special bedtime ritual with Jeff. Although Jeff still sometimes cuddled with his mother, these were now brief episodes.

We consider it likely that the relative inhibition of masturbation which occurred in this boy and his turn to his father for the support of his growing sense of masculine identity were in reaction to Jeff's initial acknowledgment of the sexual anatomical difference. (1980a:805–827)

Galenson and Roiphe's interpretation ignores their report that Jeff connected masturbation with efforts to engage his mother's interest and that giving up masturbation coincided with giving up libidinal behavior with her. At the same time he initiated a form of play in which he and his mother were umbilically connected in a regression to a symbolic dependent state. Intensifying his relationship to his beloved father was further denial of libidinal wishes toward his mother.

The emergence of his defensive denial was, in our view, reflected in his avoidance of further confrontation with his mother's genitals, for he would immediately become involved with various objects in the bathroom whenever he accompanied his mother there. We believe that his anxiety over the genital difference was further allayed by displacement to the umbilicus. Yet the strain of the persistent underlying anxiety made itself evident and was reflected in such "body games" as pulling his sleeves down to cover his hands, having his mother question him as to where his hands had gone, and then revealing his hands to her once more with a squeal of delight as well as a sense of relief. (1980a:821–822)

Mastery over castration anxiety is not the complete explanation of the body games. Jeff's repression of interest in his mother's genitals was paralleled by diminished interest in his own. His squeals of delight could have come from their shared pleasure in libidinally safe body games, as well as his maintaining all his parts while being pleasurably close to his mother.

Galenson and Roiphe see denial of genital interest in Jeff's diminished masturbatory activity. However, Jeff preceded this by wanting mother to play with his penis and followed it by avoidance of his mother's (we may add, seductive) availability in the bathroom. First including her in masturbatory activity, he then repressed interest both in his penis (displacing to the umbilicus) and in erotic feeling toward his mother. We note that the game of disappearance of body parts and the umbilical games also had to do with the issue of physical likeness to mother, which is such a difficult part of the separation/individuation/primary oedipal phase for the boy. Confirmation of gender identity and repression of sexual interest in his mother appear together in the next notes:

> His castration anxiety also seemed to be expressed in Jeff's new preoccupation with keys, pens, and tall trees, all sharing the attribute of their phallic shape.
>
> During the next month and a half, that is, from age twenty to twenty-one and a half months, there was some decline in Jeff's masturbatory activity, but a burgeoning of phallic derivative behavior of many types. *His relationship with his mother remained loving and tender, but there was little if any erotic quality in it.*
>
> Jeff shared many new games with his father, most of which involved large muscle activities. His father would carry Jeff on his shoulders as if they were horse and rider, and Jeff would imitate this game in his father's absence, taking the horse's role himself. He asked after his father during the day and they often spoke to each other on the telephone. He tended to obey his father's instructions more diligently than his mother's, despite the fact that his father was by no means a strict disciplinarian. (1980a:821–822)

This might be the beginning of the idealization process that is reflected in the work of Kohut (1977). Kohut observes a regularly recurring "idealization transference" in his work with borderline and narcissistic personalities. Jeff's respect for his father's instructions suggests two things: idealizing the father, and by diligently following father's instructions, using the father to keep Jeff himself under control.[5]

> It was particularly touching to see this small boy lean back in his chair, count on his fingers as his father did, and mimic his father's facial expressions and body mannerisms as he gradually seemed to be turning into a small edition of the man he now looked up to so admiringly. This identification extended to the cognitive realm as well: *Jeff was able to learn*

words from his father which his mother had been unable to teach him, and father and son played many word games together. *He also began to tinker with the stereo musical equipment, one of his father's favorite pastimes.* He was entirely comfortable with his father now, whether his mother was present or not. Jeff's whole body seemed to assume a phallic connotation for him. He played a "flying" game with his father, in which he would run across the room, head ducked forward, arms thrust behind him, while he loudly imitated the "brmmm" noise of an airplane. Reaching his father's outspread arms, he would be tossed into the air to the intense excited enjoyment of both father and son. While his mother watched this game rather apprehensively, she was also aware of her pride in her son's growing masculinity.

Only occasional disharmony occurred during this rather idyllic period: when the parents kissed or were affectionate with one another, Jeff would intrude between them and demand to be kissed by each in turn. It was obvious that he wanted to be the center of attraction for both parents, rather than wishing either of them for himself alone. (1980a:822–823)

That these were occasions of disharmony suggests a degree of tension. Why should a child who was treated so warmly by his parents lose his equilibrium at their physical closeness with each other? Jeff seemed to be at pains to prove he felt the same about them both, perhaps to counteract any difference that did exist.

When Jeff was three years old, we learned (during the follow-up visit with him and his parents), he had grown quite casual about seeing his parents undressed on occasion and paid little if any attention to their genitals. However, when a young uncle visited with the family during Jeff's twenty-eighth month, Jeff happened to enter the bathroom while his uncle was bathing. According to his uncle's account of the event, Jeff looked extremely startled and stared at his uncle's penis "as if he were seeing a penis for the first time." (1980a:823–824)

This illustrates the problem in the idea of the "discovery" of the genital difference to explain subsequent behavior. *An apparent interest in genitals reflects the state of the child's mind at the time, rather than necessarily a first opportunity to observe the genitals of others.* Galenson and Roiphe recognize this disjunctiveness of observation and their theory, as they continue their discussion:

This type of waxing and waning of the recognition of the sexual difference is a phenomenon we have noted in many of the other boys in our sample.

Could it be that this fact of the genital difference as a generalization which applies to all males and females becomes established only gradually over time, particularly in view of the boy's tendency to deny the genital difference and its possible interference with cognitive development? *Alternatively, such episodes may represent precursors of oedipal development, when temporary upsurge of erotic feelings toward the mother and rivalry toward the father may threaten the boy's previous strategy of denial and identification with the father, the defensive measure whereby the boy was able to maintain the bond with the mother through the vicissitudes of the early genital phase.*

Aside from the comparisons Jeff made between the size of his own and his father's penis and the idea that his penis would magically enlarge, there was no clear-cut indication that oedipal phase organization had yet emerged. (1980a:824–825)

Primary oedipal phase organization shows up as a two-year-old's experience, not a four-year-old's. The difference comes from the primary oedipal child's need to establish a basic sense of self, its relative lack of sophistication—compared with how it will be when it is two years older and also with how much less independent it is than it will be when it is four years old.

Overall, with Jeff, we get a sense of developmental process, but it is not completely clear from Galenson and Roiphe just what that is. The interpretation that it has to do with genital difference seems valid enough, but that emphasis is upon only one aspect of the total situation. Jeff shows how a boy in the primary oedipal phase can remain close with his mother and yet prevent psychological merger with her by repressing erotic feelings. He thus avoids intense inner conflict from feeling erotically impelled toward his mother before his gender/personal identity is well-enough established.

Protecting his sense of autonomy by damping down libidinal interaction with his mother, he reinforces it by imitating his father. In the resultant ego organization, he senses who he is through the father-identification, which differentiates him from his mother and sets up the first pattern for handling his impulses.

Accounts of Development in Girls

It might surprise a reader today that an account of primary oedipal conflict in a normal two-year-old was reported by Behn-Eschenburg in 1932, in his paper, "The Antecedents of the Oedipus Complex." The storms over both Klein's extreme assertions and the importance of closing psychoanalytic ranks about the major assertions of Freud may have strengthened the case for orthodoxy in Behn-Eschenburg's choice of title at the time of publication. A particular incident with his own daughter led him to write what he might have entitled, "The Primary Oedipal Phase." The following excerpt from his article quotes his observations and the essence of his conclusions:

Here is a scene which took place when the little girl who is the subject of these observations was about two and a half years old.

One morning she was "helping" the housemaid, as she often did, to make the beds in her parents' home. Suddenly she said to the maid, who as usual had pushed the beds apart, "Now you are not to put them together again." The maid replied that then there would be a gap between them and someone might fall out of bed, whereupon the baby said: "And when Mummy is dead, I shall sleep in her bed."

As I have said, it is sometimes a doubtful proceeding to attempt to interpret remarks of this sort, made by little children. On the other hand we often cannot fail to receive a very definite impression of what is happening in their minds. Here, for instance, we feel as if we were right in the midst of the Oedipus situation, although, to judge by the age of the child (two and a half), it seems much too early for it. We can really hardly help concluding that the mother was to be got rid of because the little girl had taken her father for her love-object and wanted to sleep beside him in mother's place.

In any case the change of object appears clear and well defined, although with regard to the change of aim we may not feel sure whether the child had really reached the phallic level in her relation to her father. (1932:178)

Behn-Eschenburg refers to earlier behavior notes to answer the question, starting with the child's observation of the genital difference. His only child, she was seventeen months old when she went to the seaside and for the first time saw a naked boy:

She immediately sat down in front of him and stared fixedly and with the utmost astonishment at his penis. At first she made some hesitating attempts to touch it with her little hand; then she gave it up and simply gazed. The boy too stood perfectly still and looked at her. The baby then began to search her own body, making little anxious sounds such as at that time she always uttered when anything was not quite right. She continued to sit on the ground in the same position and went on searching, quite unconcerned at what was going on round her. She even took no notice of the fact that the little boy had taken possession of her toys, an encroachment which on any other occasion she would have resented.

For some days the same thing went on: every time that she was undressed, she began to search and was greatly distressed at her lack of success. At last, after a few days, her interest in the matter seemed gradually to die out. In all other respects the child's behavior remained unchanged throughout this period; she was as lively and contented as ever.

It so happened that for about two months the baby had no opportunity of seeing other little children. Then, a little boy cousin (ten months old) came for the first time to stay with us in the house. He used to lie in the perambulator which she had formerly used, was bathed in her bath, and dressed on the table where she had been dressed, but he slept in another room. The little girl watched all this very attentively and was specially anxious always to be present when he was having his bath. She would then look fixedly at his penis and often try to touch it softly. Meanwhile she became markedly jealous for the first time in her life. She tried to push everyone away from her mother and it was very difficult to persuade her even to show people her possessions, still more to give them away. She was obviously relieved when the little boy went away again. (1932:178–179)

The above incident when the little girl was nineteen months old shows penis envy which was nonoedipal in quality. It was not a case of penis envy in the classical sense of a wish to be a boy (for Freud, a universal wish, because being a boy was clearly superior; for us because it is a way of being like and therefore close to father without threat of mother's retaliation); nor was it accompanied by the change in behavior and ego organization that would classically be expected. It had only to do with a sense of personal possession (augmented by the baby's use of her things). Her natural reaction was to assert possessive interest in all her belongings including her mother, as part of her jealous reaction. Behn-Eschenburg describes how on subsequent visits of the boy cousin, she behaved in the same way, "except that her attitude became less marked." Her outward behavior was so unchanged that reluctance to lend the boy her toys was the main clue to her feelings. She did watch with interest when a new friend, a boy older than herself, urinated out of doors. Again, beyond the interest at the moment, there was no marked change in her behavior.

As time went on, her jealousy of her little cousin seemed rather to diminish; gradually she allowed him to play with her toys, with the exception of a certain little glass ball. This she would press between her legs or sit down upon it if she thought the baby might catch sight of it.

Freud assumes that a further consequence of the child's discovery of castration is that the tender relation to the mother-object becomes less close. He adds, however: "One does not clearly understand the connection, but nevertheless one is often bound to recognize that in the end the mother is nearly always treated as responsible for the lack." *In our case nothing of the sort was remarked directly after the little girl's discovery:* the first beginnings of detachment which could really be distinctly detected occurred more than a year later when she first observed another little boy cousin being suckled. (1932:179)

Behn-Eschenburg need not have wondered. The "blame of the mother" is usually conjectured. Enough two-year-old girls are sufficiently verbal that we should hear many a toddler girl say that her mother "took away her penis" and why, if indeed the girl blamed her mother. What we find is only what Freud mentions: coexistent interest in two kinds of genitals and being angry with mother. To assume the "blame fantasy" is simply "reading their minds." Furthermore, for such a regular occurrence as gender identity and its ramifications to depend upon chance sighting of the two kinds of genitals would suggest that until the moment of "discovery" there is nothing going on in the child's mind about bodies, feelings, and its parents.

To return to Behn-Eschenburg, his next interpretation of the little girl's behavior followed the conventional thinking of the time. Behn-Eschenburg suggested that his daughter detached herself from her mother at age two and a half because in the sight of a baby suckling she associated her loss of her mother's breast with her discovery of the male genital at seventeen months. Weaning and toilet training by the mother, he thought, might thus have prepared the child to imagine loss of a highly prized part of the body so that not having a penis would mean to her that castration had occurred.

In his explanation, Behn-Eschenburg tried to squeeze his observation into the theory of penis-envy-mother-blame. He offers no behavior notes to support the theory, while the girl's limited original reaction to the "genital difference" contradicts it, as he states. Much later, the little girl may have computed penis = baby, although he gives no observed evidence for it. The facts are simply that after seeing her little cousin being suckled, she demonstrated her wish to have her daddy to herself in the reported oedipal scene:

At any rate the fact was that, directly after she saw the baby sucking, the child's attitude toward her mother underwent a marked change. She became highly aggressive and violent and, though at times she would return to her loving and coaxing ways, . . . [angry] feelings were very often uppermost.

And some days later, after her beloved little cousin had gone away, the scene took place in her parents' bedroom when she told the housemaid that "she was not to put the beds together again" and that "when her Mummy was dead she was going to lie in that bed."

It seems almost inevitable to assume that the little girl had taken her father as her love-object and that her mother had become the object of her jealousy. This means that the oedipus complex was already in full force. . . .

The conclusion reached from quite a number of direct observations of girl children is always the same: that the oedipus complex occurs much *earlier* than purely theoretical considerations would lead us to expect. Moreover, in the very girls in whom a more superficial study revealed nothing but a mother-fixation there were at least indications that an oedipus phase had been passed through at a very much earlier period indeed.

The results of the analysis of female patients have been similar. In cases where the mother-fixation seemed to have persisted very late or actually never to have given place to the father-relation it has yet transpired, over and over again, that the latter relation really had played a part, generally far earlier than we should have supposed, and that in some way or other it had affected the original mother-relation. Almost we might accept the parodoxical conclusion that the *less sign there is to be seen of any Oedipus complex, the earlier will it have played its part* [Behn-Eschenburg's italics]. (1932:184–185)

His apparently happy little girl reacted slightly to her first observation of a penis at seventeen months. By nineteen months, in a stronger response to her cousin's penis, she was affected by possessiveness, including toward her mother. That there was an anal component to all this may be surmised by the fact that in making peace with the situation she sat down upon her symbol of retention, which was a glass ball, hardly a penile symbol.[6]

When seeing a baby being suckled, she precipitously showed full-blown oedipal behavior. As we do not know anything of her thoughts on baby making, it is hard to know whether Behn-Eschenburg's assumptions are correct that her reaction was based upon the formula: weaning loss to anal loss (both blamed on mother) to penis loss (which he noted did not earlier seem to link up to anger against mother) such that she suddenly turned away from mother and to father. It would be just as logical and perhaps more revealing to say that she received excellent care from both parents and only the reminder that parents have babies together and mothers' importance stimulated her wish to come into her own as an effective feminine being. What is clear is that her oedipal conflict at two and a half caused dramatic changes in her behavior.

Galenson and Roiphe (1977) published data on five other two-year-old girls to show typical behavior at that age. We shall see how the children vary in manner of handling the complexities of primary oedipal feelings.

Galenson and Roiphe interpret changes in behavior they see in these little girls as resulting from reaction to the genital difference. They believe that the girls are basically angry with their mothers, blaming their mothers for absence of a penis. Close attention to this material with awareness of the primary oedipal conflict reveals the full sense of the child's behavior. If in truth the girl were involved significantly in only a dyadic relationship with her mother and suddenly became angry because of a fantasy that her mother took away a penis that the girl thought she once had, then the logical result should be ambivalence toward her mother (given continued dependency) but still relative indifference toward father.

None of the five girls selected to represent typical behavior patterns demonstrated such a pattern. Four out of the five showed *simultaneous* rage at mother and delight in father. In one case, mention is made only of her mother, for whom the child becomes subdued and compliant. We shall remember her as we consider the dynamics of anorexia in chapter 11. As perhaps with this girl, repression of oedipal feelings can mean that she cannot oppose her mother with self-defining activity. In all five cases, the girl's behavior after the "moment of discovery" is not what a dyadic model would predict.

It might be better if "moment of recognition" rather than "moment of discovery" were used by Galenson and Roiphe. In many instances, glimpses of others' genitals occur much earlier than the moment cited. Parental nudity is not uncommon. We must explain why the child recognizes the genital difference at a particular time.

Explaining girls' basic development in terms of a chance possibility that the genitals of the opposite sex will be exposed to all girls in the last part of the second year of life (and to all just then for the first time) seems to be stretching plausibility very far. Logic seems better served in noting: as genital sensations help the child develop a core sense of herself, her gender identity and her social identity are intertwined into a "self." Genital interest and the placement of her feelings affect her relationships to both her parents, whose genital status becomes very important for her. Viewing the genitals of others provides impetus for her to deal with her sexual feelings when she is at the point of being absorbed by all these issues. That oedipal conflict is also joined at this time is clear in the following behavior notes complete as published by Galenson and Roiphe:

Excerpts from our data will illustrate the many different patterns and types of reaction in the girls of our sample, following their discovery of the genital difference.

Lilly, who had been investigating her genital area both visually and manually, began at eighteen and three-fourth months to inhibit both these activities. At the same time, she became irritable and clinging, her play less zestful and inventive, and her doll play consisted of labelling all dolls as boys. She called for her father consistently and became distinctly antagonistic toward her mother. (1977:49)

The "moment of discovery" for Lilly[7] is not described, nor are what previous opportunities Lilly had to observe male genitalia, let alone what else was in her mind when she first evinced awareness of the differences between the sexes. We know only that after a period of interest in her own genitalia she became ambivalent toward her mother, wished for her father, and inhibited her genital play. In this context, we can recognize a familiar pattern. *Lilly showed strong ambivalence to her mother,* focused her energies on establishing male gender for little beings that looked like girls (as most dolls do), and *simultaneously reached out for her father.* This is exactly a form we might expect her behavior to take in the working out of her oedipal feelings if Lilly repressed her sense of femininity in order to feel free to reach out to her father without seeming disloyal to her mother, all the time angry that her dependency upon her mother required this adjustment.

The next child formed a very different resolution: "In Peggy at fifteen and three-fourths months, all exploration and manipulation of her genitals ceased. She became her mother's well-dressed, neat, subdued, and obedient little girl. Her dolls still remained her prized possessions at four years of age, when she was last seen in follow-up" (1977:49–50). Peggy's giving up genital pleasure coincided with her becoming an extension of her mother, not a freewheeling, independent little being. Nothing is said about her father in Peggy's pattern.

In the follow-up at four, Peggy still did not inspire comment on her oedipal development. Oedipal development even by four can be repressed in a child whose primary oedipal feelings were not apparent when she was two. We are reminded of Behn-Eschenburg's comments about what it means when oedipal feelings are not demonstrated at the appropriate age. This good-little-girl-close-to-her-mother demonstrates the kind of compromise that can involve grave consequences at adolescence, when sexuality is still harder to deny, as in cases of anorexia.

The next case shows various influences on the child's timing of her genital interest:

Winnie had fluctuated in her level of manual masturbatory activity from her nineteenth month on. At twenty-two months, while bathing with two little boys, she examined her own genitalia and asked where her penis was. After her baby sister was born, when Winnie was almost twenty-three months old, her doll play flourished remarkably, whereas her genital play subsided. At twenty-four months she persistently tried to open her father's underwear and to grab for his genitals. At twenty-five months she started to masturbate again, and at twenty-six months tried to urinate while standing up in imitation of a boy. She had remained an extremely avid doll player when last seen in follow-up, at almost four years of age, and her fantasy life was rich and varied. (1977:50)

No note of behavior change distinguished this account of Winnie's "moment of (recorded) discovery." The birth of her sister had some impact, however, for that is when her avid doll play and decreased genital play were worth recording. Interestingly, Winnie's trying to touch her father's penis occurred soon after. The assumption appears to be that Winnie's grabbing for her father's penis was a hostile act in terms of penis envy, but nothing from the material as presented tells what her emotions were. We do know that shortly after her sister's birth Winnie both tried to touch her father's genitals and subsequently again enjoyed pleasure from her own genital play. Winnie's fascination with her father's penis was followed by a period of masturbation and then an effort to imitate him in urinating. It is possible that this seemed how to be close to father by being like him in a more acceptable way than trying to touch his penis. We cannot tell if her identifying with her father upon urination reflected a persistent need to maintain closeness with him only through identification, but she was able to maintain a feminine identity as shown in continued intense doll play. Her rich inner life at four suggests a good deal of success in achieving a sense of individuality. This makes sense in light of her apparently having achieved a workable primary oedipal resolution.

The next case was observed masturbating on a toy horse before she showed awareness of the two sexes:

Jenny, our early passionate horsewoman, was still masturbating this way when last seen in her third year, although there was occasional manual touching as well. She had established ownership of several of her father's pens at the time of the birth of her sister when she was seventeen months old, during a period when her anger at her mother had mounted, and she had made many errors in boy-girl labelling of people as well as pictures. By twenty-one months, she constantly preferred her father in the flesh, or his pens if he were not available. She had also attempted to take possession of her baby sister, with whom she was a very strict and unpleasant disciplinarian. (1977:50)

Again the birth of a sibling, in this case another girl, is tinged with oedipal behavior. Jenny's treatment of her baby sister, suggesting identification with a strict mother whose role she tried to take over,[8] seems an unmistakable primary oedipal phase behavior in the context of her demonstrating a "constant wish" for her father (whom she preferred "in the flesh") by wanting his pens when he was not around. Jenny, like Lilly, showed mounting ambivalence toward her mother as she became clearer in her wishes for her father.

In the fifth case, Shirley, it is interesting to read the account as if the child were already four years old and to note what diagnostic thoughts arise as to her oedipal status:

Finally, Shirley, whose genital manipulation had become intense and was accompanied by definite arousal at sixteen and three-fourths months, showed extensive preoccupation both with long rods, which she stood upright, and with her bathinette hose, at the same time as she stared at her baby brother's genitals over and over again. Her formerly very close relation with her mother began to be superseded by a definite wooing of her father, crying and calling for him when he was away, excited about him when he returned, whereas she refused to allow her mother to read to her or dress her, and she was often sulky. She, too, developed an "abiding" preference for two of her dolls at this time and was busily engaged in much make-believe play. (1977:50–51)

We assume Galenson and Roiphe selected Shirley to demonstrate their theory that the persistence of feminine interest in dolls from the second year of life is supposed to be linked to penis envy. What is fact is that Shirley was very much interested in genitals, her own and the masculine kind, and that she simultaneously rejected her mother, "wooed" her father, and began imaginative (we assume feminine) play with dolls. She, too, demonstrates behavior of the primary oedipal phase.

Conclusions

It is fortunate that all this material is already available in print. Kleeman was not interested in the issue of the primary oedipal phase, and Galenson and Roiphe disbelieved in serious oedipal resonance in the behavior of children they describe. Behn-Eschenburg did write in order to prove the existence of significant oedipal conflict during the two-year-old period, but he was obviously stimulated by his daughter's crystal-clear declaration of her feelings rather than moved to prove a previously held idea. These cases show also the difference in the reactions of boys and of girls. The weight of all this evidence proves that two-year-old children contend with oedipal feelings and that must affect how they respond to their own genital excitement, the separation/identification process, and their behavior with both their parents, embodying the significance of the primary oedipal phase.

8 Evidence for the Existence of the Primary Oedipal Phase: Treatment of Young Children

This chapter presents evidence of the primary oedipal conflict in the difficulties of very young children who require psychological treatment.

Sachs described her treatment of a two-year-old boy in oedipal terms, although the title of her article refers only to "A Case of Castration Anxiety Beginning at Eighteen Months." At eighteen months, this boy became terrified of noises, difficult to handle, and frequently unable to sleep through the night because of his bad dreams. "A few days before his second birthday he had a frightening dream of falling and awoke screaming. One night he called out for Daddy and asked him whether something had happened to him" (1962:332). Later he told of wanting a house with no toilets and no flushes. At this point Cyril was brought to Sachs for treatment. She related:

In play sessions we played out the toilet situation with a miniature toilet and doll. He was reassured that the little doll on the toilet seat would not fall in or lose its penis. It was pointed out to him that "the frightening noises" reminded him of the flushing of the toilet, that he was afraid that his father would want him to fall into the toilet bowl or have his penis fall off in punishment for his wish to have his mother all for himself. He was reassured that his father loved him, . . . did not want him to fall into the toilet . . . did not want him to lose his penis, and that it was all right to love Mommy and to want her for himself. "Daddy understands," he would echo me repeatedly in a reassuring way. He gradually quieted down. The noise phobia disappeared. His nightmares decreased in frequency, and [with his anxiety abated] he permitted his mother to change his diapers again. (1962:332)

Generally Cyril's mother was permissive and his father stern, Sachs tells us, giving next Cyril's reactions when his mother was more controlling: "Sitting in the bath tub and crying after a great deal of nagging and scolding by his mother, he said, 'I don't want my penis. I want to "weewee" from my "toushy" like mommies do.' But the next day he again told his father that he loved his penis" (1962:353).

Cyril's brief negative oedipus followed controlling behavior on his mother's part. Cyril's reaction was to give up his male identity. It is interesting that this change came from pressure to give up his autonomy. His mother had not told him to give up his penis. For Cyril, *autonomy meant possession of his penis.* To continue with Sachs' account:

"From . . . two years and nine months old Cyril began to show identification with his father. . . . He refused to wear "baby clothes"[1] and asked for shirt, pants, and ties like Daddy's. He wanted to play "Daddy games" and played "writing papers" and "reading books like Daddy does" (1962:353). In her summary discussion of the case, Sachs says:

Certain aspects of this case suggest the possibility of an oedipal conflict. His initial toilet training was accomplished with ease, anxiety symptoms being absent and developing later in time. He had fears, probably covering up wishes, concerning his father's health, so that he awoke one night to ask him whether anything had happened to him. The child's frightening dreams of barking dogs and large objects chasing him and overcoming him are typical dreams of the oedipal period, the barking dog and the large chasing objects representing an angry father punishing him for incestuous desires. . . . He stated repeatedly, . . ."Now I am a big Daddy," and "I have a big penis, almost big like Daddy's." . . . He urinated, standing up, over and on his parents' bed in an exuberant, almost orgastic mood. . . . He developed the habit of holding the urine in until he had an erection, which he would exhibit, giggling, to his mother. . . . *The disappearance of symptoms when interpretations on the oedipal level were given and the child's subsequent strong identification with his father also support the possibility of an oedipal conflict. . . . Although we cannot accurately mea-*

sure the influence of his unusual mental development, his high degree of verbal proficiency, and his parents' insights, it is possible that these factors merely facilitated the observation in his case of an oedipal conflict that might actually be more common at such an early age than is generally assumed. (1962:335–336)

   Cyril in his second year of life demonstrates complexity of mind. We can agree with Sachs that his verbal ability helps us to recognize his primary oedipal conflict and its successful resolution. Within the toddler's understanding of adult behavior, he then exhibited a strong identification with his father and felt safe with his libidinal feelings for his mother. His ego had direction, purpose, and organization based upon these developments.

   McDevitt included the next case in "Preoedipal Determinants of an Infantile Neurosis." He describes Becky, who was just three when her illness began. However, he begins with her situation during the preceding year:

Becky's relationship with her father had been close. In addition to being affectionate toward her, he often took care of her and played with her. He was also vaguely aware of harboring sexual feelings toward her. *For more than a year before the onset of her illness,*[2] she had frequently seen him naked in the bathroom and had expressed interest in his penis. . . . On occasion, she would speak of how large his penis was and would ask her father if she could hold it. (1971:203)

   Throughout this period, Becky was extremely ambivalent and difficult with her mother. McDevitt discussed the fact only in terms of separation/individuation, but the quoted behavior with her father occurred simultaneously. Furthermore, "Since the problem of separation was of such critical significance in Becky's life, it is interesting to note that she was in fact seldom physically separated from her parents" (1971:208). McDevitt explains that her mother was almost never away from home for more than a few hours during the day, and only occasionally in the evening. Rare separations lasting more than a day were kept quite brief, and Becky was cared for by familiar and reliable persons (e.g., her grandmother or the maid) in her own home. McDevitt then states, "*She showed no unusual reactions after these absences*" (1971:208). Becky did not suffer when she and her mother were actually apart.

Just prior to the illness, "a definite change occurred in the relationship" with her father:

She now became frightened when he expressed the slightest anger, or when he rode her on his back or tickled her in the ribs—*experiences that she had formerly enjoyed with excitement.* For fear of being bitten, she was no longer able to play a favorite game, in which her father would hand her a pill to place in his mouth.

Her mother, being sympathetic and concerned, did not leave Becky unless it was absolutely necessary. Nevertheless, the mother's efforts to calm and comfort Becky were only partially successful because of the child's severe anxiety and extreme ambivalence. She frequently whined, complained, provoked, and fought with her mother. (1971:203)

Although McDevitt records Becky's illness as beginning with separation anxieties and refers only to issues of separation/ individuation preceding them, he reports that Becky had backed away from sexually exciting play with her father, showed fear of her father going out of control (his anger and his biting), and gained sympathetic attention from her mother in the time predating the illness. In this we can see that she was already dealing with oedipal conflicts even before the severe separation anxiety manifested itself. When Becky was almost three, temporary absence of her parents over two successive weekends triggered a neurosis, which McDevitt treated successfully. His description of Becky's neurosis makes it clear that the fears connected to the father figure were not as intense as those involving her mother.[3]

She suddenly developed a marked fear of being bitten by a mustached man (imagined or perceived) and reacted to any indication of physical separation from her mother by clinging and crying inconsolably, and by insisting that her mother stay with her. . . . Her fear (expressed verbally, in dreams, and in anxious clinging) that her mother might leave her, never to return, seemed to disturb her to a far greater extent than did her fear of being bitten. (1971:202)

McDevitt describes the course of treatment as follows: "Becky showed excessive concern and love for her mother, who now became the 'good' object, while her aggression was displaced onto the analyst, who correspondingly became the 'bad' object" (1971:203).

We note the significant use of splitting and good/bad dichotomization, both characteristic of the slightly younger two-year-old age: "Early in the analysis, at which time Becky occasionally masturbated in the office,[4] her masturbation was related to the wish to be tickled by her father. Later in the analysis, it was related to her frightening wish to be penetrated and to have a baby" (1971:207).

McDevitt concludes his case description with a summary in which we can see recapitulated the evidence of primary oedipal material but that he interprets chiefly on the basis of its so-called preoedipal significance.

Although Becky's analysis was replete with primal scene fantasies, the parents were certain that the child had not witnessed their sexual relations, and the analyst's material provided no clear indication of her being consciously aware of these relations.

The need to tease and provoke the mother, and the later frightening wish to be sexually "attacked" by the father, were re-enacted repeatedly in Becky's analysis. She threw, broke, messed; she not only threatened to, but on occasion did, urinate on the floor. After her fears had subsided, she would ask to be tickled or spanked, or else to have a finger poked in her eye.

The fear of the mustached man reflected an attempt on Becky's part to evade her awareness of forbidden and frightening wishes (oral-sadistic and masochistic) toward the father. Similarly, the fear of the witch was an effort to shift the area of conflict away from the mother. Although her fears of being bitten were determined in part by conflicts that were specific for the phallic-oedipal phase, the intensity of these conflicts and her failure to resolve them were in part the result of earlier circumstances. The early history and the intense separation anxiety suggest that this symptom had a complex origin: its determinants arose in part from the phase-specific conflicts (and the consequent regressions) of the phallic-oedipal phase, but to an even greater extent they stemmed from disturbances that had their origin in the preoedipal phase. (1971:208–209)

We recall that Becky showed no disturbance on the few occasions before her neurosis began when she was without her mother. Her neurosis was precipitated by the parents going off together for two successive weekends. We might consider whether Becky's apparent separation anxiety masked something else, namely, an oedipal struggle against her mother's hold on her. Again taking up McDevitt's account:

The analysis revealed that the fear of being bitten by a man with a mustache expressed Becky's fear of her father, with an upward displacement, in her fantasies, of the penis and the pubic hair surrounding it. There were two sources for this fear: (1) the projection (onto her father) and displacement (onto mustached men) of oral sadistic impulses directed toward her father's penis, which stemmed from her intense penis envy; and (2) the displacement onto mustached men of the masochistically wished-for, yet feared, sexual attack by the father, which she experienced regressively as a fear of being bitten.

    After several months of treatment, Becky's fear of being bitten by a mustached man shifted to a fear of being bitten by a witch. Fear of the witch was also the result of the projection and displacement of oral-sadistic impulses, this time directed against the mother. Becky's dread of being abandoned by her mother was a consequence of death wishes directed and projected onto her mother, whom she also loved and whose protection she sought in her fear of the man with the mustache or the witch. (1971:203–204)

    McDevitt's interest in presenting this case lay in sorting out the nonoedipal elements of Becky's neurosis and including oedipal elements only from the standpoint of their effect when she was three. Still, in keeping with Coltrera's statement that oedipal concerns do not suddenly appear for the first time in the (classical) oedipal phase, we can view the longitudinal aspect of Becky's oedipal feelings in McDevitt's material.

    When a two-year-old girl follows notable ambivalence toward her mother with intense attachment (even though the mother is rarely absent from her) and the child does not show, as McDevitt puts it, "age-typical turning to the father," we must ask why. Why need the child resolve such contradictory feelings toward mother by forming an exclusive bond with her?[5] McDevitt describes Becky's mother as depressed and emotionally withdrawn but as very concerned and indulgent about Becky's clinging. Was there not a message in this for Becky that her mother needed Becky to be bound to her? I believe so. From at least two years of age, Becky was greatly involved with her father in an erotic way while she displayed ambivalence toward her mother. Becky might have felt strongly her mother's power to disappear with father two weekends in a row. It is clear that right afterward Becky produced symptoms vehemently to deny the erotic wishes for her father that became evident in her analysis. McDevitt says in his discussion that oral sadism based upon penis envy contributed to Becky's choice of symptoms. Yet in the history he gives, Becky expresses only the wish to hold her father's penis, while the oral-sadistic elements show up in the "exciting pill game" between her father and herself. Although her neurosis manifested itself when she was almost three, her symptoms make sense in terms of efforts at separation/individuation from her mother while she contended with oedipal conflict.

As Becky proceeded toward the classical oedipal phase, her symptoms were analyzed in treatment straightforwardly according to oedipal feelings. Becky's oral-sadistic fantasies about a witch emerged in a form parallel to her first symptom (a fear of being bitten by a man), after she gained inner permission through her analysis to be conscious of her desire for her father's sexual interest. The case history shows, however, that by two years of age, Becky was pleasurably attracted to her father's penis and involved in exciting play with him at the same time as her behavior toward her mother was ambivalent and intensely difficult.

Becky's patently oedipal behavior at two is not seriously considered as such in McDevitt's theoretical discussion. He gives an excellent, learned explanation of the precursors of her illness almost exclusively in nonoedipal terms. Issues of separation/individuation, splitting and anal sadism, which McDevitt underscores, are indeed critical aspects of the primary oedipal complex, but they do not in themselves specify the core issue in the genesis of Becky's illness. McDevitt does not venture why the parents' taking two weekends together triggered such panic in Becky that she then had to repress her desire for her father and develop symptoms that hid her wishes.

When viewed in terms of oedipal rather than separation/individuation issues, this can perhaps be more easily understood: previously, Becky did not panic when faced with separation from her mother because such a separation was not perceived as a threat. However, her mother leaving for an extended period with her father made her mother seem too powerful a rival, leading to her regressions and fears.

Becky's symptoms relate directly to her experience with her father long before she was three, and thus treatment was successful in terms of what I call the primary oedipal phase. By this I mean that Becky's level of ego organization during her illness was the primary oedipal level. She showed intense difficulties with separation/individuation, basic fantasies involving oral and anal elements, splitting as a major defense, dichotomization of good and bad. McDevitt does not describe Becky at the end of treatment, but by the point he mentions, she no longer was compelled by symptoms that were diagnostic of primary oedipal functioning.

The next examples of very young children illustrate the distinctive form the primary oedipal conflict takes in the boy and the importance of resolving in treatment any such issues not previously settled.

Herzog describes his work:

I saw twelve little boys between the ages of eighteen and twenty-eight months whose chief complaint was a syndrome resembling night terrors. . . . The little boy would awaken early in the course of the night after falling asleep with greater or lesser difficulty. He would seem terrified, disoriented, and call for help. Often, he would sob, "Daddy, Daddy."[6] The mother would attempt to comfort her child . . . to no avail. Initial inquiry revealed a strikingly consistent family constellation. In each of the cases, the parents had separated or were divorced in the preceding four months. In eight of the twelve cases, the father's departure had resulted in a change of sleeping arrangements. In four of these cases, mother and son were sharing the same bed; and in four . . . [the] same bedroom. To . . . demonstrate the consistent refrains, I shall present three cases. (1980:223)

It is useful to read what Herzog selects as the important material without considering the child's age but only the nature of its communication:

Gary was a tall, blond, attractive boy who separated easily from his mother and ran smilingly into the playroom. He immediately got into my lap. Staying in constant physical contact with me, he began to play with some clay. He rolled it into long loglike pieces and then broke them into smaller parts. He laughed, seemingly with pleasure. I introduced a puppet into the play who picked up one of the pieces. The puppet could be taken for an adult male—a Daddy perhaps. Gary looked very frightened and said, "Daddy hurt, Daddy hurt." I thought Gary was indicating that the Daddy was hurt and I said, "What is the matter?" There was no response. Then I asked, "Who can help?" To this Gary brightened and said, "Daddy help Gary—please." He hugged me hard at this point. At a later time, a little boy puppet was sleeping in the same bed with his Mommy. Suddenly, he jumped up. I got out a pencil, called it a dream-machine, and put it on the little boy puppet's head. "What's happening?" I said. "Let's see if we can see what's happening to him." Gary peered through the pencil dream-machine and then looked very frightened. "Scare," he said. "Scare me—Daddy hurt quick get Daddy—Daddy help Gary." I had the Mommy puppet get up and try to comfort the little boy puppet. "No, no," shrieked Gary, looking very afraid, "Daddy hurt, get Daddy." I then introduced the adult man puppet. Gary put him next to the little boy. Then he had the man put the little boy in a separate bed and return to his wife's bed. "All better now," Gary said happily. (1980:224–225)

Gary began his therapy by mastering anal-phallic anxieties. When the analyst had a "father" show interest in the pieces of clay, Gary responded with fear and, "Daddy hurt, Daddy hurt." It is not clear whose "penis" was broken by whom in Gary's mind, but the next material that is reported concerns the bedroom. We are re-minded of Gary's presenting symptom, panic, associated with being in bed with his mother.

We know these facts: Gary had fantasies about a large penile object being broken and became frightened when a father figure became involved with the fantasy. This material led to Gary's insis-tence that he wanted his father to help him. It was also clear that being only with his mother intensified Gary's fears. The solution did not give Gary his father to himself but placed his father in charge, returning Gary to his own bed while father and mother slept to-gether. This could relate just to his wish for a happy home with a father back in the right place. Yet while it certainly contains that symbolic meaning, the fantasy does center specifically on sleeping arrangements, which suggests an interpretation in primary oedipal terms: attraction to his mother, rivalry with his father, and fear of engulfment that the sleeping with mother would stimulate, all be-ing abrogated by the happy solution. Gary's other symptoms such as the "penis splitting" are also given meaning by the primary oedipal interpretation.

Herzog's second case was Ira:

Ira was a very tired-looking boy with big sad eyes. He, too, separated from his mother and caretaker with great ease, taking my hand and saying, "You will help me. Are you a Daddy?" We began to play and, before long, I produced my dream-machine. Ira said, "This little boy is having a bad dream. I have them too. He is dreaming big bird. He eats the boy's head. The boy is scared." "What can we do to help the boy?" I asked. "Get the

Daddy," Ira cried. He was literally in tears. "Why the Daddy? How can he help?" I asked. "He is like the boy. He can because he knows the boy. He is not a Mommy," Ira cried. (1980:226)

Against the background of Ira's main symptom the material tells poignantly of Ira's fear that he is endangered by an overwhelming male (symbolized by the bird and referred to as a male in "he eats the boy's head") and yet needs male help to differentiate himself from his mother.

The third example is Marvin:

Marvin's mother did not seek assistance when her son's sleep was initially disturbed. She concluded to her satisfaction that Marvin's symptoms were a response to her husband's departure. When three weeks later, however, Marvin, who was then twenty-two months old, developed a daytime phobia of dogs, his mother decided that professional assistance was indicated. Marvin became afraid of Baba, his word for dog, and would shake with terror whenever dog or Baba was mentioned. (1980:227)

Herzog mentions earlier: "In happier times, Marvin and his father had played a 'doggie' game . . . [taking turns at being dog or person. Marvin] refused to attend his nursery school and grew ever more frightened and restricted" (1980:226). Describing the treatment, Herzog states:

Initially, Marvin was wary of me, as was his mother; but by the second interview both had become very attached and Marvin began to refer to me as Bubu, a name which to my ears was very similar to Baba. At this time, the little boy's language was quite impaired and he said very little. Whereas he previously had been able to leave his mother easily, [he could not now.] Marvin presented a full-scale phobia. His entire day revolved around the avoidance of Baba. Initially, the play was comparably monothematic. Baba was a merciless creature who attacked, and attacked, and attacked. Over time (a ten-month period), a modification occurred: Baba could be controlled by Bubu. Bubu originally and for a long time stood for me, but ultimately became a part of Boy-Boy.

Marvin said that Boy-Boy needed to have Bubu in order not to be afraid of Baba. Bubu could become part of Boy-Boy, because they were alike, not the same, but alike. Eventually, we learned that Baba was a part of Boy-Boy too. At the end of the treatment, Marvin, then four years old, said that Boy-Boy should now be called Bart. Bart was big and well and he contained Boy-Boy (sometimes now called bye-bye), Baba (sometimes called angry or mad), and Bubu (frequently called you-you). (1980:227)

Marvin shows coexistent splitting: good versus bad, self versus not-self, aspects of the primary oedipal complex. That Marvin at twenty-two months was capable of a full-scale neurosis is not surprising when one recognizes the impact of the primary oedipal conflict. The feared Baba was seen in all dogs, reminding Marvin of his special game with his father. Treatment was directed at Marvin's working through his need for individuation in league with the good father-person (Bubu). There is no mention of the libidinal situation, but a question could be asked: What was there about his father's leaving that could make Marvin feel so endangered by an angry father if Marvin did not hold strong wishes of not wanting his father? It would seem he desperately needed his impulsive self/father under control by a good father to enable Marvin to assert his own maleness. Perhaps it is not fanciful to query whether Marvin's fear of his father's wrath related to his drive to closeness with his mother.

As with Gary and Ira, Marvin's symptoms erupted around sleeping and sleeping arrangements. His neurosis left Marvin uncertain of his maleness and gave him leave to cling to mother during the day. At night, however, the libidinal situation was overwhelming.

Herzog is impressed mostly with the hostile elements of the boy's reactions with a passing reference to possible confusion of libidinal and aggressive drives. He explains the night terrors in terms of lowered barriers to control of aggression. For these boys, however, sleeptime was also when they found themselves literally in father's place.

Herzog does not say whether he generally tried to affect the sleeping arrangements or assist the mothers to get help with their need to use the children as substitutes for the former husbands. He did help to get Ira's father back into the home. Herzog's successful treatment centered on the boys' need for a father and dealing with the boys' fears and angers. However, Gary's prescription for his own happiness was his fantasy of appropriate sleeping arrangements.

Illustrating more of what we can now recognize as evidence of the primary oedipal phase, Herzog points out that his cases:

appear to be overwhelmingly concerned with oral and anal-sadistic issues. Their aggressivity feels to them as though it is out of control, and their cognitive status does not permit rational assessment of the true state of affairs. The loss of the father seems to them to be their own doing (Piaget 1936) and simultaneously deprives them of the wherewithal to control aggressive drives. (1980:228)

At eighteen months, well into the primary oedipal phase, the boy has sufficient sense of self for both oedipally based ambivalence toward his father and a sense of responsibility for his own behavior (including thoughts and fantasies). The seeming triumph of his forbidden wishes to be rid of father must add to his sense of being out of control, heightening his panic at taking his father's place in bed with mother at night.

Herzog concludes: "A boy needs his father for the formation of the sense of self, the completion of separation-individuation, the consolidation of core gender identity, and the beginning modulation of libidinal and especially aggressive drives. I call the affective state which exists when these needs are not being met *father hunger*" (author's italics) (1980:230).

No better statement can be made on the plight of the primary oedipal boy who does not have a father at home, particularly when, as in Herzog's cases, the mother seductively brings the child into bed with her. The aggressive components that Herzog emphasizes are a significant part of the anal/separation/individuation/primary oedipal phase, stirred up especially in a child of divorce. However, the aggressive components do not explain why the two signal issues of all these boys are: the sorting out of identities; and sleeping near his mother in his father's stead.

The father's presence reinforces the boy's feeling of being different from his mother and thus assuredly separate and autonomous. The father's presence also puts control over the expression of the boy's libidinal drive, which otherwise impels the boy into frightening closeness to mother. Herzog's cases exemplify the primary oedipal situation of the toddler boy. If we planned an experiment to learn about such a boy's development should his mother be blatantly seductive and his father absent, we could hardly have a better test of primary oedipal theory.

There are two more cases in the literature provided by Sachs, her title this time citing oedipal conflict beginning at eighteen months. Both children's difficulties came to Sachs' attention because their mothers were in treatment with her. She successfully offered help by developing insight on the part of the mothers into the boys' conflicts.

Like Herzog's cases, one of Sachs' was a boy who reacted with night terrors to his father's having left home. He wanted to sleep with a lollipop boy his father had given him, and became panicky when the lollipop broke. He was also very clinging to his mother, but it was what she considered as signs of his femininity that caused her to ask for Sachs' help with Claude. In describing Claude, Sachs brought out Claude's *pars pro toto* thinking and anal/genital interests in keeping with his age. An example of the latter was Claude's wish to diaper young women he liked, showing his lack of sense of generationality as well, in spite of his extreme precocious verbal development. Sachs' summary of the case emphasizes her reason for writing about it, the eighteen-month-old boy's central oedipal conflict.

[Re: Claude] we deal here with a boy who caresses and kisses teenage girls, who expresses interest in their genitals[7] . . . who wants to marry them all as well as his mother. [Expecting his father to holler about this], he is terrified of loud noises.[8] [He] shows castration anxiety in dreams . . . [and] most clearly when he becomes frightened playing with father the game "I Take Your Nose Off." Later, probably in an attempt to master his anxiety, he plays the same game with Nixon's nose depicted in a cartoon. His desire to hold a big knife would be explained as an attempt at mastery of anxiety, too, since we know of his frightening knife dream. . . . His extreme concern over the broken lollipop-boy could be explained in this vein. His interest in collecting pens, pipes, dressing and acting like Daddy (identification) suggest the nearing of the solution of the oedipal conflict. . . . As a side remark, it seems that a full-blown oedipal conflict is possible even though the father visits only once or twice a week and only for an afternoon or evening. (1977:61–62)

Sachs next considers why Claude refers to the jealous father in his dream as a "bad man" rather than as an angry man. She concludes that Claude projected onto his father his own feelings about the nonacceptability of sexual drives, having developed enough super ego to explain "a great deal of guilt" (p. 62). Sachs' discussion underscores preoccupation with the good/bad dichotomy and the consequent appearance of guilt in the personality development of this example of a primary oedipal child.

Here is another Sachs' case from which I quote only to illustrate her thesis about the existence and significance of this toddler's oedipal conflict:

[Craig] is the case of a little boy who at the age of seventeen and a half months developed nightmares of large monsters who first act friendly with him by kissing him, then chase him and bite into his ear. His desire to marry Mommy he whispered to mother. Only, "I'll marry Santa Claus," he tells me and his father. He hits father furiously for kissing his mother and plays at disposing of him in a garbage can.

He shows much more anger at his father than Claude, who has an easygoing, playful Dad who brings gifts every Sunday and who comes home only on a visit, while Craig's father comes home every night, is strict and constantly disciplining the child. Craig, in turn, is preoccupied with doing away with his father. His Santa Claus tale and his panicky behavior when mother mentions to father that Craig wants to marry her show his fear of father. The harsh and forever-doing-away method of handling father by having him carted away with the garbage and dumped shows the child's great anger at and fear of him.[9] The question arises whether here is realistic anger superimposed on the (neurotic) oedipal anger because of father's harshness to him?

Of interest is the fact that these dream monsters behave (first kissing, then biting) almost like father in reality: when father comes home, according to mother, there is first a big hello and embrace, but soon an argument between father and son develops, with father punishing the child severely.

It should be noted that these two cases of Claude and Craig presented in this paper, as well as the one of Cyril . . . (Sachs 1962) were boys. No such early case of oedipal conflict in a girl was observed by me. It is my experience that the oedipal period in girls is less stormy . . . less easy to spot in a very small child and thus bound to be overlooked. (1977:64–65)

The last comment, along with the others quoted above on the matter, tells us two things: The intensity of the primary oedipal period is impressive when observed in either sex, yet it is easy to misinterpret if accompanying manifestations of anal conflict and struggle over individuation/separation absorb our attention. Sachs states, "We should perhaps consider revision of our thinking as to the chronological occurrence of the developmental stages—at least in some children if not in all" (1977:66).

The seven cases in this chapter together show effective treatment of children for pathology that began when they were well under three years of age. In all cases treatment was based on sensitivity to a child's struggles with primary oedipal phase issues, whether the issues were so named or not. The pathology in each case reflects the primary oedipal complex in keeping with the level of ego development characteristic of the toddler-aged children and the theory of the primary oedipal phase.

9 Evidence for the Existence of the Primary Oedipal Phase: Treatment of Adults

Before looking at evidence of primary oedipal–level ego organization in adult treatment cases, I wish to underscore Behn-Eschenburg's observation (chapter 7) about the significance of an apparent lack of achievement of oedipal development. He stressed that the more completely oedipal involvement is repressed, the earlier and more serious the actual occurrence will prove to have been. Here is one corroborating experience of mine. It concerns a patient whom I saw for her second analysis.

When she was in her early twenties, Colette entered into treatment with a well-recognized, competent analyst. She felt she gained a great deal from her analysis during that time, but the analyst told her that she was limited from mature relationships by not having ever reached the oedipal stage. Her father had deserted the family when Colette was three, which certainly affected her development. However, it was when her mother died twenty years later that Colette found herself so distressed that she began a second course of treatment, with me. Fragmentation of her ego was her most dramatic symptom. Her transference to me, dreams, and acting out with her husband showed the aftermath of a significant oedipal conflict dating to her earliest years. Working through the primary oedipal issues resulted in Colette's attaining new freedom in her relationships and, most significantly, a much stronger sense of personal integration.

The lack of signs of oedipal reaction in Colette's previous analysis fulfilled Behn-Eschenburg's warning. The derivatives of the primary oedipal stage have a broad-based, pervasive quality when they surface in the behavior of adults because they date to the time of first ego organization, a process encompassing the child's entire psychological life. I believe that the four cases detailed in this chapter show this.

Case of a Man: Philip

I selected this case because of the generous detail Socarides (1973) provided. Philip's gender identity confusion and fragmented ego draw our attention to lingering primary oedipal issues in his personality. One of Philip's symptoms, sexual perversion, is much more commonly found among males than among females (Greenson 1968). When we examine his case in detail it will demonstrate gender-related pathology stemming from oedipal conflict during the period of establishing gender identity. At the beginning of treatment Philip "suffered from multiple perverse sexual fantasies which, at times, he would carry out in reality. These included homosexuality, voyeurism, exhibitionism, sexual masochism, transvestitism, and transsexualism" (1973:432). Socarides uses this case to explain his view of the origin of sexual perversion, a synthesis of his own opinions with those of the mainstream of psychoanalytic thought until that time.

Socarides quotes many studies of the subject in his discussion and investigates the possible dynamics in the origin of such illnesses in terms of males. The essence of the current view is that fear of engulfment by the mother is countered by the toddler boy's felt need for dependency on her. Still, this alone does not explain why boys should have the conflict so much more severely than toddler girls. It can, however, be explained by adding that the boy's gender identity is at stake (which current theory includes) and that, since his gender identity is at the core of his idea of himself, his sense of separate existence is threatened in a more basic way than a girl's would be. Moreover, with his genital sensations making him want to be close to his mother, there is a level of urgency to his situation that the girl never faces.

To appreciate why primary oedipal factors are crucial in these conditions we must remember that we always refer to *sexual* perversions; we readily today speak of nonsexual early factors that are basic to the etiology of sexual perversion, but how can the essential diagnostic factor of sexuality be a secondary matter attached to the syndrome of sexual perversion later on? From the evidence here of the primary oedipal phase, we can appreciate how inevitably a person with the other symptoms of the sexual pervert will also present distortions of his sexuality. We can withhold consideration of the sexual element for purposes of understanding the rest of the behavior of a person who has sexual difficulties. However, as Socarides' patients with sexual perversions will show, we can be sure that any such patient will also display sexual difficulties when we do look into that area of his adjustment. If he clearly has severe separation/individuation difficulties, he will inevitably have sexual difficulties, too, because that is the nature of the primary oedipal complex. Current theory does acknowledge one aspect of primary oedipal theory, which states that ego differentiation requires the triadic perception the child obtains through the idea of the primal scene. Socarides quotes Fenichel as saying that sexual perversions arise in terms of experiences relating to the primal scene.

Unfortunately, Fenichel's observation is not much used theoretically. The traditional explanation is that there is a primary feminine identification that all children undergo because of their closeness to their mothers and that these patients do not get past a primary feminine identification although they are males. However, a universal stage of conceptualized gender identity as mother does not exist. We know this from the toddler's unisex classification of "baby." We also know that the earliest time of ego organization (and thus potential for feminine identification) for which we have evidence coincides with (does not predate) the earliest demonstrated time of development of gender identity. Primary oedipal theory emphasizes that boys and girls from the beginning of any sense of self at all are already engaged in a primary identification based upon their classification of themselves as to gender.

The usual course in development is for boys to appreciate themselves as boys and girls to appreciate themselves as girls, although oedipal conflict may create fleeting, often teasing, cross-references. If the problem in self-identification were simply one of separation from mother, we could expect many problems in relation to independence and autonomy, but there would be no reason why these should involve an inextricable sexual element. Therefore, in a case like Philip's, we must consider the relationship between a boy's problems in separation/individuation and his sexual impulses, which are so clearly intertwined in behavior as an adult. When he thinks of himself as being like his mother, this means not only being powerful but also being spared sexual impulses that drive him toward an intimacy that threatens engulfment. *The girl's gender identity is not at risk because of her sexual impulses.* The danger she fears from a rivalrous mother complicates her development, but not because she dreads losing her entire sense of self in a confusion derived from feeling this danger through the very impulses that provide self-definition.

The traditional view of the etiology of sexual perversion offers much to bolster our assumption the psychopathology dates to the primary oedipal phase. The usual statement includes the idea that the sexual pervert "has been unable to make the progression from the mother-child unity of earliest infancy to individuation. As a result, there existed a fixation in the preoedipal period, with a concomitant tendency to regression to the earliest mother-child relationship" (Socarides 1973:433). The basis for making such a statement is that all of "this was manifested as a threat of personal annihilation, a loss of ego boundaries, a sense of fragmentation, and a fear of engulfment" (1973:433). However, ego boundaries and integration involve gender identity. The possibility of annihilation through engulfment means a degree of separation/individuation must already have taken place.

Socarides accepts Freud's formulation that such "'pre-oedipal fears' are then compounded by the superimposed castration fears of the oedipal period" (1973:434), trying thus to account for the sexual aspects of the pathology. We must keep in mind that sexual behavior is the basis of his diagnosis. The idea that this behavior is a secondary accretion hardly seems adequate to explain why sexual problems are always found with all the other behavior that we readily ascribe to the two-year-old period. Socarides makes it clear how desperately Philip needed to establish and protect his sense of identity and that Philip's difficulties came from the earliest years of his life.

Clinical Material

In this review of the excellent clinical material Socarides provides on Philip, I first underscore the primary oedipal complex and then Philip's oedipal concerns in relation to the level of his ego organization.

At the outset of Socarides' account of Philip, he tells us that he made the technical decision to pursue analysis of Philip's symptomatology in the transference, regressive as the material seemed. He tells us of being "rewarded by the patient's being enabled to be relieved of his 'stones,' as he called them" (1973:443). Philip's metaphor for his difficulties suggests that his problems relate to his experiences during the anal phase. Another derivative of the anal phase might be Philip's struggle to feel some sense of control over his existence (with oral overtones in his allusion to taste), as we learn about this in his second session in treatment:

He complained that he felt the air above him in the consultation room very "heavy and round" and he could sometimes feel or see "curved forms," could even almost taste them, "a heavy, oppressive feeling all about." He had experienced these phenomena many times before, especially when he lay down or thought "certain things." Then they could be prolonged at will and often were pleasurable. (1973:438)

The conflict about wanting to be able to taste the "curved forms" and yet feeling oppressed by their presence showed his need to establish some control through thought and will. In a later session he tells of feeling as if he were "forced to be floating around like that, like I am in a black room floating for such a length of time that I can't find myself anymore. Like a little spot of my brain is my whole being, just whisping around" (1973:441).

The second picture seems to be a counterpart of the first. In the second he finds himself almost out of control, with just a small part of himself existing with any sort of identity of its own. Both of these experiences show the earliest possible mental concept formation of the self. We see also problems about what is inside and what is outside implied in these fantasies. It is important to the understanding of Philip's primary oedipal complex to know that the feeling of being powerless, and no more than a tiny spot of his own brain, was expressed right after his telling Socarides about his fears of personal dissolution.

Fears of dissolution of his self-representation pervade him whenever the optimal distance from and closeness to his mother could not be maintained. "I think I might be dead and there is no contact with my body. I can't feel my body, afraid I'm lost. I can't get back to myself. I'm separated from my body and it's a real crazy sort of thing. The sensation isn't frightening sometimes because it is very close to a sexual sensation. But I don't know whether I will be forced to remain like that forever." (1973:440–441)

The importance of sexual sensations in these most primitive problems of maintaining identity shows us how the primary oedipal conflict works in the male. The inner statement amounts to this: "My sexual feelings give me a sense of being myself; but in allowing myself to be aware of my sexual feelings, I endanger myself because these feelings make me want to be so close to my mother. Knowing what is myself and what has to do with my body gets all mixed up with these feelings. I must be careful to maintain an 'optimal distance' so that I feel my sexual sensations without being engulfed."

There is much more material from the treatment of Philip that offers evidence of the primary oedipal complex in his case. These examples are quoted exactly and fully as they appear in Socarides' presentation but not necessarily in the same order that he brings them up.

Socarides tells us about Philip: "He fears castration and anal, oral, and aural penetration, cannot feel his penis, as if it has disappeared. He is convinced he is entering the mother's body or he is being penetrated through his bodily orifices" (1973:441).

In addition to the oral and anal confusion, this material shows poor integration of body ego. Further, Philip's body sense is susceptible to distortion, another sign of the primary oedipal level (cf. chapter 13): "His mouth begins to get smaller and smaller, the perioral region becomes numb" (1973:441). Distortion of body image is understandable seen in a child of two or younger who is confused and conflicted (cf. chapter 12).

As an example of splitting in Philip: "He screams in order to regain himself. 'Like I'm getting back to myself' . . . through [splitting of the ego]" (1973:441). It is interesting that sound production, the precursor of speech, helps him to establish consciousness of self, but accompanied by split organization: he has a self observing whether he is himself.

Ideas of violence would intermittently overwhelm him. This aggressiveness was a defense against his unconscious feminine wishes. "The ideas may start with loving feelings. Like I would incorporate you, like becoming part of my hands, hold you so tight that there is no room for you except within me."

He has an impulse to embrace the analyst, and also at the same time an impulse to attack him. "Almost like it's the same thing. There's no clue to which is which. I can't tell them apart." (1973:442)

What we see here are two aspects of the primary oedipal level of functioning. First, Philip's confusion about inside and outside is severe. Second, we can see in this that ideas of violence and aggressiveness are required when his loving feelings impel him to wanting sexual closeness. All of this is clear in another excerpt:

"I can feel something building up in me, a slow anger, anger like somebody is chopping my penis off. A penis with a hole in it. It's chopped off, turning in, and it turns into a vagina and swishes into my body. It's like it could really happen. Now this kind of fantasy is very calming, as a matter of fact, and I am very pleased with it. I have the feeling I have figured out something. The pain in my eye just went away. It's strange, it's so mixed, like I don't believe it and I do." (1973:443)

Confusion of dichotomies and the denial of good sexual feelings are in Philip's statement: "Then I have ice-cold, burning sensations. I think 'This is the way a woman feels'" Then he concludes the passage with the statement, "I always felt a woman had more of the secrets of life than a man does" (1973:444).

We see here not only the cognitive confusion that besets him in his struggles with his primary oedipal feelings but also the rela-

tionship between cognition and his sense of his mother's omniscience. In another place Philip says he is not able to pursue success
in cognitive activity in spite of his excellent ability. He feels conflict
between wishing to have his own full powers and fearing that he
must give up his identity as a male in order to know what might be
known, for "knowing" is a power of the mother.

In discussing his keeping himself from a clear identification
of gender and his inability to pursue successful work, Philip demonstrates both the oral elements in his terrors and the dichotomy of
being either all-powerful or completely helpless: "The same thing
applies to jobs. It goes back to a fear of being swallowed, destroyed,
losing my individuality. Also I sometimes feel I can do anything—
sculpt, paint, compose, write, influence people—be, I guess, all-
powerful, and at those times I feel like my mother" (1973:440).

Philip goes on to ascribe a penis to his mother, a body image
distortion that is a way for Philip to feel safe to keep his own. He
desperately seeks some way of allowing himself masculinity, power,
and the capacity to know. However, he is too drawn to his mother to
be able to manage this when he and she are clearly of opposite
gender. It is worth noting that Philip's mother was seductive.

The travail Philip experienced over separation from his
mother was demonstrated by Philip's memory of taking "a bus trip at
school, when age eight, without first discussing it with [his mother]
he experienced a severe panic reaction mixed with feelings of overwhelming loss, loneliness, pains in the chest, and feelings of confusion which necessitated his being brought home" (1973:439). We do
not know whether the material Socarides presents is in the order of
its unfolding in therapy or as he found it sensible to organize it for
reading, but he tells us next that "Philip recalls that during his
earliest years his favorite game was to 'crawl all over his mother.'"
Just after this statement we learn about the other side of Philip's
ambivalence. This is an exact statement of part of the boy's primary
oedipal problem: "If I were only able to be like my father it would be
a touch with reality. I would thereby avoid being totally swallowed
or engulfed by her" (1973:439).

It is striking how Philip feels the relationship between having
a firm sense of his own gender and feeling in touch with reality. He
recognizes fantasy in his feelings of engulfment by his mother. If he
were able to feel confident of his gender, his engulfment problems

would not exist. Primary oedipal theory explains Philip's tragedy. Being able to be like his father meant for him in two-year-old terms becoming his father in his father's role with the mother, and thus the whole shaky problem of maintaining his individuality was too difficult for him.

Such application of primary oedipal theory demands proof from Philip that he actually was involved in oedipal conflict at the stage of separation/individuation. The excerpts already quoted from Philip's material demonstrate a complex of behavior typical of the two-year-old experience, including concern about gender identity. Now I quote specifically oedipal material of the same caliber.

After saying that Philip drew a woman teacher's attention to himself in school by signs meaning intercourse, Socarides reports how in his teens Philip would swim out dangerous distances "where it was difficult to swim back to shore" (1973:440). We see here the relationship between suicidal ideation, which is typical in the primary oedipal complex in relation to the sexual problems of the person, in this instance of Philip's in relation to a likely mother-figure, his teacher.

In the light of all of this we can appreciate why for Philip:

The heaviest "stone" of all was the mounting dread and horror he experienced up to the age of eighteen as dusk approached and the darkness of night descended. This fear of nightfall was shown to be his wish for and dread of engulfment by the maternal body. "I would even run home after school to get there before dark, to be where there was light." (1973:440)

The question comes, why should nighttime be crucial in his ambivalence about engulfment if there were not a sexual connotation to his conflict?

In more direct sexual material, coprolalia occupied some of Philip's fantasies, using foul language to a woman being a complete substitute for intercourse. This is an example of the confusion of anal and genital impulses, as well as an example of splitting in the substitution of fantasy for bodily activity. Philip's coprolalia has a further significance. It was accompanied by behavior Socarides recalls in terms of the Gilles de la Tourette's disease syndrome: "repetitive spastic contractions of various parts of the body . . . interspersed with bizarre screaming, shrieking, hissing and gasping, and strange explosive, barking noises" (1973:445). We recall that primal-scene fantasies enter into the development of the self, as Jacobson points out, and thus play an enormous role in the primary oedipal complex. Philip's primal-scene fantasies involve him in the utmost terror about aggressive feelings on his own part based on anal violence and his terror about engulfment.

A primal-scene memory of Philip's that went back to the age of four "or even earlier" reminded Socarides of Fenichel's statement (1945) that "screen memories of parental intercourse find a parallel in the symptom formation of perversion."

Another example of what well might be primal scene material is this:

On one occasion he began to utter the strange sounds. "Oh, oh, I'm being touched and I don't know where. They are touching me. That doctor, the one who gave me injections when I was a child." He screams. "Just a few minutes ago I had the feeling that this had happened to me before, this convulsive thing that goes on. Oh, oh, oh, I got an awful headache then." His voice changes, it is an angry groan, the snarl of an animal. (1973:441)

Consistently, Philip's sexual material comes in the context of other issues of the primary oedipal phase. We can see in Philip how the issue of maternal engulfment is intertwined with the need to be close to the mother, not merely for comfort but for sexual expression. If Philip's deepest problem were separation/individuation alone, we should expect instead of sexual perversion at least most of the perverted behavior to be in symptoms that are chiefly oral or locomotor or perhaps oral and ocular and locomotor. Instead there are no psychological syndromes that include serious difficulties in the oral, visual, and/or locomotor systems that do not include sexual difficulties as well, as we can predict from primary oedipal theory. If the deepest issues were apart from sexual ones and we assumed that people could be so involved in the earliest developmental issues as not to achieve the (classical) oedipal stage, then we should have ample cases of symptomatology that omits sexual issues. Instead, we see sexual perversions. We readily accept that the primitiveness of all the other symptoms of the sexual pervert constitute a sign that the person's difficulties developed from the earliest time of development. We must use the same logic to recognize that sexual material that consistently emerges on that level of primitiveness in particular individuals is also due to difficulties in the earliest time of ego formation.

Case of a Man: Kenneth

We understand from Socarides that Philip's treatment was successful strictly on the basis of analysis of his fear of engulfment by his mother, and oedipal matters as if they came only later. The material on protective identification with his father gave enough opportunity to Socarides to help Philip understand this derivative from the primary oedipal phase. Labeling it as coming from the primary oedipal experiences was not necessary for therapeutic effect. Nonetheless, a brief excerpt from treatment of a similar case will show this: there is a therapeutic advantage in an analyst's being aware of the primary oedipal phase.

This case comes from Boxerman (1981). Kenneth was a man in his fifties, intellectually gifted, yet had something of a shady career in business. He was in treatment because he recognized that there was something wrong with the way he was conducting his life and also with his uncontrollable tendencies to expose himself to young girls.

His material had the intense quality of the primary oedipal struggle. Several associations were to the two-year-old period. Castration material linked up with oedipal conflicts, his surgeon father being mentioned as a butcher. However, the problem of loss-of-self-in-closeness and the intertwining of this issue with that of sexuality shows that Kenneth's major conflict was still on the level of the primary oedipal period rather than the classical (where competitiveness with father would be the sole focus.) This impression is confirmed by the chaotic quality of his inner organization. Adept use of splitting was demonstrated by the contrast between the poised appearance he made in business and social situations and his fragmented inner state.

Anal and oral material poured forth with violent ideation. Fantasies were primitive in spite of Kenneth's high intelligence. Part-object preoccupation and concrete symbolization pervaded his associations. His material during analytic sessions was chaotic and fragmented as if he were frankly psychotic. The only sign of integration was that he mostly spoke in sentences. A sample of his material comes from Boxerman's verbatim notes:

A cousin, Wendy, she was twelve and I was eleven. I looked up her sun suit. Peach-stone, I called it. Her cunt. Pee-stone. There is a statue in Belgium, a little kid peeing. Something solid, peach-stone, hard instead of a nothing. So I cut off my toe instead of what? Instead of what? And when Blanche said you cut me off, I said no. You cut me off. Father's scalpel—he butchered people with it. Cut as a prick slice down the middle. So I have to cut off my toe and endure it without any pain pills. So how bad is it? So what did I do so bad? If I did see the—my parents—I want to put it in there so no one else—Daddy—brother can put it in there. I'm in there. A fetus with the feet hanging out. My feet are hanging out and I pulled them back in. Obviously can't breathe in there. Now my brother was in there. I was two years old. My brother was in there with my mother. . . .

Yellow fat man. You're still peeing yellow. I haven't started to ejaculate yet. Saturday Night Fever he gave it to the other couple because he didn't earn it, fucking. [Reference to film in which hero gives up a prize for dancing.] I'm angry. It's got to be my father.

Tying this material to previous sessions, Boxerman felt that the key was Kenneth's fear of "peeing himself out," through his penis. He relates:

I just kind of wondered, speculated, something like this: Think of how it must have made sense to you when you were two. See, father gets a baby out of his penis into mother and if you get too close to mother—you must have been frightened—wondering what would happen. The baby will come out and go right into mother's vagina. Since you yourself are still a baby, the baby will be you. You will have peed yourself out there, right out through your penis.

Kenneth's response to the interpretation was unusual for him because he was able to agree with it. Furthermore, he was able to proceed with a theme for more than two sentences, as in his very next remarks: "Certainly. All these years I couldn't get an erection with a girl makes sense. Because I could shoot myself right up there. And my needing milk, as if part of me is gone, replenishment after masturbating. And masturbating didn't even involve coming." Kenneth continued with these ideas but too fast for recording.

When later in the session the analyst reviewed the primary oedipal interpretation, Kenneth again was able to develop a theme, although the change is noticeable only in contrast to the intense fragmentation of his thought just before:

Mother's jungle of hair [meaning her pubic hair], I can't breathe, I can't breathe. I'm opening my mouth. She's opening her cunt. 69 is safe because my mouth is occupied with her cunt. So my prick can't go up her. And fire engines are *rose-colored*. [Reference is an association to his mother in a concrete symbol he used often for her, combined with sexual material and strong feeling, in the metaphor of putting out a fire.] I wish to give up mother, the heart, the fire and put it all in Blanche. She's bright, she's lovely, she's capable. It's all fine. We touched on it once—enough. I want to run away. Peter rabbit, I'm a rabbit, I'm a rabbit and I'm going to run away. I'm going to get my Peter out of here. I want to find some opening in you. Daddy doesn't just put it in. Must be a closeness. So I won't let any affection in. Yet I'm open to ideas. I hate neckties. I run around with nothing on. Always the opposite. So the opposite: a girl being very distant and no erection is a woman being very close, and having some erection.

In this flow of associations, one can appreciate how the sense of it lies in the primary oedipal time. Feeling back with this patient to how it must have felt to be himself during that period gave Boxerman a basis for meaningful interpretation. Kenneth's material immediately following that interpretation was more focused than the previous material, less an outpouring of early feelings, more an effort to grasp their relationship to his present feelings. Two interpretations do not make an analysis, but it is interesting to see how quickly such an interpretation can have at least a temporary effect, which can help toward further exploration.

Kenneth is interesting to contrast to Philip. Kenneth, unlike Philip, managed to marry, be involved with his son (although on the basis of identification), and after a divorce, to have a relationship with some women, mostly one at a time. Also, he managed to conduct a business in which he used his high intelligence more fully than Philip could his. Kenneth was closer than Philip to an approximation of the classical oedipal phase. However, in relation to his sexual perversion, he presented the same chaotic, fragmented ego state, full of oral and anal fantasies containing part-objects and suicidal and violent ideation, use of splitting as the chief but meager defense, and overwhelming separation/individuation/primary oedipal conflict that characterized Philip, too. The material quoted here brings into relief the fact that their sexual perversions can best be understood in terms of the complex emotional situation of the two-year-old trying to establish a personal identity out of its flux of feelings and its relationships with both of its parents.

Case of a Woman: Pam

Pam was a severely obese woman in her mid-thirties. After seven years of useful work with another therapist Pam became my patient when her first therapist moved away. She had had deep depressions that lasted for weeks, when she refused to talk to anyone, mostly stayed in bed in a darkened room, and barely managed to give minimal care to her children. Paranoidal features were pronounced with no insight into how she had provoked rejection when it really did exist.

    Pam's case reflects a primary oedipal bind: she was caught in a multigenerational lockstep, separation/individuation with oedipal overtones presenting an unresolved problem from grandmother to daughter to granddaughter. Pam was treated as a "bad self" split-off of mother. Her material demonstrates the interrelationships of this with her persistent categorical "good versus bad" thinking, inner strain over autonomy versus dependency, anal elements in maintaining a dramatically messy appearance of person and home, and submergence of her physical attractiveness by oral means. Pam's transference to me alternated between using me as an idealized, all-knowing, all-powerful mother who alone could manage Pam's life for her and a rejecting, supercilious exploiter who could not tolerate Pam's anger. Conversely, her self-image vacillated between a dangerous, bad person needing control and an incompetent, resentful dependent.

    At the time of the work presented here, Pam was still locked into an angry dependency on her mother. One conflict between them concerned Pam's wishes for a career and her mother's seeming desire that she be interested only in men. Her mother's ambivalence showed even during Pam's childhood, when her mother insisted

Pam think of herself as fat. Pictures of Pam from childhood, however, show a rounded child whose weight was well within normal limits.

For years during treatment, I tried to point out to Pam that her mother confused Pam with a split-off "bad" self of her own and was comfortable only when Pam was completely dependent on her. (Infantile behavior expressed by Pam was unacceptable to her mother for herself but reassuring to her mother when she could feel in charge of Pam.)

An example of how this worked from the other direction (the mother absorbing the daughter's "good self" into her own ego) was a time that Pam's mother found a picture of Pam in which Pam looked very attractive. Her mother picked it up and showed it to a visitor as a picture of herself, even though she had never been to the scene and did not resemble Pam in either features or coloring.

An example of how Pam was affected by her dependency bind with her mother was the time when she expressed to me her interest in a particular kind of job. She demanded angrily: "Why did that other person get just the job I want and not me?" When I asked Pam how she had gone about trying for the job, it turned out that she had not tried to apply at all.

A turning point in Pam's treatment came when, after some years of effort, she gradually formed a plan to start a career she wanted. Three things occurred in close sequence. First, Pam was devastated because a friend had done something that Pam considered to be bad and that Pam felt she herself would not have done. For a while Pam could only reiterate what happened. She then began to see that someone else whom she respected could be bad in a way that she herself would not be. When this issue came up earlier, in the transference, her need to idealize me kept her from even remembering experiences with my fallibility. She now talked about the possibility that she and her friend both might be good and bad.

Second, in the next session, Pam described a horrendous fight with her mother. As Pam was going through a divorce from an unreliable husband, her financial difficulties were very great, especially in regard to care for three children. Pam's mother complainingly but reliably supported the family.

The fight started when Pam talked about going out of town to live and establishing financial independence. Her mother became vituperative. She screamed that Pam was too fat to get a job, that Pam would come to a bad end. Pam interpreted that her mother did not want Pam to progress or to feel better about herself, etc. I raised the possibility that her mother reacted to Pam's threatening to become more independent. Pam turned immediately to describing great tension over her fourteen-year-old daughter's bad choice of friends.

This association reflected their intergenerational lockstep. First Pam's mother protested Pam's independence as leading to something bad. With that issue in focus, Pam immediately produced material about bad results from independence in her daughter, treating her daughter as a split-off "bad self" of her own.[1]

Third, Pam realized that on the very day of the fight, when she showed her mother that she had only torn, dilapidated shoes to wear, her mother, in the midst of argument, wanted immediately to go get Pam a new pair. It was clear that her mother was not reacting to Pam in the way she was because Pam was bad but only because her mother struggled to establish her own sense of worth and goodness.

I then reviewed the story of her mother and Pam's fat, as far as I knew it. I wondered whether her mother's reaction to her fat from the time that Pam was small was unconsciously to stimulate Pam to maintain the fat. What she did to look as if she were against Pam's fat simply sent Pam to the sugar bowl. She never acknowledged any weight loss Pam occasionally achieved. Perhaps Pam's fat was a gift from her to her mother.

It seemed to me that Pam's mother really did not want her to have a man of her own. The only man her mother accepted in Pam's life was the unreliable husband who helped to keep Pam financially dependent on her mother, as her mother was required for supporting the whole family even when the husband nominally lived at home. The husband constantly involved himself with other women and acted as if he were not committed to Pam.

Elements of her symbiosis with her mother and the self-torturing character of Pam's relationship with her abusive husband, in addition to Pam's overweight, seemed to come into focus as Pam began to reach for self-determination. I thought out loud about the primary oedipal predicament. Pam and I reflected together on what life might have been like for her in her earliest days of recognizing being an individual, spinning a tale about it. The story seemed to have great meaning for Pam.

The next day Pam for the first time accepted with some comfort her mother's buying her new clothes. She obtained a job within a few days. Her personal grooming improved. She also mentioned statements men made at her new place of work to the effect that her face did not go with her figure (a reference to the beauty of her face). When Pam mentioned such statements to me in the past, it was with cynicism. This time she showed pleasure.

In immediately succeeding sessions, Pam had increasing clarity not only about her feelings about herself but about her relationships with other people. The idea of people using others as split-offs of their own "bad" selves did not seem so scary for her to see, even in relation to her own daughter and herself. She became less categorical in her reactions to an increasing list of friends. She observed that in addition to maintaining her obesity, consuming sugar affected her clarity of thought, something she now felt she must protect.

Pam dieted effectively and lost twenty pounds within five weeks (initial weight loss being rapid for the dieting obese). She began to establish order in her house. She would joke about her feelings that anything bad that happened to anyone important to her must be her own fault. She insisted upon good treatment from men she knew. All of these achievements made a simultaneous appearance that I could not ignore, even though long, hard work stretched ahead of us before Pam could consolidate them. Pam's striking response to a direct primary oedipal interpretation was instructive because it demonstrated a whole complex of behavioral derivatives.

Case of a Woman: Fleur

Fleur, a patient of mine in her late twenties, spent several years in sporadic efforts at psychotherapy with me before deciding upon analysis. She displayed oral/anal concerns that caused her digestive complaints, impulsivity and immediacy of need, and reliance upon her appearance in searching for a sense of identity. These features of her primary oedipal complex are not my reason for presenting her case. Her separation/individuation problems linked up with sexual difficulties in such a way that we could see her use of splitting in her handling of body anxiety and trace the condition to the primary oedipal phase.

During the period of psychotherapy, Fleur revealed ambivalence about closeness, confiding some of the bizarre things her mother used to do. One was to cleanse Fleur's vagina while Fleur was on a table in the bathroom each morning as the father shaved, continuing until Fleur was at least nine and a half years old.

Her father was passive in this situation, but otherwise he was an active force in Fleur's life. Their relationship was a highly charged, emotional one. However, her father was obsessed with his work and complained of her mother's unwillingness to participate in it. When Fleur returned from college with broken marriage plans, her father wanted her to work for him in his small manufacturing business. She did so, but taking up treatment again, she also completed her degree and fell in love with a young man she was happy to marry. Then she discovered that her husband was sterile and he refused to adopt children. The stress of this situation inescapably exposed the problems in the marriage. Fleur entered analysis quite distraught and determined to work until she felt she had resolved the inner sense of confusion with which she still struggled. The following excerpts are from sessions during the second year of analysis.

Fleur began one session with the importance she placed upon having contact with a man. She spoke about the feeling of needing to feel filled up somehow by a man. She realized she could have turned to any of her many close women friends with her current problems, but she did not choose to do so. Seeking to understand why, she said, "Being with a woman is just like masturbating." The implication was that it was a trivial experience. She said that being with women only meant talking about their problems with men anyway. Then she went on to describe differences between Jim (a lover), Herman (her husband), and her father. There was also Bruce, to whom she turned, as she put it, for the sexual expression of her relationship with me. (This latter matter about

Bruce came up at an earlier time, too. It was clear then that she was managing her sexual tensions in the transference by having an affair with Bruce, with whom she had had an intellectual relationship since college days.) They enjoyed introspecting together. As to her feelings about Jim and Herman, they were as follows:

Jim was very much like her father in providing a great deal of physical contact, a sense of protectiveness, great energy, preoccupation with business, the wish for a partner in his activities without being able to tolerate the surrender of any of his own importance, and a sense of excitement combined with a certain sense of danger. Herman, her husband, she saw as a source of safety. His emotional strength and independence attracted her. He was of her stature, both of them being 5'2" and slight of build. Their bonding had a quality of twinship. Sexually, she lost interest in him once they married. Her sense of stability and safety with Herman was shaken by his unwillingness to adopt a baby, and the marriage fell apart.

To return to the material of the session, Fleur found herself rejected by Jim that day. Also feeling rejected by her father and by Herman, she turned again to Bruce. She rejected my idea that this expressed a need to find safety in a male sexual extension of myself but repeated her earlier remark that to be with a woman to fill her emptiness seemed an inadequate or trivial kind of solution.

Fleur then raised the question of why it should be that she should need to have this fulfillment from a man. It seemed to her that it might have something to do with the fact that her mother gave her what she needed only when she was very, very young.

At that point I was guided by my rumination about the possibility of a primary oedipal conflict. I found myself interpreting this material in such terms. I wondered aloud about Fleur's linking that statement "being with women is like masturbating" to the fact that her mother supplied her well during the earliest days of life. It reminded me that a very young baby has not differentiated herself in her mind from mother as an entity. We knew from earlier material in Fleur's analysis that when she was in the second year of life her father began to play an especially important part in her life because her mother withdrew emotionally from much of Fleur's care. Therefore, she might have associated recognition of herself as a separate individual with her response to her father as a source of both supplies and excitement.

Fleur broke in as I spoke and really completed the statement with considerable spirit and conviction. She recalled saying in this session that working with a woman was perfectly all right. She had thought of going into business with a girlfriend of hers and this presented no difficulties. It was only in relation to the feeling of personal fulfillment, to sexual feelings, and to her security in a relationship that the issue of whether it was with a man or a woman became important.

The following sessions reflected a dramatic change in Fleur. She discussed ways of establishing her own individuality. She was concerned about not being too dependent on any one person, in contrast to her previous preoccupation with how her parents and others frustrated her efforts to be taken care of by them. She was now not reacting to Bruce as an extension of my sexual self but as a separate person from me.

Several weeks after the session that brought the primary oedipal feelings into sharp focus, Fleur told me she was finding it difficult to share her feelings with me. What she did discuss were questions of safety. She recalled her reasons for missing a scheduled appointment the previous week. She explained that while driving to my office she had bumped into a truck. There was no serious damage, but she felt it was important for her to understand why she had allowed the incident to occur. She was not able to pinpoint the reason. She only knew she was having some thoughts about sex, and she felt it was her reaction to these thoughts that let her attention wander so that she ran into the truck. The question of safety came up also in regard to the fact that earlier that day she had had an argument with her father, who criticized the quality of her work for him. Subsequently she walked into a glass showcase, which she well knew was there. While lying down, being given ice for her bumped forehead, she thought about how nice it was to be taken care of.

Her next associations were feelings of discomfort over being sexually involved with four men, two of whom were lawyers. She recalled when the lawyers had been liars. She then thought of what had happened during the day preceding the accident. She had learned that her father had given a raise to another employee. Fleur felt that she was not getting as much. The employee sympathetically said that her father's treatment of Fleur derived from her being his daughter.

As this came up after the "lawyers or liars" remark, I asked Fleur about the possibility that she felt her father had lied to her about her salary, promising her more and not coming through with it. We then went over the figures. It turned out that he was paying her a very large salary because he was contributing to her support in various ways and periodically giving her lump sums. The fact that it was not given on a regular basis had made Fleur feel he was unreliable and powerful. It raised again the question of safety in relationships with men.

Fleur voiced apprehension about dating a new man. Like every other man she knew, he was overwhelmed by the extraordinary quality of her personality as well as her physical beauty. Then a question of safety intruded because she anticipated that after a while he, like all the others, would withdraw from her.

The session was almost over, so I offered Fleur my reactions to it. I suggested that her difficulty in talking to me at the beginning of the session had to do with our separations the week before; she had been out of town, and then the accident prevented one session. I remarked that whenever there was a break in our schedule upon her return she found it difficult to communicate with me freely. There seemed to be a connection between *separating from me* and the issue of safety with her father and other men.

Fleur's thought went back to the truck accident. Just before she hit the truck, her mind was on the physical quality in sex, which also preoccupied her during this session. It seemed to her that much as her response in sexual situations had been physical before, she was aware of the physical qualities in a new way.

That was the note on which we started to end the session, but I recalled its beginning because it seemed important that she had also mentioned the two accidents (the truck and the glass case). Was she pointing out that the physical aspect of sex was somehow linked with the question of her physical safety?

Fleur told me that she had a feeling that this question of safety also was somehow related to very early excitement with her father. She said that something about how she felt made her think about being thrown into the air and being caught. This was such an abrupt association, it seemed of special importance. Fleur said it did not have to do with physical safety. She pictured her father tossing her into the air and catching her securely. I asked her how old she thought a child might be when her father would toss her into the air and catch her, and she said, "Oh, about two years old, maybe the second year of life." Then she said, "This reminds me of a long time ago when you and I talked about a feeling of excitement with my father during that age period." I recalled the discussion. She said, "Wasn't there something about sexual feelings for fathers at that point, that you were talking about?" I recalled talking about the oedipal period in relationship to an incident when she was over three. Fleur seemed to be talking now about an earlier time than we had been dealing with when we had explored oedipal feelings previously. I told her that it reminded me of many cases, but not necessarily her own. I really did not feel strength in the connections between what she had now gone to and the earlier material in today's session. I told her that my theoretical interest in what she told me at this point centered around the idea of the child needing to do something about the overwhelming quality of her excitement with her father and how she then required amnesia of focal sensations she had in relation to her father. I mused that this might be why girls do not always indicate total awareness of their genitals even during the oedipal phase, let alone after.

Fleur said yes, that really made sense to her because she had had no idea about having a clitoris. It seemed to her that she must have had access to it because there it was, readily available; yet it was only when she was well into adolescence, upon reading Frank Harris and learning explicitly about a woman masturbating, or being manipulated at the clitoris, that she masturbated that way and had an orgasm.

A fascinating thing about this is that Fleur's amnesia could not have been of the vagina (as is more common) because, in Fleur's life, her mother kept that channel in awareness by cleaning it every morning, all the way through to her ninth year. Amnesia of part of the genital system is a maneuver in handling overwhelming forbidden feelings according to the dichotomous thinking of the two-year-old. In Fleur's case, as she could not ignore the (deeper, usually more secret) vagina, perhaps she was amnesiac about the clitoris in connection with the early excitement. This is strongly indicated if we can put credence in Fleur's chain of associations during this session.

Fleur confirmed this possibility in her next association: "The danger I am talking about does not feel physical. It must have to do with my own feelings because I am so much calmer now." The factors of separation/dependence (as shown in the transference to me), father/mother loyalties (also seen in the transference), and the need to punish herself (through the accidents) or deny the extent of reaction to father seemed to be interrelated issues spelled out in this interview.

When Fleur returned to work after the session, she and her father quarreled. For the first time he told her she should stop therapy. Stating that he could not afford to subsidize her further, he wanted her to devote herself to the business. No compromise she offered was acceptable to him. She felt she had to tell him that if it was a matter of choice between himself and herself, as much as she would find it difficult, she had to put her self-preservation first. She broke off the discussion, furious. The next morning, before our session, her father apologized to her. He told her that he found it hard to understand her need for treatment. Fleur had brought up parity with her sister, who had been in treatment on an intensive basis for eleven years, but he could not see Fleur as being as needy as her sister. He also said that he was not going to go on a projected business trip to New York with her. He felt he needed to take a holiday and planned to do so on his own soon. It seemed clear that on some level he was responding to Fleur's emphasis upon her needs apart from himself. Fleur also felt conscious of saying to herself during the day that she had to remember she could never please him no matter what she did because she realized, at the end of the session of the day before, the ultimate pleasing of him could only be if she were to become his sexual partner, something neither he nor she could possibly allow.

Her treatment swung into a new phase. It seemed to me she explored ways to establish control now of her feelings of yearning for her father. A clue was her wanting a very objective, managerial sort of young man to join the business organization as a buffer between her father and herself.

In the weeks that followed, Fleur concentrated upon treating her father more objectively. Simultaneously she developed a relationship with a young man living in another city, Paul, who was very like her father. Some of her dependency conflict with her father she handled by leaving often to see Paul. Thus she stimulated her father's anger, and afterward placated it, a painful cycle that she came to recognize. She began next to encourage her father in more of his possibilities to establish an emotional life with another woman. He had not really done this in the years since his divorce from her mother.

A month after the sessions described above, Fleur returned from seeing Paul with the following report: she felt she required a clitoral orgasm and Paul tried to produce this. However, she could not come to a climax. Paul suggested he make entry and she agreed. She felt an inner sense of connectedness. It was tremendously exciting and satisfying physically. She was aware of a feeling of wholeness rather than a segmented feeling. The same weekend she found herself not needing to be distraught with jealousy in regard to other attractive women. She closed the session with an account of more constructive behavior with her father. As she left, she turned and gave "good-mother-me" (my interpretation) a hug.

It is important to record that at no time earlier in Fleur's analysis did the subject come up of clitoral versus vaginal orgasms. Thus it was not because of suggestion on my part that the changes occurred.

The material cited above shows how Fleur struggled with separation/individuation, managing her primary oedipal conflict by splitting off her knowledge of her clitoris. This helped her to repress her early sexual excitement with her father, maintaining the secrecy of these feelings in spite of her mother's vigilant attention to her vagina. She used a split mother imago, with me as the good one, to gain permission for herself to allow these feelings into consciousness. Thus she could integrate them as part of her childhood past and not be so much controlled by them in her adult life.

Comparison of Pam and Fleur indicates how much individual patterns can vary in the course of the primary oedipal phase. Yet in both of them it is apparent that their developments were long stymied because of continuing effects in their personalities from that basic period.

Patterns that linger from such early experience are pervasive in the personality and take very long to restructure. Nonetheless, in all the cases in this chapter in which primary oedipal interpretations were given, there was an apparent effect on increased ego integration at that point of time.

10 Comparison of the Two Oedipal Phases

We have now developed the picture of the tasks and conflicts facing a two-year-old child, which we have called the primary oedipal complex. By the time the child reaches the age of four he or she has completed a number of these early tasks, such as establishing gender identity and achieving initial separation/individuation from the mother. Therefore the pattern of interlocking challenges and tensions at the classical stage is somewhat simpler.

The term *oedipal stage* is normally used to denote the period from approximately ages four to five and a half, when a child develops intense feelings of rivalry with the parent of the same sex over the parent of the opposite sex. Driven by its now focused sexual urges, the child fantasizes about marrying the opposite-sex parent and becomes intensely competitive with the same-sex parent. This gives rise both to anger directed at the parent of the same sex and to fears of retribution from that parent. At the same time the love and dependence the child feels for that parent leads to concomitant feelings of guilt over its desires. In addition, the child identifies with the same-sex parent as part of the process, this identification going beyond the level of classification (e.g., gender) and extending to an identification with the parent's role. This leads, at the resolution of the conflict, to an establishment of the child's idea of a role in the greater world according to gender. At this time the child ceases to be concerned with sexual feelings for its parent and concentrates on learning about itself in relation to the outside world.

This chapter deals with similarities and differences between the primary and classical oedipal phases. The similarities are due to similar kinds of experiences—inner and outer—that create the oedi-

pal conflicts and shape the child's handling of them. The differences are due to the differing capacities and ego development of
children at their younger and older ages.

The child's comprehension of the two oedipal stages is very
different from our own. We can understand what is happening in
scientific terminology. So young a child has limited capacity to
conceptualize its complex emotions. The toddler girl, for instance,
does not understand why father is so exciting or why she feels tense
when her mother enters a room where she and her father are playing. Nor can she sort out rivalrous feelings with her mother in the
same terms as when as an adolescent she might find that she and
another girl want attention from the same boy. It is because of the
child's limitations in comprehension, powers, and options at the
youngest ages that so much difficulty exists in resolving oedipal
conflicts.

Similarities that exist between the primary and classical
oedipal phases are not accidental. The classical phase builds upon
the primary oedipal and in many ways is a resetting of the earlier
scene. A second recapitulation occurs at the adolescent stage, as is
commonly recognized in terms of the classical oedipal (Lidz 1976,
among others, pointing this out).

*Each oedipal drama is coincidental with establishment of a
definition of self,* characterized by striving for greater autonomy and
independence. The primary oedipal phase occurs as the child first
gains the muscular and mental faculties required for self-control.
When the classical oedipal phase takes place, this child is able to act
autonomously within the family. The adolescent phase is the point
at which a youngster can develop independence in the larger world.
Each stage also brings successive psychosexual definition: during
the primary oedipal phase the child establishes its gender identity
and focuses its primitive sexual feelings. In the classical oedipal
phase the child is involved in a "family romance," bringing its
sexual feelings under genital primacy. In adolescence the same
basic issues are worked out with peers instead of family as sexual
feelings are finally placed outside the family. Our understanding of
these processes starts with clarity about the relationship of the classical and primary oedipal phase.

Both oedipal phases occur at about the same ages in most
children. Each is preceded by a period of ego expansion sufficient to

stimulate heightened organizational activity and defining of ego boundaries (primary) or roles (classical). Neurologically patterned developments such as achieving a sense of time influence the child's formulation and resolution of both stages. This is why most children go through and resolve the oedipal stages at about the same chronological points.

Perception of sexual feelings, differentiation of the parents, and the need for affirmation of personal uniqueness all exist in both periods. Beyond such minimal ego development, the difference in levels between the primary and the classical oedipal periods creates the differences we see in behavior. The way in which ego development and the child's handling of its oedipal conflicts are intertwined becomes clear in the contrast between the two oedipal phases. During the primary oedipal phase, oedipal concerns are bound into the nascent ego because a sense of gender is the core of personality organization at that time. During the classical oedipal phase, as Freud pointed out, the child's sense of role, according to gender, becomes the basis for a more sophisticated personality organization.

Regardless of the child's degree of maturity, it faces oedipal conflict, problems of rivalry, and loyalty struggles in creating and maintaining ego organization. The degree of ego development the child has achieved at the time determines whether the child is at the primary oedipal level or at the classical oedipal level. In turn, *the way* in which the child uses its resources to cope with the oedipal situation makes for the patterning of the ego. The *sine qua non* of an oedipal phase, what makes it so important, is that the resolution of the conflict heralds a new level of ego organization.

A criterion of successfully reaching the ego level of the classical oedipal phase is to achieve primacy of genital organization. Sexual interest and fantasies then center on enjoyment of the genitals with other body parts being of lesser importance. Corresponding to this achievement is a central sense of one's role as a member of one's own sex and later, as an adult,[1] resulting in a capacity for mature human relationships. At the point of resolution of the classical oedipal conflict, all of this is but sketched out. Many years of development must yet come. Still, the criterion of genital primacy denotes a significant change in the ego, even by five and a half. On the other hand, when the child is younger, at the primary oedipal level, genital impulses are vitally important. We have seen that they form the core of self-identity and are the basis of the child's psycho-social orientation. Yet so much of personality is as yet unsettled in the two-year-old, its impulses all seem to jumble together, which makes for difficulty in discerning the impact of its genitality.

Thus, in the primary oedipal child, oral and anal matters are not apart from sexual feelings and interpersonal issues. Only by the fourth year has the capacity of the ego expanded to permit integration and order sufficient for genital primacy to develop. This earlier situation results in pervasive sexual interest. That is why inevitably adults who are considered to be borderline cases according to their problems of self-differentiation always show concomitant confusion of oral/anal material in their sexual themes (e.g., finding orgastic pleasure in spanking).

I was helped to understand this by a patient named Heidi, a recent widow, who was so beset by feelings of badness that she could permit good feelings for herself only through the agency of another person. Although she managed to function while at work, manifestations of the primary oedipal complex almost overwhelmed her personal life. Her dreams and communications in the transference revealed part-object imagery—active breasts, anuses, buttocks, and penises. In her sexual fantasies, impersonal beings inflicted macabre tortures. Anal and oral material predominated. She often kept her eyes closed during our sessions to enhance a feeling that she could keep secrets from me. Gender confusion appeared in both sexual fantasies and problems with intrapsychic separation/differentiation. At times her thought process was fragmented and chaotic. As her analysis later proceeded to a point where she began to evince genital primacy, she also displayed pleasure in her femininity, used whole-person sexual fantasies, dealt effectively with other people of both sexes, enjoyed new professional opportunities, directly sensed her own feelings, communicated directly to me her wishes for limits to my knowledge and power in regard to her, and eventually, a keen sense of generationality in regard to her teenage children.

In other words, ego organization and genital primacy develop simultaneously with psychosocial maturity. At a time of fragmented ego organization, we glimpse the disorderly and confused inner world of the very young child. Oedipal issues occur crucially in the context of this inner world, just as it is well known that they do in the context of the inner world of a child of five.

Degree of Ego Organization

The organization of the personality after the primary oedipal stage is loose compared with the outcome of the successive replays of oedipal tensions at the classical oedipal phase and at early adolescence. Personality organization becomes increasingly clear as the spiral of development reaches more sophisticated levels. At the level of primary oedipal conflict the immaturity of the toddler puts its conflict into a more primitive form than restricts the relatively mature child of the classical oedipal age. In the latter case, it is relatively easy to see the connections between the child's responses to both parents and its oedipal stirrings because the child verbalizes them in terms of future plans. Easier to observe at the primary oedipal level are differences in the child's relationships with both parents, so loosely integrated with much other behavior. Perhaps, too, as great as the repressive barriers are against memory of classical oedipal feelings, they are even greater against recall of the primary oedipal counterpart, buried in the prelinguistic past and so fundamental in its effects.

The classical oedipal phase comes at the culmination of the child's development of its basic faculties: body sense, perceptual capacities, a repertoire of ways of handling anxiety, etc. The child is now ready for integration of these components of its ego, at this point making for a much more stable and rich personality. The primary oedipal stage comes at the *beginning* of the child's burgeoning sense of its future potential, just as it leaves infancy. Its basic faculties are still developing, and the organization of its ego can only be tentative and fragile.

There are already schemas for describing childhood development in terms of object relations (autistic, symbiotic, etc.) and in terms of the self (Kohut) and cognitive development (Piaget). All of these are valuable as components for understanding various vectors in child development. It will facilitate comparison of the primary with the classical oedipal phase to add one more schema, acknowledging all the others and based upon observations of periodicity in stages of child development (Gesell and Ilg 1940; Piaget 1962).

We think of a person in terms of a characteristic ego-state. Operationally, we might call the first state in ego development the *pre-self*. The child chiefly extends itself in various ways, accumulating new information and abilities, even though creation of ego-nuclei begins by birth. With signs of object permanence, there is evidence of inner mental structure. That development then leads the child into ego integration, the primary oedipal phase as it crystallizes its sense of gender; it has a working plan that Gesell and colleagues (1940) saw when they called typical three-year-olds "little ladies and gentlemen." This period corresponds to the phallic phase, except that I suggest the name *accumulative/expansive–2*, in parallel with the preorganizational stage. The child is focused upon learning its own possibilities. (White [1959] lists the child's expanding interests at three years old in a way that is reminiscent also of the latency child.) As the child's sense of future time progresses, it imagines itself growing up to marry the parent of the opposite sex. This prospect allows for reintensification of oedipal feelings, and the child is plunged into the classical oedipal phase. By around five years of age, the child matures to the point of recognizing generationality. It knows that parents, too, continue to change, that married adults have partners and not parents in each other. Questions about death typically arise at this age (Gesell and colleagues 1940), which we can now understand as part of a child's coming to grips with generationality. This child has a sense of a "historical self as well as a present self," including a past and a future (Gesell and Ilg 1946). The child accepts its status in its family, retaining its relationships with its parents and looking forward to a mate of its own in its own generation. Its energies are again focused upon the finding and development of the personal possibilities in the third accumulative/expansive phase, latency.

Behavior in the second accumulative/expansive phase (between the two oedipals) includes exploration of possibilities the child finds in the world around it and its personal potential. Competitive feelings that have to do with one's abilities in general are heightened in attitudes about penises, and thus the name *phallic phase* was first given to this period. This name, as well as being too specific, leaves out the importance of the many positive feelings a girl has about her body.

However, using the name *accumulative/expansive phase–2* rather than *phallic phase* underscores the basic dynamic of the child's behavior, which is the nature of the child's ego development. Oedipal strivings are set relatively aside, as they will be more completely still in latency after the great organizational task of the classical oedipal phase.

Others have also made efforts toward more satisfactory nomenclature for behavior of children during what I call the second accumulative/expansive phase. Greenspan (1980) suggests "dyadicphallic" phase, presenting the case of S. to illustrate it.[2] Knowing about the primary oedipal complex and the nature of the period between it and the classical oedipal phase, we can better understand material from treatment that Greenspan gives of his patient. This case provides an excellent example of how a child handles oedipal strivings at the primary and later at the classical oedipal level of ego organization.

I select it for further discussion here (see chapter 4) because Greenspan investigates oedipal development in S. and shares much detail from S.'s treatment. In it we see evidence for the existence of both oedipal phases in succession and find material to contrast the two.

The manifestations of the primary oedipal phase that S. showed at the beginning of treatment were: difficulties in separating from her mother; admiration for men and resentment of women expressed in life-and-death terms; gender confusion; heightened sexual curiosity with emphasis on the genitalia (part-object as opposed to whole-person responses); preoccupation with disappearance and annihilation; control of high anxiety through anal mechanisms (e.g., by going to the bathroom during sessions); split between thought and feeling as evinced by her high I.Q. and appropriate secondary process thinking in contrast to tumultuous primary process behavior demonstrated in the sessions; categorizing herself frequently as "bad and mean;" and an "impersonal but intense (needy) quality to the way she related." Her behavior was fragmented, and her fantasies were dominated by oral and anal material. Greenspan determined that she had achieved some degree of object constancy but had not been able to solidify this achievement as yet. A *presenting symptom was preoccupation with her father's penis in a way that stimulated seductive feelings on the part of her father and that her mother found competitive with herself and disconcerting.* Greenspan utilizes the idea of object relations in the preclassical oedipal picture by referring to dyadic relationships, but he cites S.'s triadic involvement as relatively insignificant because of the child's immaturity. He tells how the evidence for oedipal concerns before the classical oedipal phase is presently considered:

At the proposed dyadic-phallic stage, we have an emerging phallic drama with phallic-oedipal trends being played out on a stage that is limited in its capacity to tolerate such a drama. Therefore the drama remains constricted and shallow, organizing more around underlying preoedipal trends rather than the richer and potentially more intimate oedipal themes, even though the latter may be both defensively hypertrophied and fearfully pursued. (1980:595)

We reconsider this traditional view. The problem of oedipal feelings exists for the child in the very fact of its organizing a sense of self in its psychosocial world. The child has little capacity to deal with the problem, and its primitive mental equipment creates splits and lacunae in the ego, making it all the more important rather than of little significance that the oedipal pressures exist. If one decides that all is preoedipal before the classical oedipal stage, then all oedipal signs must be interpreted as "attempts" at oedipal interest. It is only when we take into account the naturalness and inevitability of the child's earliest oedipal feelings that we can begin to understand the uses of psychological resources that a growing child makes and how there can be gender-specific psychopathological development based on the experiences of the earliest years (1980:588–589).

Greenspan cites the simultaneous existence of: "the fears of general bodily injury, damage to the emerging sexual identity, loss of love, loss of the object, annihilation, being overwhelmed by the instincts, and fusion with the dyadic object" (1980:597). He places fusion with the dyadic object correctly as a fear reaction, but he does not take into account the intensity of the interest the child has in the parent of the opposite sex.

After the above quotation, he describes S. It is clear that she is enormously involved in sexual matters, but in a chaotic, frenetic, driven fashion (characteristic of the primary oedipal child). In describing the subsequent shift in the child to the (classical) oedipal phase, as treatment progressed, Greenspan states, starting with his view of the period before the classical oedipal: "The patient will present pseudo-oedipal concerns in a narcissistic, phallic context and evidence fear of moving into the true intimacy of an oedipal situation which optimally is permitted to develop, often for the first time in the patient's life" (1980:599).

That the child exhibits "pseudo-oedipal" concerns is in a circular fashion decided on the basis that the child has not shown classical oedipal–level ego organization. Indeed, the progression in ego organization does allow the child to handle its oedipal strivings in a new way. *The fact that the oedipal strivings of the younger child do not appear in an organized form is a fact that comes from the general lack of ego development at that stage rather than from any "pseudo" quality to its oedipal feelings.* Greenspan makes the observation that "there are phallic wishes toward the dyadic object, mother, and emerging phallic-oedipal wishes toward objects in a triangular configuration, the latter still unstable" (1980:593). This is indeed true because the dependency of the child is still so great on its mother, in the girl, and masculine organization is still so fragile in the boy.

Nonetheless, as Greenspan tells of working through some of what we can call the primary oedipal phase issues,

especially the sense of entitlement, desire to control everything, jealous rage at her sister, and sense of badness, permitted a shift to triangular oedipal level concerns. With further development and differentiation of ego functions, a greater degree of object constancy was secured, symptoms were given up, and there was a sense of internal security as evinced by improved functioning at school, at home, and with peers. Differentiated ego functioning was evidenced in the analysis through "the doctor game," where the patient at this time showed in a dramatic fashion the capacity for an observing ego in the context of a therapeutic alliance, e.g., in the doctor game she observed themes that emerged and "made connections." While being the "talking doctor" had its own dynamic significance, it also represented a capacity for higher-level defensive and synthetic functioning. In this context the emergence of the patient's washing-machine fantasy regarding "shrinking her mother," and taking mother's place, feelings about "things popping out of her," fantasy about father "cutting open her mother at night in bed," wishes and fears of being cut open, poisoned, and phobic concerns about the elevator may have indicated oedipal concerns and elements in the organization of her infantile neurosis. It is interesting to note that her primal scene fantasy of father cutting mother open was organized along phallic aggressive lines where she could take either role. (1980:589)

We recall that one reason her parents brought S. into treatment was her obsessive interest in touching her father's penis and her mother's sense of rivalry between S. and herself in this behavior. Therefore what we can notice in this account is the shift not from dyadic to triadic interest but from relatively undifferentiated ego formation to relatively differentiated ego formation.

We appreciate the contrast between this transitional picture of S. and the following description of S. as she progressed through treatment. Greenspan noted: "The shift . . . to triangular patterns . . . [solidifying] in the stable delineated internal representation of self and object, thereby stabilizes a number of core ego functions including the capacity for distinguishing internal from external, reality testing, impulse regulation, organization of emotions, and the integration of thought and affect" (1980:592) and "the patient's increased associative range and depth in the context of an observing ego and overall movement into latency-type activities (improvement in peer and family relationships and attitude toward school)" (1980:589).

We can see the drastic difference in ego organization of this child. As the basic issues got worked through on the primary oedipal phase level, her ego strengthened in its capacity to deal with feelings. Classical oedipal behavior appeared in stable triangular patterns. S. was then able to have a "more delineated regression" in which she processed again themes around dependency, loss, and fusion. Working through these very early issues in the context of greater ego strength, S. evinced knowing future time and being able to plan ahead, turning to her peer group rather than being bound to her family in oedipal terms.

I wish to call attention to one more contrast between S.'s primary and classical oedipal behavior. A hallmark that differentiates the two oedipal phases is the use of elaborate fantasy rather than crude fantasy or direct representation in dealing with oedipal feelings. During S.'s treatment when she was at the primary oedipal phase she had a fantasy in which, according to the extremeness of that period of development, all females were killed and she alone survived with Daddy-people because she was a tomboy, although with some ambivalence because "girls can wear nice things." In the classical oedipal phase, S.'s fantasy was to shrink her mother in a washing machine. The primary oedipal fantasy was a life-and-death matter in which she gained freedom from guilt by confusing her gender. The classical oedipal fantasy was a compromise that preserved her mother while yet diminishing her. This fantasy utilized cognitive sophistication, perhaps humor, and certainly the idea of the possibility of change.

Summary of Characteristics of Children in the Primary and Classical Oedipal Phases

In S. we saw demonstrated many points of contrast between two-year-old behavior and five-year-old behavior as reflected in the primary and classical oedipal phases. We will now go through a more complete comparison between the phases item by item (based in part on the process of child development as noted in chapter 2).

1. *Primary process dominates use of language in the two-year-old.* Thinking is in primitive terms with concrete symbolization, *pars pro toto* symbolization, literal interpretation of words, and little form to the language structure.

   Secondary process characterizes the language of the five-year-old. There are the rudiments of logical analysis and understanding of cause and effect. There is use of all the major structures of language at this point, giving skill in understanding and applying ideas in dealing with relationships.

2. *Oral and anal elements are prominent in the behavior of two-year-olds.* By the beginning of the second year of life, the child is ostensibly not an eating machine as its younger self seemed to be, but orality is very important. Due to the enormous intrapsychic importance of maturation of its sphincters, the ego focuses on bathroom activities and power control. Oral/anal/genital impulses are poorly differentiated.

   These matters continue to be of importance to the child, as indeed eating and excretion are all our lives. Nonetheless, to a significant degree, *the five-year-old presents a parallel with mature genital primacy.* For the five-year-old, oral, anal, and genital impulses no longer swirl together within its personality.

3. *The two-year-old's attachments are characterized by intensity and lack of commitment.* By contrast, *the five-year-old exhibits firm object-constancy,* which brings with it confidence rather than desperation in relationships.

4. *The two-year-old is preoccupied with the issue of good versus bad.* The five-year-old is no longer rent by a sense of excruciating extremes. *The five-year-old is able to make some excuses* and have some sense of *gradations between extremes of good and bad.*

5. *The time sense of the two-year-old is still limited to the immediate moment.* It is a matter of a couple of months before the child gains primordial concepts of past and future. *By five years old, the child has a clear idea of its own existence in the past and that it will become an adult,* particularly like the parent of the same sex.

For the two-year-old, its time sense stretches from the concept of "now" only to some sense of past and an incipient sense of the future: babies seem genderless. The future includes the self as it is, but bigger. In the time sense of the child of the classical oedipal period, continuity has been established between itself as a baby boy or baby girl who has reached its present estate and can look forward to changing further into an adult who will still be the same person. Limited to a sense of the immediate, a two-year-old is intolerant of frustration compared to the four-and-a-half-year-old with its sense of future possibilities.

The primary oedipal child sees only helplessness or omnipotence. Its fantasy is to take the place of the parent of the same sex immediately. The classical oedipal child, with its sense of future time, can conceive of growing up, having a role—not just the appearance of an adult—and marrying the parent of the opposite sex at that point. It does not yet recognize that the beloved parent is also on a time continuum. In the further development of the child's sense of time, it comes to the concept of generationality. It recognizes that its parents are also getting older. This enables the child to repress the sexual wishes for the parent of the opposite sex entirely and prepare for an independent adult existence as part of its own age group. This is the reason that the resolution of the classical oedipal complex occurs at the same general age from child to child. By six, a child has sufficient concept of generationality to enter latency, waiting to be an adult before having sexual relationships, outside the family.

6. *The ego of the two-year-old is so poorly integrated* that fragmentation of mental processes is still typical of the child. *By five*, or even four and a half, *there is a great deal of integration* which we expect to have taken place. Fragmented behavior at that point is a sign of distress.

7. A *sense of gender is the great achievement of the two-year-old*. It is the outcome of the primary oedipal phase. However, while this is being achieved, confusion about gender is often expressed. The confusion has to do with the intensity of the primary oedipal conflict as well as cognitive difficulties. The five-year-old already has a clear sense of its own gender. *The outcome of the classical oedipal conflict is for the child to have a clear sense of role* that is implied by that gender.

8. *The super-ego of the primary oedipal child is primitive and brutal.* In keeping with the fact that all issues are seen in extremes, the judgments of the two-year-old are severe, and fantasy content about the forbidden includes the most threatening of oral and anal violence.

   By contrast the super-ego of the classical oedipal child leaves room for compromise. It is still harsh compared with adult judgment, but it is not any longer nihilistic. Omnipresence or annihilation are no longer the only two possible outcomes of judgment.

9. *Identification with the parent of the same sex is accomplished for the child at the age of two in terms of appearance* (Ceaser 1977). *Identification based upon role is*

characteristic of the five-year-old. The two-year-old might exhibit role playing of a very basic kind, as in a little girl arranging her dolls or a little boy strutting as he wears his father's shoes. Imitation describes such behavior. This is not on the same level as the behavior of the five-year-old who tries for a personality with the emotional qualities of its own gender as it perceives them in the adult state, with a sense of meaning in its activities.

10. *Secrecy as a protection against mother's omniscience for the two-year-old is accomplished only through repression.* The child can really believe that a forbidden act was not done by itself. The child becomes extremely upset if someone presses the idea that it has done a bad thing that it cannot accept for itself. What the child does not want its mother to know of its own thoughts, it must "disown" knowing itself.

    In contrast, the five-year-old is quite capable of lying to protect secrecy and can understand that it is possible to have thoughts that are not magically known to the mother.

11. *The ego boundaries of the two-year-old are fluid.* The child has some real sense of itself as an entity, but intrapsychic fusion of itself with its mother can also seem real. *In contrast, the child at the time of the classical oedipal period has fixed ego boundaries,* which makes it possible for it to feel more autonomous than a two-year-old can feel.

12. *The concept of loss for the two-year-old is total annihilation.* Mere absence can mean the impossibility of return. *The concept of loss for the four-and-a-half to five-year-old is not as absolute.* The lost can be found or replaced. The concept of loss also includes the idea of death as a real occurrence that mostly affects the old rather than the young, and it can accept the idea of another place, such as heaven, where the departed continue to dwell.

13 *The sense of place is precarious in the thinking of the two-year-old,* as this sense is tied to the sense of immediacy. This is true because space and time are not sepa-

rate concepts for the two-year-old. Thus, having a right to existence for the two-year-old is the same as holding a particular place in the immediate moment. The desperation of many a two-year-old's battles can be connected with this fact. *The four-and-a-half- or five-and-a-half-year-old by contrast has a sense of rightness in having one's own place.* The definition of one's place is not simply having possession of a particular chair or seating space or place in a social situation. There is a sense of comfort about one's knowing that it is appropriate that one has the particular spot one occupies. This relates also to comfort within the family group wherein the child feels clear about its place and comfortable being a child in a family led by two adults.

14. *The two-year-old is immersed in the all-or-none dichotomy.* Making a choice that is required may be difficult because choices seem absolute. It is this feeling of absoluteness in making a choice that makes a borderline personality so vulnerable to difficulties in making decisions. Clinically, these are often seen as choices between parents or between objects mentally linked to parents. *By contrast, the child at the point of the classical phase can utilize gradations in its thinking.* It can accommodate both parents in different ways. This is seen in such a child saying to the parent of the same sex, "Mommy, you can live in the attic (while I stay in the house with Daddy)," or "Daddy, you can live in the garage (while I stay in the house with Mommy)." The ability to accommodate two opposites relieves the child of pain in decision-making.

15. *In relation to issues of power, the two-year-old feels intensely.* Inner and outer control are combined in the mind. According to its dichotomous way of thinking, either oneself or another can have what it wants, not both. Expressions of great hostility accompany the power issue. There is a developing sense of order accompanying the power issue, which has to do with being able to control oneself and one's world, and which

can lead to obsessive-compulsive behavior when the control issue becomes desperate.

By contrast, the child at four and on has the concept of cooperation, which develops increasingly as the issues of the primary oedipal phase are settled (and can characterize even three-year-olds [Gesell and colleagues 1940]). The idea of compromise and the ability to postpone satisfaction enable the classical oedipal child to respond more flexibly to situations than it could at two. Its combined sense of autonomy and of future time together make this possible.

16. As to relationships with their parents, *gender identity is still developing for the primary oedipal boy. He must maintain a relationship with his father for the purposes of identification,* to continue to solidify his gender identity, and to protect himself from engulfment by his mother and subsequent loss of his sense of personal identity, and therefore must repress his yearnings for his mother. This means not merely giving up dependency but making himself confident of his masculinity.

By contrast, the boy entering the classical oedipal phase has consolidated his gender identity as a result of the resolution of the primary oedipal phase. Having consolidated his sense of himself, *he can now allow himself competition with his father for his mother.* Also, with his sense of gender set, he is able to allow himself tender feelings of love in addition to sexual wishes for closeness with her, which characterizes the mature love attitude of a male.

For the girl, her dependency needs are still paramount during the primary oedipal conflict, and therefore gender identity is something that she can most easily allow herself by retaining a sense of fusion with her mother. It may seem perilous to be autonomous because she is not ready for rivalry with her mother. Feeling a degree of fusion with mother, and/or herself to be an extension of mother, makes it more tolerable to entertain fantasies about herself and father at that level. *At*

the time of the classical oedipal, the sense of independence of the little girl and confidence that her mother's
anger will not be nihilistic are adequate so that *she can
attempt competition with her mother for her father*
toward the possibility of a future with him.

Comparison of What Children Achieve in Resolution of the Primary and the Classical Oedipal Phases

1. *After resolution of the primary oedipal conflict, the child
has a sense of a place in the family because it knows who it is as a
separate entity. After resolution of the classical oedipal phase the
child can show increasing readiness to be a part of the larger world
beyond the family because it knows itself as someone with a role to
play.*
During the primary oedipal phase, the child feels a sense of
parity with adults, which is why its power struggles are so vigorous.
The sense of parity with adults is diminished after the primary
oedipal phase so that the child expects to marry the waiting adult
when it becomes big enough. It is no longer a baby and feels an
equal force with other members of the family, which makes the
establishment of power important. In its mind, men and boys are
the same and women and girls are the same. Gender is clear, but
generational differences are not.
In resolving the classical oedipal conflict, the child differentiates people by both sex and generation. It is content to be a child
with a future, who can look for status increasingly outside the family.

2. *Sexual fantasies after resolution of the primary oedipal are
tied to the idea of growing up and marrying the parent of the opposite sex.* A hierarchy of impulses is not established, and sexual
fantasies are infused with oral and anal elements.
In contrast, *after resolution of the classical oedipal, sexual
fantasies are not about parents.* Mythical persons, such as princes
and princesses, kings and queens, are the subjects of these fantasies,
but particularly princes and princesses because there is recognition
of generational status. Sexual fantasies are focused on genital sensations.

3. *The primary oedipal child resolves the conflict with a sense of personal identity. The classical oedipal child resolves the conflict with additionally a sense of social identity.*

4. *In both stages, at resolution, the child experiences a lowered degree of anxiety* because of its new sense of certainty and of confidence in its new ego organization. Apperception of future time, to the degree each achieves it, in each instance now allows the child to feel a degree of certainty in the face of constant change, creating the relative calm of both postoedipal stages.

5. *The significances of the primal scene at the two stages can be compared.* During the primary oedipal phase, the primal scene (by fantasy or actual observation) stimulates the child's sense of its individuality through its similarity to one sex and a special relationship to the other, the different one. However, the child's interpretation at that age reflects the violent fantasy typical of the anal stage. The importance of primal scene fantasy at this level can be seen in the fact that the impressions of it are strong enough to be stored in the memory system of the toddler and available for reactivation at the classical oedipal period. That the four-year-old's primal scene concerns date to this earlier stage is evidenced by the form that the fantasies then take, as in the case of Freud's Wolf Man (1918). During the classical oedipal phase, recovery of thoughts of the primal scene may serve to reinforce the child's previous achievement of gender identity and the child's current need to redefine in a much more sophisticated way what it means to be a member of its own sex. Exclusivity and feelings of loving intimacy are part of the classical oedipal child's primal scene fantasy rather than violence, lending sharpness to the child's jealousy, but also redefining the child's picture of adult interaction in terms of gender. A child's relationships with both its parents form the familiar triad by means of which the child superimposes a sense of role upon its own gender identity.[3]

Case Examples

It is of theoretical interest that when progressing through treatment, people do not seem to require periods of expansion/accumulation in parallel with the phallic phase and latency. Successful integration of the ego on the primary oedipal level is directly followed by movement into the classical oedipal phase. These characteristics are apparent in close study of a child. Using the art and science of psychoanalysis in a remarkable tour-de-force, Lopez details his work with a boy named Monroe (Lopez and Kliman 1980).

Monroe, an inner-city child, presented a special therapeutic challenge. When he was two-and-a-half, a defective brother was born. His mother suffered a psychotic break and was hospitalized for the next nine months. Monroe's father and paternal grand-mother took care of him until his mother returned, whereupon they both left at once, permanently. The mother, on a heavy drug sched-ule, remained emotionally withdrawn for the full two years of Monroe's treatment.

At four years of age, when his treatment began, Monroe was almost unreachable. This description of dominating oral and anal fantasies and intense ambivalence in ways of relating shows his primary oedipal status: "He would kick, bite, spit, punch, scratch, and make a shambles of the classroom, create chaos and drive the teachers to near despair. . . . As infuriating as Monroe might be one moment, as lovable he became the next" (1980:345). Typical of the way in which Monroe expressed oral-anal impulses, he seemed insatiable in stuffing himself with food and fantasized swallowing the feces of beloved people.

A first transition toward ego integration followed after Lopez interpreted Monroe's anger at the birth of his younger brother when Monroe was two and a half. Lopez recognized that the critical issue to Monroe was that his mother's sexuality excluded him. Monroe's anxiety lessened by this acknowledgment. Monroe strove for a mas-culine identity, particularly by yearning for a paternal figure he might love and admire and in whose strength he might participate. Lopez points out that this kind of masculine identification had more to do with manner of dressing than manner of behavior. We can recognize here a key difference between the primary oedipal child's focus upon the appearance of gender and the classical oedi-pal child's sense of role in it.

Gradually Monroe seemed to be developing toward the (clas-sical) oedipal phase:

Then a shift in the material occurred. What had been an ebullient seeking of association with men to gain a feeling of strength became rigid, compel-ling, and clearly defensive in character. It became a means of escaping from closeness to women—in the nursery, from closeness to teachers.

The turn of events was, at first, puzzling. My focusing on Monroe's longing for a father to rescue him, and on guilt causing him to turn aggression against himself, as manifested by his suicidal gesture,[4] was probably at least partially valid, but it seemed not truly to hit the mark.

Finally, information conveyed by Monroe's therapeutic companion[5] shed light on what was happening. His mother's condition had deteriorated. She had become even more inert and less involved with her children. (1980:351)

Understanding the nature of the primary oedipal phase, we can see why Monroe was suicidal. His mother's withdrawal extracted the dreaded price with which the primary oedipal boy is threatened for asserting his masculine identity, namely, losing contact with his mother. This was especially poignant for Monroe because he had just begun to project his sexual feelings with his female teacher. A self-assertive quality in Monroe's suicidal behavior is clear from the fact that he not only did hurt himself but he also threatened to do so in a way to frighten his caretakers. This indicates the way in which his need to be self-assertive and the need to be self-destructive were joined.

After much working through of feelings on the primary oedipal level until the final nine months of treatment, Monroe's firm transition to the classical oedipal phase was accomplished in the following manner. Starting from a striking effort to separate psychologically from his mother, as Lopez describes it, Monroe's behavior showed good progress in his ability to handle separations until periods of confidence were:

interspersed with episodes in which he would call desperately for [his mother]—at times insisting that her hospitalization or even her death was imminent. Vomiting, complaints of stomach aches and head pains, painful minor accidents, and another threat to jump from the balcony on the stairwell outside the classroom accompanied his tears. However, no relationship between these episodes and his mother's actual condition could be discerned from home visits and interviews with her.

It dawned on the nursery team that the key to understanding these episodes lay in Monroe's concretistic mode of thinking, causing intensely experienced ideas to become confused with reality. Thenceforth I related these episodes interpretatively, not to Monroe's mother's imminent departure, but rather to Monroe's own efforts to detach himself psychologically from her both by functioning independently and by going beyond her inadequate mentation. In each instance my efforts were rewarded: Monroe regained his composure rather quickly and resumed his progressive development. *For example, Monroe was carrying on in his all-too-familiar provocative, obstreperous, sadomasochistic manner in a session which followed one in which he had responded to an attractive female observer by being stimulated to ecstatic heights of phallic exhibitionism.* When I focused on this shift in his material, Monroe sobered, turned to me, and said, "My brother killed my Mommy and sent her to the hospital." I verbalized Monroe's wish to be rid of his mother, especially after having been exposed to the visitor of the previous day, his guilt over this wish, and his displacing responsibility onto his brother. Monroe stopped and nodded sadly. He then engaged in a variety of activities, including instructing a boy with a tested I.Q. of more than 130 on how to make bow and arrows out of drinking straws; hugging a teacher and two children affectionately; and playing at being an Indian warrior battling imaginary adversaries on the nearby hill. (1980:361)

From this point on, Monroe presented clear, classical oedipal material in relationship to his man therapist and a beloved woman teacher. He created age-appropriate, elaborate fantasies for handling his feelings: "He enacted being caring and affectionate to the family he had created and set up a home for it. He took me, as his son, for a walk, gave me money, and bought gifts for me. Finally, he built a handsome phallic structure of blocks for Mrs. Solomon, his wife" (1980:362).

A transitory reverse oedipus yielded quickly to interpretation,[6] and Monroe moved firmly toward realistic relations with the adults in his milieu treatment center and with his peers.

The case of Monroe shows the contrast between the way in which sexual wishes are handled on the primary oedipal level of ego integration and on the classical oedipal level. When at the former level, Monroe's conflict was imbedded in fragmented behavior, dominant oral-anal fantasies, rapidly shifting ambivalences, primary process in use of language, the use of men by a boy to establish masculine identification in a rigid, compulsive pattern based upon appearance, intense, ambivalent attachments, the need for immediate gratification, and exhibitionism. At the classical oedipal level he displayed an integrated sense of the male role, being protective and giving in relationships, capacity for commitment in relationships with both children and adults, patience, the rise of secondary process in his thinking, and relative decathexis of oral and anal impulses.

Monroe was freed to make this transition in two stages when it was possible to interpret for him his hitherto unconscious primary oedipal conflict. The first stage was after acknowledgment of his anger that his mother had made his baby brother with his father and not with him, excluding him sexually. This interpretation freed him to seek out strong masculine figures such as firemen and workmen with whom to identify in terms of appearance. The pattern changed from a "happy, ebullient" one into a "desperate, rigid" one when Monroe's mother began to deteriorate. The second stage was the exploration of the connection between Monroe's sexual mother-imago and his fears of engulfment by his mother.

Typical of the work toward the transition is the statement about his alternating sexual interest with offensive behavior. Monroe first expressed his sexuality in the primary oedipal mode. Second, he revealed his need to resist the engulfment by his mother that he feared when his sexuality was aroused. Monroe's immediate positive response to interpretation is characteristic of my experience with patients when they are contending with such material, although, as Lopez notes, the working-through period is lengthy.

Monroe's transition from the primary oedipal phase into the classical oedipal phase was possible because Monroe felt free from the terror of engulfment by his mother and the preoccupation with annihilation his sexual impulses had thus imposed upon his development. At this point Monroe rapidly developed age-appropriate classical oedipal behavior. Follow-up reports show that Monroe subsequently moved smoothly into latency, happy among his family and his peers and eager to learn in school.

A brief account of a transitional point in the life of an adult patient of mine also illustrates the differences between the two oedipal phases. Carla, a woman of thirty, was my patient as an adolescent and young adult. Her separation/individuation problems had been acute. Eventually, she resolved them enough to be able to move to another city than the one in which her mother had lived. Suicidal tendencies abated, and she fell in love with Edgar, who was supportive and treated her well. All of these were achievements that contrasted with her earlier behavior, when her tie to her mother dominated her life. As in so many instances one sees, the mother had considered Carla her favorite child because she looked like herself, intensifying Carla's confusion in trying to establish herself as an autonomous being.

After Carla moved away, I received many letters and telephone calls from her, which enabled her to wean herself from me gradually while continuing her analytic work. By the time she met Edgar, I was hearing from her only on the rare instances that she visited her old home town. I was surprised therefore to receive a long-distance call from Carla at the point I now describe.

Carla started off by telling me that things were "good and bad." Two main themes were: she antagonized a woman superior at work by being difficult and demanding (although she felt right in what she stood for); and Edgar's new job required him to be away except for weekends during the next six months, and Carla feared destroying their relationship by being unfaithful to him. The fear of separation, seeing her sexual impulses as bad, putting herself disadvantageously in a position of defiance to a woman in authority, and seeing *herself* as bad all erupted together. She was able to recognize the old pattern. She could see the next six months of repeated separations from Edgar (which she knew had nothing to do with her personal worth) as an opportunity to work further on her feeling that someone she loved would leave her because she was bad, or that she could not have a man of her own because a woman in authority (her supervisor) wanted her for herself.

This material lets us see the contrast between the levels of ego functioning in the two oedipal phases. Carla's leftovers from the primary oedipal phase were preoccupation with the split between good and bad, seeing herself as bad, identification of sexuality with badness. The difference in Carla that reflected her achieving the classical oedipal phase we can see in a higher level of ego functioning: she was aware of both good and bad in herself and did not need to feel suicidal or swamped by oral and anal impulses or resort to part-object fantasies. She had a sense of personal worth and a role to play in the larger world (I'm good at my job, my company needs me) and considered the antagonistic mother figure as having good as well as bad qualities. She after all did not need to respond to the separations from Edgar as signs of her having no right to him because of the opposition of her mother imago. She could operate in terms of future time, not being emotionally bound by the limitations of the present. For Carla this permitted seeing herself as an adult.

An example of the value of recognizing the role of generationality in the resolution of the classical oedipal complex comes from my patient named Lynn. At this point in her analysis, Lynn was acutely aware of her competitive feelings with me, which were highly significant now in the transference. Simultaneously, she newly allowed herself household help. Before this, she felt she did not deserve any, even though she could have afforded it financially. She could not, however, allow herself to be pleased by the work the maid did for her. At issue was this: Lynn's mother had required her to do household chores, and as Lynn remembered it, this eventually seemed to mean doing her mother's job. The experience was complicated by her mother's giving Lynn the job of making her father's dinner whenever the mother and father fought, as they did very often. Lynn tried to handle the blurring of generational boundaries by keeping herself inferior to her mother, who in Lynn's mind was never pleased with what Lynn did. In her present-day treatment of her maid, Lynn enacted the role of the mother, still keeping the maid/ Lynn in her place. Using roles for self-definition rounds out the classical oedipal complex. Lynn several times lost or misplaced her wallet (which she associated with a grownup identity and ability to take care of herself) when she caught herself entertaining thoughts about having a fine man of her own. This contrasted sharply to former, primary oedipally based behavior, Lynn becoming suicidal because she noticed a shadow that resembled her father in a painting she had interpreted to signify rampant sexuality.

Summary and Conclusions

We can summarize the psychological status of the primary oedipal age child and the child at the classical oedipal period.

The primary oedipal child is characterized by use of language dominated by primary process, oral and anal elements in its fantasies and behavior, intense ambivalence and lack of commitment, preoccupation with good/bad dichotomy, splitting as its major defense mechanism, and dichotomous thought processes about omniscience/total ignorance, omnipotence/total helplessness, autonomy/dependence, immediacy of time sense, lack of differentiation between adults and children, fragmented mental processes, and the need to consolidate its sense of gender.

Five-year-olds will seem primitive in these respects in comparison with adolescents who contend again with strong needs for individuality and sexuality. However, compared with the two-year-old, the five-year-old child is characterized by the ascendancy of secondary process, instinctual elements that are relatively under control, a high degree of object constancy, which give stability both to the self-image and the image of others, the sense of future time, the sense of generationality developing rapidly, an integrated ego with a sense of roles, of a social role in consonance with its gender, the ability to wait, the ability to tolerate ambiguity, and a sense of degrees of goodness and badness.

With all of this, the child at both ages handles as best it can impulses toward self-actualization and sexual impulses toward the parent of the opposite sex.

Jacobson (1954) speaks of the advance from *fantasies of being* the parents to *striving to become like* the parents. The sense of future time along with a sense of one's real possibilities together define the resolution of the classical oedipal period and the onset of latency. Or, as Thomas (1963) put it, the child looks forward to its future as an adult but for the present is content to be a child. This child can then set about learning how to become an adult.

Part III A Test of the Concept of the Primary Oedipal Phase: Applicability to a Gender-Specific Psychopathology—Anorexia

11 Introduction to Anorexia

The main purpose of part III is to provide a test of the theory of the primary oedipal phase. An opportunity for such a test lies in the fact that there are certain severe psychopathologies that puzzlingly occur most often in one gender group or the other. I refer to such conditions as anorexia nervosa, sexual perversions, the incidence of threats of suicide, the incidence of commissions of suicide, obsession-compulsion, and hysteria, none of whose gender specificity has been adequately explained. All of these conditions are associated with developmental difficulties before the classical oedipal period.

The theory of the primary oedipal phase offers explanation of the gender specificity of such conditions, as we have seen in the chapters on patterns in males and females. A good test of the theory, then, would be to examine one of these gender-specific illnesses in depth to see whether the theory adds significantly to our understanding of the psychodynamics of the illness.

Studying in this manner the extent to which the theory may apply to all gender-influenced clinical entities would be an encyclopedic effort well beyond the scope of a single volume or indeed one person's ability. I can try to test the theory here by selecting one condition to explore. I hope that others in the field will be intrigued by the possibilities of this approach and test the proposition further.

For purposes of this initial study of the primary oedipal phase, I shall investigate anorexia nervosa. I pick anorexia because there is a great deal of information on it and because there is a great deal of interest in it as well, partially stimulated by a possible increase in its occurrence. In addition, there are a number of features of anorexia that make it a particularly good "test" in that they seem by their number and complexity to defy the possibility of a simple and natural explanation. Anorexia always appears in the matrix of a particular syndrome. Furthermore, that syndrome can appear in matching degrees of severity as a unit in patients within a wide range of other psychopathologies. Also, anorexia in many patients alternates as a symptom with bulimia and/or obesity, providing a test for the theory to explain such shifts. Finally, although much more prevalent among females, the syndrome does occur on occasion among males, and the exception as well as the rule needs to be explained.

In attempting to relate anorexia to the primary oedipal phase of life, we are fortunate that two distinguished analysts report very fully their respective treatments of two child anorexics. Therefore, we need not rely simply upon reconstructions in trying to evaluate the relationship of a putative primary oedipal phase to the etiology of anorexia nervosa.

Statement of Theory

[Anorexia nervosa is a condition characterized by the willful avoidance of food even though it is plentiful. This symptom is the most dramatic and life-threatening aspect of anorexia and has therefore received most of the attention. However, Sours (1977) has established that, in fact, anorexia exists as a definable collection of symptoms, a complex pattern that is always present no matter what other disease entities (from mild depression to schizophrenia) may exist in conjunction with it in a particular patient. The pattern he described includes the following: refusal to eat, denial of the problem, hyperactivity, problems in separation/individuation from the mother, amenorrhea, denial of sexuality, secrecy of thought, splitting as a defense, and preoccupation with oral and anal matters.]

The combination of sexual and separation/individuation problems with such other two-year-old issues as oral/anal concerns and ownership of thoughts as well as the reflection of such two-year-old thought patterns as categorical denial and splitting will, by now, be recognized as forming a primary oedipal complex.

It will be worth going through the logic of how specifically the female pattern of the primary oedipal complex can lead to the anorexic's collection of problems, to provide a framework that can be referred to, before we enter into a detailed discussion of the evidence for the application. We recall that the process of ego formation for the girl contains components of self-definition from modeling herself on her mother, from the separation/individuation process, and from recognition of her own feelings, which include the intense sexual feelings that are directed toward her father. One of the major conflicts that comes out of this for the girl is that which arises from her connection between her sense of self and her sexual feelings on the one hand and, on the other, her dependent relationship with her mother. This can lead to strong guilt feelings on the part of the girl. One strategy she can employ to deal with the guilt-causing situation is to repress her sexual feelings.[1]

When this happens early in the primary oedipal phase there are several unfortunate consequences. A girl normally develops much of her sense of gender and hence her sense of self on the basis of her sexual feelings. Also, the very intensity of those sexual feelings help to set the little girl apart from her mother and thus to initiate a sense of separate identity. By denying herself her sexual feelings early on in her ego-forming process, she retains a vague, poorly organized sense of self. In addition, at this early stage her dependence on her mother is especially great, making her all the more vulnerable. There develops an almost desperate drive for security. This is, again, at the earliest time of the primary oedipal phase, when oral matters dominate. Mother is so connected with food in the child's mind that, in regard to issues that will later date back to this time, food will remain a metaphor for mother. We thus already see how sexual issues, issues of autonomy, and eating become intertwined.[2]

Assuming that a girl's very early psychological development contributes to a later anorexia, the basic condition is her early connection between sexual feelings and her sense of self on the one hand and, on the other, the girl's dependent relationship with her mother, as epitomized by the feeding situation.

This extremely early primary oedipal conflict can be expected to be generated more often when the baby girl is both in close contact with her father—inducing early intense sexual awareness—and with her mother—strengthening the bond of dependence. Such intensely emotional, close-knit families are indeed characteristic of those in which anorexic children appear. Evidence shows further that implicitly or explicitly there is stress on choosing between the parents (Minuchin 1974).

In a practical sense, the girl's response is one of becoming "Mama's good little girl." She is extremely dependent, an extension of her mother really, being compliant in every way to assure that she will not lose the security she requires. It is worth mentioning that at this stage such compliant behavior receives a good deal of adult reinforcement as well. Without being in touch with her sexuality, which might bring inner tension, and without feeling the strength of self to act more independently, such a "good girl" remains thusly tied to her mother into her childhood. (She is also often mildly to severely obese at this time, demonstrating her further allegiance to mother in oral terms.)

An example of how one such early compromise appears to an observer is in the case of Peggy (Galenson and Roiphe 1977; cf. chapter 4, this volume). At age fifteen and three-fourths months, Peggy demonstrated awareness of anatomical differences between the sexes. Peggy did not draw attention to any interest she might have had in her father after this. The reaction Galenson and Roiphe noted was that she became her mother's subdued, compliant little girl, patterning herself after her mother without conspicuous signs of separation/individuation.

This pattern of behavior would be expected to continue right through the classical oedipal age without signs of conflict, since the little girl has firmly repressed her sexual feelings and does not have the degree of ego organization needed to approach the tasks that are normally worked out in the classical stage. Indeed, Sours (1974) points out that the most severely disturbed anorexics have a history of no obvious oedipal behavior.

Thus we see that being "Mama's good little girl" has become a trade-off: the girl earns her mother's continuing care but is not a (gender-defined) individual in her own mind. Whatever independence/autonomy she does allow herself, her separation/individuation is shaky because she cannot advance without intense oedipal conflict. Often she will not permit herself to have even girl friends as she clings to her mother before adolescence. If she does allow friendships in childhood, she suddenly dissolves them as adolescence approaches (Palazzoli 1978).

[It is understandable why most cases emerge at adolescence. The physical changes of adolescence make her sexuality apparent. The precarious balance breaks down. Her cultural support also breaks down as the expectation is suddenly that she will break the apron strings and become independent. Yet she has never achieved a prior sense of real selfness that would allow autonomy, nor has she ever gained inner permission for her own sexuality.

Her initial response to the intensified sexual impulses she feels is to follow her old pattern and try to deny them. That is why anorexics typically develop amenorrhea months *before* they stop eating (Thomä 1967), as opposed to the physiologically explainable order where amenorrhea would follow self-starvation.

Finally drawing on the resources of her primary oedipal ego organization, the girl reacts by becoming "anorexic": she gives up mother/food to gain a degree of autonomy. Desperately, as with constant activity, she strives to prove that she can survive without her mother. At the same time, by losing weight she minimizes her feminine form, denying her sexuality. Along with sexual repression, this appeases her mother by reaffirming her position as a nonrival. There is also the self-punitive aspect to it; feeling guilty over her sexual feelings and independence, she cuts herself off from the symbol of her mother's caretaking, rejecting food before her mother can withdraw it.]

[The extreme conflict behind her behavior also shows up in the girls' inconsistencies. Often the girl will hide secret caches of food, the giving up of good (mother) not meant to be self-destructive. Also she will symbolically display her sexuality in safe ways that are never followed through such as buying very feminine clothes but then keeping them in a closet and never wearing them. She wants to strike out independently and to enjoy her femininity, but she is trapped by her guilt and fears and lack of ego development.

In understanding how girls become anorexic we can also see why boys, by and large, do not. They have a different set of primary oedipal conflicts, although the boy may grow up burdened with difficult leftovers from that period. He has separation/individuation problems and is as prone as his sisters to oral frustration, but what is different for most boys is that *they do not link up sexuality with simultaneous rejection by themselves of both mother and autonomy.*]

A boy's sexual feelings do not make him his mother's rival.

Instead, the pattern we have seen is one where to overcome his fears of engulfment the two-year-old boy splits off sexuality and autonomy together from dependency, distancing himself from the object of his desire. When, however, a mother is both overwhelmingly seductive and controlling, he may not be able to overcome his desires and fears enough to make such a split. Herein lies the origin of male anorexia when it does occur. Since he has not gained enough autonomy or moved close enough to his father for successful self-modeling, such a boy will have a weakly formed ego and sense of gender. A second solution therefore available to him is to avoid engulfment by making his father the object of his sexual strivings. This tenuous adjustment, which carries much conflict and confusion, is the reason that male anorexia develops only in the context of acute gender identity problems and why the prognosis for male anorexics in treatment is particularly grave (Sours 1974, cf. chapter 14). Unless such a boy is able to consolidate a sense of male identity and role during the classical oedipal stage, his only recourse to avoid engulfment can seem to him to be a denial of his need for his mother. Since such a condition is again established by breakdowns in the earliest stages of ego formation, when orality predominates, once again the mother is symbolically connected with food. By denying food the boy can simultaneously reject both his sexual attraction and his dependency urges toward his mother and stave off the engulfment she threatens.

This explains another difference in the form anorexia takes in girls and in boys when it does affect them. The girl denies her hunger to deny the fact that she has dependency feelings, but the boy feels the hunger and takes pride in resisting it, gaining ego strength from holding off mother, the engulfer.

Yet by turning his sexual urges from his mother he loses the ability to model his sense of gender and identity on his father. And keeping his mother at a distance, he cannot pattern after her fully either. The subsequent inability to take on a masculine role deprives him of support from his peer group and adults and thus keeps him from enjoying the kind of acceptability the pre-anorexic girl maintains for herself during latency. *Therefore, the male anorexic may become symptomatic even before adolescence.* The work of Falstein, Feinstein and Judas (1956) as well as that of Sours (1974) bears out these speculations (quoted in chapter 14).

Thus we see how understanding the forces that shape the early ego can lead to a comprehension of the causes of both the anorexic condition in the female and the rare case in the male. Before considering clinical evidence for the primary oedipal complex as the basic determinant of the anorexic syndrome, previous theories must be put into perspective.

Identification of Anorexic Behavior

We begin with a brief review of the historical setting of attention to anorexia. Palazzoli (1978) tells us that the ancients probably were aware of anorexic behavior. She points out that later descriptions of "witches" and other unusual women during the Middle Ages demonstrate that the anorexic condition probably attracted notice then. However, medical descriptions were offered only much later, in Italy and in England. Simone Porta in the sixteenth century gave a general account. The first detailed description, by Richard Morton in 1689, listed the hallmark signs: amenorrhea, lack of appetite, constipation, extreme emaciation, overactivity, and indifference to the condition.

Toward the end of the nineteenth century, Lasègue (1873) cited anorexia as a modern clinical entity. He noted in his Victorian time the close-knit familial setting that Bruch (1973), Minuchin (1974), and Palazzoli (1978) point to now as typical for anorexics. Gull (1874) named anorexia, drawing attention to it in the English-speaking world.

Most of the work on anorexia for a long time after Gull was devoted to description and categorization. Freud (1905) noticed anorexic behavior in his patient, Dora, after her sexual encounter with a father-figure, Herr K. Freud concluded that there was a relationship between depression, the giving up of sexuality, and anorexia. Diagnosis of anorexia proved a problem, however, because the anorexic syndrome could be found in cases varying from otherwise near-normal behavior[3] all the way to schizophrenia. Sours (1974) finally recognized the specific syndrome that could appear in combination with various other conditions. Etiology remained perplexing.

Theories That Have So Far Contributed to Understanding Anorexia Nervosa

A physiological explanation for anorexia was the first to be widely accepted. In 1914, Simmonds discovered a disease of the pituitary that caused emaciation. For a long time afterward, anorexia was regarded as symptomatic of Simmonds' disease. Treatment was based upon endocrinal manipulation and surgery. Only gradually did mounting evidence lead interest back to psychological factors. Even today Halmi (1978) raises the question as to whether physiological factors might predispose certain individuals to anorexia. Halmi's chief concern, however, is treatment for harm done by malnutrition.[4] Summarizing the evidence of endocrinal and neurological disorder in anorexia, Drossman (1980) discovered little of causative significance. The anorexic's willful avoidance of food and resistance to treatment, Palazzoli emphasizes, seldom appear in cases of physical illness.

As anorexia became recognized as a psychological problem, psychoanalytic thinking about anorexia centered chiefly on oral aspects of early experience or on the relationship between mother and child. Benedek (1936) and Thomä (1967) among others, traced the oral-aggressive fantasies of anorexic patients to early disturbance in the feeding situation. However, this presents a problem as the total explanation of the anorexic syndrome because it is not gender-specific. A boy's experience in the early feeding situation can be as frustrating as that of a girl. The early genito-oral connections with ego differentiation and interpersonal relations with both parents would seem hard to ignore in theorizing about anorexia, but so they have been.

In keeping with her concept that the sexual element can be ignored as a causative matter in anorexia, Palazzoli believes that the early relationship with the mother is solely responsible for proneness to anorexia. She sees an oral-incorporative basis for avoiding preservation of bad objects or continued taking in of bad objects. She states (1978) that contrary to the speculation of Anna Freud in 1965 (and others) that early feeding disturbances account for the later emergence of anorexia, disturbed relations with the mother produce an *oralized expression* of what is essentially a power struggle. Palazzoli counts herself as a follower of Melanie Klein in seeing anorexia as an effort to deny cannibalistic impulses to destroy the mother. In explaining why these impulses would be so strong, Palazzoli comments on the feelingless way in which a typical mother of an anorexic presents the breast to her infants. This characteristic of the mother does not explain differences between the child who grows up to be anorexic and the same mother's other children who do not become anorexic. Furthermore, the typical description parents give Palazzoli and other workers is of a child whose early feeding seemed very satisfying to all observers. The anorexic's pattern includes periods of being quite round and even obese prior to the anorexia and sometimes after the onset of anorexia, in alternation with it. Bruch (1973) even states that bulimia always accompanies anorexia. Even if Palazzoli's explanations were close to the cause of eating disorders in these patients, that still would encompass a range of behavior and would not specifically describe the cause of the anorexic pattern.

Clear-cut evidence that physiological factors are secondary appeared at least in a single case with Wiener's report of identical twins (1976). By definition genetically, and from their history environmentally as well, they were physiologically indistinguishable, but were nonetheless discordant for anorexia. (Psychological explanations of the case fit with primary oedipal theory. See chapter 14.)

Ceaser believes that anorexia and bulimia are both attempts at restitution following object loss. He is struck by the oral-incorporative issue in four anorexic patients of his whose mothers had died of a wasting illness. "The patients were unable to accept the loss of their mothers, due in part to the role of aggression in their relationship. Each patient's reaction to her mother's cachexia and death contained striking guilt feelings and revealed excessive ambivalence" (1977:482).

Again, we are left wondering why such dynamics would apply so frequently to females only and why the feelings about the mother caused anorexia (as was true in all four cases) only when a girl encountered her own sexuality years after her mother had died.

Bruch (1973) looked at oral incorporation from a different perspective. She proposed that anorexic patients have an acquired perceptual disturbance characterized by a failure to distinguish hunger sensations from other bodily needs. She hypothesizes that this confusion resulted from inappropriate maternal responses to the infant's cues when the infant was in a state of nutritional need. Such a developmental defect in body identity, to Bruch, underlies what she observed in true anorexia nervosa: the prideful, relentless pursuit of thinness as a means of conquering an overwhelming sense of ineffectiveness and lack of autonomy.

This implied a relationship between ability to distinguish bodily sensations and the issue of autonomy. From primary oedipal theory we can glean an interpretation of why such difficulty in distinguishing bodily needs (other than in cases of mental retardation) appears along with acute problems in separation/individuation: the child cannot permit itself perception of its own bodily needs if it wishes or feels compelled to maintain a sense of fusion with its mother. Inside/outside must be blurred. It is then understandable why the symptom Bruch emphasizes should be part of a syndrome produced by sexual conflict.

Jessner and Abse (1960) found that anorexics project relationships with both a feeding and a starving mother in the transference. This is background for applying Mahler's observations about toddlers during the rapprochement subphase, in seeing that period of life as related to subsequent anorexia. However, we know that both imagos of the mother are mental constructs that the child creates. Splitting is useful for ordering experience when one's mental equipment is still very primitive. Kramer (1977) cautions us that sensitivity to the child's intrapsychic processes is needed in trying to understand its development, not to see transferences as simply reflections of parental behavior. Transference manifestations reflect *inner reality*, which is an amalgam of the child's experiences with its wishes and fears. These must include the psychic events of the primary oedipal conflict.

Nonetheless Masterson bases a useful system of therapy on Mahler's codification of the separation/individuation process. Noting that the anorexic accepts pleasure for herself only in the context of a symbiotic mother–child dyad, he emphasizes the interplay between pathological ego-rewarding and ego-withdrawing aspects of her functioning. He helps the patient to see how rewards are used defensively to avoid anxiety and pain in experiencing withdrawal from the mother, the "abandonment depression." Yet, why should needing mother less cause such anxiety and pain? Why should feeling sexual automatically mean giving up mother? And why should the child's awareness of being sexual at adolescence be the specific reason to revert to this exact oral expression of her conflict, along with the rest of the anorexic syndrome? Intuitively it is understood that these matters are connected. *The next step is recognizing that the anorexic crisis is a restatement of the whole conflict of the patient's second year of life, although the part played by separation/ individuation can be seen conceptually in itself.* The relationship between the girl's need for separation/individuation and her special feeling for her father can be glimpsed in two anorexic cases of Masterson's. He includes them in a study of aftereffects of treatment of adolescents (1980). Marie showed minimal residual impairment and Jean a greater degree.

The therapeutic work with Marie had centered on separation/individuation from her mother. Eighteen months afterward, she was free of anorexic symptoms. The report emphasized her feeling confident of being able to say no to boys and to end relationships with them without depression. Although the primary oedipal conflict was not explored with Marie, significant therapeutic work was done with her father. The father came to understand that he had fused Marie in his mind with her namesake, a sister of his who had died of anorexia. "Gradually he was able to separate the two, which enabled him to become a father to his daughter" (1980:111).

On the other hand, there is no statement about successful work with the father in the case of Jean, who was followed up after six years: "Since her discharge, her principal symptom had been sexual acting out. . . . She was currently seeing an older married man" (1980:134).

Other factors may well have entered in, but it is striking how the cases differed in the therapeutic program and in outcome. Marie's relationship with her mother was deeply explored, but also her father was helped to change his unconscious signals to Marie. Marie was then able to proceed with her life with little impairment. Jean came to feel more independent of her mother and thus could give up her need for either anorexia or obesity. She no longer needed to deal on the primitive symbolic level of the primary oedipal phase; however, the same issues were in focus, now at the classical oedipal level. "She had to avoid her mother" as the price for having a father-figure (an older, married man). When note is taken of these data, they suggest that the object-relations problems of the anorexic are triadic and not dyadic in nature.

In appreciation of the importance of the separation/individuation process in the anorexic syndrome, Palazzoli (1978) is one who points to the girl's new roundness of form as she comes into adolescence as a reminder of identification with her mother. This could not apply to the many girls who are obese, thus very round, before they become anorexic. It is secondary sexual characteristics that are of real concern as these girls enter adolescence. Her roundness of form would not mean anything horrific to the girl if the significance of femininity, i.e., sexuality, were not included. Nonetheless, even if it were possible for the roundness of maturity to be a significant factor without reference to sexuality, it would not explain the inevitability of other aspects of the anorexic syndrome that are also so much part of it, such as secrecy of rituals (e.g., in bulimia), guilt-ridden, compulsive gum-chewing, a primitive space/time sense, anal preoccupation, such as the use of laxatives and emphasis upon cleanliness, interest in clothes without the wearing of pretty things she owns, or the feeding of others and the interest in studying gourmet recipes. A total syndrome that we have seen makes sense as a reflection of the primary oedipal phase.

There is more to be said about the role of physical change at adolescence. Shainess (1979) finds the bodily changes of the girl important because they seem to be a point of difference from boys. This is true enough but does not make clear why it is those bodily changes plus increased awareness of her sexuality that together precipitate a girl's anorexia.

In considering the situation of boys, it is also true that boys have their own difficulties with changes in their bodies, contrary to Palazzoli's estimate. A lack of muscular coordination as the boy has sudden growth spurts, his new hairiness, his lack of conscious control in wet dreams and unruly erections, etc., give the boy ample cause for bodily concerns. One could imagine that many boys might respond to these conditions by attempting to constrain growth by not eating. Another possibility would be for them to become obese in an effort to control the growth process. Still another possibility would be to be obese as an effort to avoid separation from mother, i.e., to remain tied to her through oral incorporation. All of these behaviors are seen clinically in males, but the fact is that eating problems are very much less common among males than among females. Possible reasons for this disparity will be explored further below, but basically the primary oedipal situation does not produce in many boys an inner conflict over wanting father for himself and feeling rivalrous with mother. Shainess (1979) accurately predicts that if she saw a male anorexic he would prove to have severe gender identity problems. We have seen how such a negative oedipus can emerge as a defensive resolution for the primary oedipal conflict, by including severe gender identity problems.

Chediak also sees a possible connection between the separation/individuation phase and the etiology of anorexia. Thinking particularly of girls, he starts from the facts that consolidation of gender identity continues throughout adolescence and that "dieting which triggers the anorectic syndrome relates to sexuality in early adolescence, e.g., menarche, beginning of dating, masturbation, desire to be attractive, feelings of fright associated with actual or fantasied sexual activity, promiscuity, etc." (1977:465).

Chediak, then, refers to Mahler's suggestion that the intrapsychic task of becoming a separate individual is generally more difficult for girls than for boys during toddlerhood and that it is because a girl's lack of a penis increases the disappointment and ambivalent ties to mother typical of all children at the age. We know that a boy's possession of a penis does not forestall his being more likely prey to gender confusion than is a girl and that when a boy becomes anorexic he is likely to be prepubertal. Therefore, it must be clear that there is more than penis envy involved in the sexual aspects of conflict over separation/individuation. Also of interest is that penis envy is not overt enough in female anorexics to be mentioned as a major characteristic in the various descriptions of the typical syndrome.

Chediak further refers to Kowalski (1976) on Barnett's theory that girls' study of the vaginal orifice results in their finding it mysterious and uncontrollable and thus anxiety-provoking. However, as Rado (1933) points out, *any explanation of the girl's attitudes toward her body must emphasize the universal fact of good feelings in her genitals.* If that is kept in mind, the problematic feelings a girl has about her body can be understood as stemming from conflict, and then the nature of that conflict can be known.

Bruch (1973) looked to cultural factors to explain the incidence of anorexia.[5] She was interested in doing so because, although the condition was described so early in medical history, she had been aware of a recent increase in its incidence. The cultural factor that she thought contributed to the increased incidence of the illness was present-day emphasis upon slimness. Bruch realizes that this factor would not explain why some who diet as teenagers become anorexic while the vast majority do not. Furthermore, it is hard to see why the emphasis upon slimness that permeates the mass media would affect mainly middle-class females, among whom is the highest incidence of anorexia. Finally, the cultural message in fostering slimness is to create maximum sexual attractiveness, a message that anorexic girls deny in their symptomatic syndrome. Indeed, it might be the other way around: that the cultural emphasis upon slimness as a feature of sexual attractiveness coexists with other factors in the culture, such as sexual permissiveness, which also impinge upon the population and are the real cause of the increase in anorexia. Furthermore, anorexic girls are often specifically concerned about having an appearance of abdominal bloat and looking pregnant, which is not connected with cultural questions of overall slimness.

Another cultural factor that Bruch lists as contributing to the increase in incidence of anorexia is indeed the recent increase in sexual freedom. Bruch mentions that, while commendable for other reasons, sex education in the schools has triggered the onset of anorexia in some of her cases. The present-day child does not have much chance to slow down her developing interest in sexuality until she can handle it well. For the girl who is particularly conflicted, this can mean great susceptibility to a resurgence of her primary oedipal complex.

Another factor affecting the rise in incidence of anorexia may be the increasing number of nuclear families in our culture. These are particularly seen in the upper middle class, from which most anorexics come. Bruch (1979) tells of a study done in England. In schools with children from upper middle-class families, the incidence of anorexia was one in two hundred; in schools with children from working-class families, the incidence of anorexia was one in three thousand. Sours (1980b) and Crisp (1977a) note that in the relatively rare cases when girls from so-called blue collar families are afflicted with anorexia, the history usually shows sexual traumatization. Sours specifies "rape and other aggressive sexual encounters." Palazzoli brings out the point that the culture of working-class families supports protection of girls from sexual involvement to a greater degree than that of upper middle-class families. On top of this cultural difference, small nuclear families, which are more prevalent in the upper middle class, foster the most intense emotional involvements among their members, and this could maximize the sexual aspects, too.

A powerful cultural effect may come from the current emphasis upon youth at all ages, as Adler (1984) points out. She cites two aspects. First, mothers of teenagers do not look as much older or relatively asexual today as mothers of previous generations did. Our culture supports a degree of blatancy in sexual interest which may be reflected in a mother's behavior, thus increasing a daughter's sense of parity with her mother and fostering the continuation of old oedipal confusion. The mother's wariness about the daughter's rivalry with her could also be stimulated by her own blurring of generational boundaries in her pursuit of eternal youth, which is stimulated so much through the media. This situation could lend a surreal quality to the daughter's primary oedipal predisposition to see herself on a par with her mother if she dares to think of herself as a separate person from her mother, plunging the daughter into an illness which dramatizes primary oedipal concerns.

The second observation of Adler is that even grandmothers do not appear to age as obviously as they used to do. Therefore part of the natural preparation for death as part of the cycle of life is diminished, increasing anxiety over separation. This might also be within the ken of an early adolescent girl in our culture, adding to the intensity of her conflicts.

These considerations about family structure help also in understanding why anorexia does not appear to occur in tribal societies (Bruch 1973). In the first place, such societies, although they exist in diverse patterns, tend to provide extended family structures rather than close-knit nuclear families. Second, to maintain their cultures, they tend to provide clearly understood guidelines and controls on sexual behavior, many separating male and female parents during the child's earliest years. Girls in such societies thus do not contend with ambiguous intense relationships within the parental–child triad. Nor do those girls contend with feelings of almost complete responsibility for their own sexual behavior. These conditions are opposite of what a child experiences in the upper middle class of modern urban society.

Lasègue said in 1873, after citing the upper socioeconomic class status of his anorexic patients: "This description would however, be incomplete without reference to their home life. Both the patient and her family form a tightly knit whole, and we obtain a false picture of the disease if we limit our observations to the patients alone" (Palazzoli 1978:5)

This quotation could have come from Bruch, Palazzoli, or Minuchin in discussing the current view. Minuchin and Palazzoli find another characteristic: indirect communication within the family, making it difficult for members to deal with messages. Also, the identified patient becomes the focus of great concern through her illness, which, as a secondary gain, gives her a sense of power. The family dynamics no doubt exist as these authors describe them. However, such dynamics do not alone explain why a particular girl in the family develops anorexia or why others in the family do not, or why the anorexic syndrome includes all the symptomatology typical of the condition.

The closeness of the family becomes important in understanding the nature of anorexia when we put it together with Thomä's point (1961) supporting Minuchin that there is intense loyalty struggle within families of anorexic patients. Overtly or covertly, he finds, there is pressure on the child to side with one parent against the other. Viewing a child in a close-knit, nuclear family in which there are strong messages from both parents demanding special loyalty, we can imagine a child being drawn into these dynamics early in her life. Why a particular daughter is caught by these pressures might have something to do with her unique sensitivity to expressions of feeling when she is very young. She might also feel herself especially involved because she is what I call the "self-child" of the mother—the one who most resembles the mother according to the mother's own perception.

Sylvester (1945) describes a child anorexic who was identified in the family by the time she was two as being most like her mother. I have seen several instances in which a daughter's resemblance to her mother made for confusion in the feelings of both mother and daughter. For the mother it seemed to resuscitate her own early difficulties, which she would try to rework in her relationship to the daughter, who reminded her of herself when very young. For the daughter, this circumstance seemed to heighten her own confusion about who was who participating in the oedipal drama, as she tried to establish separation/individuation from the mother. Powers (1981) tells of an anorexic patient who resembled her father's family and who for this reason was treated seductively by her father and rivalrously by her mother. Masterson's case, Marie, received special messages from her father, who unconsciously identified her with his sister. The qualities of a child might from its earliest days compellingly uncover or rekindle oedipal concerns of the parents. Thus, a particular child may get different signals from the parents than do the other children in the family when it comes to handling its own oedipal feelings and separation/individuation.

Conrad put the situation exactly in telling about her work with families of anorexics: "The child had a pathological but necessary function to fill in the family, that of taking care of the father for mother, and keeping the parents apart because of their fear of intimacy. This role reversal between mother and daughter represented a blurring of generational boundaries" (1974:491). Blurring of generational boundaries would keep a daughter from being able to resolve her oedipal conflicts even during the classical oedipal period.

There are two more points to note about the family constellation. First, Bruch underscores how utterly helpless the anorexic feels and what this means to her behavior in the family. Palazzoli believes that adolescence stimulates the girl's desperate efforts to establish a sense of personal power, that adolescents typically rebel and anorexia can fit such a need. It is evident that the anorexic develops a sense of power in her family through her insistence upon her symptom. However, the power that she shows first is in commanding her own body. She develops a sense of power in relation to the family through her new-found importance only as her illness develops. The power issue, which is not gender-specific, provides only secondary gain in anorexia as far as family dynamics are concerned.

The last point about family constellation is that anorexics are usually first- or second-born children. Considering how often impregnation fantasies turn out to be part of the symptomatology (Sours 1974), it is not surprising that so many anorexics were children who were followed by siblings. The case studies of Behn-Eschenburg and Kleeman (chapter 7) and Sylvester's young patient (chapter 14) show how stimulating it is to a small child to witness its mother's pregnancy. In my experience the anorexic syndrome can be associated with a girl's mother having been pregnant while the patient was in the primary oedipal phase.

All the theories under review here point up important contributory factors to the development of anorexia. However, most people presenting these different theories comment on a continuing sense of mystery that lets them know that there is yet more to be understood. The crucial questions of why this child, why this syndrome, why so seldom a male child, remain impossible to understand until the workings of the primary oedipal complex are appreciated. Before looking more closely at the way in which the anorexic syndrome reflects the child's development during the primary oedipal phase, it is necessary to examine the evidence that oedipal concerns are of vital importance to these patients.

Anorexia and Sexuality

The onset of amenorrhea often appears before the oral symptoms develop in anorexics (Thomä 1961; Sours 1974). This would seem to be a clear sign that problems with sexuality are basic in this illness. Sandler and Dare (1970) mention oedipal concerns and instinctual pressures of adolescence as the precipitating cause of the condition. In his treatment of anorexics, Crisp (1977b) explains to them that their dieting is a metabolic device for reducing scary sexual feelings while trying to handle attachment to mother.

Nonetheless, many do not give credence to the importance of sexuality in anorexia. Palazzoli devotes a chapter in *Self-Starva-*

tion (1978) to the reasons why she does not consider sexual matters to be primary. She is persuaded by the fact that there is a massive turning away from sexual interest on the part of anorexics. Examining this issue throws into relief the primary oedipal conflict in anorexia when we explore and find that sexuality is the basic problem for these patients.

The literature on anorexia provides much evidence on the subject. Palazzoli's is of interest because we know she did not select it to prove this point. In the context of family interaction when one member is an identified (anorexic) patient, Palazzoli quotes the following clinical material:

One characteristic of these parents, that has also been noted by other authors, including particularly Minuchin and Barcai, is their reluctance to assume personal leadership of the family. In particular each of the parents feels a need to blame his or her decision on others. Here are a few examples [italics and asides according to Palazzoli]:
Mother: "I don't let her wear miniskirts because I know her father doesn't like them."
Father: "I have always backed my wife up. I feel it would be wrong to contradict her."

Mother: "My husband had decided to spend his holiday by himself in our country cottage [a place she loved herself] but I was simply forced to follow with the whole family and my old parents *on account of my father*. You see, Father wasn't well and he had to be near a doctor." [Her husband was a doctor].
Father: "My wife and I never went out because Angela [their elder daugher] protested. Now we have Anna [the i.p.]. How can we even feel like going out?

The arguments used in the following two examples are even more intricate:
Mother: "Angela came back from school with a peculiar look in her eyes. 'What's wrong with your eyes?' I asked. 'Did you get hit?' She told me that a school friend had applied some brown eye-shadow. 'Ugh,' I said, 'How can you put on brown eye-shadow? What horrible taste!'"
Therapist: "Were you disgusted by the brown colour? Would blue have been all right?"
Mother: "Well . . . the fact is that my husband cannot stand girls who look like painted hussies."

The same mother also produced another gem. Her husband had accused her of living like a recluse. It appeared that the patient, Anna, had for some years been friends with a classmate, Patrizia, and that the two families knew each other.

Father: "But *whom* are *you* friends with? With no one. You have even stopped seeing Patrizia's mother."

Mother: "Well, how could I be friends with Patrizia's mother? You know perfectly well that Angela [the elder daughter] can't stand Patrizia's father" (1978:208–209).

In all four instances, which Palazzoli presents in terms of showing the nature of leadership in the family, her point is that the way in which issues are handled is always indirect. Interestingly, in all four examples it is the mother who is carrying the message. Also, in all four the message is strong: daughters and fathers had better not get too close. It is worth a bit of interpretation to see this.

For example, in the case of the daughter wanting to wear mini-skirts, the father makes a weak statement that he will not contradict the mother, rather than an assertion on his part that the mother reads him correctly in what she says. In the second example, the mother permits herself to be close to her own father only through her husband, denying any feeling on her own account or of her father's wish to be with her. In the third example it is blatant that the father responds to sexual provocation and the mother is concerned about it in reference to the daughter. In the fourth case, again the mother's behavior shows that she is comfortable about daughters and father-people being kept apart. When the mothers seem to be saying, "Do not dress in the way father disapproves," the girl hears who is doing the complaining. The issues are the girl's seductiveness, the father's vulnerability, and the mother's control. The message is the mother's injunction to her daughter that girls must not want their fathers. Interestingly, Palazzoli picks exactly the examples that reveal the underlying problem in order to show how the family operates its indirect communication. These mothers are very clear in their basic messages, warding off daughters' and fathers' closeness.[6] The issues are both sexual and oedipal.

Another interesting example of this sort comes from Minuchin and Rosman. They present a composite picture of families at the start of treatment:

[Having set a meal for the family] the therapist leaves the room and asks the parents to get the child to eat, emphasizing in extreme cases that if the child doesn't eat she may die. This dramatic approach serves to draw out the ineffective ways in which the family interacts. For example, the mother may consistently mollify the father's demands that the child eat. Even though she wants the child to eat, she can't help protecting the child from the father's demands. Therefore, he redoubles his demands and the mother increases her efforts to soften them with conciliatory comments. (1980:4)

Even with the daughter's life on the line, mother's chief message is that the daughter should not do what will please the father with her body. It seems fair to assume that when so sensitive a set of clinicians as Rosman, Palazzoli, and Minuchin select these examples to show how the family works, they are intuitively responding to a subject for communication that is typical in the anorexic's life with her parents.

We can see that the same oedipal issues we observe from our outside perspective are paramount from the girl's point of view, too, by examining accounts of anorexics. In a poignant statement of the anorexic girl's plight, Palazzoli offers an autobiographical sketch, which she reproduces exactly as it was given to her by a patient. The girl starts with a short preamble describing her early childhood. This is followed by a longer statement of how her illness developed. In the first part she takes herself back to middle childhood and tells how her sister and her mother, the nuns at school, and her father all looked down upon her. The only person who stood up for her on one occasion that she can remember was the maid. This is in contrast to the more frequent picture one gets of the anorexic girl as a very "good" child. We do not know whether this child seemed as naughty in the eyes of her parents as she was in her own eyes. However, we would expect the typical "good Mommie's girl" to harbor such bad feelings about herself since guilt is a major force in precipitating her, in reality, compliant, behavior. In any case, I wish to quote the paragraph with which she ends the reminiscences of her childhood:

At home I was rarely praised for anything. One day I went into my father's study which was a most mysterious place to me. He was writing at his desk.

Suddenly he looked up and smiled "Come over here, skinny, let's see if you have grown." I approached him warily. "Come along now, lift up your skirts," he said. I obeyed with a vague feeling of embarrassment, remembering the nun's oft-repeated warnings that little girls who lift their dresses go straight to hell. "Ah, I can see that your little bottom has grown a little fatter," he said, tapping my bare thigh. "Come over here, let me give you some caramels." And he opened the drawer of his desk. I felt deeply ashamed but happy. I took the sweets and went out into the garden. I straightened my skirt properly, lay down on the ground and thought: "My father and I will both go to hell." I was certain my father had done me a great injury. I didn't eat the sweets he had given me." (1978:170)

That this is her own idea of the point of the early recollections is reinforced in what she says about the onset of her illness. She starts by describing herself as being withdrawn and living in a world of fantasy, getting along poorly in school, but with considerable drive to achieve. She speaks of wanting to be clever "for the Lord's sake." She suffered because she did not feel as good as Jesus would have liked. She mentions her tantrums, her envy of her sister's seeming successes, and her idealization of her father, who was away at war.

However, when her father returned she experienced great disappointment and reminded herself of rejections that her father had dealt her in the past. The desire to please him seemed to be swept aside. In school she did poorly at this point, to her father's great disappointment. It is clear throughout that her father was interested in her schooling while her mother seemed more interested in her general behavior. At her school she admired an excellent student who appeared very slim. She felt herself inadequate and gross compared with this person. She began to try to identify with the slim, successful student. At the same time she developed contemptuous thoughts about her father. She then says: "And when I saw that I could get nowhere with him, I turned increasingly to my mother" (1978:183). However, that was troubled, too. Her mother misunderstood her. They had unending quarrels. Her wishes were almost always, in her perception, set aside by her mother.

Crisis developed on an occasion when she witnessed a violent quarrel between her parents and became aware that they followed this with lovemaking. She says of the aftermath of the quarrel before the parents became reconciled: "Little by little we[7] managed to calm her. Father reappeared for supper, looking furious and not saying a word. Mother turned her back on him, *refusing to eat.*[8] And all of us went to bed in silence" (1978:184).

It was immediately after this incident that the patient became aware of her parents' lovemaking and realized that their arguments were a preamble to their becoming sexual with each other. After recording this, she exclaimed, "I would never be like my mother . . . a woman who had gone to seed and had grown fat" (1978:186).

The family was to return to a place where they formerly lived and where the girl had felt less conflicted. In relation to spending the summer there, she says:

In the summer we all went back to S. Now I had started eating, and was putting on weight to my parents' obvious delight. *My father seemed particularly pleased with me.* I had asked a very clever school-friend to join us, but I felt rather ashamed of our poor house, and right from the start made a point of doing all the tidying up so that the place would not look too shabby. (1978:188)

This respite was short-lived. The friend who was invited pressed the girl about thoughts for her future, which was the last straw. The sexual pressures she had just seemed to escape by going back to the scene of her childhood were reactivated by the threat of growing up. At that point, she tells us: "At supper that night I refused to eat more than [the friend] did. My mother was surprised. 'What does this mean? Only a few days ago you were eating like a horse. You have put on weight at last, . . .' and she looked angrily at my friend. 'You are just a copycat,' she spat at me" (1978:189).

Ignoring her mother's hostile tone, she decided that her mother wanted her fat and that she would resist. Her dream was to be slender but academically successful and independent. The father's interest in her academics is again to be kept in mind in understanding her pattern of pleasing him in a nonphysical way. She continues, "From time to time one of our neighbors would exclaim: 'My goodness, how thin you have grown. And to think that you used to be just like your mother!' That was enough. I intensified my efforts" (1978:189).

She completes her account by telling of her return to the city where she had come to recognize her parents' sexual involvement and where she had had her first anorexic reaction: "We returned to the city. The new term was about to start. I felt confident. My father shook his head and muttered: 'You used to be so pretty, and now you look like a scarecrow!' 'Pretty was I? You just like fat women. Of course you do, you can do what you please with them. And I know what pleases you most!'" (1978:190).

At this point it was clear to the father that she was anorexic, and he brought her for treatment.

The sexual and oedipal factors are clear enough in this account. They are also in Ceaser's four patients, each of whom lost her mother after a wasting case of cancer. Ceaser stresses the dyadic object-relations aspects of experiencing such a trauma. Without minimizing the importance of this to each of the patients, it is still noteworthy that the losses of their mothers occurred when they were respectively three, eight, twelve, and sixteen years old. All four reacted to the loss of the mother, immediately, by resort to vigorous oral incorporation, becoming obese. Anorexia was precipitated "at the time of the first kiss, intercourse or fellatio" (1977:482). Ceaser sees the girl's conflict as stemming from ambivalence over closeness, yet much more is implied in kisses, intercourse, and fellatio than the idea of closeness. They are all sexual activities involving a man. "Stuffing" themselves was sufficient to keep the girls feeling psychologically comfortable until they confronted their sexual wishes. It was then in each case that the girl was compelled by unconscious reasons to reject her former sign of wanting to keep mother with her and she stopped eating. Such material demonstrates how pervasive oedipal issues in the family are for girls who become anorexic and how traumatic it is for them to meet their own sexual impulses.

Palazzoli (1978) tells us in discussing therapeutic technique with these patients that it is important not to press interpretations about sexual feelings. She speaks of this resulting in "dire consequences." This extreme judgment underscores the importance of sexuality to these people. In fact, Crisp (1977a) reports good results in treating anorexics on the basis that they are punishing their bodies for sexual impulses. Sours says of typical development in the most serious cases of anorexia that the girl tries to postpone entering into early adolescence, but "heterosexual fantasies emerge causing her to look to the mother of early childhood for protection. . . . Her ego ideal is that of a sexless, affectless and perfect autonomous being" (1974:572).

The teasing question is, why do heterosexual fantasies drive the girl back to "the mother of early childhood?" With this much evidence of the causative significance of sexuality in anorexia, it is appropriate to consider evidence that the anorexic syndrome is a reactivation of the primary oedipal complex.

12 Anorexia and the Primary Oedipal Phase

The Nature of the Anorexic Syndrome

Sours (1974) reviews evidence that anorexia appears in a variety of emotional settings ranging from the relatively mild to severe, including schizophrenia. In degree of intensity corresponding to the severity of the refusal to eat, anorexia is accompanied by a characteristic list of other symptoms. We shall learn that this syndrome is a manifestation of the primary oedipal complex.

In establishing that anorexia is a syndrome and not an isolated illness, Sours differentiates three groups of patients. The first group is the most severely disturbed. He includes here patients who have diagnoses ranging from borderline to frankly psychotic. These are the cases (along with Sours' group III: male anorexics) who may display a chaotic disorder with severe cachexia and even death through circulatory collapse.

In his thorough discussion of the developmental histories of his group I, Sours emphasizes the severity of maternal control in the patient's life and the mother's efforts at maintaining her daughter's dyadic attachment to herself. This promotes a sense of fusion between mother and daughter rather than nurturance of a separate individual. Sours further observes in these cases: "The developmental history is surprisingly lacking in [classical] oedipal phenomena. It is as though the child passes inconspicuously and calmly from senior toddlerhood to latency, with the social awareness and need for mastery of children during that time of development" (1974:572).

We can think immediately of Behn-Eschenburg's (1932) admonition that in cases in which the oedipal conflict is not clinically evident, the condition is most grave. In chapter 11, a brief quotation from Sours described the onset of anorexia in this group. Even though oedipal feelings were not recognized in these girls when they were younger, he told how heterosexual fantasies threatened what little autonomy the girls had achieved during latency.

We now consider further the question of why she turns to "the mother of early childhood" for protection from her own heterosexual fantasies, if heterosexuality has never before been of importance to her. Why would she not simply deny any interest and continue undisturbedly in her symbiosis with her mother? Or, to put it another way, *why should any adolescent's needs for separation/individuation be tied specifically to sexuality?*[1] Why should being perfect mean being sexless? The answer must be found in an earlier compromise, repressing her sexual feelings and sense of independence together in order to remain psychologically fused with her mother and thus conflict-free. Seeking perfection and affectlessness is a derivative of the primary oedipal child's dichotomous thinking and splitting mechanisms.

Sours describes a second group of anorexic patients as being much less disturbed. In these cases, he notes, oedipal behavior had been previously observed. Their symptomatology is the same as far as the anorexic syndrome is concerned, but the manifestations are less severe and their pathology in general is less grave. This clinical distinction between the first and second groups of anorexic patients makes excellent sense in terms of the theory we have been discussing. In a psychopathology determined by intensity of primary oedipal conflict, those patients who were not able to display oedipal feelings at the normal times would have been left with a more fragile ego than patients who were able to display their oedipal feelings at an earlier time but who are overwhelmed in trying to cope with the recurrence of such feelings at adolescence.

Sours' third category of anorexic patients is composed of males, who mostly present the syndrome in prepuberty or early adolescence. These patients are also gravely disturbed. They

are extremely tied to the mother with whom they identify and by whom they have been overfed. . . . Her exhortations are experienced by the child as a maternal directive to assume a more masculine role and to gratify his seductive mother as a genital male. Through food refusal and starvation a male anorexic attempts to control his sexual feelings toward the mother, to kill the incorporated mother, eliminate his ("feminine") body fat and subdue passive-feminine wishes. (1974:574)

This depiction shows the male anorexic suffering from difficulties around gender identity because of his mother's seductiveness. Sours emphasizes that, as we might expect from such core difficulties, male anorexics tend to be very ill:

Phasic food refusal and perverse pleasure—sometimes orgastic—from vomiting and bulimia are much more common in male patients, although these symptoms can also appear in the first group of patients who show serious ego defects. This combination of symptoms is usually found in patients with incorporative fantasies with aggression turned toward the self. In these cases an overt psychosis is apt to be masked by anorexia nervosa. (1974:574)

Sours' observations on male anorexics are confirmed by Falstein, Feinstein and Judas (1956). These authors also describe anorexia as part of a syndrome that appears in patients of various diagnostic groups and various depths of psychopathology.

From these studies we learn that the anorexic syndrome occurs with greater or lesser severity in accordance with the general diagnostic status of the patient. We see that the earlier and more completely oedipal feelings are repressed without being used as the basis of ego organization, the greater the pathology the patient displays. Corroboration of this view lies in the nature of the anorexic syndrome as it reflects the issues of the primary oedipal phase.

The anorexic syndrome typically includes, in addition to rejection of food and sexuality: uncertainty of bodily integrity, image, sensations, and control; severe difficulties in separation/individuation; feelings of helplessness and futility; massive denial; preoccupation with good and evil; anal preoccupation; splitting as a major defense; suicidal behavior; secrecy; kleptomania; primitive sense of space/time; hyperactivity; amenorrhea.

The place to find the anorexic syndrome is in case studies. As a starting point to recognizing the primary oedipal nature of the syndrome, we have a case of Lorand's (1943). She was a twenty-four-year-old whose anorexia began when she was twelve years of age and who did not improve under various treatment programs until her successful treatment by psychoanalysis. Although this work preceded Mahler's insights into the process of separation/individuation, Lorand treated his anorexic patient in terms of a pathological early attachment to her mother. He recognized, in addition to fright and defense against sexual drives, more diffuse disturbances in her whole personality structure. He elucidates:

What was once an oral desire for the breast and food became a craving for all that could be taken and eaten up, the mother's breast, everything the mother possessed, including the father. As this oral craving suffered increasing frustration by the mother, it became directed toward the father, charged with the same fear and guilt which were created in infancy by the frustrating mother. (1943:282)

Nonetheless, Lorand tells us:

Long after the disturbed feelings towards her mother diminished, the emotional problem caused by her father remained active. It was not until the end of the second year of analysis that she was able to sit through a meal with him. . . . Previously such an occurrence [brought] abdominal pains, stomach symptoms, and eating difficulties that would last for days. (1943:284)

Lorand further tells us:

It was apparent that her seeming ignorance about sexual matters was merely the result of deep repression. [Actually], she knew a great deal about them, and knew from experience about genital sensations. However, she rejected the knowledge in order not to be disturbed by it. She expressed repeatedly the desire to be sexless, and when father talked about her getting married, she wondered about it because father and mother's union was unhappy. She knew they never liked each other.

In her early childhood, she remembers being like a little beast who wanted to eat up and tear up everything and everybody. Her jealousies started with sibling rivalry as early as the age of two. At this early age, her father became linked with her oral cravings. From then on, these desires carried sexual charges. The desires which primarily concerned mother's breast, food, and getting love from mother became in later stages identified with desires to have everything mother possessed including father's love . . . associated with early ideas of oral impregnation.

The analysis of this patient proved . . . that the oral symptom—her reaction to food—served to realize other fantasies which were of primary importance. . . . In a symbolic way, eating was equated with sexuality, just as in instances noted by previous authors, especially Waller, Kaufman and Deutsch (1940) and Rahman, Richardson and Ripley, (1939). All symptoms centering around eating could really be transposed to her problems of sexuality. In the deepest layer, there was the primary desire for impregnation, to become fat, to have a big abdomen. The guilt, however, associated with that desire, resulted in the expression of the opposite, namely a denial by expulsion, or vomiting out of the stomach content, all of which indicated the danger of "getting fat." The fantasy of oral impregnation was clearly proven in the course of analysis, when she used as a defense nausea and loss of appetite to prevent her dates with men. (1943:285, 289)

Two facts stand out in this account. First, the patient had severe problems in separation/individuation, as shown in the diffuse disturbances in her whole personality structure and unresolved primitive attachment to her mother. Second, by at least the age of two she linked together her oral cravings, sexual feelings and feelings about her father. Her persistent difficulties in developing a strong autonomous ego complete the basic picture of a primary oedipal determinant of anorexia for the future adolescent.

From a fragmentary report by Deutsch, unearthed by Roazen (1981), her interaction with an anorexic patient also demonstrates the primary oedipal complex. Deutsch's patient presented the mixed bulimic and anorexic symptoms that Bruch finds diagnostic of "true anorexia." The young woman began her analysis with a strong positive transference to Deutsch but soon shifted to a hostile one in the following manner: she first binged, then got into bed with her mother and confided Deutsch's interpretations of pregnancy fantasies. Her mother was predictably outraged with Deutsch, whereupon the patient used her next analytic hour to demonstrate a hostile split-transference to Deutsch. Simultaneously the patient expressed "a positive relationship to mother, a hate against father" (1981:508). The content of her material showed, according to Deutsch, sadomasochistic, delusory use of binging/starving in relation to resistance to mother/Deutsch's supposed omniscience and feelings of emptiness and loneliness, with her body variously representing the world, her food/mother, or the state of pregnancy.

The patient next expressed her struggle to separate/individuate by missing several analytic hours.

When the patient returned, Deutsch sensitively offered her a daily option on whether or not to use a promised hour. Deutsch concluded with the words, "Now you are free." The patient immediately responded, "Now I will tell you something. You see that a lot of my ceremonials is obedience and disobedience to father. I have been good because he wants it and I do the contrary by a disobedience" (1981:509).

Deutsch continued her account:

And after I said, "You have absolute freedom," then she brought out she cannot stand the freedom and how terribly she needs the obedience to father. Father says eat and then she has one of the eating spells. She says, "You see, I am eating, eating, eating until I burst!" And then comes the not eating: "I am disobedient but I have my punishment and I am dying." In this there really was some enlightenment. (1981:510)

We see how this anorexic desperately needed to warn mother/Deutsch that personal freedom (separation/individuation from mother) could lead to the acting out of oral pregnancy fantasies under father's domination. *Such primitive involvement with the separation/individuation process in a patient invariably means equally primitive involvement with oedipal feelings.* The rest of her primary oedipal complex reveals itself in the patient's concern with maternal omniscience, splitting as a defense, sadomasochism, life/death ideation, and delusory use of her body in a primitive system of concrete symbolization.

Of major importance in the cases just discussed is the connection between oral symptoms and impregnation fantasies. This connection is common in the anorexic syndrome. Sours (1974) lists it as the source of the prevailing fantasy among the group II patients, those who manifest oedipal feelings at least during the (classical) oedipal phase and whose pathology is relatively mild. Oral impregnation fantasies are not surprising in patients whose distorted perceptions of their bodies center upon a false idea that they are bloated in the middle. We note that such fantasies come into play when an adolescent girl who has previously been unable to differentiate herself from her mother suddenly becomes aware of her own sexual impulses. We ask why this circumstance should produce a well-defined syndrome, so similar from person to person, if the connection were not regularly made between orality, sexuality, and the issue of individuation. That these critical connections are evident in the anorexic syndrome regardless of the degree of pathology the patient otherwise displays tells us that the connections are not achieved in a haphazard way. The marvelous variety in human development would surely affect the anorexic syndrome if critical connections between orality, sexuality, and the issue of individuation were not laid down during the very early primary oedipal phase.

Whatever other meanings the refusal to eat may hold for the anorexic, it involves resistance to the tie to the mother. It provides overriding proof of not needing mother in the most fundamental way. Girls who will become anorexic get through their childhood years by maintaining a sense of fusion with their mothers, which does not dissolve in the period of intrapsychic separation/individuation/primary oedipal conflict. Lorand was apparently able to document in his case that the anorexic syndrome was a replay of how the patient felt about herself, sexuality, and oral impulses when she was no more than two years old, partly in relation to her mother's pregnancy.

The Primary Oedipal Connection Seen in Early-Onset Anorexia

We now have a view of anorexia as a complex pattern that is unified by its connection with the primary oedipal phase. In many cases of anorexia, only reconstruction enables us to know what probably happened. However, two cases in the literature offer detailed accounts of treatment of young girls who developed anorexia when barely two years old and earlier than four, respectively. We can see in them quite directly the effects of oedipal conflict upon the separation/individuation process and the origins of the anorexic syndrome.

Sours (1980b) raises the question of diagnosis in child cases. It is true that they are rare: the literature yields only three treatment cases, two of which were presented with sufficient detail to be quoted here. We can understand the rarity of child cases. It is due to the nature of the primary oedipal solution of the pre-anorexic: re-

maining psychological
maintain until she faces
　　In doubting that
exia of adolescence, Sou
tensions involved in eatin{
dren. Milner's and Sylveste
cern over their not eating, e
syndrome with sufficient sev
ization for dehydration and c
　　After thorough investig
next chapter, the second will a[

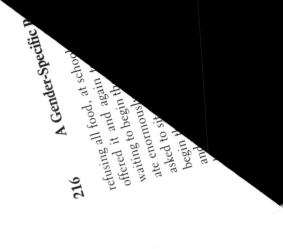

A Gender-Specific

216

refusing all food, at scho
offered it and again
waiting to begin th
ate enormous
asked to sit
begin
an

The Primary Oedipal Complex
and the Anorexic Syndrome

A child was brought to Milner (1944) for treatment of an anorexia
that began when she was two years old. Milner calls the child
Rachel.

　　This was her feeding history: Born a month prematurely
Rachel gained weight slowly until she was five months old, after
which she gained satisfactorily. She responded well to spoon feeding
begun when she was ten months old. Her mother reported difficulties in getting her to take food starting in the high chair. We are not
given Rachel's age at this point except that it appears to have been
later than at ten months. The stated history skips to the fact that she
was in the parents' bedroom until she was eighteen months old,
when she developed the measles. (The parents said that she always
seemed asleep when they had intercourse.) Rachel was then moved
out of her parents' bedroom. This was when Rachel stopped paying
attention to food. Mother had to interest her in something else in
order to get the food in. In Milner's words:

Difficulties increased until one day she ceased to eat or drink (she was just
over two) and signs of dehydration developed. A specialist suggested leaving bits of food about the house and this worked for a time. After this she
insisted on sitting on her mother's lap and saying "Mummy feed me," for a
period of six months. Then she went to a nursery school and again began

and at home, and screamed when her mother
ook nothing at all for three days. While she was
e analysis her mother sent her to her grannie, where she
and was happy, but when her mother arrived she at once
on her lap and again refused to eat. She was brought home to
e analysis and would eat a little for breakfast if her father gave it
her mother was not in the room. [However, for the three days just
before the beginning of analysis she would eat a little, provided that she
could feed her mother with half of it from her own plate. (1944:54)

Her mother described Rachel's general behavior as "extremely independent, always refusing help at school, wanting to do what the older children did and wanting to use an adult knife and fork at meals; she played happily by herself, had many friends and slept very well" (1944:54).

What we learn from this mainly is that Rachel presented no feeding problem through weaning at ten months. Sometime later, when her mother no longer held her to feed her, Rachel began to be difficult. When Rachel no longer slept in her parents' bedroom around an illness at eighteen months, a power struggle over feeding began. Her severe anorexia at the age of two was obviously connected with Rachel's intense conflict over dependence and independence in relation to her mother. The nature of this conflict and its emotional concomitants became clear in the process of Rachel's analysis. Rachel's case reveals the origin of the anorexic syndrome, which we can only surmise from the behavior of older anorexics.

To begin with a picture of Rachel, here is Milner's first impression:

She was a pretty, dainty, intelligent little girl, and the mother reported no other symptoms; but under analysis it became clear that she had many deep-seated difficulties; her charming ways had a hint of artificiality which soon showed itself to be an expression of very deep mistrust of herself and others. (1944:53)

In the overall pattern of Rachel's behavior in treatment we get a sense of the high energy and constant activity typical of anorexics. Rachel gives orders and rescinds them or orders Milner to be defiant but always judges that Milner does it unsuccessfully. In the same way, she assigns identities and then denies them. Fragmenting, destructive play, as in hours of cutting up papers, is interspersed with imaginative play, mostly using herself and Milner but also the materials in the room to show her confusion about what is inside and what is outside. Her confusion includes the meaning of feces and urine and their relationship to eating and to dangerous poison. Her vocabulary is usually age-appropriate or advanced, but she also uses neologisms and baby talk. We see Rachel's extensive use of splitting when we contrast this behavior with how adultlike she tries to be outside of her treatment sessions.

A few of the primary oedipal issues that are clear in Rachel's material, as indeed in that of older anorexics, are:

Ambivalence with an almost constant rhythm of shifting from one psychological position to its opposite, and alternating in identifications;

Separation/individuation as a source of confusion played out in terms of whether her mother is to be with her or not and whether Rachel is herself or her mother;

Much anal material;

A constant power struggle, which is dramatic in the transference, Rachel constantly giving and withdrawing instructions to her therapist;

Preoccupaton with being bad or good;

Splits between being a "good girl" whose behavior is all-conforming (but has an artificial quality that is clear to Milner), and a hidden "bad girl," and also between being someone who is very intelligent and capable, in contrast to the tempestuous, helpless, infantile child within;

The oral apparatus being connected with oedipal concerns expressed in part-object concrete symbolization (as in oral impregnation fantasies and identification of her father with a voice, her mother with food).

These issues are manifest in the material of Rachel. I have selected below typical passages from Milner's account as illustrations.

Overview of Rachel's Treatment

Milner saw Rachel on a daily basis for a period of about six months. Rachel's separation problems were so difficult that the analysis began with Rachel's mother in the treatment room. In the first hour,

Rachel foreshadowed a major theme, tantalization. Rachel perched on her mother's knees, looking at the objects in the room and gnashing her teeth. Throughout the treatment, as a kind of ritual, Rachel brought in fuchsias from Milner's garden, commanding her to eat them and then shouting, "Don't!" The underlying meaning, according to Milner, seemed to be that mother had something Rachel wanted but could not have. In the second hour and repeatedly afterward, Rachel scratched at the door of a painted house, insisting there was a man inside, and searched drawers that she was told belonged to someone else.

By the tenth session, Rachel was able to tolerate her mother's staying in the waiting room, although Rachel frequently visited her there or brought her back into the treatment room. Four sessions later, Rachel demonstrated a loyalty struggle in leaving the treatment room to go tell her mother that she wanted to bite Milner's finger.

Milner began to learn from Rachel what eating meant to her. Food was "the actual people who were the objects of her longings and angers, [Rachel] showed a whole series of doubts and fears about what it was she really had inside and what happened to it" (1944:55). The loyalty struggle intensified in the nineteenth session, Rachel pretending to cut Milner's clothes, wanting Milner to retaliate, and hallucinating that her mother was calling her.

I interpreted her fear of retaliation from me for her wanting to cut and bite me, and as she went in to her mother she said to her: "Someone bit my finger" . . . in the fourteenth hour she had wanted to bite mine. *It was after this hour that her mother reported a very marked improvement in her eating.* (1944:55)

Milner's interpretation ameliorated Rachel's fear of her mother's retaliation. This enabled Rachel to feel safer in taking in food/mother. There followed a long period in which Rachel came somewhat to the sense that the anger and greed she expressed were her own feelings. An important part of her confused behavior stemmed from her perception (according to Milner) that eating means biting, eaten things diasappear, and she did not know what they turn into: "Fæces and urine were part of the mystery for her, including the possibility that what one ate became dangerous inside. . . . She also felt that, in her anger, and jealousy against her mother who would not let her have her father, she wanted to attack her mother" (1944:54).

At the same time Rachel's material showed that: "what she wanted, and felt that she could get by eating was all that her mother had, then she could not feel sure that her mother was not a dangerous person who was robbed from and eaten up" (1944:55).

This material is reminiscent of Lorand's interpretations reconstructing his anorexic patient's experience at age two.

In Rachel's fiftieth hour:

She said, having just put two bricks in her own mouth: "You're greedy, you want to bite my voice, take away my voice." And in the fifty-second hour she showed, I think, the connection between voice and her father's penis by interrupting some interpretation of mine, in which I mentioned Daddy, by screaming, "You mustn't, that's my song, you mustn't," and hitting me and adding: "He's my Daddy, not yours, you haven't got one." (1944:55)

Rachel continued from this material by concentrating between the fiftieth and the seventy-sixth hour on feelings that something she injured was inside herself, attacking her. Processing her feelings in this way, Rachel came to sufficient comfort in her rivalry with her mother to begin to glimpse new solutions. Thus, in the seventy-sixth hour, Milner reports:

To deny this feeling, . . . [Rachel] began by tearing the flowers she had brought and putting them in two piles, and then said "I can skip," and began to demonstrate it. She then found a leaf and said: "Does it prick? Let's pretend it's pricked us both and put cream on!" Then she found a torn bus ticket, and put it in her mouth and said: "My leg doesn't hurt." And then she saw the loose leg of a stool which she had previously tried to pull off and now touched with her foot, saying: "It pricks," and then threw the stool away. Here I think we can say that she wanted to show me that she could skip in order to try to feel that she was all right inside, full of life and skills. (1944:56)

It is interesting that Rachel's hyperactivity in showing skill and ability was expressed around this material. Milner speaks of Rachel proving she had a good penis inside. (In the same session there was material [kicking away a stool leg] to get rid of a bad penile object, which Milner connected with defecation.)

It is important also that Rachel thought of an erstwhile resolution of her oedipal conflict during this session: the phallic object pricked both her mother and herself, and they could both make themselves feel good about it. Perhaps this was a way of using concrete symbolization to suggest that she and her mother could both be the objects of her father's attention, albeit in a sadomasochistic manner made acceptable in the fantasy by administering cream.

In the next sessions, however, the competitive quality of her oedipal strivings again overwhelmed her:

She gradually showed how she felt herself to be such a danger to her mother and everything inside her mother that she felt that she herself ought to be got rid of, that she herself ought to be dead. In fact, it is material which seems to me to show that the refusal of food had in itself a suicidal intention, as well as being the attempt to protect herself against taking inside something which she felt . . . would . . . attack her and destroy her from inside. (1944:56)

Working through the lethal implications of separation/individuation in hostility to her mother and her efforts to handle her oedipal longings eventually brought Rachel to a second milestone in her treatment. She went on a month's holiday with her parents, hardly eating the first week but eating normally the rest of the time whether or not her mother was present.

In the ensuing period, as might be expected from primary oedipal theory, Rachel progressed in ego differentiation so that she now referred to herself and Milner by their names and experimented with ways of getting rid of the omnipresent mother. "Spit it out if you don't like it!" Milner became aware that the food/mother was a nasty lady inside of Rachel who made her do bad things.

The playroom stood . . . for her own inside with me as the nasty lady. For she began to cut paper while I held it, and then said "You made me tear it, you made me drop the scissors, you're a horrid Mrs. Milner and I won't open the door to you," and while saying this she put the paper over her mouth. By this last gesture with the paper she seemed also to throw direct light on her symptom, as if by refusing to eat she could avoid having the nasty lady inside. When I interpreted that she felt I was the nasty lady she

. . . said "You aren't." . . . She made us spend a long time dancing gaily around the table in a very free and happy way. She had often danced before, but it had always been in a highly sophisticated way, wriggling her body and swinging her arms like a music-hall dancer. . . . But now she danced just like a little girl and finally stopped, saying: "It's nice, isn't it? I'm going to tell Mummy." She brought her mother and made us all three dance, then ran and gave her mother an affectionate hug. In this hour there was none of the rivalry and possessiveness that had been so frequent before, and it is particularly interesting that this capacity to show genuine affection followed directly after the interpretation of the . . . nasty lady. (1944:59)

This freedom to be herself was a milestone in Rachel's progress.

Milner's understanding that Rachel felt controlled by the bad mother inside her who made her do bad (sexy) things enabled Rachel to dance like a little girl instead of imitating a seductive woman. However, at this stage, Rachel's greater sense of reality in terms of knowing who she was and who her mother was required her to distance herself from her father. This consequence makes sense when we remember that remaining fused with her mother was a way of being safe with her mother, a defense against her oedipal feelings. From primary oedipal theory we could also predict that at this point Rachel would display penis envy as the only acceptable (safe) way of showing desire to be her father's kind. She shifted from wanting to be the kind he would choose to being the kind he was. Milner tells us:

Her rivalry material now showed more aspects of penis envy. After saying one day, "You haven't got toys in your room—I have," she added, "We've got to hide from Daddy," as if to say that if she takes the penis her father then becomes the enemy. Actually her mother now reported that Rachel was very clinging with her and uneasy with her father, which reversed the earlier situation. (1944:59)[2]

At the same time there was renewed emphasis upon anal and part-object material ("Mummy, why does kaki and weewee come out of there and not out of legs and eyes?"). Rachel was able to free herself of what Milner called a "subtle artificiality" in all her behavior to the extent of screaming with real emotion when she was angry with Milner.

She had shut me out of the lavatory and when she came out I interpreted her not wanting to have me there as to do with feeling that she had bitten me up, like the torn leaves, and now wanted to get rid of me, and that the kaki would show what she had done. She indignantly interrupted with "I don't eat kaki and weewee; you said I do, I don't." The connection between fæces and the nasty lady has already been seen, and here she was showing the fear that whatever she ate turned into fæces. That it was poisonous fæces and flatus which were the danger to the new baby[3] was shown when later she tucked her doll, Belinda, into the wheelbarrow and said she was ill. In a dreamy voice she explained: "She got in my pram and in the wind, catch the wind, and she didn't like it and she ate some leaves, poison stalks."

Then she took some plasticine from the drawer and ran round with it, shouting "let's pretend there's a real monkey" and shrieked when near the supposed monkey and called out in a different voice "I don't like you, Rachel Sheridan"; then in her own voice "Then I don't like you, monkey." She made the plasticine into rolls and said she was making lovely things for Belinda, and cuddled her, but added: "The monkeys say they don't like my yellow plasticine." Here the monkeys seem to have stood for both the real mother outside and the super-ego mother inside, both telling her she must not poison the baby with her yellow fæces. (1944:60)

We see in this last session that the lethal super-ego of the primary oedipal complex begins to be integrated into a whole-self-object that offers judgment and control that she can live with as a whole Rachel Sheridan.

Her mother stopped treatment at this point in spite of Milner's strong protests because she claimed that she could no longer bring Rachel and Rachel was now completely normal. Six months after termination, the new baby was born. Rachel was sent away for six weeks. For a brief period upon her return, she was withdrawn but ate voraciously. By the time of Milner's follow-up, the mother reported that Rachel was fine.

We get little picture of the family dynamics in Rachel's case. What we do know is that the mother was cooperative enough with Rachel's treatment to permit the child to bring her into the session, or wait on another floor as the child determined it. We also get the impression that the father was active in Rachel's care from his participating in the feeding at one stage. However, in keeping with Kramer's point (1974) that we pay attention to the intrapsychic factors in anorexia, Rachel was deeply involved in a particularly intense (primary) oedipal conflict, the dynamic in her illness. Milner underscores the fact in her discussion of the case.

Summary of Rachel's Course

Rachel's treatment shows how the process of separation/individuation and the handling of oedipal feelings are intertwined. Tantalized by her mother's having her father, she felt that the food/mother would retaliate from inside Rachel if Rachel ate (robbed) her mother. When Milner helped Rachel to identify her own wish to bite (destroy), the child was relieved enough to start to eat in a normal way, although Rachel's eating continued to be symptomatic during many vicissitudes of her development during treatment.

Rachel used Milner as both an alter ego and as a mother-figure, while Rachel alternately took the opposite role. Either way meant her intense conflict. She gradually became more able to identify her own feelings, finally assuming a whole-person identity with her own name. In this process Rachel learned first that the nasty (food/mother) lady inside did not control Rachel's own sexy feelings. Her immediate relief at this interpretation enabled her to act freely according to her own age while she was in the session.

Late in the analysis Rachel found another solution. Her fantasy was that mother and Rachel were both "pricked" and they shared ways of making themselves both feel good about it. We might conjecture that this was a shift away from all-or-none thinking and thus, she could imagine that she and her mother would both survive while sharing her father. Overwhelmed by competitive feelings, Rachel then shifted into a negative oedipus, during which time she again could eat. We might theorize that becoming more conscious of her wish to destroy her mother, Rachel chose to preserve her instead. However, this required her to give up her oedipal wishes for her father and settle for being like him. In her further development, Rachel showed increasing confidence to handle her hostile feelings.

When Rachel began treatment, she was in the throes of the primary oedipal conflict. By the time she left treatment, there were signs of her integrating her ego. We have postulated that primary oedipal issues are at the root of anorexia. In consonance with this idea we see that as Rachel began to be able to combine individuation with resolution of oedipal feelings, she no longer was subject to the primitive self-punishing symptom of anorexia. In the next chapter I shall use details from Rachel's treatment to see how the full syndrome of her anorexia illuminates our understanding of the anorexic condition in general.

13 Rachel as Guide to the Formation of the Anorexic Syndrome During the Primary Oedipal Phase

In the following pages, I draw from Milner's account of Rachel's treatment to illustrate each symptom that is regularly considered to be part of the anorexic syndrome. The later emergence of the same syndrome in cases of older anorexics then becomes unmistakable. The common factor proves to be the primary oedipal complex.

It is rare to find anorexia in so young a child. The typical patient represses her primary oedipal conflict without developing an autonomous ego in terms of it. She achieves psychic equilibrium by remaining in her own mind a psychological extension of her mother, until she is too hard-pressed by her sexual impulses during adolescence. In Rachel we are able to see what can happen when a child cannot attenuate the primary oedipal conflict in the usual way or postpone dealing with it as do those who develop anorexia later.

Rachel developed the anorexic eating disorder. In other respects most of her behavior, if it at times extreme, seems age-appropriate for a two-year-old. For example, Rachel's oral-anal-genital fantasies, which would be regressive in an older patient, are in fact appropriate because she was, at the start of the treatment, in the period of transition from oral to anal/genital dominance. What we shall observe, however, is that the rest of the behavior complex that age-appropriately accompanied Rachel's anorexia is precisely the complex of symptoms that we have seen invariably accompanies adolescence-onset anorexia. This firmly establishes the connection between the origins of anorexia nervosa in the time of the primary oedipal phase.

As we would predict from primary oedipal theory, she shares with older anorexic patients the rest of the syndrome. Rachel's oral/genital fantasies cannot be the result of regression because she was only two when she became anorexic. During her primary oedipal phase a tight association between oral and sexual impulses gave rise to Rachel's behavior in her illness. However, most such behavior seems age-appropriate for a two-year-old. It is only the degree of Rachel's disturbance that attracts attention.

Rachel as Guide: The Role of the Primary Oedipal Conflict in Anorexia

In Rachel's case we need not speculate about whether she had a severe oedipal conflict by the age of two, nor whether this was the basis for her developing anorexia at this tender age. Her analyst tells us of Rachel unequivocally:

Her central anxiety seemed to be fear of what she might do, or felt she had done, in connection with her oedipus wishes, and what might be done to her in retaliation and punishment; and she felt her oedipus wishes largely in oral terms. Thus if she ate she felt she robbed her mother, her mother then becoming an enemy. (1944:60)

Strong early connections between oral primacy and oedipal strivings predispose a child toward anorexic solutions to her conflicts. The fact that she encounters her sexual feelings and impulses toward her father while oral organization is still the most effective part of her ego predisposes the girl to handle her oedipal feelings in genito-oral terms. A significant example was Rachel's bringing in fuchsias (a flower with a long slender bell slightly fluted at the end). She gave them to Milner to eat, then shouted, "Don't!" Symbolic oral-genital use of the fuchsia continued throughout the analysis, although by the last session the tone of the play was different.

No symbolic interpretation is necessary to understand Rachel when she shouts at Milner, "He's my daddy, not yours. You haven't got one!" The rest of her symptoms reflect the state of the ego in its first organizational efforts during the primary oedipal phase, in striking similarity to the anorexic syndrome.

Rachel as Guide: Anorexia

The most imposing symptom in the anorexic syndrome is the willful refusal to eat. This behavior stems from various connections the primary oedipal child might make between food and her conflicts. Rachel's main fantasy proves to be that taking in food/mother puts a "nasty lady" inside her. This nasty lady makes her do bad (sexy) things, controlling what Rachel does. Another part of Rachel's difficulty is primitive guilt that is associated with her rivalrous wish to destroy her mother:

She introduced the material by showing how she felt she got her mother inside, that is, through her bad and greedy mouth. For she brought in a fuchsia flower which was open and said: "This has a mouth, tear it up." (Actually, some time after this, the mother reported that at home she said one day: "Mummy, I could eat if I didn't have to put it in my mouth.") (1944:57)

And in another session: "Having shown this projection of her desire to bite by the feeling that someone outside had bitten her, she gradually began to show, during weeks of analysis, how she felt that the thing she had injured was also inside her and attacking her from inside" (1944:56–57).

Rachel clearly expresses her fear of retaliation from the food/ mother. In addition to this central oedipal meaning of her anorexia, Rachel demonstrated the fantasy that she took in her father's penis, giving her impetus to add skill to her hyperactivity, thus showing (in Milner's words) "a good penis inside her." This idea of ingesting the wished-for penis is a major theme, also, in Sylvester's young patient (see chapter 14). Oedipal conflict required that child to vomit the fantasied penis out, as a sign of loyalty to her mother.

Rachel also expresses poisoning fantasies, which in her case are fostered by a projection of guilt she feels over her destructive urges in combination with anal fantasies that bad stuff comes out of her.

Although they are not obvious in Rachel, who was already anorexic before her mother became pregnant, for Sylvester's anorexic child patient, oral impregnation fantasies were important. Perhaps this is related to the histories of Sylvester's patient and many other anorexics with siblings who were conceived early enough in the patient's life for the mother's pregnancy to be obvious during the patient's primary oedipal phase. This was apparent in Lorand's case, previously noted. Sandler and Dare (1970) describe adolescent girls who, in strongly rejecting pregnancy wishes, face a resurgence of oral impregnation wishes and fantasies. They cope with these by becoming anorexic. We can see in the anorexic how early formation of fantasies of oral impregnation can be traced because they reappear in later pathology.

A blatant meaning of anorexia is that the mother is not needed. Rachel showed this in her refusal to eat in her mother's presence. Refusal to eat is the ultimate in resistance to mother's power. As self-deprivation it eases the conflict in oedipal tensions. Rachel at some points was able to eat if her father fed her, provided that her mother was not in sight. This also explains why Rachel and Sylvester's patient were able to eat, respectively, at her grandmother's and in the hospital, removed from the site of conflict. In another example, Rachel used food to show that at best she did not need her mother more than her mother needed her. After the first analytic session, she was willing to eat if she and her mother shared equally the food from one plate.

As food was the metaphor for mother, in Rachel's two-year-old mind to be translated literally, not taking in food meant preventing her mother from becoming a nasty lady inside herself who wished to do sexy things or from becoming something poisonous in the form of feces to get back at Rachel for Rachel's destroying her. "The next hour showed how she felt herself controlled and at the mercy of the nasty lady inside, how she felt she had a real bad agency within herself. . . . By refusing to eat she could avoid having the nasty lady inside" (1944:59).

Refusal to eat in order to avoid ingesting her mother was an important dynamic in Rachel's anorexia. Milner underscores another theme that attaches meaning to food that Rachel indicated in her very first sessions. This was that her mother had something she was not letting Rachel have, which proved to be a man. Milner explains this danger to Rachel's feelings: "What she wanted and felt that she could get by eating was all that her mother had" (1944:56). The giving up of food was in part to avoid her mother becoming a dangerous person who was robbed from and eaten up and then from within Rachel would be a source of harm to her. Rachel, in giving up food, was also denying that she wanted what mother had. As long as she could deny that she wanted what mother had, she was free to be close to her father. In another effort at solution, a period of reverse oedipus, Rachel did not need to eschew food, but then Rachel clung to her mother and ignored her father.

Food can also have a specific symbolic meaning. For example, Mary, an anorexic/bulimic patient of mine in her twenties, mentioned throwing up after eating a pickle. Her only association, given with embarrassment, was to a penis. Recognizing an unconscious connection between the pickle's elongated form and her conflicts is not the same as conscious avoidance of pickles because she believed they were penises. However, Rachel shows us that there is a time early in life when primary process dominates thought, when the concrete symbol is consciously treated as if it were the original part-object. In chapter 4 a quotation describes how Rose, a normal two-year-old (Galenson, Miller, and Roiphe 1976) used her father's pens as concrete part-object symbols of him. Early in the primary oedipal phase, concrete symbols and their objective correlatives may seem interchangeable to the child. In the anorexic's replay of feelings from that phase, specific foods can trigger conflicted behavior on such a basis.

There are other meanings that anorexics attach to their refusal to eat. These too stem from linking together orality, sexuality, and the issue of individuation. We know this from the amenorrhea that often precedes weight loss and the fact that the onset of self-starvation is timed with heightened awareness and then rejection of sexuality.

In a dramatic series of sessions, Rachel demonstrated that in eating she felt she took in a "nasty lady" who made her do bad (sexy) things. Taking in "food/bad mother" meant to Rachel that she acted on two conflicting wishes: wanting to be seductive like her mother, and needing to be on guard with her mother for fear of her mother's retaliation (through both poisoning and subsequent attacking feces). Milner describes Rachel's concern that what one eats is aggressive because of the biting impulses involved. "Wee-wee" and "kaki" next represent aggressive forces, transformations of food once the damaged, angry mother is ingested.

Ceaser (1977) describes the ambivalent taking-in of mother in obesity: holding on to her by ingestion and destroying her at the same time by making her disappear. Clearly, his anorexic patients (see chapter 12) felt the reverse by not eating, resisting merger with food/mother and at the same time (as these patients were dealing with denial of death wishes) preserving her. *These were not child patients, but the form of their thinking about food corresponds to the material from Rachel.*

The relationship between anorexia and other oral manifestations of the primary oedipal conflict is important. Ceaser presents an example of another symbolic use of food when food means all of mother. He quotes an anorexic patient of his as saying, "When I gorge I lose myself; there is nothing but myself and the food altogether. Nothing else matters or exists" (1977:483). In this example, the food equals mother and the patient uses it to prove her wish for losing herself in a merger with mother.

Ceaser's other patients employed the concrete symbolism of food/body/mother in overeating when they lost their mothers. After being aroused sexually, each one wished no longer to use oral incorporation to "retain" mother; indeed, she felt compelled to do the opposite, to starve herself, in terms of the same symbolism. The girl's sense of fusion with her mother at the time of separation/individuation serves a defensive purpose in helping to avoid oedipal conflict. Food provides a link with her mother, which fits into the daughter's confusion of what is inside and what is outside of herself. Such use of primary process derives from an early connection a patient has made in handling her feelings when she did not as yet have the verbal equipment to resolve problems through the use of secondary process.

The same level of functioning is reflected in intentional vomiting, another form of rejecting food. The anorexic's use of vomiting is sometimes an orgastic experience. We can understand this when we consider that anorexia is based upon the primary oedipal conflict. Thomä (1977) reports a case of anorexia in which his patient talked of the mouth and the vagina interchangeably. This patient's fragmented, chaotic stream of thought bespoke an early ego-state. It is understandable that in a child's early experiences of her body, orifices involved with pleasurable feelings seem equivalent. Thus vomiting can become an orgastic experience in that it is a convulsive use of the oral apparatus. Vomiting can seem to be strictly a self-punishment, but sometimes by putting her fingers down her throat, the anorexic can feel she is reproducing the sexual act.

Use of her own mouth/vagina and penis/fingers in fantasied intercourse in the process of vomiting allows her to feel that she is not disloyal to her mother in having sexy feelings. Particularly when erotic fantasy is completely repressed, foods may be used as phallic symbols (e.g., hot dogs)[1] to satisfy a fantasy of oral intercourse and then vomiting them back in denial of sexual feelings and the wish for father.

Symptoms are metaphoric expressions for what a person cannot put into verbal terms. We see in all the above examples the variety of fantasy connected with refusal of food. However, the different possibilities all involve feelings about mother, separation/individuation, and sexuality. Anorexia, bulimia, obesity, and compulsive vomiting all consist of the same fantasy elements and deal with them on the same two-year-old level. This is why the various eating disorders may exist serially in a given patient, in the same way as someone can rework a fantasy from different perspectives in successive dreams. Under different circumstances, the patient has different responses to her basic conflicts.

We see in Rachel how such age-appropriate meanings of the anorexic symptom appear in a two-year-old child. We can now review the other elements of the anorexic syndrome and note how each of them makes sense as a significant manifestation of the primary oedipal complex.

Rachel as Guide: Bodily Concerns

There are four kinds of bodily concerns that are typical of children at the primary oedipal level. There is evidence that all of them occur in patients with anorexia.[2] These concerns are: uncertainty of bodily identity; uncertainty of bodily image; uncertainty of bodily sensations; and uncertainty of bodily control.

Uncertainty of Bodily Identity

In keeping with the barely organized ego-state of the child in the primary oedipal phase, the anorexic often treats herself as if she were an extension of her mother: the body/mother. The following sequence states Rachel's confusion about what is inside and what is outside in terms of what is her body and what is her mother:

After herself tearing the fuchsia she said to me: "Cry and say 'I'm the Mummy cooking the dinner.'" In the light of her reference to the mouth I can only assume that she meant, in feeling she was the mother, that she had taken her inside through her mouth. She then argued about this, trying, I think, to deny it but at the same time, wanting it; for she said to me: "You're not the Mummy, you're only three and a half." . . . She then gave me some stalk to eat, saying, "Spit it out if you don't like it," introducing the idea, which she developed later, of getting rid of the mother she had taken inside. (1944:57)

Anorexics also show this confusion of self and mother that means to the anorexic only one of them can exist as a separate being. They often display an interest in feeding others, as Palazzoli and others mention as part of the identification with mother that the girl wishes for ambivalently yet desperately. She gains control of the feeding situation, holding the power for herself, being mother and not her victim. When Rachel took in her mother through her bad mouth, she *became* "Mummy cooking dinner."

We might well imagine that the question of what is inside and what is outside thus overshadows the child's certainty about her own bodily impulses. Just as she is not sure about the form of her person, so she would be even more likely to be confused about whose sensations she is experiencing and under what circumstances. Therefore the inside-outside confusion of the child in the primary oedipal phase would predispose her to confusion about bodily sensations and their significance to her when she was later overwhelmed by a resurgence of primary oedipal issues.

The fact that the child has confusion over body identity becomes significant in that the child's conflicts must be dealt with within the framework of that confusion: for example, how can the child get rid of a rival if it is unsure of who is self and who is rival? This confused context can be seen in the handling of destructive wishes and sexual feelings. We have seen much material showing that Rachel's urges about the mother/body were partially destructive in nature. Milner writes how Rachel's confusions about eating and what it meant for the mother/body gave rise to inner turmoil:

> She felt that taking food inside her was as if she was taking in the actual people who were the objects of her longings and angers, but also showed a whole series of doubts and fears about what it was she really had inside and what happened to it.
> "This has a mouth, tear it up," [and] "Mummy, I could eat if I didn't have to put it in my mouth." (1944:57)

This inner destruction of uncertain consequences meant, to Rachel, that her mouth itself was a dangerous organ. The same uncertainty in personal identity influences the way in which sexuality is perceived and dealt with. This was seen with Rachel in the way she was able to be free to dance like a little girl instead of a seductive woman when Milner gave the interpretation that showed her that eating the food/body/mother did not put inside her the nasty lady/mother who made her sexy.

Older anorexics show a similar pattern of perplexity in implementing hostility due to their body identity problem. We have seen that anorexics older than Rachel also have confusion about body identity in relation to mother. We have also seen that the sexual repression of the anorexic occurs as a guilt response directed at mother. Thus it is clear that, as with Rachel, her sexual feelings must be tied to the context of the mother/self identity rather than simply to mother per se. We saw this sex/identity connection earlier in Deutsch's anorexic patient (chapter 12), whose body at various times represented to her the world, her food/mother, and the state of pregnancy (a state she fantasized her father was trying to induce in her by making her eat).

Uncertainty of Bodily Image

Anorexia, Bruch (1973) points out, always includes distortion of the body image. This confusion is, in fact, implied by confusion in body identity such as Rachel displayed. If you do not know who is who, you cannot learn to recognize one from the other by appearances.

This ego defect is not strange in a child in the second year of life. The child is then in the process of organizing for the first time an inner representation of her body image and possesses a still shaky perceptual/recognition system. The young ego freely takes advantage of this perceptual fluidity in handling problems. Thus, when Rachel needed to hear her mother, she hallucinated her mother's voice. As a child's ego and sensory abilities mature during the primary oedipal phase, its definitions of bodily image are normally resolved.

Anorexics, however, display bodily image concerns reflective of having not resolved the question fully. The preoccupation with her appearance, which Palazzoli recognizes as a form of preoccupation with body image, reflects the anorexic's concern about identity and which image she will reveal. The purchase of many clothes, hardly to use them, when examined turns out to be another effort to move toward femininity without really being able to allow herself to do so. We remember that, at the primary oedipal stage, the child's basis of identification is through appearance. "I am as I look." I am reminded of a healthy two-year-old, Catherine. She stood in her mother's shoes before a mirror and exclaimed, "Pretty!" (Newman 1967). Such freedom to enjoy being herself is what we hope for in the child.

In contrast is my patient, Sally, an anorexic in her early twenties. Sally struggled each morning to decide what apparel she would wear, a question of what image she would present. Ultimately it became clear that the choice Sally struggled with was between clothes in which she might look very feminine and even pregnant or clothes that gave her a boyish, highly stylized appearance. Her more feminine clothes, much as she loved to buy them, remained in the closet. Like Rachel, she could not see herself as feminine without conflict. The anorexic does not have inner permission to enjoy her femininity.

Palazzoli's patient whose diary is quoted in chapter 12 screams at her father that she refuses to be plump like her mother and attract him sexually. One of Ceaser's interpretations of his patients' overdetermined anorexias is that they must look like their cachexic mothers upon becoming sexual. Given this background, it is not surprising that anorexics will look at their emaciated bodies and insist that they see fat. Any curvature of the abdomen is taken as a sign of being pregnant. (Lorand's patient cited in chapter 12 displayed a reaction-formation to fat on her abdomen, covering up her real wish to be pregnant.) Any sign of femininity of form seems a dangerous sign of the girl's hidden, sexual feelings. For the anorexic, these are crucial matters because the level of her ego development is still at the stage of fully equating her sense of self with her appearance.

It makes sense that an ego defect permitting such distortion comes from the earliest time of ego organization, when the child was just beginning to organize its intrapsychic bodily representations and simultaneously to define itself as either good or bad. A defect from such an early time would be at the orally dominated early end of the primary oedipal continuum. Intense oedipal conflict at that point would interconnect orality, sexual feelings, and a loosely organized body ego.

Uncertainty of Bodily Sensations

As with uncertainty of bodily image, unsureness about bodily sensations is partially implied by a two-year-old child's confusion over bodily identity. Not being sure about the form of its person, the child is even more likely to be confused about whose sensations it is experiencing and under what circumstances. The inside–outside confusion makes for confusion as to where impulses come from, who is hungry, and so on. This bodily sensation confusion also stems from the primary oedipal child's physical state of development, which does not yet include a coordinated, sophisticated body sense and the ability to identify feelings with words.

Rachel, during most of her treatment, demonstrated confusion as to which feelings were inside her body and which were outside of it. Milner gives the following example: "Having shown this projection of her desire to bite by the feeling that someone outside had bitten her, she gradually began to show, during weeks of analysis, how she felt that the thing she had injured was also inside her and attacking her from inside" (1944:54).

Once again we find that this two-year-old's difficulty is found in (older) anorexics as well. A major aspect of the anorexic's concern with the body has to do with misinterpretation of body cues and the difficulty of identifying her own feelings.

Bruch (1973), Minuchin and Rosman (1980), and others point out that indirect communication and distorted perception of feelings are typical styles of an anorexic's family. However, these dynamics do not explain why a particular child uses such mechanisms to the extent that the anorexic does. If we appreciate her confusion as to who she is and, most especially, what is inside and what is outside her body, her behavior becomes understandable.

These confusions lead to great anxiety. Chediak conceptualized "anorexia nervosa primarily (in the sense of etiology) as a psychological problem in which impulses coming from one's body are greatly feared." (1977:472). From our understanding of the primary oedipal phase we realize that both her oral and her sexual impulses can so often frighten a child that the familiar asceticism of the anorexic is her only recourse.

However, although anorexia is the most dramatic and major oral symptom, bulimia, vomiting and guilt-ridden, compulsive gum chewing, also appear in the same patients, as well as pre-anorexic obesity. She may ignore hunger pangs, but she allows herself sensations that accompany these other oral symptoms. For example, during an intense anorexic period, she will stuff more and more sticks of gum into her mouth as a wad gets chewed down or the sweetness disappears and she tries to maintain the feeling in her mouth that she wants from the gum.

As with Rachel, whether or not any anorexic will allow herself to be accurate in her perceptions of her inner state depends on the subject of the moment. She can repress all sense of nutritional need, or she can be inordinately aware of minute stimuli. Her behavior is determined by her fantasies about what she is doing. When Rachel's guilt feeling toward her mother was sufficiently reduced, her ideas of how dangerous she was were less distorted. She became freer to express real feelings. Symptomatic behavior could thus be replaced by a truer sense of reality of her physical state and acceptance of her feelings.

Uncertainty of Bodily Control

For the anorexic, not eating is, among other things, a way of establishing control of her body. It is inevitable that concerns about bodily control are great in the anorexic. The sexual nature of her automatic physical changes in adolescence makes her desperate to control her body. Because she is confused about who she is, establishing control of her own body helps her to believe that she is independent from her mother.

The anorexic's control of her body through self-denial thus fulfills a tremendous need. Her feeling is that only by excluding mother/food/body can she be herself. In this ironic and reality-reversing way, her self-starvation preserves her sense of selfness; only because she is mired in the ego-state of her two-year-old self is this dilemma played out through the concrete symbolization of food (as in food/mother/body). Heightened sexuality has brought with it the full intensity of her too shakily resolved primary oedipal conflict, including her early confusions in separation/individuation from her mother.

In studying Rachel, we learn how hard it is to believe in one's control of one's own body when the body-ego is still fragmented. An example is Rachel's fear that Milner would steal her voice: "Thus after frequently telling me that I must not talk because I was a baby, she said one day in the forty-sixth hour that I must not have any toys, and when I asked why she said it was because I had taken her voice" (1944:55).

The products of the oral apparatus and all of its uses became entangled with the child's idea of her relationship to her body and to those around her.[3] At an extreme, this can lead to regarding the body as an object separate from the sense of self. An anorexic's ability to split off her feelings from her body is in part derived from such a development.

Rachel as Guide: Separation/Individuation

Difficulties in asserting their own autonomy is a basic problem of anorexics and a key factor in identifying the source of the anorexic's pathology in the primary oedipal phase.

Evidence appears throughout her material that Rachel was in the throes of separation/individuation, as indeed she had to be at only two years old. In the very first session it was clear that she could not permit herself to separate from her mother. It took nine sessions before Rachel was willing to let her mother stay in a waiting room on another floor. Even then she frequently dashed out to see her mother, often inviting her back into the treatment room. Later Rachel played a game in which she assigned places in the room to

Milner and her mother. The action consisted in Rachel taking those places for herself.

In the same period we get the following material, which shows the ongoing conflict about who was who and how oedipal feelings entered into her difficulties in establishing a personal identity. (Recall that the "nasty lady" was a construct of her mother, which, internal to herself, blurred Rachel's identity):

"I'm going to cut out the nasty lady." Now these two pieces of material coming together suggest, I think, that the nasty lady was the mother who would not allow her the penis or baby, and that this rival mother was not only an imago precipitated by the external experience of frustration, but also the rival mother which she felt was inside herself (inside the drawer, in her play) and which she wished to cut out of herself . . . an instinctual impulse within her—but she could not think of it as that, she could only try to deal with it in terms of the frustrating mother who stimulated it. (1944:58)

Toward the end of the analysis, Rachel provided more evidence of the individuation process she was going through. Rachel "took her mother in through her own bad and greedy mouth" and then became the "Mummy cooking dinner." The action was interspersed with her telling Milner, "You're not the Mummy, you're only three and a half"[4] and then reversion to destructive behavior, taunting Milner. The conflict was not only in knowing who was who, but in reconciling her wishes to be the mother-person with the reality of her own state. The swing from being the one or the other showed her conflict over the danger she felt if she were to be herself and autonomous, in which case, her symbolic destruction of mother as rival produced overpowering fear. When she was most confused about who was who, she managed her conflict by not eating (being independent of mother) and acting as if she were grown-up (an extension of mother). It is of interest that when Rachel reached the point where she could think of herself as Rachel Sheridan and see her mother and Milner as distinct separate people, she no longer showed pathological restraint from eating.

Effective separation/individuation changes the quality of the super-ego to a more gentle one, as Rachel demonstrates. In her last session with Milner the super-ego/mother/monkey offered stern judgment of Rachel but did not threaten danger. When she was able

to move beyond the primary oedipal level of personality organization, Rachel was no longer the prisoner of a brutal super-ego, and
she no longer required such cruel self-punishment of herself in
managing her conflicts. Inner permission to be more of a person in
her own right implies a degree of resolution of oedipal conflict.
While her oedipal tensions were not as yet settled, she no longer
needed to be anorexic. This progression is paralleled in the case of
Sylvester's anorexic child patient (chapter 14).

It is while ego organization is at the primary oedipal level,
when separation/individuation from the mother is so tenuous, that
oral/anal concerns, the dichotomies of omnipresence/annihilation
and good/bad, oedipal fears, and guilt-feelings combine to turn the
child's beginning sense of responsibility into a cruel super-ego. This
archaic super-ego can require extreme behavior. As separation/indi-
viduation becomes more certain and the child's ego is capable of
more sophisticated thought, the super-ego is modified to allow for
more comfortable compromise: such a resolution as anorexia is no
longer required.

Rachel as Guide: The As-If Personality in the Anorexia Syndrome

Deutsch's (1941) "as-if" personality comes to mind when we consider the anorexic syndrome. By this Deutsch meant that the child
does not cathect certain images of itself. Therefore, it might operate
in a way that others approve of yet within itself gain no credit or
satisfaction for doing so. Anorexic girls are usually described as
others as being "good" and compliant in their pre-anorexic behavior
(Bruch 1973). The patient's self-evaluation can differ from this
markedly. We learn, for example, in the diary of Palazzoli's patients,
that she considerd herself to be mean and unmanageably bad.
Lorand's patient described herself similarly. Anorexic patients I have
known appear outwardly as sweet, helpless little beings; yet they
describe themselves as really mean, inside. Their feeling because of
this split is not of a person but just a creature going through the
motions of expected behavior.

An interesting sidelight is that anorexics I have seen were
excellent mimics, as Storey (1976) observes to be true in his experi-

ence. Milner makes the point about Rachel, also. Perhaps ability in mimicry contributes to a child's confusion of being herself or not. Success in mimicry might add difficulty in ordering inner and outer experience in the process of forming an integrated, autonomous self. The pre-anorexic child's ability to mimic might be stimulated, in any case, because (operating on the basis of faulty separation/individuation) she must observe her mother closely in order to learn to behave as much like her as possible, thereby fusing with her. Being an as-if personality would lead the pre-anorexic to skillful mimicry.

Regardless of the role of mimicry, we have from Milner the following comments about Rachel:

> I think that the doubt about her own feelings partly explains what was a marked feature of her behavior in general, that is, a subtle artificiality. . . . It was as if everything she did was half pretence, as if she felt that to express her real feelings was far too dangerous, since these were so jealous and destructive. And it was only quite near the end of the analysis that she was able to burst into a fury of genuine indignation on discovering that I possessed a bicycle. (1944:55)

The expression of feelings that seemed genuine coincided with Rachel's assumption of a personal identity. She was able to separate because her guilt feelings toward her mother were sufficiently reduced so that she could bear responsibility for her own impulses. The meaning of the bicycle to Rachel is not explained by Milner. Its importance lay in Rachel's ability to show what Milner termed real feelings.

In Rachel's seeming adultness she was certainly an "as-if" personality. The "as-if" personality is an important concept in understanding anorexia because it helps us to understand how the child maintains the equilibrium she shows during the latency period, and even before for that matter, by remaining fused with her mother and undifferentiated in her own mind. She is not really emotionally invested in the pleasing personality that she presents. For the as-if personality, "My badness is me." Her very sense of self, based upon gender identity, is unacceptable. All ability to be mature in her behavior had to be used in an artificial way, as if it were not she herself doing the good things because being separate from her mother carried with it too much weight of oedipal guilt. In

Rachel's case, she could be an effective child, rather than a pretended little adult, only when the hostility to her mother and her early fantasy of a food/mother controlling her from the inside were interpreted.

An interesting sequence by way of illustration is this segment from Rachel's analysis showing her struggle to become a whole person: "Rachel said, 'I'm Rachel Sheridan. You're Mrs. Milner.' Then 'No, you're not,' etc."[5] (1944:58). This occurred subsequent to blatant oedipal material, around which Rachel's mother reported renewed difficulties in eating, Rachel now refusing her favorite foods. Rachel returned to the next session making a ferocious attack on Milner, hitting her hard on the face. She then left saying that Milner was a darling but that Rachel herself was not one. In reaction to Milner's insisting that the session was finished, Rachel was able to scream, and for the first time Milner felt that this was with deeply felt emotion.

We can understand this sequence as a milestone in Rachel's struggle for personhood. She had found that being an individual carried her into the middle of her oedipal feelings, and her punishing avoidance of food temporarily had to recur. However, when Rachel found that showing her worst self and being responsible for bad feelings did not destroy Milner or her mother, she was unable to feel sufficient relief of guilt that she could express her own emotions directly. This crucial fact we recognize as being vital in the improvement of older anorexics, who must also find the courage to be themselves without the cover of an "as-if" personality.

Rachel as Guide: Helplessness

Bruch (1973) considers the feeling of helplessness as a cardinal aspect of the anorexic syndrome. We know from examination of the primary oedipal complex that the two-year-old is preoccupied with the dichotomy between omnipotence and utter helplessness. Rachel demonstrates the significance of this problem, which confirms the reasons for being an "as-if" personality. Milner tells us:

For by controlling her own behavior according to some imposed pattern, continually acting a part, instead of allowing herself to behave freely and spontaneously according to her own impulses, she felt she could be safe from those impulses. And by so often trying to control me and make me copy exactly what she did, she was, I think, showing me what she was doing inside herself, as well as trying to avoid the responsibility for her impulses by sharing it. For it seemed to me that her method of defence by control here included the idea of getting all her external objects, including me, inside herself, and the failure of this defense was shown in her intense anxiety when I did not know what she wanted me to do without being told. It was as if her artificiality was a picture of her internal situation, in which *she felt so dominated by the people she had taken inside that she could not be herself at all.*

Rachel's difficulty in handling the dichotomy between omnipotence and helplessness stems from how dangerous and unacceptable her own impulses seem. She must defend against feeling helpless lest she act out those impulses. Being an independent person is frightening because it means being responsible for one's impulses; so she must imitatively cling to her superficially perceived patterns of adult behavior to avoid acknowledging that she holds unacceptable impulses. Her sense of helplessness contrasts with her desperate urgency to prove to herself that she can do without what mother offers, namely, food. Her need is to be perfectly competent; her terror is to be completely helpless because that means being swamped by her own impulses as well as vulnerable to the bad mother of her mind. It is true, as Bruch, Palazzoli, and others point out, that the anorexic finds power in the importance of her illness in the family. However, this is only a secondary gain, which develops as her symptoms do. The underlying situation is the one Milner described in the quotation above.

This poignant description tells us the role in Rachel's illness of her feeling helpless. It also illuminates the primary oedipal level of similar feelings among older anorexics.

Rachel as Guide: Denial

Denial is one of the most unfortunate aspects of the anorexic syndrome because the patient's denial of her difficulties thwarts treatment. From the first, descriptions of anorexia have included the fact that such patients deny having a problem. If the girl were to admit that she is symbolically ridding herself of mother, she would automatically become aware of her real struggle: the effort to be her own person and avoid destruction because of her own sexuality. She settles for anorexia and the satisfaction that neither her mother nor anyone else can control her feeding.

We do not have direct evidence of Rachel's use of denial in respect to her food or the state of her body when she starved herself. However, there is ample evidence of her use of denial as a mechanism of defense, indeed, as one of her main defenses.[6] It is typical of Rachel's agitated ambivalence that she sets a scene and then denies it. We find in Rachel's material repeatedly the command that Milner do something and then the denial that she has succeeded. In the case of an interpretation concerning her wishes in regard to feces she indignantly interrupted with, "I don't eat kaki and weewee; you said I do, I don't!"

By denial, Rachel tried to avoid the fact of her own smallness and dependence, a denial that was shown in her taunting rivalries with Milner. Milner points out in regard to anorexia Rachel's fundamental feeling that her mother "had it all." Therefore if Rachel could believe that she had all she wanted, and that it was the best, then she felt she would be saved from her dangerous anger at not having. Earlier in this discussion Milner makes it clear that the "all" that Rachel wanted (and that her mother had) was her father. Milner emphasizes the ebb and flow of denial on Rachel's part in trying to deal with this yearning.

Ceaser (1977) tells how the anorexic's retaliation upon the body/mother helps to explain the delusional denial of thinness. He says the denial of weight loss allows these patients to continue the aggressive assault on their bodies with lessened guilt. In other words, what the anorexic is really denying is her fantasy/wish to destroy her mother. This explanation fits with our general understanding of the condition from Rachel. We also saw destructive fantasy wishes about mother in the case of Rachel, whose two-year-old ego-state permitted the use of similarly massive denial.

Rachel as Guide: The Good/Bad Dichotomy

Mogul (1980) is the latest to point out asceticism as a characteristic of the anorexic. This emphasis upon purity, perfection, and goodness versus badness derives from the primary oedipal child's psychic pain over her sense of her own (sexual) badness. Such preoccupation with goodness and badness can be seen in Rachel. In discussion of Rachel's chief defenses, Milner referred back to a session in which Rachel had frightened herself by revealing her wish for her father and cites again: "projection: she tried to feel that I was the person who wanted to bite. I was the bad and greedy child, not she" (1944:60). The two-year-old can imagine only extremes of good and bad. If bad feelings exist, they must all be lodged within one person; and if one is bad, then the other must be good.

Rachel demonstrated how upset she was by her own destructive urges when she accused Milner of being horrid. Such dramatic incidents invariably derived from feelings on Rachel's part that she was controlled by the "nasty lady" inside and that her behavior was very bad. Typically, following such a sequence Rachel instructed Milner to pretend she was punished with bodily injury and then ordered her about, castigating her for always being wrong.

It is easy to see how such agony over goodness and badness and guilt feelings in a child who relied on the mechanism of splitting would result in an emphasis upon asceticism and the denial of body feelings (as the source of badness), bringing her to the anorexic solution for her oedipal conflicts.[7]

Rachel as Guide: Anal Preoccupation

Thomä (1967) draws attention to the anorexic's anal preoccupations in emphasizing cleanliness and heavy use of laxatives. Compulsive use of enemas and laxatives suggests the anorexic's attempt at resolving the primary oedipal extended into the early part of the anal phase, when control of the excretory process started to be an issue. The work with Rachel contained a great deal of messing in the playroom. Rachel constantly demonstrated a struggle for control in her interactions with Milner. In addition, her material is replete with frequent lavatory play and talk of "kaki" and "weewee." One of her greatest fears was that whatever she ate turned to feces, dangerous because of the association with the "nasty lady" inside. We might speculate that the violence of Rachel's fantasies stems from the fact that anal/power concerns were, expectedly, a very important matter at her age.

In another session Rachel connected anal material with pain in her stomach. An anorexic patient of mine also complained of pain in her stomach each time after a bulimic spell and felt she required massive use of laxatives. Pain in the stomach as self-punishment is part of the anal fantasy of the anorexic patient. The punishment in Rachel's mind came from the dangerous nasty-lady-mixed-up-with-feces. One of the least controversial ideas about psychopathology is that a child's stresses and strains during the two-year-old period engender anal preoccupation later on in life.

Rachel as Guide: Splitting

Splitting is a chief defense mechanism of the child in the early days of ego formation. Therefore it must appear in the behavior of anyone whose psychological illness stems from the primary oedipal phase. Indeed, Thomä (1961) and Sours (1974) point out the use of splitting in the anorexic. Masterson makes it the focus of his treatment of anorexia, emphasizing "good" and "bad" mother and self images. The splitting off of sexual feelings, the splitting of good and bad feeling from each other, etc., are glaring examples of how the anorexic keeps thought and feeling separate. They tell us how early the basis for this syndrome is laid down.

Rachel demonstrates how the ego is first organized in terms of splitting. We see this, for example, in her shifting from one role to another, splitting off various aspects of her ego in each role; in her extreme concern with goodness and badness; and in feeling that she must act without expressing her true emotions while she maintains an adultlike guise in her behavior outside of her therapy sessions, split off from her age-appropriate (although extreme) behavior with Milner. In addition, as with all anorexics, she splits off her wish for food from any bodily sensations she might feel. Rachel wanted to feed Milner just as older anorexics will prepare gourmet meals for others, but these interests are not connected to promptings from her own body to take in food.

Rachel as Guide: Suicide

The anorexic girl, in keeping with her massive use of denial, says that she is not hurting herself by not eating. She typically feels herself to be in fine physical condition. Nonetheless starvation is harmful to herself and in a number of cases leads to death.

Suicidal ideation is another primary oedipal issue because the girl's conflict involves the question of having a right to her own space. She has difficulty in figuring out how her mother and she can coexist as individuals. Lynn brought this home to me graphically when she said to mother/me, "If I am in charge of my own life, then that is kind of like killing you off because the part of you that used to control me no longer exists." If she existed as an individual, it meant mother's/my destruction. It is in this spirit that the anorexic girl denies her intention to kill herself, just as she denies her wish to be rid of her mother, but her behavior is unmistakably self-destructive in her guilt-burdened drive to become independent, totally rid of her mother. She cannot permit herself to acknowledge these feelings. When we see that anorexics are capable of denying even their bodies' promptings for food and their sexual feelings, it should not be difficult for us to imagine that they defensively deny ideas of suicide.

Milner was most interested in the suicidal quality of Rachel's anorexia, giving as an example:

When I gave an interpretation beginning "Whatever I do, you say it's wrong because . . ." she interrupted with "Whatever I do I cut myself" and then "D'you know, Mrs. Milner? My Mummy got a bleed with a pin." I then interpreted that the hurt Mummy was inside, like the nasty lady, and she went on pretending to cut her own arms and fingers, then threw the scissors away and said: "Let's pretend we're dead. We must take our shoes off." She began cutting the brown fur trimming off her slippers and then suddenly hugged her tummy. Here she seemed to be saying *that she could not cut out the nasty lady inside without feeling dead herself,* also that she felt the nasty lady as equivalent to fæces, that is, the brown fur on her slippers. (1944:58)

In another excerpt Rachel shows how these feelings are part of her using anorexia as a means of handling her primary oedipal conflict.

She gradually showed how she felt herself to be such a danger to her mother and everything inside her mother that she felt that she herself ought to be got rid of, that she herself ought to be dead. In fact, it is material which to me seems to show *the refusal of food had in itself a suicidal intention, as well as being the attempt to protect herself against taking inside something which she felt was injured.* (1944:56)

These examples from the accessible material of Rachel tell us much about what might be occurring in the thoughts of older anorexics. We can see how they share with Rachel not only self-starvation and the oedipal conlfict but, as reflected in behavior, the judgment of her primitive super-ego that she herself ought to be dead.

Rachel as Guide: Secrecy

Palazzoli (1978) points out the importance of secrecy in the thinking of the anorexic. One sees it especially in bulimia and vomiting, which are performed as secret rituals. In the diary of a patient of Palazzoli from which we have already read such important material, one of the most poignant statements is the girl's account of her pain when she feels that her whole secret fantasy world was about to collapse by the intrusion of treatment into her life. We are reminded of how, in the struggle to develop a sense of independence and autonomy, any young child needs to feel capable of secret thought that no one else, not even mother, can know.

Some anorexics, as Palazzoli and others mention, keep secret caches of food. In these cases, secrecy over eating derives from the need to protect the integrity of her mind from the all-knowing mother (just as secrecy is an issue in all syndromes that hark back to the primary oedipal phase).

Rachel displayed a typical primary oedipal/anorexic ambivalence in her conflicting wishes for autonomy and ownership of her feelings on the one hand and, on the other hand, wishes to escape the rage of her mother that such autonomy and self-ownership would bring. She demonstrated an obsession with secrecy in the way she handled both sides of the conflict.

At any early point in her anorexia, Rachel could take food from her father if her mother was not around or if the food was left for her to take secretly. We can understand this as an expression of the first part of the ambivalence over whether to be autonomous or dependent. Having secret food that is unconnected with mother is possible to the extent that the girl feels safe in being autonomous. Then she can have secret thoughts. When she feels too guilty over her own forbidden (frequently sexy) thoughts, absolute safety from mother's anger could exist only if the girl and her mother were fused, the extreme form of dependency, or if she avoided food entirely.

Rachel demonstrated the other side of the ambivalence in a "frenzy of anxiety" when Milner did not know what she wanted without Rachel telling her. To feel safe, Rachel needed to feel fused with mother/Milner. That implied omniscience on the therapist's part. Facing evidence of the lack of such omniscience, Rachel felt unfused and left responsible for her own thoughts—a situation that terrified her.

A corollary of this is the question of trust. Untrustingness and suspicion also characterize the anorexic. Rachel shows how her mistrust of her mother is related to the hostility she harbors for her mother and therefore feels must have its counterpart in her mother as well. This mistrust of herself and her mother contributes to the need for secrecy of thought. The anorexic's urgent need to keep her secrets is understandable in her conflicted efforts to gain a measure of autonomy and, as in Rachel, to avoid judgment for her rivalrous feelings about her mother.

Rachel as Guide: Amenorrhea

Rachel's age precludes inclusion of amenorrhea as part of her anorexic syndrome. However, we can see how her conflicts, if undiminished because she had not dealt with them further, might well later on have prevented her from becoming an adult, sexual female. Combined loyalty to her mother and fear of her made Rachel extremely anxious about her own sexual feelings. When relieved of some of her guilt feelings toward her mother, she could behave appropriately as a little girl her age and move toward a sense of personhood. With a modified super-ego, she could tolerate her own sexual impulses without chaotic self-punishment. On this new basis, we can imagine that Rachel would not need to repress her sexuality in adolescence or to starve herself because of it.

Rachel as Guide: Kleptomania

Thomä (1967), among others, mentions kleptomania as a prominent symptom in the anorexic syndrome. We can understand kleptomania as a symptom by which symbols of part-objects seem to restore what one feels to be missing. The *pars pro toto*, concrete symbolization of the primary oedipal child's mentation leads the anorexic to feel that what she steals is of magical value to her. Plucking the fuchsias from Milner's garden was a ritual in Rachel's treatment. Another kleptomanic act was taking from drawers objects that she knew did not belong to her. These objects were symbols of getting her father for herself away from her mother. In comparable thought process, Rachel told Milner that she must not talk and that she was a baby and had no toys because she had taken Rachel's voice: "You're greedy! You want my voice!"

In the use of the fuchsias, Rachel tantalized Milner. She sometimes gave the flowers to Milner to eat and then shouted, "Don't!" Her wariness lest she be deprived and her zest in tantalizing Milner reveal why Rachel felt she must take things. She tried to counteract her sense of deprivation and inferiority by gaining a part-object symbol of what she wanted. We recognize the same thought process in understanding the kleptomania of older patients who are anorexic.

Rachel as Guide: Hyperactivity

Hyperactivity is almost always cited as a basic part of the anorexic syndrome. Observers are amazed by the contrast between the emaciated state of the patient and her level of energy. As Palazzoli (1978) points out, an anorexic's level of energy output and activity can belie her wasted state up to a point of actual physical collapse.

Reading Rachel's case material gives us an idea of the hectic, often frenzied pace of her activity. Milner specifically mentions her level of activity in the nineteenth session, when Rachel showed confusion about who was who. She elaborated this in terms of who had a penis. Milner was reminded that a week before Rachel had wanted to bite Milner's finger. Rachel now told her mother that Milner had bitten Rachel's finger. Milner said that Rachel felt something outside had something better than she did but that it was forbidden to Rachel. Rachel's idea in the biting seemed to be that if she had a penis inside her, then she could be very active. The high level of activity seemed to Milner to counter "dead feelings" from Rachel's hopelessness and guilt in her rivalry with her mother. Milner also felt that Rachel displayed good feelings in her intense activity because she wanted to show that she had a good penis inside of her. In terms of this Milner said, "she wanted to show me that she could skip in order to try to feel that she was all right inside, full of life and skills" (1944:56).

Milner's essentially oedipal interpretations are undoubtedly true, but primary oedipal theory requires attention to the issue of autonomy, too, since the major importance of autonomy at this stage is part of why the primary oedipal conflict is so great. One reason for the anorexic girl to be constantly active is her effort to prove that she is in charge of her own body. We understand this in Rachel when we note that the above material appeared in the context of Rachel's confusion as to who was who.

Rachel as Guide: Perceptions of Space-Time

Following the idea of Kuhn (1953) and others, Palazzoli observes that her anorexic patients concentrate upon the immediate in their experiences and isolate themselves within units of time. What appear to be sequences of time to others are experienced disjunctively by such patients. In the same manner, these patients feel isolated in space, which includes having no place in human relationships. It seems impossible that there can be a place for both mother and self as separate individuals when both want the same thing (father). We recall Patty's chant in her suicidal moment: "There's no place for me." The immaturity of space-time perception in the primary oedipal child is another significant factor in the eating disturbance syndrome.

Low frustration tolerance is a consequence of this state for the anorexic, as for any two-year-old. The ability to wait is clearly not developed and is related to the perception of time. Rachel demonstrates low frustration tolerance throughout her therapy. She plays a game in which Milner as a baby is shut into a cage. Rachel tells Milner that she will not be gone long and then commands that Milner as baby retort, "Yes, you will!" Rachel then furiously bangs the door shut on Milner. This difference between the adult perception of time and how the passage of time feels to a child is apparent in the behavior of normal two-year-olds.

Palazzoli gives an example of an adolescent anorexic toward the end of her treatment. The patient, Liliana, looks back upon her perception of time and space during the period when she was ill. Liliana tells Palazzoli:

I have at last discovered the meaning of days. My days used to end every night; they never continued into the next day. Each morning, I had to start all over again, somehow to purify myself from the "pollution of the last day." It was my way of being ready for anything. But in the evening I was oppressed all over again. At night I just had to vomit. Each morning was just one long chore. I had to clean myself all over (baths, enemas), rid myself of the encrusted dirt, of everything that clung to me inside and out, and start from the beginning, all clean. Perhaps I was desperately searching for my true self.[8] (1978:141–142)

Palazzoli further describes Liliana's new sense of time and space, which accompanied a new sense of self. Space and time meant differentiated opportunities for her existence. As we would expect from our understanding of the primary oedipal phase, Palazzoli points out that the new spatial experiences Liliana enjoyed included her sense of her own space in interhuman relationships. Liliana felt able to define her own wishes in relation to others and to maintain her own preferences without feeling they had to be set aside because of the wishes of others.

The discovery of the anorexic's characteristic perception of space-time is extremely important theoretically. Their characteristic level of use of the space-time concept is recognizable in the primary oedipal age child. Nothing in any theories of anorexia that have been presented prior to this one explains why this should be. We can understand the condition in relation to the primary oedipal phase, from which standpoint the anorexic's sense of space-time is to be expected. Primary oedipal theory predicts that the perception of space-time should be as Palazzoli describes it in her typical patient, Liliana. The changes in Liliana's sense of space-time that occur with her increased mental health also are what we expect when we understand the nature of personality development that follows the primary oedipal complex.

Rachel as Guide: Anorexia Nervosa

In Rachel we have seen evidence of every one of the identified elements of the anorexic complex, with the single physiologically explainable exception of amenorrhea. We have also seen that in her case these elements were understandable as two-year-old age-appropriate behaviors. Thus, not only can the set of conflicts that a girl faces in the primary oedipal phase logically explain the anorexic's eating disorder; but in addition, by placing anorexia regressively in the time frame of that same period of life, it can explain why all of the anorexic's symptoms are found together.

14 Further Evidence of the Primary Oedipal Phase as a Dynamic in Anorexia: Children, Adults, Males

With the manifestations of the primary oedipal complex in anorexia clearly in mind, we can now further test the implications of the theory: that the anorexic syndrome dissipates as the ego advances to predominantly classical oedipal level organization; that the syndrome is the same in child and adult; and that the different primary oedipal situation of the boy explains the rare incidence and characteristic form anorexia takes in the male.

Another Case of a Child Anorexic

We are fortunate to have in addition to Rachel another child anorexic whose analysis is available for study (Sylvester 1945).[1] This child's experience is of interest for three reasons: First, she reveals the dynamics of her anorexia, including its primary oedipal phase aspects. Second, she demonstrates a contrast between behavior that is symptomatic of the primary oedipal phase and the classical oedipal behavior she developed through her treatment, with a consequent sturdy, healthy ego. Third, in relation to the question of a physical component in the etiology, it took six months before the diagnosis of this child's condition was made, until thorough physical tests established that her condition was purely functional.

It is interesting to speculate why these little girls were susceptible to anorexia so young. High intelligence is typical of anorexia (Sours 1980b), and these two children were particularly precocious. They also shared history of eviction from the parental bedroom in a traumatic way. Milner's case was transferred when she became ill with the measles, and Sylvester's when her father returned after a long absence and her parents decided she was disruptive to them while sleeping in their bed. Both children experienced two concomitants of the mothers that are typical of the pre-anorexic situation: strong early maternal identification with the child, and fostering of a precocious maturity (by the age of two in these instances). In any case, we can look carefully at more material to test the relationship between primary oedipal phase development and the syndrome of anorexia.

The patient was the third of five children born within six years. She seemed to thrive after she was born but had to be weaned abruptly at four months because her mother was pregnant again. The consequence of this seemed to be excessive thumb sucking, which her mother tried unsuccessfully to stop. The child started to talk at seven months of age and was completely toilet-trained at nine months. Also, when she was nine months old, her father was arrested for passing bad relief checks and sent to jail for two years.

Four months later, at the age of thirteen months, she had a mild attack of measles, coinciding with her mother's returning from the hospital after the birth of her younger brother. She had a prolonged convalescence during which she lost considerable weight, gave up walking, resumed soiling and wetting, and became a feeding problem. She had temper tantrums whenever the mother nursed the baby and was generally very difficult to manage.

There was a striking change in the child when she became two. She appeared to be highly identified with the mother in a constructive way. She became oversolicitous of the younger brother, insisting that she share her food with him. In general, her behavior was "very grown-up, reliable and self-sufficient. . . . She showed remarkable intellectual achievement, took complete care of herself and was very eager to help in the house" (1945:170).

When the father returned she was "not quite three years old." She at first refused to go near him. Her older sister soon became the father's favorite. The patient had slept with the mother until the father returned and reacted so violently to being evicted that the mother took her back into her bed. The child then developed a habit of vigorously sucking her fingers and her hair to a degree that was very annoying. She also was blatant in trying to separate her parents, wishing to sit or sleep between them. Simultaneously, she regressed in her behavior. Her speech became babyish. She was shy, listless, and withdrawn.

The preamble to her illness included the following facts: Her mother developed toxemia of pregnancy with severe vomiting. The little girl developed pica (eating dirt)—perhaps expressing anal-oral fantasies of impregnation. Taking ashes from the stove, in addition to flowerpot dirt and paper, for which she was severely scolded, directly preceded her own symptom of vomiting. At the same time she gave up food. "From time to time, apathetic behavior changed into hyperactivity that appeared incongruous with her nearly marantic condition" (1945:168). Along with this behavior came the anorexia in conjunction with bulimia. She became extremely emaciated. At four years of age she weighed only twenty-three pounds.

After tests for physical causes proved negative, she was kept on the general ward of a children's hospital to be given intensive psychoanalytic treatment. It continued for over seven months. Her first session is worth quoting in detail. First sessions often contain the essential story, after which a patient works on the barriers to resolution of conflicts then presented (Bettelheim 1961). So it was in this case.

During the first session the solemn little girl appeared surprisingly independent and self-sufficient. She devoted herself exclusively to play with plasticine which she molded and smeared on the furniture while producing grunting and belching sounds. She did not respond when spoken to. Her awareness of the analyst's presence manifested itself only in her grabbing plasticine out of the anlyst's hand and in a fiercely defiant look when· she attempted to eat the plasticine. No resistance was offered to this but candy was placed on the table when she repeated it. She ate the candy and greedily, asked for more and more, and after stuffing herself demanded to be carried around and rocked in the analyst's arms. The aggressive smearing was handled by acceptance and the offer of candy seemed to substitute gratification for self-punishment.[2]

Being carried around and allowed to stuff herself with candy in addition to actual satisfaction meant reassurance, and enabled her to bring her first confession in a very impressive performance with a set of dolls. The father doll fed clay balls to the whole family, and the mother doll and the doll representing the patient herself vomited. She repeated this play throughout the whole session, at the end of which she made her first verbal communication, a request to be called by her older sister's name rather than by her own.

What she expressed was this: her own and her mother's symptoms are alike and are connected with the father. She evidently identified with the pregnant mother and disclosed her oral impregnation fantasy. Confession, however, is followed by denial. When she asks to be called by her sister's name she expresses the wish to be the father's favorite and to be free from symptoms. (1945:172)

Remembering the child's prodromal pica, the anal element of this material is of interest. Subsequent material centered upon her impregnation fantasies with strong oral components and issues of sibling rivalry and separation/individuation. When she learned from her mother's visit that another baby had been born, she had a severe vomiting spell. Some other pertinent material is worth quoting:

Following the next visit of her mother she had an attack of wetting and soiling. . . . [She investigated the analyst's mouth, looking for a baby]. [She further portrayed] theories about impregnation: The mother doll ate large quantities of plasticine and when the analyst, in response to a question, denied that this was going to make a baby, she had the father doll and the mother doll kiss each other and again asked the same question. The next step in her play was to put father and mother to bed together with the father lying on top of the mother. The father then stepped on the mother, making her cry out. The mother doll now broke into pieces and had to be fixed by the analyst, after which the patient delivered the baby through the mother's abdomen and put it on the mother's breast.

We note several elements pertaining to her sex theories: The first is a fantasy of impregnation through eating. The oral concept is maintained in the second phase of her play, the gratification being given by the father. In the third and final, repeatedly staged phase of the play her sadomasochistic ideas about the primal scene became evident. However, the significant point is that the rage against the pregnant mother evokes these fantasies and these are benevolently modified only when the analyst forgivingly repairs the mother doll. As long as the child is assured of the possession of the kindly analyst she can allow a doll baby to be born and to nurse. (1945:173)

While working through primal-scene material, she often assumed a masculine identity. Vomiting recurred. A boy-dog-self named "Whoof" carried out a campaign of killing the whole family of dolls in her play: "The next day Whoof and the entire family were put into a box which the patient closed and rattled furiously. 'They fight,' she said. Upon opening it with many precautions she decided that 'he killed them all'—and 'now I will do it too'" (1945:175).

Sylvester interprets this excerpt as a sadomasochistic fantasy of the primal scene. She is sensitive to her patient's enactment of gender confusion. The child adorned female doll figures with penises on the head and chest, insisting they were still girls, affected a deep voice, and played with flashlights and guns. Sylvester traced those behaviors to the patient's wish to be like her brothers and father and enjoy their advantages with her mother. Sylvester attributed the vomiting to conflict over oral-aggressive impulses and self-punishment.

Sylvester's interpretations focus on the meaning of vomiting, not on the refusal of food. She just took note of whether the child ate or not. However, the retention of food is also of enormous theoretical importance. The refusal of food brings us back to the point that it is conflict with mother that is involved. The patient fused with mother to achieve intrapsychic balance as a "little adult" when she was two. The adjustment broke down when her parents' interactions produced a new pregnancy, upon which the child continued her identification with her mother, except on a hostile, self-punishing basis. If we remember this, then vomiting takes on a different significance. We remember that the patient's symptoms began when her mother vomited while pregnant and scolded the child for eating dirt. We know from the play in the patient's first session that she had the fantasy of the father performing oral impregnation with clay, a dirtlike substance. We can now relate both the girl's vomiting and her decorating girl dolls with penises on their heads and chests to a libidinal rather than aggressive wish for the penis. The vomiting is explained as a guilt-given rejection of the father's oral impregnation; and, in keeping with the child's protests that the dolls were still feminine after the penile additions, the dolls were merely possessing the penises, as in Rachel's and Rose's use of that part-object to represent having males to themselves, not becoming males (as in Sylvester's analysis). This interpretation is substantiated by such material Sylvester quotes from the same period as:

> Her brother Gilbert, she played, also came and gave her the candy she asked him for. He was represented by a little boy doll with a golf club. While the patient insisted that he was really big and gave her everything she broke his golf club and fed it to the girl doll. Finally she selected all the broken or injured toy soldiers, put them in a box with the girl doll and said, "She gets all the candy from all the Gilberts." (1945:175)

In this play, the oral incorporation of Gilbert's golf club/penis is put in the context of getting a sweet. The perspective is one of possessing something she wants; the penis representing Gilbert is someone who is nice to her, not someone she envies.

Interestingly this material was followed by a period of regressive play. In terms of primary oedipal phase theory, retreating from the state of gender to babyishness would have given relief from the conflict of loyalties that would arise for her in relation to her mother after touching on sexual issues.

> Now came a period of regressive play: she lay on the couch, kicked like a baby and talked baby-talk. She demanded that candy be fed to her. She apparently wishes to avoid the hostility connected with her rivalry and achieves this by regressing to a level at which gratification was not yet endangered by hostile competitiveness. *Eating under such conditions does not call for punishment as the hostile meaning is eliminated. She is free from her symptom while this stage lasts.* (1945:175)

Being a baby subjectively precedes the separation/individuation process and the sense of self that involves gender identity. *As she feels she does not have a gender as a baby, she does not need to have symptoms, even though there was an early feeding disturbance in her history.*

At this point in treatment, the patient was still developmentally at the primary oedipal level. Her use of splitting was still very important. Preoccupied with the question of goodness and badness, she proclaimed that it was Whoof who did bad things and not she. Next, however, *she managed a giant step in separation/individuation.* She proved to herself that she could survive well in the hospital while her analyst was on vacation, spontaneously withdrawing from the analyst for several days after her return. She did not need to vomit.[3] Her analyst's subsequent willingness to respect her need to reciprocate by making the analyst do without her enabled her to consolidate her gains. She now proclaimed that she wanted to return to treatment and learn "to sew like you." This was an age-appropriate form of identification in which she wanted to learn how to be like the analyst in feminine ways. From this point on the signs of classical oedipal behavior became stronger. For the first time since the beginning of her anorexia, she was able to handle sibling rivalry in a constructive way. Sylvester describes the period:

She is no longer fully overwhelmed by her hostile fantasies. It is for this reason that she does not have to resort to vomiting. Increasing ego-control becomes manifest in her attempt to solve her conflict with the analyst by identification. Superego factors become obvious in her attempts to be good and socially acceptable. Reaction-formation appears when for a time she has to pass on everything that is given to her. But when, later, she asks again for candy, adding "for Philip," the little boy who is the object of her most intense sibling rivalry, she shows a true conscience reaction. Aggression against the analyst and sibling rivalry now emerge again but they are handled on a distinctly different level. When she gets angry at the analyst she now no longer attacks her, her aggression takes socially acceptable forms as when, after tearing up paper or cardboard, she insists that we clean it up together. (1945:178)

　　Sylvester points out that one can see the patient's progress from her previous attempts to differentiate sharply between good and bad, a preliminary step in a child's progress in reality testing. By the point in treatment now achieved, the patient could be comfortable about the "badness" within herself. Being "bad" no longer destroys the "good." In fact, badness can be rectified, as in cleaning up her messes. This achievement freed her from the rule of dichotomies and polarizations that gives a mythic quality to the two-year-old's version of the world. She had new ability to distinguish between fantasy and fact, a hallmark of the transition to the classical oedipal phase and its resolution. She now could tolerate different perceptions of the same object, herself as "good and bad" rather than needing to be split into "good or bad."

　　The cognitive ability to tolerate ambiguity permits a child to develop an emotional basis for the dominance of secondary process in its thoughts. Thus this child could now apply real, integrative insight to understanding herself. For example, she interpreted an attack of vomiting that had occurred when a boy who was a sibling substitute on the ward was presented with birthday cake. She took the biggest piece but ate only a few bites. When she had to throw up afterward, she could say, "Because it was too much and I was angry" (1945:178). Ability to label feelings is another critical development in the advance from the primary oedipal phase into the classical. Further development of the expanding personality is told by Sylvester:

The span of her creative activity widened considerably. She began to sew, to draw, to cut out and to paint. . . . Analytic material as shown in her play now had direct reference to her conflict and its mastery: Whoof was cautioned against peeping into a house that was full of little dolls because it would make him "too mad," but later he was allowed to look together with the analyst. She said, "We look together and he does not bite any more." Still Whoof was accused of making candy "black and bad." She fought him with the analyst's help until he became harmless and ridiculous and she made fun of him. (1945:179)

Whoof was originally the bad self/boy/dog the child used to express unacceptable feelings. With her new capacity for self-acceptance and insight, she could at last enjoy her femininity without feeling guilty. The child now for the first time demonstrated an inner freedom to show interest in men on the ward. "She chatted with orderlies and interns and to the analyst bragged about the attention they gave her" (1945:180). Here is an interesting excerpt from this stage:

Integration of the reality testing capacities became apparent in the next period: she took the role of the father, the analyst became the mother, and her doll became her own surrogate. The doll was bad; bit, spat, and vomited on the mother. The patient, as father, examined her with a stomach tube and decided that the doll was not bad but sick and had to be fixed in the hospital. (1945:181)

The final phase of treatment began with a defensive angry resistance. As her anxiety diminished, hiding games led to showing Sylvester her secret: She "proceeded to suck one hand while she masturbated with the other one. . . . She talked freely about her mother [noting the analyst's greater tolerance]" (1945:182).

Once, while masturbating, she told me that at home she had gotten a licking. Then she said to me, "But you would not mind." She invented a game called "Who took the sticky?" [hiding a pencil between two sheets of paper, recovering it triumphantly, and attributing it to preferred males]. . . . She again played at tube-feeding the doll. The doll had it done as punishment for trying to swallow the tube [i.e., for oral incorporation of penile object. J.K.T.]. Then she sprinkled the floor with the same bottle and tube which she had used for the tube-feeding, and stated, "like a boy doing number one." After this had been discussed she decided to let the doll get well without washing her stomach, to sprinkle the floor "like a girl" without using the tube and to use the bottle as a symbol of the womb. [She developed a crush on one intern, calling him] "my doctor and not yours" and decided to save her candy for him. When the analyst gave her special candy for this purpose she clearly differentiated her relationship to the two objects of her attachment in referring to him as "my darling doctor" and to the analyst as "the good ice-cream lady." (1945:183)

Summarizing the work Sylvester tells us,

She is finally able to test out the possible consequences of her other presumptively bad impulses such as genital and voyeuristic tendencies after the anxiety connected with her hostile oral tendencies had been dispelled; and she shows realistic differentiation in her object relations to father and mother figures. (1945:185)

Comparing these achievements with her early behavior, we recall that this little girl was precocious at nine months, when her father was still at home. She became difficult soon afterward when her baby brother was born. Suddenly, at two years of age, she fused with her mother, adopting very mature behavior. Material in her treatment identified an older brother, Gilbert, as a caretaking father-figure with sexual overtones. We can conjecture that in the absence of their father her relationship with Gilbert was significant during her two-year-old period, as he would then have been five (at the height of his classical oedipal period, when his behavior toward her might have been libidinized). Such speculation on my part might be completely fanciful. It is fact that when the father returned after the next year her conflicted wishes for him overwhelmed her.

In treatment she demonstrated masturbating with one hand while she sucked her other hand. She told of being spanked for this, which fits with the history of her anorexia as given by the mother. This reported her irritating her parents by sucking her hand while she lay between them in bed. The child might have felt sexually stimulated while lying between her parents and tried to resolve her loyalty conflict by masturbating and simultaneously sucking on her other hand (the latter being reminiscent of the bond with her mother before the father's absence).[4] Strong parental disapproval of the masturbation-sucking behavior would have forced her to find another way of resolving her dilemmas about separation/individuation, sexual feelings for father, and loyalty to mother. Her solution was to give up being an extension of her mother (the two-year-old "as-if" personality she had tried to maintain), regressing in her behavior. Simultaneously, she "gave up" mother in the form of food, developing a dangerous anorexia, and she vomited repeatedly to demonstrate she was not retaining father in the form of his baby-making penis. The hopelessness of her marantic state, devoid of object relationship, was relieved only by occasional hyperactivity. The latter sign of a still active ego was reinforced when she was hospitalized.

Removal from the home allowed her to reveal her basic conflict in the first session of her analysis. By the culmination of her analysis, the child reached the point of acting out in session her wish to masturbate and suckle at the same time. She knew her analyst would not mind. With good mother/Sylvester's permission for her sexuality, she could then operate mostly on an age-appropriate classical oedipal level. She left treatment with the statement, "Eating is O.K."

To review this case from the standpoint of theory, she resolved through treatment the oedipal tensions she put into focus in the very first session. Anorexic behavior was part of her primary oedipal complex. She displayed marked ambivalence and power struggle and oral and anal ideation, including oral impregnation fantasies and sadomasochistic primal-scene fantasies.

Part-objects were important in her fantasies, as was the good/bad preoccupation of the primary oedipal child. Separation/identification was obviously a problem to her. Although she seemed to have managed an effective mother identification when she was two years old, this proved to be on the basis of fusion with her mother rather than by her being a little girl acting independently in a feminine manner. Gender confusion as a strategy took up a good deal of the treatment time. Finally, regression to being a "genderless" baby helped her to a point of feeling free of conflict. A milestone in her progress was to reject her analyst without resorting to anorexia-bulimia. She subsequently formed a new bond with the therapist based on a constructive identification and features of the classical oedipal phase. She seemed to be saying not "I must be you," which is the statement of the primary oedipal child, but "I want to learn to be like you,"[5] which is the statement of the child in the classical oedipal phase.

In keeping with this stage, she enjoyed the attention of grown men around her, but she still considered herself to be someone who could grow up to have the waiting adults for herself and thought that a baby she might have when she grew up would be cared for by the analyst. She is able to show the beginnings of tolerance of ambiguity, capacity to identify her own feelings, increased creativity and broadening of scope, impulse control (not with wholesale repression but constructive resolution, including the use of humor and capacity for verbalization, taking note of both her feelings and her intellectual understanding). The concept of generationality could be expected in time.

Such a symptom as anorexia would be out of phase in so well-developed a personality. It is not surprising but a pleasure to learn in Sylvester's follow-ups on this child that even three years after treatment and the birth of two more siblings, although the rest of her family remained troubled, this child was emotionally and physically healthy.

Adult Case

I should like to offer an excerpt from a case of mine to indicate how, in treatment of adult anorexics, recognition of the primary oedipal factors can be useful.

The case of Esther demonstrates the self-punishing quality of the anorexic syndrome and its connection with the patient's relationship to her mother and to her own sexuality.

Esther, a professional woman in her late twenties, provided the typical history of an anorexic girl. As an only daughter, she was a "good little girl" in a close family. Her childhood figure had been quite round. When Esther began treatment I accepted her version that cosmetic dieting was responsible for her extraordinary thinness. As I got to know her better, I realized that she had developed a mild anorexia during adolescence. Esther's complaints to me had to do with depression, daily difficulty in deciding upon the image she wished to portray through her appearance, and problems in her social relationships, all consistent with the diagnosis of anorexia. The basic diagnosis became clear as she lost more than 25 percent of her body weight, was amenorrheic, exhibited bulimia, compulsive gum chewing, and abusive administration of laxatives.

Our early work centered upon Esther's need to be clear about her own feelings and then to stand up for herself in accordance with them. Esther's transference to me was of an idealized, all-giving, all-knowing mother. Like her own mother, I was her reliable friend, "always there." Her one defense against feeling merged with me was to be silent while she processed her feelings. I respected her silences and did not verbally interpret her need for them during the initial phase of treatment. She interrupted treatment when she decided to live with Donald, a man about whom she had long fantasized.

Esther returned to treatment in agony over abdominal symptoms, which she now began to consider might be connected with her feelings, even though they were obviously affected by her overuse of laxatives. Her eating disturbance alternated between anorexia and bulimia. She was agitated about her relationship with Donald, who seemed to her to alternate between being paternal and showing her little interest. She complained about his lack of interest in sex, but her own symptoms made sex impossible. She mentioned her mother frequently, always in terms of her supportiveness. Esther spent hours and hours in her mother's company or on the telephone with her.

Eventually I began to hear much less about her mother. Occasionally she now mentioned her father. Esther felt she was his favorite person. The case material plainly showed that Esther felt she could not keep her man when she felt threatened by loss of mothering people.

From distress about the time of day of our sessions, we got to the fact that on mornings when she was a toddler her mother often left her in the care of her grandmother. Esther remembered how her grandmother used to force-feed her. Maternal abandoment in the transference reinstated the terrible feelings she suffered then. Between sessions she vomited, trying to expel as much of the replayed "forced-feeding" as she could.[6] In spite of all her suffering, Esther's guilt feelings over choosing to stay with the "fatherly" Donald were still too great. She felt she had to give him up.

At this point, I interpreted the primary oedipal dilemma I felt she was caught in. I emphasized the plight of her two-year-old self, terrified at her powerlessness when her mother left her and feeling guilty about her special feelings for her father.

The next session showed how much relief even an initial review of the dynamics could give. She said that she need not leave Donald after all, and she wanted to discuss her feelings. However, when Esther touched upon a wish to be like her mother, and I underscored it, she redoubled her defenses. She reaffirmed an identification with her father and avoided treatment for a while, emphasizing closeness with her parents as an alternate protection from being overwhelmed by her impulses.

From the standpoint of primary oedipal theory, it makes sense that too rapid confrontation of her feelings of femininity aroused overwhelming anxiety. As Esther's therapist, I had to recognize that anorexia involves the deepest feelings of the patient and must be approached very slowly.

Esther returned to treatment for the second time after several months. She began to clarify her feelings, particularly a determination to stand up for herself. She felt a need for regular exercise, channeling her hyperactivity in a way that was good for her, and was conscious of an increased sense of independence. Gradually she diminished her involvement with her parents. She put more energy into her professional practice and designed living quarters that pleased her. The bulimia occurred less frequently and was no longer a daily constant. As the dynamics of her case became more accessible, the transference helped her express anger at her bind in the loyalty struggle in valuing her parents. Her frustration produced memories of being her father's favorite, although he was self-preoccupied, and awareness of her mother's yearning to have more of him for herself. Angrily demonstrating that mother/me was not so important to her, Esther baited me with a series of men physicians who she said "proved" that she was not anorexic or bulimic.

In one example, her symptoms were attributed to digestive complications from overuse of diet pills she added to her laxatives during "spells" of bulimia. She was also furious in turn with each of her former doctors who had "not recognized" what the latest one diagnosed.

At this point, Esther also indicated having endured a pre-adolescent loyalty struggle when she was ten years old. She had painfully allowed herself to progress from her allegiance to her mother to her peers, including "liking" a particular boy, and then retreated to her mother again. The present replaying of the tortured split between her feelings of wanting a satisfying sexual relationship with a man of her own and her needing to handle her tie to her mother was clear, too. Deidealizing me and asserting independence of me was her next accomplishment.

Esther's treatment revealed that she suffered greatly, physically as well as emotionally. However, her pain was not over her avoidance of food. Her suffering centered on the issue of control in her life, with problems about eating and elimination, her femininity, and sexuality. These factors, taken together, we come to know as the anorexic response to ineffectively resolved primary oedipal conflict.

Anorexia in the Male

What then of the boy? He simply has not been involved in the girl's dilemma. The pattern of the boy's primary oedipal conflict explains the difference between boys and girls in the incidence of anorexia.

The boy's genitally impelled wish to be very close to his mother (and thus in his mind his danger of engulfment) and his wish to be independent (and thus his need to ignore his genital sensations) contrasts to the way in which a girl may be mired in primary oedipal conflict. He does not automatically feel he is his mother's rival when he allows himself autonomy, nor likely for that reason does he feel guilt toward his mother or expectation of her destructive rage. Issues of gender identity and the patterns of the primary oedipal phase give the boy his challenges to meet, but they are not the same as a girl's. The boy, in terms of his primary oedipal pattern, develops anorexia only as part of extreme cases of gender confusion.

As discussed in chapter 11, the male anorexic has grave problems about gender identity. His primary oedipal phase is unusually difficult because of the degree of seductiveness of his mother coupled with her emphasis upon overfeeding. Sours, summarizing the research on the subject, observes that male anorexics are "usually prepubertal, passive, chubby boys, who fear phallic aggressive feelings; they are frightened by sexual feelings toward the mother" (1980b:272). Such cases tend to be preadolescent, because boys in our culture do not receive positive reinforcement from remaining fused with their mothers. Therefore, their being "good little adults" in their mother's mode does not gain them general cultural support for their fragile egos even during latency. They do not dare to form strong egos because that would mean being masculine/sexual. The beckoning seductiveness of the mother threatens engulfment.

An interesting difference between female and male anorexics is that females usually deny hunger while males do not (Garner and Garfinkel 1979; Sours 1980b). We can understand that the girl must eschew food entirely because even wanting to consume it (except for caches secreted from her seemingly omniscient mother) is laden with guilt feelings and a sense of danger. The guilt feelings come from wanting to destroy the food/body (mother), wanting to be sexually attractive (to father), and wanting to avoid signs of fantasied, forbidden, wished-for pregnancy. Her sense of danger comes from the mother/rival's power. Admitting to hunger but ignoring it makes sense in terms of the anorexic boy's triumph in resisting the attraction of his seductive mother. He wants the food but refuses to lose his identity by becoming fused with her, as would be shown in a soft, round form (the stated reason according to Sours 1980b) and, of course, by the concrete symbolization of becoming fused with her because of taking in the food/body/mother.

Palazzoli adds exhibitionistic behavior as another typical sign in male anorexia. Exhibitionism begins to appear in young children as genital interest and self-individuation take up increasing energy. However, by the third year the child normally modifies the impulse in socially acceptable ways. A male anorexic, desperately seeking to differentiate himself from his mother, then utilizes this primary oedipal–level behavior, exhibitionism.

Knowing the difference between the male and female primary oedipal complexes, it is not surprising that only in relatively rare instances a boy's primary oedipal resolution involves anorexia. Even Kay and Leigh (1954), who consider that 10 to 30 percent of anorexics might be male, still place the greatest incidence at three cases of males for every seven of females. Most studies estimate the incidence of males at 2 to 10 percent. Sours (1980b), surveying available data on the subject, states that male anorexics (as a group compared with all groups of female anorexics taken together) have a worse prognosis in all forms of psychotherapy than do the females. He classifies male anorexics among the most disturbed who express the syndrome.

We can see the basic dynamics in three cases that Falstein, Feinstein and Judas provide in sufficient detail. The first, Jim, aged twelve, showed:

[a] basic fear of the dangerous mother who could poison and hurt him. who could desert him, who was weak, unreliable, fearful, and inconsistent. There were indications, too, of fears of retaliation because of his own wish to eat up everything, including the mother. The father appeared as an ally and protector, yet someone who carried a big gun while Jim had only a little knife. . . . It seemed that he was *unable to tolerate the implications of femininity and castration that he associated with passive submission and being fattened. . . .* There was evidence of jealousy of the mother in her relationship with the father and a *wish to take her place and to receive what father was giving her.* (1956:158)

In their next case, Joe, aged ten and a half, we learn:

Toilet training was achieved by the end of the second year, but he was almost four before he could hold his penis to urinate; until then his mother held it for him. The mother had never stopped her practice of wiping him after bowel movements. . . . He insisted that he wanted to be weak and helpless so that his mother would take care of him. He seemed to feel that his mother wanted him to be big and strong because she wanted him to go on a vacation with her. . . . He avoided further discussion by insisting that he was too young to talk about sex. . . . His concern over his masculinity was evidenced in *transvestite fantasies in which he was mistaken for a girl.* (1956:161–162)

Their third case was Dick, who was also ten years of age. We find that: "He proved to be a brilliant, passive, dependent, rather effeminate child, *very closely identified with his mother* and reflecting her ambivalence by presenting a similar ambivalent attitude toward her" (1956:164).

In discussion of these cases, the authors mention these qualities:

During latency these chlidren have a tendency to be obese. There is a very strong feminine identification and they are very close to their mothers.

The fear of growth and the masculine role, and the wish to remain in an infantile, dependent relationship with the mother become predominant and the patient begins consciously to starve himself, alternately protesting that he does and does not want to grow up, and that he does and does not want to remain weak in order to be cared for by the mother. *Oral and anal sadism pours forth.*

There appears to be an incapacity in these children to identify in any way other than by imitation.

During the struggle for supremacy, food seems to take on all of its early and primitive symbolic significance. (1956:166–167)

The case material is striking in showing the boys' plight in being intensely involved with mothers who were blatantly seductive. They could not admit to their sexual wishes for the mother without feeling helplessly engulfed by her. Only a nonsexual closeness based upon imitative identification kept them feeling safe from annihilation. However, the dependency on food/mother also had to be eradicated in order to maintain a distance that would not be threatening. Furthermore, the superficial surrender of their masculinity in making a mother-identification was ambivalent and unstable. They were in deep turmoil. To understand this we must remember that the wish to feminize was a defensive maneuver and not a deeply satisfying yearning of the boy. The boy represses his deepest impulses but can feel that he protects himself from engulfment/extinction by assuming a feminine identity. He reinforces this protection by proof of his independence of food/mother through not eating.

In the cases cited above, there is abundant evidence of oral and anal material, difficult separation/individuation problems with the mother, identification on the basis of appearance and imitation, great ambivalence, power struggles, distortions of body image and concrete symbolization of food, all remainders of the primary oedipal phase (and all characteristic of the classic anorexic syndrome as well). When a boy cannot form a sufficient core gender identity to move beyond this phase for the kinds of reasons demonstrated by these cases, he may become an anorexic. The primary oedipal involvement of male anorexics is comparable to that in the most disturbed cases in Sours' classification of female anorexics. Only the most severe psychopathology, comparable to that of the sickest of female patients, produces the syndrome in the male, accounting for the relative rarity of the condition in the male group. Their degree of involvement with primary oedipal phase issues explains both why they are anorexic and why anorexia appears so much less often among males than among females. The issues involved in anorexia in an adult can operate on such an intense, primitive level only as leftovers of a struggle poorly settled in early childhood. That struggle originates in the primary oedipal phase, the beginning of the time of good/bad ideation when sense of self and independence, along with awareness of different feelings for mother and father, fixes these matters as a syndrome in the child's developing personality.

In the still more rare instance of a male anorexic whose general ego development permits a favorable prognosis, the operation of the primary oedipal complex is visible. A sexually related psychological trauma during the primary oedipal phase can occur in conjunction with other predisposing psychological conditions and act to elicit a later anorexic condition in the male or female. This can happen even when the child has shored up sufficient ego strength to keep its underlying primary oedipal problems from attaining the degree of pervasiveness that handicaps most anorexic boys. Such an example is Paul, a case of Wiener's (1976). He has added interest for us as an identical twin, discordant for anorexia. The fact that his twin, John, was not anorexic throws into relief the dynamics of the condition.

From the available information, Paul was the more energetic of the pair. It is not known how early he came to seem the more tense twin, but otherwise the boys' development seemed quite similar. Paul and John had similar fantasies "albeit with different shadings" (p. 532). They both contended with the birth of a younger brother when they were two years old and with "rather typical family dynamics" (p. 533). Neither twin differed from the other in an unremarkable feeding and training history nor, of course, genetically. However, when Paul was three, he displayed interest in his father's penis to which the father reacted with panic and "vigorous disapproval and prohibition" (p. 526). That the father still talked about it eight years later (even though Paul did not repeat the behavior) gives some idea of the intensity of his feelings. The father successfully encouraged both boys in athletics, but although Paul was the more forceful of the two, the father's message to Paul allowed only for the appearance of masculine behavior, not freedom in sexual thought. Taking note that Paul did not suffer any early oral disturbance and that the only significant difference between him and his twin was the blatancy of the father's message about sexuality, we can look for the meaning of his anorexia.

Typically for male anorexics in contrast to female cases, Paul was prepubescent at onset and expressed concern about not eating. He saw his self-starvation as an attempt to establish control over his body and impulses, but he also could not swallow, particularly his saliva. Initially after hospitalization, Paul continued to lose weight. He expressed concern that he might cause his parents to divorce even though from what Wiener gleaned, the marriage was a sound one. Paul demonstrated the primary oedipal level of his concerns by confusion about what was inside or outside of himself, preoccupation with being good or bad, hyperactivity to prove autonomy in spite of his emaciation, confusion of body parts (stomach for uterus, mouth for anus as in saliva being equated with excrement), fear of his body's going out of control (splitting). The first breakthrough in his psychotherapy came when Paul imparted his terror of his urges because "he had for so long relied on imposed or artificial controls" (p. 530).

Paul was able to accept a guarantee from Wiener that he would help Paul to learn that he could trust himself and his body. On the following day, the boy began to eat a regular diet. He needed further reassurance that his stomach would stay flat. In less than a month he had regained eight pounds, was cheerful in mood and could be discharged to outpatient care with only his delusions about his saliva as a continuing symptom.

Paul now confided his sexual conflicts. He felt guilty and ashamed of his early heterosexual fantasies. He defended himself with fantasies of oral impregnation and anal birth. The second and final turning point occurred when he wrote out and discussed his fantasy involving the "anal" saliva. Reminiscent of Sylvester's case, Paul gave food and his saliva male significance as that which enters, his own stomach serving as the receptive female organ: thus swallowing became intercourse. It was his "policeman" (father/super-ego) that inhibited his eating so that he could not complete his impregnation fantasy.

Two days after these revelations, Paul was free of "anxiety, obsessional thinking or difficulty in swallowing his saliva and was essentially symptom free for the first time in a year" (p. 531).

In his discussion of the case, Wiener emphasized the ego strengths of both boys. They were academically, socially, and athletically adept. As to psychopathology, Paul's twin, John, indicated in an interview that he had similar conflicts over heterosexuality as did Paul, but expressed his difficulties in phobias and a more dependent pattern of behavior compared with Paul. The mother is described as controlling but nurturing and "appropriate" (p. 531) toward her sons. It makes sense that John was able to manage his life otherwise successfully on the basis of symptoms which excused his desire for closeness with his mother. Both twins struggled with guilt and shame over heterosexual wishes, but it was Paul who engaged his father's intense involvement. We might speculate that the father's insecurity about his own masculinity made him need to be especially in charge of the sexual impulses of his more active son. Paul's vulnerability to this behavior of his father's might well have been heightened by the meaning to him of his mother's pregnancy and the birth of a younger sibling while Paul was in the primary oedipal phase, a speculation that derives from Paul's obsession with keeping his stomach flat.

Paul's primitive reactions to his oncoming adolescence make sense in the light of his father's treatment of him on account of his sexual interest, on top of what he shared with his twin of oral/anal/genital fantasies and bodily concerns. From the guilt feelings and shame both boys expressed about their heterosexual fantasies, we know that whatever homosexual fears the father may have had, the sons responded to his passionate interest in their athletics (bodies) by recognizing his claim to them. Paul's defense against the particularly strong message he got from the father was the primary oedipal unisex fantasy which created his anorexia.

Traces of the Anorexic Syndrome in Nonanorexic Cases

We have seen that the anorexic syndrome consists of an extreme exhibition of the primary oedipal dynamic resonating in adolescence or young adulthood. We should expect on that basis that the same collection of symptoms in milder form would be observable in conjunction with other, less severe forms of eating disorder, such as mild compulsive eating or moderately severe dieting not classifiable as anorexia. We see such mild playbacks of the primary oedipal phase in the following two patients of mine.

First, Barbara gives the formula for anorexia in inverse form. She began one session by showing me pictures she had taken of her pretty two-year-old niece, greatly resembling Barbara at the same age. After some critical comments about Barbara's sister-in-law, the niece's mother, Barbara was reminded of her own mother's feeling that Barbara had been too fat. She next again criticized "mother people," daring to imply her really feeling superior to them. Abruptly, Barbara moaned, "I wish I had no body." I asked her why. "Then I wouldn't feel fat [said in tone of disgust] . . . or have other [pause] feelings." I asked her what the other feelings might be. "I suppose sexy feelings." She explained that being fat meant being unattractive, but it somehow was associated with having sexy feelings. If she had no body she would (1) have no sexy feelings and (2) be good.

Barbara's constellation of inner forces produced a different face of that coin, but clearly for her, as for anorexics, the two-year-old experience—competition with other females, body image, sexuality, orality, and the good/bad dichotomy—formed a symptomatic syndrome.

Another young adult patient of mine, Alison, also sheds light on the syndrome. Although slender, she was not anorexic. Her presenting symptom was depression. Her mother having suffered a severe depression the year before, Alison's depression seemed overdetermined, with a need to suffer like her mother as one factor. The focus of our work was on her need for a sense of greater separation/individuation.

Alison was feeling better about herself in general when she suddenly developed excruciating menstrual cramps. Nothing she tried seemed to help to diminish them. Her associations led to thoughts about the pain of childbirth. These thoughts reminded her of her mother's tales of trouble with pregnancy and sex. Before this point in her analysis, Alison had told me nothing about her father except how much she disapproved of him. In this session, however, she imparted happy early memories of his exuberant play with her, particularly before her siblings were born, when she was younger than two years old. This treatment experience came as Alison began to value her sense of self. In other words, being like her mother in suffering over sexuality, happy excitement with her father when she was under two, and self-differentiation all came together in this session. Interpretation in terms of the dilemmas of the primary oedipal phase seemed to give her some ease.

For two years I heard no more about menstrual difficulties. By this time she had become a geographer (her mother being a cartographer). She felt that she was going her mother one better in her professional choice. She began to feel free to explore relationships with men. For some time we worked along without dramatic incident. Then Alison called me in great agony. She was menstruating and again experienced pain in her pelvis which seemed to her like childbirth. She panted, "Something *must* come out—I go to the toilet, but nothing happens!"

She was in the fourth day of a previously uneventful menstrual period. That morning we had had a session in which Alison told of delight in her femininity. She looked forward to that night's Christmas party, where she anticipated the attentions of a particular young man. She thought of herself not just as playing a role, but as being really beautiful. From our session, Alison had gone to her health club, where she had run joyfully and then attended an exercise class. Up until that point in the day, Alison was completely comfortable, planning for the party.

Daring to think of men noticing her at the party seemed to trigger a backlash in her feelings. Later in the day, while she was at work, Alison thought of the many pelvic movements she had performed in her exercises: wide open movements and postures like the birthing position. Alison realized how sexual those movements in exercise class were.

Her thoughts went to getting her hair cut for the party, but she worried what her supervisor (who was about her own age yet, according to Alison, was like Alison's mother) would think of her looking so mature. Beginning to feel acutely uncomfortable, she began to talk about her pains with a friend at work and found herself discussing her parents. She was given tea, but it made things worse. She left work early, driving to her apartment in a state of terror because she felt the pain was too disturbing to let her drive safely. Alison took Tylenol and tried everything else that anyone told her to do. None of this was ameliorative.

In giving me this account, Alison noticed that her pains crescendoed whenever she mentioned her parents. She talked of how they tried to control her. Describing her mother's reaching out to her in a conversation, Alison exclaimed that she could feel the "red-clawed hand" of her mother coming through the telephone. Alison felt particularly that her mother wanted to intrude on Alison's sexuality (which in fact had been largely repressed until she came into treatment). It seemed to Alison that her mother's depression made her desperate to live through Alison. Another pressing matter was Alison's coming to believe in her own right to sexuality. It was as if Alison had to suffer like her mother for being sexual.

Alison said to me, quite seriously, "I'll just tell her what she wants to know—my whole sex history. I never told her about the latest person; I'll just give it up if that's what she needs to stop this pain!" Alison clearly felt that the pains came from her mother in order to punish her. We contemplated: Even if she did give up her sexuality to her mother, could that really satisfy her mother or make her happy? Her mother would still be herself and Alison herself.

Alison seemed to feel better with this idea. She told me about adolescent fantasies she had had about being either Maid Marian or Robin Hood. Maid Marian went to a nunnery when she could not be with Robin. He was active, just as it was important for Alison to be physically active. She now decided she could be her own kind of Maid Marian, active and strong. Alison told me that she was feeling better. We agreed that she would call me several hours later if she wanted to and to work further at that time if she felt the need for it.

Alison did call. She told me she had been sleeping. She now felt fine. She wanted to eat, but she was not sure that it was wise. Milk seemed to be the perfect idea. Then she said to me with the sense of great discovery, *"This must be what anorexia is all about!"*

Alison had not mentioned to me any worries about her being anorexic before. It was striking to me that her integration of primary oedipal phase issues now gave her simultaneous relief and insight about anorexia. The previous time she reported severe menstrual pain it proved to be about punishment for early happy memories of herself and her father when she began to feel independent. In the intense work of this day she expressed conflict over whether she could be independent of her mother and sexually attractive without paying for it by suffering her mother's afflictions. Primary oedipal-level fantasies of birth were prominent in this material, in both oral and anal components. (Swallowing something [tea] "caused" child-birth pains; "something must come out" into the toilet to relieve the pains.) Gender identity was another primary oedipal issue that she joined. Finally, Alison was able to consolidate good feelings about herself as a (genderless) "sleep and eat" baby. She stretched from the adolescent version of her gender confusion back to the earliest forms of reassurance. Then in her insight about anorexia, she seemed to integrate the elements that she had been experiencing fragmentally. She went on to enjoy the party.

Several months later, she was dining with her parents when her mother's efforts at controlling Alison became blatant. Alison had a brief return of menstrual pain. It lasted only for twenty minutes as Alison became aware of reacting to her mother's behavior and recognized that she was feeling caught in the old family triangle. The pain subsided, and Alison relished her meal.

Even though overt anorexia was not one of Alison's symptoms, we can see in her case the binding together of orality, sexuality, and ideas arising in the second year of life, the same complex of symptoms Sours and others described for the anorexic and that we observed in two-year-old behavior patterns. Along with her mild compulsive dieting, these symptoms include: hyperactivity (exercise program a prerequisite for feeling good); problems in separation/individuation from her mother (concern about going beyond her mother professionally); menstrual difficulties (although not as disturbed as amenorrhea); repression of sexuality (an initial condition as she began treatment); secrecy of thought (feeling she had to tell her mother everything in order for her mother to stop causing her to suffer); splitting ("Maid Marian" and "Robin Hood," feminine and masculine parts to herself); and preoccupation with oral/anal matters (as seen in her impregnation and birth fantasies).

Sexuality for the usual female case remains connected with rivalry with her mother over her father. Therefore, when the upsurge of sexual impulses in adolescence reinstates great yearning, the hapless girl feels plunged back into the drama of her earliest days. Thomä (1961) observes that often an anorexic patient even goes back to using the utensils of her childhood. Yet she is no longer a tiny child, and her conflict cannot this time be managed simply by repression and denial. Her possibilities for sexuality are much greater and more pressing, while what she gives up for continued dependence upon her mother is more obvious. In an interesting circle, anorexia illustrates the power of the primary oedipal complex, and the primary oedipal complex enables us at last to understand anorexia.

Summary and Conclusions

Summary of the Theory

This book presents and gives evidence for the theory of the primary oedipal phase. The theory of the primary oedipal phase is developed by integrating the various psychological events that occur simultaneously instead of simplifying the situation to the perspective of a single event. By so doing, understanding of human personality is furthered in appreciating rather than reducing the awareness of its complexity. As the theory unfolds we see that:

1. Gender identity, ego formation, separation/individuation, body-ego formation, awareness of sexual feelings, and gender-based role modeling all develop simultaneously, *and each is given definition by the others.*
    a. Intrapsychic separation/individuation from the mother is possible only because the child achieves a sense of self through formation of an integrated ego.
    b. Ego formation develops from the simultaneous establishment of separation/individuation, gender identity, awareness of sexual feelings, gender-based self-modeling, and the body-ego.
    c. Gender identity forms in relation to awareness of sexual feelings, self-modeling on the like parent, and ego growth.
    d. Sexual feelings arise physiologically but are focused only by the development of gender identity and of the ego.

     e. Self-modeling is possible only through the establishment of gender identity and of ego growth.

     f. Body-ego develops in relation to all of these plus physiologically timed growth.

2. Conflicts are inherent in this process, and the nature of these conflicts is different for each sex. These conflicts can be separated into three groups. However, these groups of conflicts are separable only by the observer. Their simultaneity and their importance to the child make them inseparable to the child.

     a. One set of conflicts includes those arising from simultaneous, growing awareness of sexual feeling and awareness of *both parents* while working through separation/individuation difficulties. For the boy, this means that sexual attraction opposes individuation. For the girl this means that sexual attraction threatens being a traitor to the one to whom she is still linked via dependency.

     b. The second group of conflicts arise from self-modeling based on the parent who is simultaneously becoming a rival due to awareness of sexual feelings (in the boy's case) or who is simultaneously the one from whom separation/individuation must be achieved (in the girl's case).

     c. A third group of conflicts arises in the resolution of the separation/individuation and autonomy–dependence conflicts.

3. This primary oedipal conflict thus arises naturally, so influencing how the child thinks and feels that the proper name for this period in the child's life is the primary oedipal phase.

4. The many other factors in the toddler's life, such as oral dependency, sphincter maturation, growing cognitive skills, and psychosocial cueing by the parents, all get represented during the creation of the child's nascent ego according to their meanings in the other processes and conflicts. The limited cognitive development of the two-year-old in turn determines the manner in which those conflicts can be handled and the way in which their resolution molds the developing personality.

5. In order to manage so much, the child utilizes the developmental fact that language and consciousness arise gradually and are added on to preexisting imagistic thought and emotional capacities. Therefore it can leave unconscious (i.e., not label in conscious thought) those feelings that it deems un-

acceptable to itself. The mechanism of splitting, involving denial and repression, thus becomes a natural help in handling emotional conflicts at this age.

6. The primary oedipal complex, as it develops in each child, is unique to that child, but it always involves oral and anal elements, as well as the patterning of thoughts and feelings, including attitudes about independence-dependence and about the parents and the self in terms of their gender.

7. A primitive super-ego coalesces at the same time. The child's sense of self engenders a sense of responsibility. Therefore, as intuited in the Bible, it experiences guilt and shame from knowledge of self and sexuality. The first super-ego formation is created out of the primary oedipal child's oral and anal sadism, its preoccupation with the dichotomy of good versus bad, and its confusion about omnipresence and annihilation in the experience of object-absence. Violent fantasies deal with uncertainties as to the consequences of separation/individuation in the context of oedipal feelings.

8. The complicated combination of all these factors in the child's inner life is what I call the primary oedipal complex. I call it that because the child's oedipal feelings are the dynamic expression of what it means to the child to possess whichever gender identity is at the core of its ego.

9. Since the nature of the primary oedipal conflict is substantively different for boys and for girls, it results in different behavior patterns among them.

10. Because of these behavior patterns, gender-related differences affect all the developmental processes, which must be taken into account in understanding both early personality development and later personality disorders.

11. Depending on whether things go smoothly or whether there are hitches and obstructions, well-defined behavior patterns and in some cases psychopathologies derive from the primary oedipal phase. Some examples of such psychopathologies are anorexia, suicidal ideation, and disorders of gender identity.

The incidence of these conditions is different among men and among women because the primary oedipal phase takes a different course in boys than in girls. Whenever the incidence of a severe psychopathology is different between the two gender groups, the condition is traceable to the patients' primary oedipal phase. This fact explains the nature of the syndromes that make up severe pathological conditions. Conversely, whenever, as in borderline personalities, the pathology is known to derive from the two-year-old period, in addition to problems over separation/individuation and splitting as a defense, patients will display other remnants of the primary oedipal phase: their relationships with other people will be troubled in terms of gender; their sexual fantasies will be filled with oral and anal elements; and their egos will be poorly integrated.

12. The difference between the classical oedipal phase of the child of four and the primary oedipal phase of the child of two is not the degree of oedipal involvement on the part of the child. The difference is in the levels of ego development of which each child is capable.

13. The nature of ego organization at the resolution of the primary oedipal phase and then at the resolution of the classical oedipal phase and finally after adolescence forms a guide to understanding degrees of psychopathology and appreciating the individual's achievements in mental health.

With the help of this understanding we can reconsider where the two-year-old "primary oedipal" phase fits into the greater context of child development and what factors influence the individual differences we observe in human personality.

Reflections Through Life

So immense are the complexities of development in human personality that, in order to present the primary oedipal phase with clarity, I have concentrated on the mere fact of its existence. Only having established this can we now turn to look for the place of the primary oedipal phase along the developmental continuum. Earlier in the book, I also purposely omitted systematic consideration of factors that affect how a particular child experiences and resolves its earliest oedipal conflicts. However, as we put the primary oedipal phase into perspective, we can now take note of some of the factors particular to a given child that affect its personality formation along the way.

The Developmental Field

There exists a large and diverse literature on personality development, which must be taken into account in seeking the significance of the primary oedipal phase. I draw upon the work of object relationists, ego psychologists, and cognito-geneticists in their various subdivisions. All these workers center, as do I, on the idealized "universal child."

Previous models have been a series of mutually corrective pictures, each emphasizing things that the others left out. Thus Freud's visualization of the ego as "the residue of abandoned object cathexes" (1923) led through Klein to Fairbairn's statement that normal development and psychopathology are both to be understood strictly in terms of inner and outer object relations (1944). The corrective extreme of this is the cognito-genetic model preferred by Piaget (1954), McGraw (1963), and Chomsky (1968), somewhat exemplified by Kagan, Kearsley and Zelazo (1980) and Thomas and Chess (1980). This model holds that the obvious timetable of maturation controls the shaping of personality. Ego psychologists such as Kernberg (1968a) view these developments chiefly in terms of inner processes that seem to exist, especially associations of similarly charged feelings. Sullivan and Kohut focus on interpersonal shaping of the self. Current trends (Saretsky, Goldman and Milman 1979) seem to be bringing the various lines of observation closer together. In keeping with this trend, the ideas presented here take the form of a synthesis of all of these lines of work to attempt a clearer sense of the ego-integration process.

The Earliest Years

In drawing a timeline for personality development, a major question is where to start. I have invested some effort in this book to showing that ego formation, sexual feelings, triadic interactions, and so on are all simultaneously being developed by the time of the primary oedipal phase. Yet we must address the question of whether ego formation could begin still earlier, as far back as at birth or even in utero. The number of excellent workers who have theorized about such early ego determinants demands that we take the question seriously.

Evidence that pre–early oedipal trauma has no detectable effect upon later child and adult personality is negative evidence, not to be regarded as conclusive. (An example is the Viedemar 1979 study in which a girl with severe congenital esophagus dysfunction, which totally prohibited swallowing, was operated on only months after birth. Yet in careful follow-up, she developed no eating disorders or other psychopathologies, becoming a normal adult.) We have also already given evidence that many key prerequisites of personality formation do not arise before the primary oedipal phase, such as the capacity for object permanence and linguistic thought. Yet one could postulate that imagistic, prelinguistic experience could greatly influence the form of later ego growth. Indeed, this is an approach that many have taken.

In some previous psychoanalytic models, elaborate choreographies of abstract forms have been conceived to occupy the inner life of an infant. The worry one must have is that, in ascribing such complexities to the infant from our adult perspective, we are engaging in anthropomorphization. This problem was noted by Guntrip (1971). He pointed out how much anthropomorphizing about infant personality by psychological theorists comes from reconstructions with adult patients. He emphasized the need to remember the rudimentary state of a baby's powers in guessing what mental constructs might be counterpart to the baby's behavior.

Then how can the truth be known? Does the infant have a complex inner life, or is that just anthropomorphizing? For us the crucial question is not the state of the infant's mind but rather whether that state has any major significance for the later personality. If it does, then we should find evidence for it in later behavior. Certain psychophenomena have indeed been attributed to this earliest time. It is by close scrutiny of these phenomena that we shall find our answer.

Most of the theorizing about leftovers from early infancy has centered on part-object fantasies and in particular breast part-object fantasies. Detailed examination of the claim that such fantasies are derived from this period is also important in that it gives an indication of when the child actually forms permanent images and thus inner object relations.

Fortunately, our society provides a simple test for the claim. The test is based upon the fact that babies in Western cultures are usually bottle-fed. Conservative sample figures from over the last five decades are that 50 percent of all babies are fed by bottle from the beginning of their lives and 72 percent after the first month. (American Academy of Pediatrics Committee on Nutrition 1979).[1] *If it were true that fantasies about part-objects derived from an oral period preceding the beginning of the primary oedipal phase, those fantasies would have to involve bottles, not breasts.* At least, that would have to be true in a tremendous number of cases. To the bottle-fed infant, the detail of its mother's breasts must be much less important than the bottle she extends to it, her face, or her hands. It simply makes no sense that a young baby who is fed exclusively by bottle would have complicated fantasies engendering the strongest affects about mother/milk and express those fantasies in terms of breasts.

However, by the time the child is a toddler, it is conscious of breasts in terms no longer on a par with bottles. Distinguishing between the sexes is by that age a way the child has to organize its own genital feelings and impressions of an interpersonal world, at a point of its maturation that permits permanent memory of form. Breasts make a fine distinction between male and female bodies when the child becomes sensitive to such categorizations. Thus by the time of the beginning, orally dominated part of the primary oedipal phase, fusion of oral interests and oedipal concerns is likely to produce mental constructs. There are other examples of early fusion between oral and genital experiences denoting awareness of genital differences during the late oral period, for example, the "swallowing vagina" psychotic fantasy (Robertson-Rose 1983). Only if patients' fantasies reflected actual experience during the pre-self oral period would we be justified in assuming that their most primitive fantasies arose directly from the first months of life.

If not from early experience (as the bottle example shows), then could we propose that such fantasies do derive from early infancy but are inherited rather than experienced directly (i.e., a genetic sense of breasts)? To answer with a question, is it reasonable to ascribe an infant's affects in primordial fantasies about breasts and mother to its experience and yet insist that the breast/mother symbol is in itself a genetic given? We must conclude that it is not.

If, as we are driven to believe, early infancy is not a direct contributor to the later personality structure, then we must have another model for it, since the first nine months of life are not a mere holding pattern for toddlerhood, but rather are filled with dynamic development. I propose the following model based on the evidence that the ninth-month period for most babies is a time when neurological functioning quickly becomes more organized and stable. Along with other evidence presented in chapters 2 and 3, EEG studies (Metcalf 1979) are striking in this regard.

The child from the prenatal state on gradually develops in cognitive capacity and range of emotional expression. Its perceptions also gradually increase in scope, starting with what adults recognize as parts, and eventually include organized wholes (Arieti 1976). Affective responses are global and become associated with concurrent events. These are shifting states, however; only gradually as the infant approaches its ninth month do such experiences regularly become the basis of anticipatory responses. Good and bad become significant concepts for the child and not merely an observer's interpretation of tropistic behavior. Ego-nuclei, which are formed out of autonomous ego functions, become a network that enables a child of nine months or so to begin to organize a sense of self. Awareness of parts of self and parts of others in conjunction with a capacity for object permanence can be put to use by means of an ability for concrete symbolization. The uniqueness and intensity of genital sensations give focus to all these accomplishments. For the next year and a half, the child is in the primary oedipal phase and its business is integration of its ego.[2]

This model includes the mental processes delineated in a great deal of careful psychoanalytic work. However, it suggests that the timetable of personality development be reconsidered. This model also takes into account evidence that much motivation for infantile behavior comes from a natural tendency to utilize expanding capacities. Freud foreshadowed recognition of this when he wrote in 1938 that the biological course of infant development was ultimately more important to the personality than the specific nature of early experience. Thomas and Chess (1980) stress "goodness of fit" of experience to the particular child's developmental state at the time of the experience in order to understand effects upon the personality from that experience. The capacities for mental identification and then imitation of behavior grow from dim beginnings to become the source of major mental activity by the time the child is two years old. The effects of experience must be understood in this context. The human infant is neither a glob of putty nor a pre-formed jack-in-the-box.

There are many great and fascinating questions we raise about the child's mechanisms for response to experience and how and why effects of experience take place. It will help in our continuing explorations to consider the developmental setting of the primary oedipal phase.

A Sketch of the Developmental Continuum
We have seen that the ego begins to coalesce in the primary oedipal phase. In chapter 10 we saw how the later classical oedipal stage may be viewed as a replay of the primary oedipal stage. The two oedipal periods punctuate these other periods, which also may be viewed in parallel with each other. The overall pattern fits observations by Gesell and colleagues (1940) and Piaget (1954) that there is periodicity in childhood development.

The preorganizational state of the child's mind up until the primary oedipal phase increasingly involves organizational activity, but experience-gathering and exercise of newly unfolding capacities are still more pronounced. We might think of this first stage as a time of accumulation and expansion of ego nuclei. As mapping of the body and interpersonal relations coordinate with ability to consolidate the ego, the child enters the primary oedipal phase.

By the time the child reaches three years of age, the stormy, self-defining passions of the two-year-old resolve into the relative calm of the next phase, often called the phallic. However, as Gesell and colleagues (1940) and White (1975) point out, the three-year-old is a well-developed personality, reminding adults of "little gentlemen and ladies." More accurately we can consider such a period as another time of accumulating experience and expanding capacities. Now that the parts of the body are recognized and the sense of self is defined by physical form, the bodily interest of children of both sexes has to do with effectiveness. Thus, what one can do with special parts of the body is intriguing and fosters competitive feelings.

The differences between the sexes are important from this standpoint, and the phallus is highly cathected. However, girls are not limited to visual perception of phalluses as they develop attitudes toward their own bodies. They have ample wonderful feelings in the genital area. They also can identify with their highly effective mothers, the least effective of whom are vastly more capable than a three-year-old. "Phallic phase" is an unbalancing concept that ignores the broader processes within the personality, and it particularly distorts the situation of the girl. We need an appropriate name for this second period, in which again accumulating experience and expanding capacities is the main psychic thrust.

Gradually, a new stage of consolidation and ego organization emerges as the child gains further confidence in its ability to develop and also a sense of future time that suggests it will grow up to be like the parent of the same sex. In the throes of a new organization of self in terms of role, this child is then in the classical oedipal phase.

The next stage of development we are in the habit of calling latency, but that is another unfortunate choice of term. Its use derives from the obvious change in expression of sexual interest. However, sexual interest per se continues to develop all through the middle childhood years (Gesell and Ilg 1946; Fraiberg 1972).

What changes in this way after the classical oedipal phase is that parents are no longer consciously the objects of sexual aims. Furthermore, conscious sexual interest toward the parents does not dominate the feelings of adolescents. Such content is not merely latent after the classical oedipal phase but definitely repressed.

Fundamentally, resolution of the classical oedipal phase leads the child into another period of emphasis upon accumulating experience and expanding capacities. As with the three-year-old, the child's preceding achievements in ego organization are the firm platform from which it operates. A strong sense of identification by gender and age group becomes the basis for following segmented pursuits and expressing competitive feelings. Fantasy is clearly segmented off and demarcated, including oedipal themes only symbolically, as in fairy tales.

Adolescence, of course, is the next period of large-scale organizational acitivity of the ego (Lidz 1968). In the adolescent, heightened sexual ability intertwines with the prospect of adult independence, a considerable challenge to the preadult. Dealing with this intertwining produces an emotional upheaval reminiscent in all ways of the oedipal phases. Similarly, it leads to a level of organization of the ego based upon new possibilities, the adult self.

Factors Making for Individual Differences
in Resolution of the Primary Oedipal Conflict
Until now we have chiefly considered the developmental line occurring in every child's life. It is the long list of factors specific to each child, however, that makes for the uniqueness of a personality.

In this section we take some note of biological, familial, and cultural factors that make a difference to each child's development. All of these and more affect the child's first organization of its ego. Conversely, how the child responds in terms of these same factors later on in its life is much determined by the outcome of its primary oedipal conflict; that is, by the nature of its synthesis of its first ego.

Biological Factors Affecting the First Organization of the Ego. In development of an ego, there are biological factors that make for individual differences as well as for the similarities that distinguish all of humankind.

This survey starts with *genetic factors*, raising the nagging question of how much is nature and how much is nurture in explanation of human personality. Theorizing about hyperactivity is an example of why the debate seems endless. A child may be hyperactive for genetically based reasons, but its constant movement and short attention span also have inner defensive value in escaping the engulfing mother (remembering that the child's perception of its mother's engulfingness is influenced by primary oedipal conflict). In turn, a particularly controlling mother might treat her hyperactive child according to her perception of its defensiveness. A reciprocal pattern can ensue, which is thus caused by nature *and* nurture.

There are two complications in our efforts to understand this process. First, there may be tertiary effects (e.g., the child's perception of itself as out of control and bad), which can be attributed only to both nature and nurture and which in turn characterize the child's behavior. Second, and still more difficult for purposes of scientific clarity, a specific expression of nature might not occur except in the presence of given nurture. Furthermore, with any characteristic, this will happen in varying degrees in different individuals due to each one's special qualities of nature and nurture and feedback effects. No wonder we are far from precise understanding of the nature–nurture relationship.

At least we know that nature and nurture both exist. In the study of an individual child, we can look for signs of the ways they interact in producing that child's personality.

One major genetic factor is the sequencing of various physiological capacities. EEG studies (Metcalf 1979) show that there is a neurological stabilization that occurs at around nine months of age. Studies by Torgersen and Kringlen (1979) show that, in contrast to the infant of two months, the infant of nine months has established patterns of rhythmicity and reactivity. There are in fact many examples of rapid higher-level maturation of the organism at this age. However, these genetically determined periods do vary. Particular children might not become typically stabilized by nine months, taking an extra month or two to develop certain functions, whereas others might be precocious. The same points relate to the rise of language and the capacity to conceptualize. Whether these various forms of maturation occur simultaneously or some of them occur earlier or later, what the child has available for its beginning sense of self must affect how it forms its ego. For example, a child whose motor capacities during ego formation permit it to be much more mobile than the average child of its age is perhaps less prone to scotophilia than the child whose motor capacities are slower to develop. This second child might cathect visual experiences more than the child who is able to respond to the environment in a more active way.

Individual patterns of reactivity affect the child's general way of experiencing (Petrie 1967). The range extends from those who seem to augment the intensity of given stimuli, to the majority, who operate within a moderate range, and to those who respond to stimuli by seeming to reduce intensities. In this aspect of processing stimuli, some individuals will be sensitive to much slighter stimuli (the augmenters), while others will require more intense stimulation in order to gain a particular level of response (reducers). The former would perhaps be more prone to rely on inner experience for gratification, while the latter, seeking stimulation, would experience the world differently and be treated differently in turn.

These factors show up even in neonates. Stroufe and Waters (1977) found that neonates could reliably be classifed according to those which, regardless of who held them, were comfortable being held tightly and those which were comfortable only when being held loosely. There is not information on how longlasting those particular neonatal patterns are, but it stands to reason that such sensitivities and thresholds for stimulation of infants in the Stroufe and Waters studies apply also to other genetically determined patterns that gain stabilization by nine months. These aspects of inner experience must affect the child's self-perceptions.

Throughout the primary oedipal period, that is, from approximately nine months to about two and a half years of age, there are characteristics of what used to be called the instinctual life of the child that vary at least to some degree in terms of genetic givens. For example, in the early part of the primary oedipal phase, children are still teething. The way in which a child feels about its body and feelings about feeding and therefore mother are likely to be affected by the difficulty or ease of the teething experience (Hoffer 1949). Sometimes an absence of certain enzymes makes digestion of milk difficult, which has consequences for the child's attitude toward mother and feeding. The strength of anal impulses and anal eroticism might be affected by the amount of anal mucosal tissue, which varies from child to child. The maturation of the sphincters is another genetically determined factor that has consequences in how the child experiences itself and the way in which it comes to understanding of its own acceptability—or nonacceptability—and encounters the various emotions involved in the toilet-training process. Key factors may allow for normal development even when related, seemingly necessary ones are deficient. For example, the presence of genital feelings enables an infant to organize a clear sense of self as a being with gender even when its genitalia are ambiguous in form.

The individual timing in development of certain specific capacities such as the ability to walk greatly affect the child's sense of autonomy and the ability to see itself as a truly separate, functioning organism. What produces frustration differs in ways that are influenced by its genetic makeup.

The child's *physical appearance* is another biological factor to consider. Its physical resemblance, whom it seems like both physically and in apperceived personality traits, can affect strongly how parents will react to a baby. Disturbing behavior may be seen not as a passing incident but as a danger signal in babies who are considered to "take after" someone whose negative qualities are feared. Conversely, greater tolerance may be extended toward another child who is considered to be like an approved-of person. Physical appearance as well as order of birth and gender can determine whether children may be used as good- or bad-self split-offs of a parent.

Its relative size can affect how the child is perceived by others and eventually how it perceives itself. A large, robust-looking child may find itself happily holding its own with an older sibling or instead suffering under pressure more appropriate to an older child. Conversely, a small, delicately constructed child will be seen in some instances as an object to be protected and in others to be scorned.

Another consequence of physical appearance is the response the child evokes esthetically. A child of apparent beauty receives different treatment from that accorded less well-endowed siblings. The effect on the beautiful child can be helpful in building a positive self-image. It also can cause difficulty because the child does not understand what it does to create the response, particularly when it encounters seductive behavior by a parent. Conversely, a less attractive child may identify with a more attractive, just older, same-sex sibling during the crucial toddler stage, confirming a positive self-image.

For all children, appearance is a key basis for organization of the ego during the primary oedipal phase. Therefore, such examples of the influence of appearance can play a formative role in the personality.

Health factors are another source of biological influence upon personality. Thomas and Chess (1980) make much of the child's experiences in relationship to the developmental point the child has achieved at a specific time. We can be alert to the degree to which experiences in health can affect a primary oedipal child's self-concept. Handicaps that exist from birth provide a different experience than similar ones that occur during the primary oedipal period. Helen Keller provides an example of this (Bleich 1976). She was a precocious eighteen-month-old when she suffered the illness that left her deaf, mute, and blind. From that time until Annie Sullivan restored the power of words to her, Helen Keller behaved like a "bad child." The famous first insight into the concept of water turns out to have connected with her level of attainment before her illness and with a feeling of goodness. In her autobiography she describes how, in her belief, the restoration of language made her feel like a self, a person, and simultaneously her behavior was transformed into lovingness and cooperation.

In the same way, less catastrophic but serious health experiences such as operations have a particular effect when they occur during the primary oedipal phase. Thomas (1963) reports a case of a twenty-month-old girl who used the experience of being under anaesthesia as part of her primal-scene fantasy. This event was highly significant in the structuring of her ego. Experiences in the hospital have impact due to the concomitant separation from the familiar home and often from parents. They also affect the child in terms of the behavior of the staff and other sick children.

The use of leg braces and other orthopedic restraining and molding devices in this critical period of life can foster attitudes that get built into the child's system of goodness and badness and its self-concept as a being of either gender. A sense of physical injury can be bound to other feelings involved in the child's self-identification. Brushes with death, feeling that one cannot breathe (as in asthma), and pain are other examples that may have a structural personality effect. The child who is sickly over a period of time may respond to the caretaking it receives by identification with the caretakers. It might also build into its ego the idea that being sick is a preferred status.

Another matter of health that can be of great significance is release from an ego-inhibiting handicap. An example of this would be new-found vigor after heart surgery, or correction of a problem in hearing or vision. How the toddler actually uses the experience depends upon the total context of its situation, but the meaning the experience has will be demonstrated by the effect that is seen in the child's ego.

Familial Factors Affecting the First Organization of the Ego. Familial factors include the child's parents and family constellations and changes also involving grandparents, siblings, adoptions, and family moves. At the top of this list comes the *parents*. Anyone reading this book is well aware that the most profound external influence upon the child's developing ego is its parents. To understand their influence upon the formation of the child's ego, we must take note of the reactions of the child to each parent and to the parents' relationships to each other. Herzog's cases are dramatic examples in point. The degree to which each parent is competitive for a child's loyalties adds further significance to the intensities of the child's own impulses toward each parent. Parental rejection is an issue that engages our professional interest, but the covert claims parents make on a child are at least as important. The sexual aspect of these claims is at last explored in crucial research by Galenson (1983). In achieving the resolution of the primary oedipal conflict, the child reacts to all of these factors.

Important *family constellations and changes* are next to consider. In the course of this book, there has been a continuous emphasis on the importance of both the parents in triadic interactions in the development of the ego. There are, however, many cases of children growing up from birth in one-parent homes: teenage pregnancies, early deaths or divorces, homosexual parents, etc., and cases of prolonged absence of one or the other parent during the early years of life (cases of extended illness, sailors, soldiers, etc.). In some cases this can have, as we must expect, horrific consequences in ego development.

On the other hand, many children of such homes develop into adults with no serious psychopathologies. One major difference from case to case may be the other people in the child's life and in the parent's life. The degree of interaction with grandparents, aunts and uncles, and the parent's boyfriends and girlfriends all vary tremendously; and how the child is able to use the various options psychologically also differs from youngster to youngster. One must expect, however, that when there is a psychological need for a particular role to be played, and when there is anyone available who could conceivably fill that role, the child will make use of the fact as best it can. Later divorce of the parents that occurs during the child's primary oedipal phase can also exacerbate the conflicts of toddlers of either sex.

In a broken home or an intact one, grandparents are often of great value to the toddler. Especially when geography permits close contact, grandparents can significantly affect the child's comfort in separation/individuation and sense of safety in its impulses. Their roles may be even more useful during the classical oedipal period, when they facilitate the child's sense of generationality. Death of a grandparent even as early as during the primary oedipal phase can be an important matter, particularly if the grandparent had lived with the family or nearby. In addition to dealing with the emotions of the parents, the child must deal with its own feelings of loss and question its own sense of responsibility. At all times, the intricacies of the parents' relationships with the grandparents plus the child's own relationship with them add special emphases to the child's emotional experience.

Siblings, as Josselyn (1948) pointed out, function to absorb some of the intensities of oedipal feelings. This is true especially at the primary oedipal level. The sex play of siblings can have enormous impact upon the self-concept of a child, including feelings of goodness or badness. Siblings are probably the first recipients of transference reactions.

Sibling rivalry is widely recognized as important in a developing personality. Libidinous sibling bonding contributes equally to the personality structure.[3] Among other things, the sibling interrelationships are important to how children will relate themselves to the large world later on. The expectations of treatment of one sort or another by people outside the family is conditioned to some degree by what happens with siblings. Particularly during the latency period, siblings may also operate as a form of "transitional object" in the child's efforts to find its place in the larger community, comparable to Winnicott's (1958) idea of the transitional object for the child in the toddler stage. Such use of siblings can be seen in a younger child's insistence on following an older sibling around outside the home whenever the latter goes on about its own business. One sees this again in school phobias and other signs of anxiety that develop when an older sibling goes off to school or to live in another place for the first time. The chosen sibling's going off can be enough for the younger child left at home to experience a sense of loss of self. This derives in part from the role of the sibling in a transference from the mother or father.

Krout (1939), in a pioneering study, found that children's ordinal positions in the family created characteristic effects upon personality. For example, a second child who is the same sex as the first-born is probably received differently by most parents than a second child who is of opposite sex. This milieu affects each child.

Also, it matters when a sibling is born. The birth of a sibling during the time of the primary oedipal phase seems to intensify a child's conflicts (White 1975). Siblings who died before the child was born or during the primary oedipal phase of the child can have presence in the psychic life of the surviving child. Such an effect was reported by Freud (1900) in his own history.

An effect of a mother's pregnancy during a child's primary oedipal phase is observation of changes in the mother's body. This can have considerable impact on a toddler who is in the process of consolidating its own body sense, as illustrated by some anorexics. Besides physical changes, the pregnancy brings other consequences for the relationship between the parents and the relationship of the child to each of its parents. What this means in terms of the child's feelings and of the impact it has upon the form of the toddler's primary oedipal conflicts will vary with the dynamics of the particular situation.

Singular events of emotional impact can become important in association with simultaneous developmental aspects of the toddler's life. Catastrophes in the family, e.g., illnesses, fires, accidents, losses, all contribute special meaning to the time of the child's life when they occur and in the wake of their general consequences. Critical for the child are the questions, Am I helpless? Am I at fault, therefore bad?

Incest is an example of an extraordinary event in which the quality of its impact varies according to the developmental stage of the child and what else the child is faced with in terms of behavior by other members of the family. When a mother does not acknowledge a father's incest, the child's problem of dealing with its guilt feelings is greatest. Another difficulty is seductive behavior short of incest, which the child reacts to as if it were incest. How such circumstances fit into or stimulate the child's fantasy life during the primary oedipal phase is a major dimension of ego development (e.g., Greenspan's case, chapter 10).

The literature is rich on the subject of the effect of separation of the child from its mother (Bowlby 1960, Spitz 1940). Similar studies relating to loss of the father are now being added. Drastic separations (as opposed to the daily rhythms of family life) such as those of death, divorce, or other large-scale events, change family constellations. Such changes are meaningful for the child in terms of the primary oedipal conflict.

A family move is another example of significant special events. A vulnerable toddler might use houses as concrete symbols of mother in dealing with feelings about loyalties when a possibility of change in relationships is dramatized by the move. This might be played out in the development of sleeping and feeding disturbances or, in extreme cases, disoriented behavior. These symptoms are often accompanied by dramatic withdrawal from the father in trying to resolve primary oedipal conflict.

The question of adoption is an interesting one from the standpoint of primary oedipal feelings. Sometimes the idea is introduced to the child during its toddler period. However vague the child's understanding, the idea of not belonging to the parents further complicates the process of separation/individuation and relationship to the father. Parental reaction to the adoption can increase anxiety, ambivalence, and/or seductiveness in handling of the child. Such experience can explain some of the anger an adopted child may feel later on about the predicament in which the biological parents left the child. The acute predicament is not the loss of a mythic mother but the accentuating of the splitting process in handling good and bad feelings about the self and the true (adoptive) mother. The child may feel an added loyalty strain in coping with oedipal impulses when at that stage the question of who belongs to whom becomes still murkier.

The effects of special events upon the toddler can be surprising. To understand them, we must remember that during the primary oedipal period the characteristic preverbal thought uses the logic of association. Therefore, other circumstances that are associated in time with the occurrence of the special event will have a generalized impact. Not only specific circumstances but the milieu in which the circumstances occur will affect the child's response. Whether the results are constructive to the early ego depends on the meaning the special event has for the child in terms of gender identification and oedipal conflict, including separation/individuation. In this context, meaning involves the child's sense of its own goodness or badness, passivity or capacity for control.

Cultural Expectations Affecting the First Organization of the Ego. Mentioning even a few of the many cultural standards that apply to a toddler's life reminds us of their importance: whether great physical restraint of children is expected/permitted, whether feeding is routinized, whether toilet training is emphasized, whether genital stimulation is treated casually or inhibited. The culture (or in our complex culture, a subculture to which the parents belong) might be ego-syntonic for a verbal child with relatively little investment in motoric activity, or vice versa. Such factors are meaningful in the ways they affect the chief bearers of culture, the parents of young children, in response to their children. This is true for less personal issues, too. Is the urban family required to keep a child quiet in an apartment with close neighbors? How do such requirements affect the parents and thus their approach to the child? Must the mother produce elaborate sterilization of food and environment to meet the culture's (doctor's, grandparent's, neighbor's) expectation of good mothering? Do paper diapers remove pressure from the mother to hurry toilet training? Television can be a peculiarly intrusive adjunct of the parents in some families. For the toddler, its significance might be greatest as a transitional object literally affecting the child's self/other perceptions; or as source of parental relaxation, television might serve to make parents more accessible for holding and cuddling.

Another frame of reference in understanding cultural effects upon the toddler child is cultural myths about children. Kagan (1980) reminds us that at different historical periods children may be seen as inherent sinners who must be curbed or as free spirits to be protected from inhibitions. These general attitudes impinge particularly upon the child's idea of itself as good or bad and its ease in separation/individuation.

Sleeping arrangements have direct oedipal implications with which the child must deal. These arrangements vary. The whole family may sleep in one bed, as in some rural areas. Children may never sleep in the same house with their parents, as in some Israeli kibbutzes.

We have a great body of information about the ways in which tribal societies and other societies more simple than our own affect their children's personalities with their particular requirements. Malinowski, Boas, Mead, Erikson, and Henry are some of the pioneers in finding the relationship between the requirements of a particular culture and the personalities that develop within the culture. In all of this important work, however, it is to be understood that the basic attributes of human personality are set in terms of such fundamental human experience and behavior that almost any kind of behavior one sees in one culture is likely to appear in any other to some degree. The declaration of Terence, "I am a man: therefore nothing human is alien to me," applies to all of mankind for all of us. Perhaps this is due in great part to the circumstances of nature that impose upon all humans the same set of psychological challenges in the toddler phase, when the first level of personality organization takes place.

Ramifications of the Theory

The preceding chapters have given much space to explaining the origin of various pathological behaviors on the basis of the primary oedipal theory. This is in large part due to the fact that by far the majority of the psychoanalytic literature, and indeed most of what is known on the subject, comes from analysis of disturbed individuals. If, however, the primary oedipal phase is truly the time of ego-pattern formation, then it must be at the root of many "normal" behavior patterns as well. In a number of instances this would appear to be the case on the basis of logical application of the model we have developed, but evidence is needed to prove the point. In this section I wish to offer a few examples of how this logic can be used, in the hope that others will be stimulated to generate the substantiation. In addition, study of possible ramifications of the primary oedipal phase might deepen our understanding of certain issues. Categories suggest themselves for such study: behavioral matters, implications for understanding certain social issues, and implications for further understanding of the process of psycho-therapy.

Explanations of Pervasive Behavioral Phenomena
Recognition of the primary oedipal phase enables a clearer tracing of ego-states in personality development. Study of *patterns of ego*

functioning might be fruitful in relation to primary oedipal conflict. A fundamental aspect is how factors specific to each child influence organization of the primary oedipal complex, i.e., ego formation. Some patterns seen in adults might be derivative.

For example, *many men do not allow themselves to get emotionally close to women.* We have seen that in the primary oedipal phase, when a male is forming his gender sense, he finds that his developing sexual impulses impel him toward greater closeness with the early object of his sex drive, his mother. Yet he is still in the process of separation/individuation. Closeness to his mother thus implies a loss of his identity through fusion. Loss of identity has two meanings for the two-year-old boy that might not be obvious from the adult perspective. First, because of the all-or-nothing thought pattern to which a child of that age is limited, identity loss literally means oblivion. This gives great force to his terror of engulfment. Second, because during the primary oedipal phase gender identity is forming at the core of the ego, and because his mother is of the opposite sex, the identity loss is translated to the child as loss of his maleness. (This terror of engulfment does not arise for the girl both because her sexual urges do not drive her toward her mother and because even in dependency she can still find a gender sense by identification with her same-sex mother.)

A common resolution to the boy's overwhelming fear of engulfment is to allow himself sexuality by guarding simultaneously against too much emotional closeness, which could swamp his ego. Thus such a male has an inability to "open up" with his sex partner because it threatens the very core of his ego, his sense of manhood.

Some men feel the need to dominate women in relationships or cannot tolerate women in superior positions. These are closely related issues to that preceding. To resolve the fear of engulfment such men can be independent, sexual individuals only by maintaining control and thus preventing women from pulling them into what they perceive as an endangering situation. The fears that set up these two behavior patterns exist to some extent in all men, as all had to deal with primary oedipal issues when young. However, those who have firmly consolidated their egos and gender identities in the primary oedipal, classical oedipal, and adolescent periods do not any longer need to erect such defensive barriers.

Male impotence is common after being laid off work. The usual explanation is that a man feels less "like a man" when he can no longer provide for his family. While this is certainly true, the reason why he needs to feel competent in an outside sense to feel sexual has always been left as intuitive. We all can appreciate the connection, but only with primary oedipal theory can it be explained logically why this must be so. Ego formation, we have seen, initially occurs during the primary oedipal stage. At this time there are three major contributors to the process in the male: self-modeling on father, separation/individuation from mother, and awareness of sexual feelings for mother. In losing his job, two of these underpinnings of the ego are collapsed. The man, in failing to support his family, ceases to model on his own father/provider and, by becoming dependent (on his wife or welfare), loses some of the autonomy that provided individuation. Sexuality declines not by any mystical connection but because, along with the other two components, it is another part of the ego-core. That is, for the young child (and at his heart for the man), sexuality is not separate from modeling or individuation. All are part of the same single task of self-definition.

Men who are athletic are usually socially competent. This makes sense since a child who learns to enjoy using his body at an early age is both gaining autonomy and modeling on his outside world–connected father. Thus his ego gains strength early on, and his awareness of his sexual urges is increased. Certainly later social factors play a great part in reinforcing this, but even some of those lead back to primary oedipal issues. For example, we shall see that girls being attracted to "exciting" physical men, which helps the athlete in further social maturation, has a primary oedipal basis.

Young men who are very studious are often socially maladjusted and often appear as weak "mama's boys." Some boys resolve these fears of engulfment in different ways than the controlling, sexual pattern described above. Especially if the mother is very dominating and/or if the father is a weak figure providing less of a model or if he is not compensating by developing efficient loco/muscular independence, a boy may not gain a sufficient level of individuation to stave off engulfment. Instead of erecting barriers from his mother he may instead protect himself by repressing the sexual urges that would drive him toward the engulfment. In so doing he does not deal with issues that are key to his psychosexual development and simultaneously he retains his dependency on his mother. Since he did not gain in autonomy by physical development, he is often not particularly strong, either. The studious characteristic has three causes. The first is that by remaining close to mother he identifies with her. Since early linguistic skills usually develop in interactions with mother at that same age, linguistic thought gets emphasized. Secondly, in repressing sexuality to maintain closeness without engulfment, the child uses a mind–body split. The esthetic, intellectual satisfaction is substituted for the physical pleasures. Finally, the anal/compulsive aspects of the studious personality find their root in the age at which all this occurs.

Women often feel guilty about sex. Young girls have a very different pattern of primary oedipal conflicts. For the girl, awareness of her sexual feelings makes her a rival of the mother, from whom she is simultaneously trying to undergo separation/individuation. She is still very dependent on her mother, and her mother/provider is clearly something good. Since at the time of the primary oedipal phase the girl's cognitive abilities have grasped the concept of absolutes but not of gradations, she thinks in terms of dichotomies. This is the origin of the splitting mechanism of organizing the world since mother is "good." Then, to the girl, anything opposing mother is "bad." Before a self-concept has been developed, there is no way to turn the idea of being "bad" against oneself. As the girl develops a (primitive) ego, she can attribute "badness" to herself and her anti-mother sexual feelings, thus giving rise to great feelings of guilt. For a woman who has not adequately resolved primary oedipal issues at that stage, or later during the classical oedipal or adolescent phases, sexual feelings can remain tied to guilt.

Women like to be "swept off their feet." One way for a girl to resolve these guilt feelings is to repress her sexual feelings. When this is done totally the result is psychopathological. However, one way she can get out of the bind and enjoy her sexual attractions is to allow herself to be in touch with such feelings only with exciting, physical men. Under such circumstances she need not feel guilt because she has abdicated control of the situation; it is the man's fault that she is excited, and she has thus not betrayed her mother/provider.

Some women need to be dominated by men in their personal lives or do not feel competent to take charge of men in their professional lives. This is a more extreme case of the same behavior pattern. These women's guilt feelings are somewhat stronger, and they are not at ease if they interact with men in any form unless they have abdicated control. To be on a par with men means responsibility for any feelings that might arise and thus betrayal of mother. This is, of course, opposing these women's own need for individuation in ego growth, which can lead to great inner turmoil.

Some women are only attracted to men who will end up hurting or degrading them. There are such women who will repeatedly get themselves into abusive situations, often complaining of them but never breaking such relationships off. Such a woman often was treated as a good self/split-off by her mother as a young child. As a girl she was, therefore, especially close to her mother and for that reason felt particularly guilty for her sexual attractions for her father. She cannot absolve such intense guilt as easily as some other women and must thus suffer for her "badness." Only by suffering, and by announcing her suffering in complaints over brutality made to mother-figures, can she gain an inner permission for her sexuality and pleasure.

Some women are "dumb blondes," pretty but not apparently very bright. At the two-year-old stage much identification is on the basis of appearances. Girls who learn to be attractive have engaged in much self-modeling on their mothers. This modeling also means that they model their attraction for their fathers on their mothers. Sexuality is not repressed, but the dependency-guilt trap is still there. Girls can avoid the guilt by developing a mind–body split. They can be sexual if they do not have an inner knowledge of their actions; they are not aware that they are behaving traitorously. Body (sexuality) is not repressed but mind is. That this occurs at the two-year-old stage rather than the classical oedipal stage (for instance) is seen in the use of the splitting mechanism. It is a successful strategy only because the primary oedipal mind operates on such a level.

Some women who are successful in business act asexual. Two-year-old girls can also deal with their newfound sexual feelings for their father by repressing sexuality and finding other ways to be close to him. They can work as adults, expressing autonomy from the mother. They achieve closeness to their father by identification rather than through sexuality. Thus they can develop into outgoing little "tomboys," or, if they do not later gain a sense of permission for their sexuality and an identification as females, into independent, successful career women who are repressed sexually.

These examples are but a sampling of many patterns that come to mind that can be explained on the basis of primary oedipal theory. Much in these patterns has never been adequately explained in a cohesive way before. Yet other, later, psychological factors and cultural reinforcement will also turn out to be important in them. Only future examination of evidence will determine how important a role each level of explanation plays in determining the patterns we observe.

Sex is dirty. Reported by anthropologists (Brown 1978) about other societies, this connotation is widespread in our own. The anatomical relationship of the genitals to urinary function and the closeness of the genitals to the anus, plus the pleasurable relief of tension associated with elimination all make the association between sex and dirtiness understandable. The fact that this association extends to "dirty words" and "dirty-mindedness," attributed badness to people, especially to women who make their sexual interests manifest and particularly who are sexually provocative, and most of all the fact that the disclaimer that sex is dirty is so often found in people who are judgmental and involved in categorical thinking suggests that the sex–dirtiness association is a relic of the primary oedipal phase. By contrast, those who show more sophistication in personality development are more likely to be comfortable with their sexual feelings.

What I have called the *intergenerational lockstep* is also a developmental matter illuminated by recognition of the primary oedipal phase. The intertwining of separation/individuation and oedipal concerns by his or her child can resuscitate the parent's primary oedipal concerns, causing a blurring of the parent's sense of generationality in relation to both the older and the younger generations. Haugh (1982) thinks of emotional patterns that seem to skip from grandparents to grandchildren. He suggests that the mechanism lies in this interplay. Further, guilt feelings and anxieties from the primary oedipal level can overwhelm a marital relationship when the couple become parents, making a difference in how they treat a child. Cohler and Grunebaum (1981) have already broken ground in studying intergenerational processes. They kept a particular eye on separation/individuation issues. The interplay of these issues in the context of the whole primary oedipal complex would seem a natural next step in such work.

Developmental issues abound as we think about these patterns. We can hope for further understanding of what kinds and degrees of stress foster regression to the adolescent, classical oedipal, or primary oedipal levels and on the basis of what earlier conditions. One more developmental matter is the combination of universal and specific factors producing the various patterns of ego formation that characterize individual children during the primary oedipal phase. Formation of an "as-if" personality is such a pattern, as we saw in chapter 13.

Further investigation is warranted on how the simultaneity of ego formation with other attributes of the primary oedipal phase produces patterns of *guilt and shame* when the child's sense of self creates capacity for feelings of responsibility for its behavior. We can differentiate between guilt (feelings that one's badness caused harm and requires reparation) and shame (feelings of badness that mask pleasure in the unacceptable). From what we have learned already, it is apparent that the primary oedipal complex explains the cruelty of some people's self-punishing and self-inhibiting systems and why these systems always involve sexuality. We must now learn the necessary details for understanding how archaic super-egos are formed. We can try to find out what facilitates the advancement of the child from the lethal super-ego of the primary oedipal complex to the merely stern super-ego of the classical oedipal complex and then to the mature and ego-dominated super-ego that emerges through adolescence. Noting differences between the super-ego of the toddler and the severely ill adult, simply because of their differences in potential, it might be fruitful to explore the two ego–super-ego relationships from the standpoint of the individual's resources in coping with sexual feelings and wish for autonomy. In the context of the primary oedipal complex, we can understand parallels between primitive super-egos of the very young child and of the most severely disturbed adult patients.

The *timing of the resolution of the classical oedipal conflict* is brought into relief through study of the primary oedipal phase. The question of when the classical oedipal conflict is resolved is presented in chapter 10 strictly in terms of ego capacity for comprehending generationality. Worth exploring might be the relationship between this biologically determined change in the organism and the familial situation subject to such variables as parental frustration of the child's sexual aims. The latter is the traditional explanation for the child's resolving its (classical) oedipal conflict (Thomas 1963). However, as we see in the case material in chapter 10, ego development (in normal children based upon maturation) is the fundamental reason. Much can be usefully learned about the mechanisms involved.

Most importantly, primary oedipal theory permits fuller understanding of the relationship between normal and pathological personality development. The vicissitudes of ego organization and functioning can be traced with greater accuracy. From this might come significantly more information on how to foster strong ego growth.

Gender-Related Differences
in Personal Behavior
Under implications for differences in personal behavior due to gender identity, we might turn attention to better understanding of penis envy, vaginal and clitoral orgasms, castration anxiety, and the fantasy of a phallic mother.

Chasseguet-Smirgel and Galenson have already established (chapter 5) that sets of domineering mothers and passive fathers characterize the situation of daughters who display intense *penis envy*. It would be interesting to see whether, as primary oedipal theory also suggests, the fathers in these cases are covertly (or subtly but overtly) seductive with their young daughters, who are so much less formidable than their wives. Penis envy is often cited as related to a girl's wish for a baby as a penis substitute. As toddler boys also may wish for a baby, psychosocial factors must also be considered. Kestenberg (1975) and others have explored the wish for a baby, but it seems logical to seek insight in terms of primary oedipal conflict.

The occurrence of intense *castration anxiety* in boys corresponds with domineering/seductive behavior on the part of their mothers during the primary oedipal phase, especially in the absence of an active father-figure or perhaps in the presence of a father who strongly signals his need for the boy's loyalty. Again, we need study of the subtleties, as in Galenson's latest work (1983).

The *defensive concept of a phallic mother* might be studied from the standpoint of primary oedipal theory: How does this fantasy help a toddler boy to feel safer with his mother? Does denial of the genital difference mean less fear that he will lose his penis (gender-self-identity) when he feels impelled toward/engulfed by her? For a girl, does a fantasy of a phallic mother protect her from needing to assert her preferences for her (phallic) father in the face of a strongly controlling mother?

Another interesting question concerns girls who *give up sense of the existence of the vagina* when, as is often observed in the behavior of two-year-olds (Fast 1979), they give up all genital pleasure. We now can recognize this as part of their solution to primary oedipal conflict. It seems that some such girls then in later, classical oedipal behavior, permit themselves only the more superficial (though intense) feeling in the clitoris. A sidelight relates to the evidence of toddler girls wanting to touch their fathers' penises. Yet there is a tendency among women to become aroused sexually upon being touched rather than upon touching (Money and Ogunro 1974). Is this because at the primary oedipal level she quickly learned to inhibit the touching impulse toward father's penis and subsequently could permit herself arousal only if the male took the initiative? What conditions of adolescence and adult life, including psychotherapy, permit these girls to feel free to enjoy all their sexual feelings? And what can we learn from them of the usual progression of ego development and impulse life?

Gender-Specific Psychopathologies

The primary oedipal aspects of gender-specific deep psychopathologies should occupy considerable attention. Part III on anorexia gives one format for such exploration. There are severe emotional illnesses more commonly seen in one gender group or the other (e.g., among men: commission of suicide, obsessive-compulsive behavior, sexual perversions, and gender-identity problems; and among women: threats of suicide, masochism, depression, hysteria). The sort of close study that was fruitful with anorexia should be useful in these instances, too, as is strongly suggested in case material throughout this volume. Narcolepsy is a symptom that makes sense in terms of the toddler's view of infancy as a genderless state. In my experience, withdrawal into the "good baby" state of sleep is a way of relieving anxiety in the wake of primary-level oedipal concerns.

Gender-Related Differences in Social Behavior
Social behavior and the primary oedipal phase is another topic to consider. The primary oedipal phase possibly affects social behavior in the character of romantic love. The oft-listed qualities of this form are reminiscent of the primary oedipal complex. The experience of love at first sight that is sometimes associated with romantic love, for instance, touches on the toddler's identification of people by appearance, not having the sophistication or the time sense to wait for deeper knowledge of the other. I do not refer here, however, to either what the French term friendship enlivened by desire or what we call being romantically in love. Tennov (1979) offers the word limerence to mean romantic love experienced as a pathological state.[4] Intense reaction to separation, problems in maintaining identity, sexual enslavement, extreme polarization of good and bad, splitting, distortion of the sense of time, and ambivalence shown in furious jealousy—all provide an emotional setting evocative of the primary oedipal phase. This is an intriguing subject to explore.

Tradition supports an idea of different patterns of activity between the sexes. This is another psychological puzzle. Since in all cultures women are extremely active in child care, the idea of feminine passivity as part of a role definition must come from something other than direct meaningful experience with mothers during the first formative stage. Children's perceptions of their own genital reactions relate to observations of parental behavior (See chapters 7 and 8). We could also study the details of how a child translates observations of physical appearance in both sexes into its own ego scheme during the primary oedipal phase and, during the classical oedipal phase, how the child translates its awareness of others' behavioral patterns into a more sophisticated self-image, according to gender role.

There are intercultural questions: the primary oedipal child's consolidation of its gender identity leads to self-definition by appearance. The more sophisticated classical oedipal child defines itself in terms of gender *role*. What implicit understanding of this may be reflected in standards of behavior in different cultures? What aspects of culture relating to gender and ego strength is the child thus sensitive to in toddlerhood, early childhood, and adolescence? How may behavior patterns within a given culture be better understood through awareness of the characteristic nature of primary oedipal experience in that culture (as cited about initiation rites in chapter 4)? How might the characteristic primary oedipal experience in a given culture affect the occurrence of various gender-related psychopathologies in that culture? Knowing when and how individuals are susceptible to various promptings by the culture can illuminate moral issues in a society such as ours. For a small example; why, when, and who might be affected by sexist jokes (with relief or anger) and to what extent at various ages? How responsible should society as a whole be for such behavior in terms of impressionability of children at various ages? It is interesting to consider how much ego is involved and/or affected.

Social Issues and the Primary
Oedipal Experience
Under implications for better understanding some social issues, we might study the gender differences in some sociocultural patterns. These patterns could include the preference of males for exclusively male society while females are more tolerant of mixed society. According to primary oedipal theory, females may resolve overwhelming oedipal conflict by opting to be like the beloved father, so that even when they grow up without easy self-acceptance (including their gender) they can feel comfortable in male society. The male human, focused during toddlerhood on establishing self-identity in terms of differences in fundamental appearance, can retain discomfort at closeness to females. Two sources of relief that are practiced in many societies, including ours, are all-male organizations, from secret clubs to the military; and hierarchical arrangements that safeguard the emotional distance as well as dominance of the male in charge of groups of women. Leftover primordial fears of loss of personal (gender) identity through (sexual) fusion are not a new idea in psychology or in anthropology. Still, clarity about the workings of

the primary oedipal complex might reveal new insights into these phenomena.

Societies often pattern members' behavior by gender-specific roles. Interrelationships may be clarified between how children experience the culture during the primary oedipal phase and how characteristic cultural patterns become ego-syntonic in terms of this experience.

Certain societal behavior such as going to war,[5] and the exercise of group prejudice, may reflect primary oedipal issues on the part both of leaders and of those who enthusiastically follow. I do not suggest reductionism here. I merely suggest that in understanding these phenomena, we might find that *adding* knowledge of the primary oedipal phase of development provides a more complete picture. To explain why many intelligent adults support war or group prejudice in their problem solving, attention might be given to the stirring up of primordial feelings. The primary oedipal complex perhaps provides the wellspring of such feelings.

The Process of Psychotherapy

Finally, implications of primary oedipal theory might be studied in relation to understanding the process of psychotherapy. In my increasing awareness of the primary oedipal phase, I have found it useful in three ways having to do with the work of analysis. First, isolating parts of the early experiences into different nonoedipal factors leaves floating the connections between all of those and a person's sexual feelings. With growing ego strength a person often spontaneously bridges these gaps emotionally. The theory of the primary oedipal phase provides the therapist with missing links, which he can use to facilitate the process. Second, guideposts from the primary oedipal level or the classical (e.g., the use of characteristic time frames) help to identify the issues with which a patient is dealing. Third, I have found a useful increased sensitivity to fuller meanings of transference behavior (and more to watch out for in countertransference!).

A form of transference that is of special interest now is the idealizing transference. According to Kohut (1977), this should be allowed to run its course. However, primary oedipal theory suggests that we might in reality be avoiding analyzing the transference because we are enjoying a countertransference boon to ourselves in accepting the split (good analyst/bad patient or omnipotent analyst/ helpless patient), if that's the case, or accepting the fusion (patient-good-only-because-part-of-analyst *or* patient-effective-only-if-part-of-analyst). It can be profitable to explore immediately the particular conditions fostering the idealizing transference instead. As this behavior reflects primary oedipal ego-organization, primary oedipal conflict should prove to be involved. Similarly, the mirroring transference that Kohut found often to follow the idealizing transference might prove to reflect the beginning of resolution of oedipal conflict on the basis of identification.

The study of therapeutic results might be furthered by attention to derivatives from the primary oedipal phase.[6] As noted earlier in this book, meaningful results often accrue from deliberately processing one or another aspect of the primary oedipal complex (e.g., orality, anality, separation/individuation, oedipal feelings per se) or not at all, as in nonpsychoanalytic therapies. Historically, this fact has been crucial for clinical purposes. It would be interesting in terms of the present extent of knowledge to investigate how recognition of the primary oedipal phase helps us to better understanding of a) possible stages in psychotherapy with various kinds of patients; b) how diminution of anxiety bound to part of the primary oedipal complex can free the ego toward greater integration;[7] and c) whether a keener appreciation might develop of the intricacies of transference and countertransference patterns in the courses of successful and unsuccessful treatment if we trace these patterns in terms of the deepest implications of the primary oedipal phase.[8]

All of these ruminations derive from clinical experience as delineated in this book. From such experience, I believe that systematic study of these matters could prove to be fruitful. However, they represent complicated issues. Recognition of the primary oedipal phase is merely a new baseline from which to increase our understanding.

Null Hypotheses as a Test of the Model

Evidence for the existence of the primary oedipal phase has been selected here on the basis of availability. I have tried to find cases in which there is enough direct material to shed light on the truth of the theory, taking care to keep any excerpted material in the context of the original report. None of the case material quoted from the work of others was originally published in order to establish the existence of the primary oedipal phase. Therefore, these examples make strong argument for it.

Nonetheless, to test the theory completely we must vigorously explore the possibility that negative examples might exist. We must also remain open to the possibility of alternative explanations for the phenomena observed. Accordingly, I suggest the following statements as null hypotheses to guide critical examination of the theory. They all test the points that problems with sexuality and with separation/individuation are completely intertwined and that the degree of difficulty of both together is a key to understanding someone's general level of ego functioning. The model would be severely weakened by the discovery of any of the following:

1. A different theory that explains as satisfactorily as does this theory the same wide range of facts, including:
   a. The gender specificity of such psychopathologies as anorexia and sexual perversions.
   b. The specific syndromes of behaviors that accompany these conditions.
2. Demonstration that, in reality, gender specificities for psychopathological syndromes do not exist and that the apparent data are artifacts of culturally forced perception.
3. A sample of closely studied children *who do not include gender identity* in the establishment of their nascent egos (through a point of successful separation/identification at approximately the age of two) but seem secure and psychologically sturdy nonetheless, *with a clear sense of self.*
4. The existence of problems of severe separation/individuation in adult cases who do not exhibit concomitant problems in the areas of sexuality and relationships with others on the basis of gender (including at best a drastic split so that there is permission inwardly for successful behavior in only the one area or the other at a time).
5. The existence of severe sexual problems in adult cases without concomitant problems in the area of separation/individuation.

6. The presence of clear gender identity, mature sexuality, and confident separation/individuation in patients whose symptoms nonetheless include fragmented egos, pervasive use of splitting as a defense, suicidal ideation, oral/anal preoccupation, and a distorted sense of time so that only the immediate moment has meaning, and who form intense but highly ambivalent relationships or brief relationships or who withdraw from having interpersonal relationships at all.

7. Confused gender identity and lack of adequate sense of separation/individuation in patients who nonetheless exhibit a degree of genital primacy, use higher-level defenses such as sublimation, are involved with defining roles and forming mutually respectful relationships (although perhaps still revealing generational confusion), possess egos well beyond a fragmented state, utilize ideas of future time, and are not beset with hopelessness.

Substantiation of any of these possibilities would contradict the correctness of the theory of the primary oedipal phase.

Coda

On the weight of evidence that the proffered model is true, we see sweeping significance to the ego in how the sense of individuality and the sense of sexuality are combined. From a sense of individuality comes the joy of competence and mastery. From the sense of sexuality develops a framework for social living. To allow oneself both is to be a complete person. However, the child must begin to integrate them both while at the very beginning of its powers and options. It does the best it can at the time, but then it continues to grow in accordance with how it has already shaped its ego during its earliest efforts to manage both individuality and sexuality.

If the child's development is relatively successful, the child's maturational processes bring it into the classical oedipal and later into the adolescent stages. In each instance, the child then has a chance to reorganize its ego in keeping with its new abilities and opportunities.

It is the miracle of the human mind, however, that not only during the classical oedipal phase and during adolescence can one reorder the early confusions and compromises. Through insight or other experiences in life, it remains possible to gain inner permission for both sexuality *and* individuality, pleasure *and* competence, social commitment *and* personal achievement, a sense of wholeness that means freedom to love truly and to enjoy using one's abilities with a deep feeling of success.

Notes

Introduction

1. There are several words and phrases that I sometimes use interchangeably and to which I at other times attach specific different meanings. These are ego, self, primary oedipal complex, self-differentiation, ego formation, nascent or first organized ego, and integrated ego. The "ego" in general is more encompassing than the idea of "self" and includes personality organization. The ego can be seen in relation to unconscious factors (Brull 1975; Bettelheim 1982); the "over-I" or "über-ich" (Freud 1923) or "super-ego"; and the "id" or "it"—the primeval forces alien to the ego (in the sense of self) that are nonetheless part of the personality. "Ego" can mean what we refer to as I, myself, or "me!" In this sense the ego includes only what is available to the personality in the self-reflexive mode. The "over-I" forces and ego-alien "it" forces are by definition not integrated into the self. Yet, they are significant parts of the personality, that is, the whole person. "Ego" can be shorthand for the more cumbersome expression "total personality." Therefore, when referring to the first organization of the ego, I include more than the child's conscious sense of being "me!" although learning it is "me!" is part of the process of forming the whole organized ego. Determining what will be unconscious is a basic process in organization of the nascent ego. Those parts of the personality—super-ego and id—which are not experienced as being "me!" are parts of the whole personality, but not the ego in the narrow sense of self. Ego organization means more than an organized sense of (conscious) self. Ego organization encompasses the broader meaning of ego, the whole of the personality including other (unconscious) institutions besides the self. The primary oedipal complex describes all psychic aspects of the two-year-old's life. Therefore it provides another way of thinking of the primordial ego, reflected in the various attributes of the nascent ego (again, interchangeable adjectives are used here with "ego"). "Nascent" or "initial ego" is the phrase I use to refer to the ego in the whole personality sense, in its earliest stages of organization. I hope that the context of these various words will make my meaning clear in each case.

The other way around, I use three words consistently to distinguish between related aspects of the primary oedipal situation: the two-year-old child's oedipal *conflict* becomes the central issue in the emotional *complex* of its feelings and thoughts at the age, thus producing the primary oedipal *phase* of its development.

1. History of the Idea of the Primary Oedipal Phase

1. Lebovici restates the hitherto traditional view of oedipal development but adds that "an apparently clearcut oedipus complex . . . . may be confused with incestuous wishes which have not been worked out" (1982:213).

2. Assessment of a Two-Year-Old's Psychological Challenges

1. Kern (1973) gathers much evidence that even early in the nineteenth century scholars called attention to the existence of infantile sexuality. The idea was sponsored by men as eminent as Henry Maudsley (1867). This material does not detract from the magnitude of Freud's contribution, any more than earlier European discoverers of North America detract from the fact that Columbus created general acceptance of the continent's existence. It does, however, underscore that infantile sexuality has long been recognized as a subject meriting serious attention.

2. Thomas and Chess (1980) summarize the evidence.

3. The context by which an infant gains its sense of gender includes its categorizations of the physical world, such as differentiations based on movement. Maratos (1973) and Meltzoff and Moore (1983) proved that infants imitate human movement by the age of one month. This is in accordance with Bower's evidence (1982) that infants recognize objects by means of their characteristic movements or positions. By eight or nine months, infants can and do differentiate between other nine-month-old boys and girls on the basis of their patterns of movement alone (Aitken 1977; Aitken, Kujawski, and Bower 1981), a feat we adults cannot do. Such perceptions can serve as a powerful adjunct in interpreting genital sensations which they become aware of at the same age.

4. Person and Ovesy (1983), reviewing theories of gender identity conclude that the psychoanalytic approach can explain pathology but not "the origin of conflict-free normal core-gender identity." In fact, only psychoanalytic theory can explain normal development (which is never completely conflict-free), but only when the primary oedipal phase is taken into cognizance.

5. Parke and Sawin (1977) summarize the burgeoning research on this. In a more recent example of what is being found, Pruett (1983) studied infants whose primary caretakers were their fathers. Sons developed stranger reactions four to eight weeks earlier than did daughters. Pruett's data support Bower (1974) and Kagan (1978) in their conclusions that stranger reaction stems from cognitive issues. For our purposes here, it is also valuable to recognize that self-other discrimination is related to gender. Pruett rounds out his contribution by noting further that as to separation from fathers, girls showed affective disturbance significantly greater than the boys and six to ten weeks earlier. I have not been able to find research about the ages at which the two sex groups who have been cared for primarily by mothers exhibit such reactions. Perhaps the custom in other studies of averaging the response codes of boys and girls together stemmed from the supposition that children so young do not differ in their responses by gender. In any case, Pruett corroborates that there is a substrate for the development of the primary oedipal complex.

6. Belsky (1980) studied the difference between findings in home observation and in the laboratory and concluded that context significantly affected findings about mother-child interaction.

7. We might raise here the question of why an infant should articulate loss of mother's support because of its own development when its overall experience is that each new achievement adds to rather than subtracts from previous abilities. Furman (1982) observes the weaning process and discovers that babies almost uniformly initiate the process. Mothers subtly but clearly let their babies know if they have some desire to prolong the early feeding stage, beginning the child's separation/individuation conflict.

8. Solomon (1980) calls attention to opponent processing. This occurs on the sensory level in hearing a "deafening silence" upon cessation of a loud sound or seeing its complement after withdrawal of a highly saturated color. It is not surprising that primitive mentation would follow the same pattern of achieving balance through dichotomization.

3. The Formation of Gender Identity

1. Greenacre (1968), Erikson (1959), Jacobson (1964), Mahler (1972), Amsterdam and Levitt (1980), Stechler and Kaplan (1980) are among them.

2. Kleeman (1976) speculated that genital awareness was not a major organizer of behavior. However, as Person and Ovesy confirm, core gender identity "locates the appropriate object for imitation and identification" (1983:221). Citing the evidence about hermaphrodites, they recognize that choice and patterning of gender is socially determined. Remembering that blind children achieve gender identity in the same manner as sighted children, we know that genital awareness is the child's basis for understanding gender identity.

3. The existence of a core self is revealed in normal subjects by Hilgard in hypnotic experiments (1977). Ludwig and his colleagues (1972) proved its existence even in multiple personalities with highly rigidified ego fragmentation, the core self alone being aware of each of the other selves.

4. Among Dominican Republicans, a hereditary disorder spontaneously reverses some children's apparent sex from female to male. In a predetermined dramatic masculinization upon adolescence, this group changes gender identity accordingly. Imperato-McGinty and her colleagues (1980) feel that these cases contradict the conclusions of Money and Stoller about the fixity of gender identity. However, the hereditary pattern is recognized in the community so that the change at adolescence is expected. The children are called by special names. We must therefore question whether these cases were reared in an atmosphere of certainty about their gender, which Money, Stoller, Lev-Ran, and Greenson all emphasize is necessary to formation of definite gender identity by the age of two years. Lev-Ran cites hermaphrodites whose adult forms contradicted the gender assignment at birth by their doctors. Having been reared unambiguously, these cases maintained their original gender identity.

5. Money and Ogunro (1974) provide a table on psychopathology in hermaphrodites. Corresponding to the findings of others cited here, their figures on hermaphrodites are roughly comparable to the incidence of psychopathology in the general population.

Psychopathology in Ten Patients with the Partial Androgen Insensitivity Syndrome

1. Severely incapacitated	
a. Episodic (N = 1 man)	1
b. Chronic	0
2. Mildly incapacitated	
a. Episodic	0
b. Chronic (N = 1 woman)	1
3. Not incapacitated	
a. Guarded and sensitive to stigmata	
(N = 3 men, 1 youth)	4
b. Confidence achieved (N = 3 men, 1 woman)	4

Community surveys of mental health status of populations yield varying results depending upon method and selection of subjects. Primrose (1962) made clinical evaluations of an entire community and found the same ratios of disturbance reported above. Money and Ogunro comment on the sparsity of psychopathology in these patients with such a magnitude of sexual problems. They suggest that these happen to be people with abnormally high competence in problem solving or that clear definition of problems may guarantee their negotiability. This comment is interesting, but is not tied to data. Ehrhardt and Meyer-

Bahlburg (1981) stress, as do most investigators of the subject, that the key variable in producing emotional stability in hermaphrodites is the degree to which parents are definite about their gender while raising them. Such interpretation makes sense in terms of primary oedipal development.

6. Gould (1983) explores this situation in depth.

7. Galenson and Roiphe conceptualize early development in terms of shock at the recognition of the genital difference, but this is their description of most children's immediate reactions: "The affective reflection of the genital-phase organization included definite pleasure in body exhibitionism in the boys—the strutting body posture, as well as direct phallic pride. The girls were flirtatious and exhibitionistic, with skirt-lifting and genital exposure during the early weeks of their new genital awareness" (1979b:14).

8. The issue of narcissistic injury becomes clear when we consider hair length. Why should a girl, who by the time of genital awareness likely has hair much longer than that of most boys, care so keenly about the lesser difference in visual impression of compared genitals? Beyond that, as Bettelheim (1954) points out, the child can compare adult forms. The mother's two breasts figure prominently, as does her enlarged abdomen if as is often the case in spacing children she happens to be pregnant while a given child is in the two-year-old period. The child of either sex has many aspects of physical appearances to react to in learning about gender. The special significance of the genitals must start with the intense pleasure that the child relates to in terms of its total experience.

9. Lerner (1980) explores the limiting effect upon a woman's therapy that derives from interpreting her penis envy as a wish to be like a man.

10. A child's name belongs on our lists of attributes for a sense of individuality. Recognition of its name is one of a child's earliest achievements. Responding to talk about itself by name is one of the earliest manifestations of a primitive self-concept, and the first in relation to others. Qualities of its name can affect how the child feels about itself. We can appreciate how much the child's name contributes to its self-concept when we recall deep relationships between one child and another that they form around the happenstance of having identical names. Bettelheim (1983) points out the importance of names in self-categorization even in adults.

4. The Interrelated Tasks in Relation to Personality Structure

1. Galenson, Miller, and Roiphe say, referring to her avid interest in such objects during the age period: "Most of these representations were similar in structure to her father's longed-for phallus and objects which he used consistently in his daily life. Thus, we have associations in structural *pars pro toto* thinking and contiguity with the loved object" (1976:92).

2. Lacan (1973) bases his system of psychoanalysis upon significance of prelinguistic thought as the patient's unconscious.

3. Garner (1980) traces the emergence of creativity as therapy freed a patient to integrate thought and feeling. Arieti (1976) terms this the tertiary process.

4. Warner (1983) demonstrates that the difference in patients' dreams, comparing those at the start of treatment with those at the end, lies in the integration of the "styles" of the two hemispheres.

5. Patterns of the Female

1. The dichotomy of omnipresence/disappearance (annihilation) carries serious implications for the toddler. A child can be strained in its efforts to determine who is good or bad in the context of severe primary oedipal conflict along with destructive oral/anal/sadistic

fantasies. The limited time sense of the toddler makes a presence in the moment seem like omnipresence. Likewise, disappearance seems total—annihilation. Yet the absent mother or father reappears. Feces are expelled. Yet the need to expel them repeatedly recurs. The sense of personal power or helplessness in these matters can be enormous.

For the toddler, total annihilation alternates with a complete switch to omnipresence. This early dichotomy can be replayed later in life. Tom Sawyer enacted a typical childhood fantasy in being (taken for) dead, thus hearing the eulogies at his supposed funeral. Troops marching off to war are cheered by crowds who massively deny the reality of imminent death. Suicides may show signs of a similar sense of unreality about death. Shneidman (1982) decribes presuicidal thought of a case he finds to be typical of his vast experience. The description corresponds to the thought processes of the primary oedipal child.

These facts are supported by study of life–threatening behavior in toddlers. Rosenthal (1982) reports seeming accidents that turned out to be consciously self-destructive even in such young children.

2. Knowledge of the vagina is often repressed by girls until adolescence (Fraiberg 1977). Commonly the toddler girl represses her deepest sexual feelings. Kestenberg takes note in her patients:

"Vaginal sensations shift to the clitoris in an incomplete externalization that makes it possible for the patient to experience a sensual focus on an external part of the genital rather than on an external object" (1975:115). But the dominance of the clitoris also implies a loss of the vagina as an organ. When the classical oedipal conflict arises later on, sexual interest is often limited to the clitoris. Giving up her most hidden, deepest feelings might accompany a girl's resolution of the primary oedipal conflict.

3. When these guilt feelings are particularly strong, the girl may grow up to submit herself to sadistically overpowering men. Aviram (1981), who studied a group of battered women, found that the women who had not experienced violence in their homes of origin were those most likely to continue relationships with men who beat them. In other words, their fantasies rather than identification with a victimized mother guided their behavior.

4. Gillespie (1976) observes that clitoral response in women accompanies a wish for penetration and does not characteristically involve an impulse to make penetration. Heidi's behavior is an example of this even though she fantasized that the penis of the man was hers. Her clitoral arousal did not stimulate fantasies of penetrating her partner.

5. Lerner (1980) explores the limiting effect upon a woman's therapy that derives from interpreting her penis envy as a wish to be like a man.

6. Patterns of the Male

1. For persons of either sex, the value of expressing anger is the sense of separateness that it automatically produces. For someone whose sense of self is shaky, the more forceful the expression "No!" the more effective it is in proving that there is a difference not only of opinion or course of action, but of personhood. This point is brought out by Levy (1953) and Parens and Parens (1979) among others.

2. Unambivalent attitude toward mother: Roazen (1975:40–41), Blum (1977:768). Description of mother, including her tempestuousness, her doting on him, general vanity: Jones (1953:3, 5), Martin Freud (1958:11–12), Bernays-Heller (1956:336–339). Early memory of mother: Freud letter to Fliess (1897:233). Attitude toward father; description of him, including his gentleness and indulgence of Freud: Freud (1865), Jones (1953:2, 7), M. Freud (1958:10), Bernays-Heller (1956: 335). Dates of birth and death of brother: Blum (1977:773). Significance of nursemaid: Freud letters to Fliess (1897:261), Jones (1953:5, 6, 9–10), Schimek (1975:850–851). Feelings about deaths of father and brother: Jones (1953:8), Choisey (1963:112–113). Freud (1900:421–425), Blum (1977:768, 772).

3. Friendships with women: Roazen (1975:62). Freud's need for an intimate friend and a hated enemy: Freud (1900:483). Freud maintained "Deed" concern even in one of his last papers: Freud (1937:258). One place where he makes this last point is in "The Question of Lay Analysis" (1926:20:212).

7. Evidence for the Existence of the Primary Oedipal Phase: Direct Observation of Young Children

1. The observations tending to be somewhat repetitive, I selected the samples that follow. I tried to include enough material so that we can follow William's development in the detail. His mother put William's age in parentheses (years: months + days) and his angle of penile erection on a scale of 0 to 3 + .

2. Not quoted here; gives examples of William's pride in his penis and his wanting mother to pay attention to it.

3. Jeff apparently had ongoing opportunity to observe his mother in the bathroom.

4. Both William and Jeff watched their fathers in the bathroom. William (Observation 19) acted as if he wished to touch his father's penis, then shifted his attention to the effect his father's penis created (bubbles in the water). Castration anxiety connected with anal concerns was now augmented. Jeff also seemed to inspect his father's penis with great interest during a time of heightened pleasure in his own genital. By contrast are descriptions of the bathroom behavior of two little girls with their fathers, S. (chapter 4) and Becky (chapter 8). They persistently tried to touch the father's penis in a setting of emotional difficulty with their mothers. S.'s mother reported feeling unhappy and competitive in the situation. Of course, these girls were in treatment because of severe problems, whereas William and Jeff are examples of normal development. For this reason I add my observation as merely a footnote of possible interest. However, a normal little girl, Winnie, described later in this chapter, started to "grab for [her father's] genitals" when she was twenty-four months old, shortly after a new baby was born. None of the girls is portrayed as attacking the fathers or as if to dismember them. We would expect girls to show the desire for pleasurable contact with father's genital during the primary oedipal phase, while boys of the same age are more interested in comparing themselves with their fathers.

5. This value in the idealization process is discussed further on pages 308–309 in relation to transference in psychotherapy.

6. Cf. Bell's observations (1965) about anal/phallic connection at this age and the notes by McDevitt (1971) in chapter 8.

7. In an earlier note on Lilly in the same article, Galenson and Roiphe tell only that she increased her toileting interests at fourteen months to include "pulling at her genitals during diapering and bathing. At seventeen months she asked to see her mother's 'penis' and inserted her fingers between her own labia." No precipitating events are mentioned for these activities nor any other behavioral effects aside from looking.

8. In a child who did not display anger toward the mother with clear preference for her father, such behavior could perhaps be considered as identifying with her mother's omnipotence, fusing with her rather than trying to displace her. That is different from what we see in Jenny, who did display anger toward her mother with a clear preference for her father.

8. Evidence for the Existence of the Primary Oedipal Phase: Treatment of Young Children

1. Again we see the dichotomy of genderless babyhood and gender identity, in this case, maleness.

2. This behavior was therefore noted when Becky was under two years of age.

3. McDevitt presents the case material in a different order, but all of it is quoted here.

As the present purpose is to demonstrate the primary oedipal phase, all the dynamics of a particular case are not germane. Therefore, I shall only mention for background that Becky was a tense infant whose mother found her difficult. It is not clear how much before she was two years old Becky began her bathroom play with father. When she was around eighteen months old, Becky's struggle with separation/individuation was so intense her mother helplessly allowed a maid to dominate both herself and the child. The analysis subsequently revealed that this maid used threats and force in Becky's toilet training. Becky responded with enuresis, which continued until she was four and a half years old. McDevitt found penis envy to be connected with this symptom. It is not surprising when we recall Chasseguet-Schmirgel's point (chapter 3) that penis envy is greatest when there is a threatening mother-figure. McDevitt also mentions that Becky was considerate of a baby sister born when Becky was twenty-seven months old but showed jealousy of her when treatment began. In another aspect, Becky's analytic material "was replete with primal scene fantasies," but data are lacking to fit their origin into Becky's course of development.

4. McDevitt says, "Masturbation was first noticed shortly before the age of two, particularly when Becky was unhappy. Since it was not excessive, the parents ignored it" (1971:207). As the analysis took place starting when Becky was already three, the fantasy content of her masturbation did not necessarily relate to feelings toward her parents when she was younger. Yet it is suggestive in the light of the rest of her history at two years old.

5. Price illuminates the paradox of the child who feels rejected but whose mother really demonstrates intense involvement with it. Price observes: "To the extent that a mother may treat the child as an extension of herself, the child may perceive rejection of its *selfness* even as it feels irresistibly drawn into its mother's orbit and absorbed by her. Such neediness on the part of a mother can intensify the child's confusion in its primary oedipal conflict" (1983).

6. We are reminded of Sachs' case, Cyril, who at the same age underwent this difficulty due to the press of his oedipal fantasies with his father in the house.

7. Claude's fantasy about changing pretty babysitters' diapers shows that his precocious verbal ability illuminates rather than bypasses primary oedipal development.

8. Sachs traced this to Claude's preoccupation with his father's hollering.

9. We see how limited time sense and anality mold the fantasies of the primary oedipal child (and nascent super-ego, giving rise to corresponding symptoms).

9. Evidence for the Existence of the Primary Oedipal Phase: Treatment of Adults

1. It is fascinating to see the effect in adult patients on their relationships with their own children when they make progress with their old confusions about generationality. Once patients begin to deal with the fundamental issues in terms of the level of ego functioning achieved in resolution of the oedipal conflict at the classical stage, their behavior toward their children becomes more clearly parental, making it easier for the children to achieve their sense of generationality in turn.

10. Comparison of the Two Oedipal Phases

1. Martin and Halverson (1983) report research highlighting the importance of the concept of sex-typing of activities to children who are at the age of resolving the classical oedipal complex. Five- and six-year-olds looked at pictures of males and females performing

various activities conventionally sex-typed in our culture. Some of the pictures depicted the usual pattern and some of them reversed the expected sex-typing. A week later, the children tended to preserve the conventional associations by distorting their memories of the inconsistent pictures. These findings exemplify the significance of sex-role at this age in the child's way of mentally organizing its world.

2. Current nomenclature terms the period from two and a half to four years as phallic-oedipal. The behavior of the child at the end of this continuum, however, is what is meant by the term *oedipal complex* and refers to the period I call the classical oedipal phase. To distinguish between the two periods, Edgcumbe and Burgner apply to the earlier end of the continuum the term *narcissistic-phallic stage*. Greenspan uses for it the term *dyadic-phallic stage*. However, all agree that the (classical) oedipal period can be distinguished from earlier stages of child development.

3. Actually witnessing the primal scene, especially if combined with seductive behavior toward the child on the part of the parent of the opposite sex, can overwhelm the child. In that case, inner permission may be stifled for individuation (at the primary oedipal level) or for determining a clear role based upon core gender identity (at the classical oedipal level.) At the primary oedipal level, this can mean repression of fantasy, the blurring of fantasy and reality being too difficult for the child to resolve. Also, such a child might not be able to advance to the classical oedipal level because it is still preoccupied with the earliest form of its conflicts. Its expressions of oedipal conflict continue to be chiefly nonverbal and its behavior typical of the ego-functioning of a younger child.

4. Monroe threatened to throw himself over a balcony and did hurtle himself down some stairs.

5. The therapeutic companion was a female graduate student whom the treatment center provided to spend one day a weekend with the family. There was also a homemaking assistant supplied by the county to help care for the family during eight hours of each weekday.

6. The negative oedipus reaction was stimulated by the imminent departure of his beloved female teacher. Monroe became withdrawn and melancholy with intermittent angry verbalization of his feelings. When these reactions were interpreted, he elatedly attempted a female identification. Lopez related the behavior to Monroe's need to identify with his depressed mother when she was emotionally unavailable to him before he began treatment. Monroe was able to integrate this interpretation and continue with his forward development.

11. Introduction to Anorexia

1. Precocity might be a factor in the development of anorexia, giving special emphasis to the early fusion of orality and sexuality in relation to the separation/individuation needs of a child with advanced neurological and cognitive maturation.

2. In an adult, a new challenge to become independent can upset the balance when inner permission for sexuality has previously remained tied to keeping herself dependent and thus "not responsible" for her impulses. Being autonomous means responsibility for one's own impulses and she must find a way to handle the resurgence of guilt toward her mother over sexuality. Anorexia can be the result.

3. A temporary grief reaction can be an example of near normal behavior involving mild display of the anorexic syndrome. One example is a case of mine whose eating behavior was previously unexceptional. At a particular time, Emily was deeply involved with a man who reminded her in many ways of her father, especially in his size, his social ease, and his wit. She had not referred to her mother in treatment for a long time. Now, however, her mother was expected to die imminently. Emily told me that her lover wanted to go on a trip

with her. She felt she could not plan such a thing at this time. What she really wanted to do was to go away alone to a primitive place where people ate a minimal vegetarian diet and required a vigorous exercise program. The combination of a self-depriving "mean" atmosphere, minimizing food, energizing the self-control of the body with exercise, and giving up her sexual partner was a striking combination in reaction to her mother's impending death.

4. Hudson (1983) approaches bulimia by treatment of underlying depression, largely by medication, raises interesting questions about the effects of starvation and the physiology of the depressed, but does not embrace the whole anorexic syndrome. One-third of his cases did not exhibit bulimia at the end of a year, with degrees of improvement in many others. As his interest is primarily clinical, the design of his study does not permit conclusions as to etiology. It complements the theory presented here to find success in treating bulimia as a mere symptom of a more general disorder.

5. Boskind-White and White (1983) approach bulimia/anorexia in terms of family culture and report therapeutic success treating groups of young women on this basis. However, the material they report is compatible with the theory presented here.

6. It is not possible to state from the evidence here that these mothers gave their daughters the same messages when the daughters were in the primary oedipal period. However, the blatancy of these mothers' messages is reminiscent of the examples in chapter 8. In that chapter we saw how competitive some mothers can feel with their two-year-old daughters in the family triad during a daughter's primary oedipal phase. Therefore, it is not a far-fetched presumption that the mothers described above express attitudes toward their teenage daughters that also existed when the girls were very young. (I thank Myril Landsman for raising this point.)

7. Patient and her sister.

8. The mother refuses to eat as a sign of her rejection of the father. It seems possible that identifying with her mother in this way was part of this girl's motivation for anorexia. The mother's refusal to eat as a way to express rejection of the father also leads us to speculate on the intensity of the mother's primary oedipal leftovers and how they might have affected her handling of this daughter at the daughter's primary oedipal phase.

12. Anorexia and the Primary Oedipal Phase

1. Risen (1983) talks of "preoedipal" issues in a successful treatment case of his but underscores the patient's oedipal conflicts as the cause of her illness.

2. This might be interpreted as a negative oedipal reaction due to the freeing up of positive feelings about mother; but, if so, why should Rachel's new comfort with her mother have required her to give up her father if her oedipal feelings were not previously engaged?

3. Rachel's parents started another child during the midpart of her treatment. For purposes of the present discussion, I do not draw much upon the material specific to this fact, which came up toward the end of Rachel's analysis, because her anorexia began so much earlier.

13. Rachel as Guide to the Formation of the Anorexic Syndrome During the Primary Oedipal Phase

1. Sylvester's case (1945), reported here in chapter 14, used the same mechanism.

2. Bruch (1973) cites these as cardinal signs of anorexia, along with massive feelings of helplessness.

3. Milner does not tell why Rachel chose the voice, but we can speculate about it from another instance in which voices and identification of daddy were associated together. The distinction between maternal and paternal voices must be useful in a child's development of gender identity. As cited in chapter 2, infants respond differently to the voices of their two parents. Perhaps taking away someone's voice could have meant to Rachel reducing the person to a state of genderless babyhood. This idea fits Rachel's telling Milner not to talk because she was a baby.

4. At another instance in the analysis Rachel called herself three years old before she had reached that age. Rachel's mother removed her from treatment when the child was only three years and three months old, so in the quoted remark Rachel was thinking of herself as older than she really was, even while reminding herself that she was still a little girl. This might have intensified her confusion about where she belonged in the family scheme.

5. This recalls the importance of a person's name in building a sense of self (chapter 2).

6. Milner emphasizes Rachel's use of denial.

7. There is also the idea of starving the body as a punishment for unbearable body urges and resulting guilt. Rachel showed this in times of greatest distress when she specifically refused her own favorite foods.

8. In passing we note other elements of the primary oedipal complex in Liliana's anorexic syndrome: anal preoccupation and lack of ego differentiation in the search for her true self. We can also raise the question of what oppressed her that caused her to need to vomit each night. To me, at least, nighttime rituals are suggestive of sexual connotations.

14. Further Evidence of the Primary Oedipal Phase as a Dynamic in Anorexia: Children, Adults, Males

1. In doubting that child anorexia is the same illness as anorexia of adolescence, Sours (1980b) cites a child's interest in food and that tensions involved in eating are expressed by both parents and children. Sylvester's and Milner's cases, however, did not express concern over their not eating, even though they displayed the anorexic syndrome with sufficient severity that both cases required hospitalization for dehydration and cachexia.

2. I believe that Sylvester interprets the patient's anorexia as self-punishment.

3. As we speculated above, she may have vomited formerly to show that she did not wish to keep close to father or make a baby with him. Surviving comfortably without the presence of her vacationing good-mother analyst, the patient did not need to vomit upon her return. These connections make sense in the context of the patient's next proceeding to develop to the classical oedipal level, including the formation of age-appropriate meaningful relationships with available males.

4. For any child of nine months that would have been at the observable start of individuation/separation, and this child was precocious.

5. The patient's wish to "learn to sew like you" was one such expression in the transference.

6. The vomiting had multiple causes, and these associations with forced feeding were meaningful.

Summary and Conclusions

1. This study surveys research going back as far as the 1930s in Britain and America. Between the 1950s and mid-1970s ever fewer babies were breast-fed. That trend is now sharply

reversed (Martinez and Nalezienski 1979). However, patients in treatment today represent the population with the least likelihood of breast feeding experience and thus maximum opportunity to discover bottle imagery.

2. Emde (1983) also refers to self or ego formation as a process rather than a fixed point. Unsurprisingly, he bases his conclusion on much the same evidence which leads to discussion of the topic here. (See also chapter 2.) Emde notes the mirror experiments by which we learn that fifteen-month-olds are the youngest to show an organized representational self, although an affective core may begin forming from the start. He takes into his account of the early ego how human experience is at that time "organized by polar opposites, continually integrated by individualized experience." We see the ramifications of this fact in the development of the primary oedipal complex.

3. Bank and Kahn (1982) have begun a more complete study of sibling relationships, but they do not focus on the primary oedipal level and possible ramifications of sibling interactions at that level.

4. The primary oedipal aspects of romantic love can show up at any time of life. A way in which primary oedipal concerns can show up as a compelling pattern in adults is in the midlife crisis. For men, sometimes the middleaged appearance of a wife suddenly touches too strongly upon the oedipal leftovers of the adolescent-self. He thus seeks another woman, much younger, who strikes others as being remarkably like his wife except that she is so much younger than the wife. Sometimes the new woman represents his own adolescent daughter, but often she rather represents the mother of his adolescence, his classical or his primary oedipal period.

When the relationship to the new woman is one of intense infatuation, then other aspects of the man's behavior may place it in the light of the primary oedipal stage. Some hallmarks of this would be intense possessiveness, cruelty alternating with slavish devotion, impetuousness derived from a sense that the only timeframe is the immediate moment, a pronounced sense of identity through dress and other forms of appearance. Thus, the confusion of the generations which is part of the ego-state of the primary oedipal child can determine the man's choice of romantic love when his wife of many years seems too much like the mother from whom he had to distance himself as an infant.

5. Herdt (1981) found constant warring to result from a need to reaffirm masculinity in tribes which foster a prolonged mother/child symbiosis.

6. The framework a child's time sense provides for the ego is crucial in defining ego-states. Often the elements of a regressive phase can best be identified developmentally in terms of the "time warp" the patient experiences, e.g., a feeling there is only the present and what is not true now can never be and/or what is true now is for always. This aspect of the primary oedipal complex is relatively accessible to consciousness. In working with it, people seem to find it easier to deal with other leftovers, which they more easily then can see as issues from an earlier time. Another example is such a case as the aforementioned Patty whose processing of primary oedipal material was spontaneously followed by changes in her patterns of intellectual functioning, eating, and the occurrence of suicidal ideation.

7. A definite replay of the second phase for accumulation/expansion of ego resources (conventionally called the "latency period") is not seen in patients in analysis as a prolonged interval after accomplishment of classical oedipal organization, before signs emerge of an adolescent phase. However, patients who got through their middle childhood years by avoiding fantasy (because it seemed too threatening) gradually show more tolerance for fantasy and more ability to utilize it (becoming freer in creativity) as they work through their oedipal feelings. We can understand this as a parallel with the usual segmenting off and recognition of fantasy as such that is usually so helpful to children in the years followng the classical oedipal phase.

8. The value of understanding the primary oedipal complex becomes apparent in three common transference situations. The first occurs in a patient who feels disoriented when confronted with missing sessions because either the patient or the therapist is going out of town. This often occurs at a point in the work when issues of separation and oedipal guilt are strongly evoked, producing resonance from the primary oedipal time. The questions of "Who am I?" and "Where am I?" can be intertwined. These questions can be intertwined during the early part of the primary oedipal phase because of the significant way in which the child is still using position or place to help it orient itself to objects and indeed establish recognition of them. Therefore, when deep feelings are being evoked in the transference, the patient's sexual fantasies combined with the fact of separation can make it seem dangerous to know who or where one is.

A second example of resonance of the primary oedipal complex in the transference is the complaint of being "empty." This one often engages our countertransference reactions because in our profession, it is easy to mobilize feelings of being an all-giving parent, in contrast to the withholding mother of the patient. We thus can respond to the patient's complaint in terms of hypothesized underfeeding or other ungivingness on his/her mother's part when the patient was an infant. Careful sifting of the material of the session, however, is likely to reveal that the patient is trying to hide how excruciatingly full he or she is of forbidden fantasy. When we are aware of the horrible danger the patient feels in the possibility of our being able to know his or her thoughts with the magic of our omniscience, we can become more sensitive to underlying issues. In accordance with the total primary oedipal experience, these are likely to turn on matters such as separation/individuation in the face of sexual wishes and the possibility of total disappearance/death.

A third example is in the charge that the analyst is mundane, or other claims to the patient's uniqueness at the expense of the analyst. This can trace to the primary oedipal situation in the following manner: "If I am independent of mother/you, that means having rivalry with you/her (on the part of a woman), or that means that I may be forced into a sexually-driven fusion with you/her (on the part of a man), unless I can establish as fact my 'superiority' to you/her in that I am free of 'common' feelings such as sexuality (which embroils me with you/her)." In this way, the patient can hold on to a sense of self without the agony of primary oedipal conflict. We remember that in the polarized thinking of the very young child, one is either superior or inferior. In that cast of thought, to be different from means also to be either superior or inferior to the other.

Bibliography

Abel, Theodora. 1978. Mashima Yukio—a psychoanalytic interpretation. *Journal of the American Academy of Psychoanalysis* (July 3, 1978), 6:403–424.

Abelin, E. 1971. Role of the father in the separation-individuation process. In McDevitt and Settlage, eds., *Separation/Individuation*, pp. 229–252.

—— 1975. Some further observations and comments on the earliest role of the father. *International Journal of Psychoanalysis*, 56:293–302.

—— 1977. Psychoanalytical theories of the self: an introduction by M. Shane and E. Shane. In A. Goldberg, ed., *Advances in Self Psychology*. (1978), p. 33. New York: International Universities Press.

—— 1980. Triangulation, the role of the father and the origins of core gender identity during the rapprochement subphase. In Ruth F. Lax, Sheldon Bach, and J. Alexis Burland, eds. *Rapprochement: The Critical Subphase of Separation-Individuation*. New York: Jason Aronson.

Abraham, K. 1921. Contributions to the theory of the anal character. In Ernest Jones, ed., *Selected Papers of Karl Abraham*. New York: Basic Books, 1942.

—— 1934. A short study of the development of the libido, viewed in the light of mental disorders. In Ernest Jones, ed., *Selected Papers of Karl Abraham*, pp. 418–516. International Psycho-Analysis Library, no. 13. London: Hogarth Press, 1942.

Adler, Alfred. 1925. *Individual Psychology*. New York: Basic Books (1976 printing).

Adler, Lenore. 1984. Private communication.

Ahrens, R. 1954. Beiträge zur Entwicklung des Physiognomie und Mimikerkennes. *Zeitschrift für Experiential und angeweissene Psychologie*, 2:412–454, 599–633. Reported in E. Gibson, *Principles of Perceptual Learning and Development*. Englewood Cliffs, N.J.: Prentice-Hall, 1969.

Ainsworth, M. D. 1973. The development of infant–mother attachment. In B. M. Caldwell and H. N. Ricciuti, eds., *Review of Child Development Research III*, Chicago: University of Chicago Press, 1973, pp. 1–94.

Aitken, S. 1977. Psychological sex differentiation as related to the emergence of a self concept in infancy. Honors thesis, Department of Psychology, University of Edinburgh. Quoted in T.G.R. Bower, ed., *Development in Infancy* (1983).

Aitken, S., J. H. Kujawski, and T.G.R. Bower, 1981. Gender identification in infancy. Manuscript in preparation, University of Edinburgh. Quoted in T.G.R. Bower, *Development in Infancy*. San Francisco: Freeman, 1982.

Alpert, Augusta and Isidor Bernstein. 1964. Dynamic determinants in oral fixation. In Bertram S. Brown, ed. *Psychoanalytic Study of the Child*, 19:170–195. New Haven: Yale University Press, 1973.

American Academy of Pediatrics Committee on Nutrition. 1980. Formula and breast feeding. *Pediatrics* (March), no. 65.

Ames L. S. 1946. The development of the sense of time in the young child. *Journal of Genetic Psychology*, 18:97–125.

Amsterdam, B. 1968. *Mirror Behavior in Children Under Two Years of Age*. Ph.D. dissertation, University of North Carolina. Order No. 6901569, University Mirofilms, Ann Arbor, Mich.

Amsterdam, B. and M. Levitt. 1980. Consciousness of self and painful self-consciousness. In Solnit et al., eds., *Psychoanalytic Study of the Child*, 35:67–83.

Anastasi, A. 1958. Heredity, environment, and the question "How?" *Psychoanalytical Review*, 65:197–208.

André-Thomas. 1909. Anorexie mentale. *La Clinique*, 4:33. In Palazzoli, *Self-Starvation*.

Arieti, Silvano. 1976. *Creativity, the Magic Synthesis*. New York: Basic Books.

Arlow, J. 1963. Conflict, regression, and symptom formation. *International Journal of Psychoanalysis*, 44:12–22.

Aviram, Yamima R. 1981. Battered women. Master's thesis, no. 2831, University of Illinois at Chicago Circle.

Barcai, Avner. 1977. Reactions of family systems to rapid therapeutic change in one of its members. *American Journal of Psychotherapy*. 31(1):105–115.

Balint, M. 1965. Instincts and object relations, Part I. In *Primary Love and Psychoanalytic Technique*, pp. 3–147, New York: Liveright, 1965.

———— 1968. *The Basic Fault: Therapeutic Aspects of Regression*. London: Tavistock.

Bank, Stephen P. and Michael D. Kahn. 1982. *The Sibling Bond*. New York: Basic Books.

Barglow, P. and M. Schaefer. 1977. A new female psychology? In Blum, ed., *Female Psychology*, pp. 393–424.

Barnett, M. 1966. Vaginal awareness in the infancy and childhood of girls. *Journal of the American Psychoanalytical Association*, 14(1):129–141.

Behn-Eschenburg, H. 1932. The antecedents of the oedipus complex. Read before the Twelfth International Psycho-Analytical Congress, Wiesbaden, September 4, 1932. *International Journal of Psychoanalysis*, (1935), 16:175–185.

Bell, A. 1961. Some observations on the role of the scrotal sac and testicles. *Journal of the American Psychoanalytical Association*, 9:261–286.

———— 1964. Bowel training difficulties in boys: prephallic and phallic considerations. *Journal of the American Academy of Child Psychiatry*, 3:577–590.

———— 1965. The significance of scrotal sac and testicles for the prepuberty male. *Psychoanalytical Quarterly*, 34:182–206.

Belsky, Jay. 1980. Mother–infant interaction at home and in the laboratory: a comparative study. *Journal of Genetic Psychology*, 137(1):37–47. (Pennsylvania State University, Division of Individual and Family Studies, University Park.)

Bemporad, J. 1980. Review of object relations theory in the light of cognitive development. *Journal of the American Academy of Psychoanalysis*, (January).

Benedek, T. 1936. Dominant ideas and their relation to morbid cravings. *International Journal of Psychoanalysis*, 17(1):4056.

Benjamin, H. 1966. *The Transsexual Phenomenon*. New York: Julian Press.

Benjamin, J. 1963. Further comments on some developmental aspects of anxiety. In H. S. Gaskill, ed., *Counterpoint: Libidinal Object and Subject: A Tribute to Rene Spitz on His 75th Birthday*. New York: International Universities Press.

Bennett, S. L. 1980. *Infancy in Child Development in Normality and Psychopathology*. J. R. Bemporad, ed. New York: Brunner/Mazel.

Bergman, A. 1971. I and you: the separation/individuation process in the treatment of a symbiotic-psychotic child. In McDevitt and Settlage, eds., *Separation/Individuation*, pp. 325–355.

Berlin, I. N. et al. 1951. Adolescent alternative of anorexia and obesity. *American Journal of Orthopsychiatry* 2:419, 196.

Bettelheim, B. 1954. *Symbolic Wounds*. Glencoe, Ill.: Free Press.

—— 1961. Chicago Psychoanalytic Psychology Study Group. Lecture.

—— 1982. Reflections on Freud. *New Yorker* March 1, 1982.

—— 1983. Scandal in the family. *New York Review of Books*. 30(11):34.

Bion, W. R. 1967. *Second Thoughts: Selected Papers on Psychoanalysis*. London: Heinemann.

Bleich, David. 1976. New considerations of the infantile acquisition of language and symbolic thought. *The Psychoanalytic Review*, 63(1):49–71.

Blum, Harold P. 1974. The borderline childhood of the Wolf Man. In Blum, The prototype of preoedipal reconstruction. (See Blum 1977.)

—— 1976. Masochism, the ego ideal, and the psychology of women. In Blum, ed., *Female Psychology*, pp. 157–191.

—— 1977. The prototype of preoedipal reconstruction. Paper presented for the Margaret S. Mahler Birthday Celebration of the N.Y. Psychoanalytical Society and Institute, May 10, 1977. *Journal of the American Psychoanalytical Association*, 25(4):757–785.

Blum, Harold P., ed. 1977. *Female Psychology: Contemporary Psychoanalytic Views*. New York: International Universities Press.

—— 1980. *Psychoanalytic Explorations of Technique*. New York: International Universities Press.

Bogen, J. E. 1969. The other side of the brain. *Bulletin of the Los Angeles Neurological Societies*, 34:35–61.

Boskind-White, Marlowe and William C. White, Jr. 1983. *Bulimarexia*. New York: Norton.

Bower, Gordon H. 1980. Mood and memory. Address at meeting of American Psychological Association, Montreal, September 1980. *American Psychologist* (February 1981), 36(2):129–148.

Bower, T. G. R. 1982. *Development in Infancy*. San Francisco: Freeman.

Bowlby, J. 1960. Separation anxiety. *International Journal of Psychoanalysis*, 41:89–113.

Boxerman, Albert P. 1981. Private communications.

Brenner, C. 1957. The nature and development of the concept of repression in Freud's writings. In Eissler et al., eds., *The Psychoanalytic Study of the Child*, 12:43–44, 206.

Bronowski, J. and U. Bellugi, 1970. Language, name, concept. *Science*, May 8, 1970, p. 669.

Brown, Cheryl J. 1979. Reactions of infants to their parents' voices. *Infant Behavior and Development*, 2:295–300.

Brown, Louise. 1980. *London Daily Mirror*, April 3, as quoted in *Chicago Tribune*, April 4.

Brown, Paula. 1978. *The Highland People of New Guinea*. New York: Cambridge University Press.

Brown, R. 1970. *Psycholinguistics*. New York: Free Press.

Bruch, H. 1973. *Eating Disorders: Obesity, Anorexia Nervosa, and the Person Within*. New York: Basic Books.

—— 1979. *The Golden Cage*. New York: Random House.

Brull,, Frank. 1975. Translations of Freud. *Psychotherapy*, vol. 12, no. 3, pp. 273–279.

Brunswick, R. M. 1940. The preoedipal phase of the libido development. *Psychoanalytical Quarterly*, 9:293–319.

Bychowski, Gustav. 1945. The ego of the homosexual. *International Journal of Psychoanalysis*, 26:114.

—— 1963. Frigidity and object relationship. Read at panel on Frigidity in Women, held at the midwinter meeting of the American Psychological Association, December 1960. *International Journal of Psychoanalysis*, 44:57–62.

Cannon, Walter B. 1960. *Journal of Nervous and Mental Disease*, 131:202–212.

Carey, W. B., and S. C. McDevitt. 1978. Stability and change in individual temperament. *Journal of the American Academy of Child Psychiatry* 17:331–337.

Ceaser, Martin. 1977. The role of maternal cachexia in four cases of anorexia nervosa. *Bulletin of the Menninger Clinic* (September), 41(5):475–486.

Chasseguet-Smirgel, Janine. 1975, 1976. Freud and female sexuality. Read at the Twenty-ninth International Psycho-analytical Congress, London. In Eissler et al., eds., *The Psychoanalytic Study of the Child*, 31:42. New Haven: Yale University Press, 1976.

—— 1976. Freud and female sexuality. *International Journal of Psychoanalysis*, 57:279–283, 285.

Chediak, Charles. 1977. The so-called anorexia nervosa: diagnostic and treatment considerations. In *Bulletin of the Menninger Clinic* (September 1977), 41(5):453–474.

Chisholm, James. 1983. *Navajo Infancy*. New York: Aldine.

Chodorow, Nancy. 1978. *The Reproduction of Mothering: Psychoanalysis and the Sociology of Gender*. Berkeley: University of California Press.

Choisy, Maryse. 1963. *Sigmund Freud: A New Appraisal*. New York: Philosophical Library.

Chomsky, N. 1968. *Language and Mind.* New York: Harcourt Brace and World.

Cobliner, W. G. 1965. The Geneva School of Genetic Psychology and Psychoanalysis: parallels and counterparts. *The Psychoanalytic Review* (1976) 63(1):51.

Cohler, Bertram J. and Henry V. Grunebaum. 1981. *Mothers, Grandmothers, and Daughters.* New York: Wiley.

Colarusso, Calvin A. 1979. The development of time sense from birth to object constancy. *International Journal of Psychoanalysis,* 60:243–251.

Collipp, P. J., ed. 1975. *Childhood Obesity.* Littleton, Mass.: PSG.

Coltrera, Joseph T. 1980. Truth from genetic illusion: the transference and the fate of the infantile neurosis. In H. P. Blum, ed., *Psychoanalytic Explorations of Technique,* pp. 289–314.

Conrad, Dorothy. 1977. A starving family: an interactional view of anorexia nervosa. *Bulletin of the Menninger Clinic,* 41(5):488, 491.

Crisp, A. H. 1977a. Diagnosis and outcome of anorexia nervosa: The St. George's view. *Proceedings of the Royal Society of Medicine,* 70:464–470.

—— 1977b. The differential diagnosis of anorexia nervosa. *Proceedings of the Royal Society of Medicine,* 70:686–688.

Dahl, H. 1965. Observations on a "natural experiment": Helen Keller. *Journal of the American Psychoanalytical Association,* 13(3):533–550. In *The Psychoanalytic Review* (Vancouver, B.C.) (1976), 63(1):59–70.

Daly. 1928. Der Menstruationskomplex. *Imago,* vol. 14. In K. Horney, The denial of the vagina. *International Journal of Psychoanalysis* (1933), 14:57–70.

De Casper, A. J. and W. P. Fifer. 1981. Of human bonding: newborns prefer their mothers' voices. *Science* (June 6), 208(4448).

Deutsch, H. 1942. Some forms of emotional disturbances and their relationship to schizophrenia. *Psychoanalytic Quarterly,* 2:301–321.

Deutsch, Helene. 1976. *The Sexual Experience.* B. J. Sadock, H. I. Kaplan and H. M. Freedman, eds. New York: Williams and Wilkins.

—— 1981. Anorexia nervosa. *Bulletin of the Menninger Clinic.* 45:509–510.

Doob, L. W. 1971. *Patterning of Time.* New Haven: Yale University Press.

Drossman, Douglas A. 1980. Anorexia nervosa/obesity in childhood. *Society's Child.* Nutley, N.J.: Roche Laboratories.

Dunn, E. 1981. Private communication.

Eber, Milton, 1980. Gender identity conflicts in male transsexualism. *Bulletin of the Menninger Clinic,* 44(1):31–38.

—— 1981. Don Juanism: a disorder of the self. *Bulletin of the Menninger Clinic* 45(4):307–316.

Ede, Donald A. 1978. *Introduction to Developmental Biology.* New York: Halstead Press.

Edgcumbe, Rose. 1981. Language development and object relations. In Solnit et al., eds., *The Psychoanalytic Study of the Child,* 36:168–169.

Edgcumbe, Rose and Marion Burgner. 1975. The phallic-narcissistic phase, a differentiation between preoedipal and oedipal aspects of phallic development. In Eissler et al., eds., *Psychoanalytic Study of the Child* 30:164, 168.

Ehrhardt, Anka A., and F. L. Heino Meyer-Bahlburg. 1981. Effects of prenatal sex hormones on gender related behavior. *Science*, 211:1312–1318.

Ehrhardt, A. A., K. Evers, and J. Money. 1968. On hermaphrodites. *Johns Hopkins Medical Journal*, 123:115.

Eissler, Ruth S., ed. 1974. *The Psychoanalytic Study of the Child*. Vols. 26, 27. New Haven: Yale University Press.

Eissler, Ruth S. et al., eds., 1945–1972. *The Psychoanalytic Study of the Child*. 25 vols. Vols., 1, 5, 9, 10, 12, 13, 18, 19, 21–25. New York: International Universities Press.

——— 1973–1977. *The Psychoanalytic Study of the Child*. Vols. 28–32. New Haven: Yale University Press.

——— 1975. *The Psychoanalytic Study of the Child: Abstracts and Index, Volumes 1–25*. New Haven: Yale University Press.

Ekstein, Rudolf. 1966. *Children of Time and Space, of Action, and Impulse*. New York: Appleton, Century, Crofts.

Ekstein, Rudolf and Richard Friedman. 1967. Borderline states in childhood and adolescence. In Eissler et al., eds., *The Psychoanalytic Study of the Child*, 22:357–374.

Eliade, M. 1958. *Rites and Symbols of Initiation*. New York: Harper & Row.

Emde, Robert N. 1983. The prerepresentational self. In Solnit and Eissler, eds., *The Psychoanalytic Study of the Child*, 38:165–187.

Emde, R. N. and J. Robinson. 1979. The first two months: Recent research in developmental psychology. In J. Noshpitz et al., eds., *Basic Handbook of Child Psychiatry*, pp. 63–71.

Engel, G. L. 1967. Ego development following severe trauma in infancy: a 14-year study of a girl with gastric fistula and depression in infancy. *Bulletin of the Association of Psychoanalytic Medicine*, 6:57.

Erikson, Erik H. 1956. *Identity and the Life Cycle*. Monograph no. 1. New York: International Universities Press, 1959.

——— 1959. Identity and the life cycle. *Psychological Issues*, 1:50–100.

——— 1963. *Childhood and Society*. 2d ed. New York: Norton.

——— 1965. Inner and outer space: reflections on womanhood. In Robert J. Lifton, ed., *The Woman in America*, Boston: Houghton Mifflin.

——— 1968. *Identity: Youth and Crisis*. New York: Norton.

Fairbairn, W. 1944. Cited in M. Hurvich, Aspects of borderline personality and psychopathology. In Saretsky, Goldman and Milman, eds., *Integrating Ego Psychology and Object Relations Theory*, p. 206.

——— 1952. *An Object Relations Theory of the Personality*. New York: Basic Books.

——— 1973. Synopsis of an object relations theory of the personality. *International Journal of Psychoanalysis*, 44:224–225.

Falstein, Eugene I., Sherman C. Feinstein and Ilse Judas. 1956. Anorexia nervosa in the male child. *American Journal of Orthopsychiatry*, 26:751–772.

Farberow, N. S. and E. Shneidman. 1961. *Cry for Help*. New York: McGraw-Hill.

Fast, Irene. 1979. Gender differentiation in girls. *International Journal of Psychoanalysis*, 60:441–453.

Fast, Irene and Morton Chethik. 1972. Some aspects of object relations in borderline children. *International Journal of Psychoanalysis*, 53:479–485.

Feighner, J. P. et al. 1972. Diagnostic criteria for use in psychiatric research. *Archives of Genetic Psychiatry*, (January), 26:57–63.

Fenichel, O. 1945. *The Psychoanalytic Theory of Neurosis*. New York: Norton.

Ferenzi, Sandor. 1930. Each adaptation is preceded by an inhibited attempt at splitting. In *Selected Papers*, 3:220. New York: Basic Books.

Fliegel, Zenia. 1973. Feminine psychosexual development in Freudian theory, a historical reconstruction. *Psychoanalytical Quarterly*, 42:385–408.

Fliegel, Zenia and D. A. Freedman. 1964. Studies in the ego development of the congenitally blind child. In Eissler et al., eds., *The Psychoanalytic Study of the Child*, 19:113–157.

Forrest, David V. 1983. Language as object—and subject. *Journal of the American Academy of Psychoanalysis*, 11:4.

Fraiberg, Selma. 1959. *The Magic Years*. New York: Scribner.

—— 1969. Libidinal object constancy and mental representation. In Eissler et al., eds., *The Psychoanalytic Study of the Child*, 24:9–47.

—— 1972. Some characteristics of genital arousal and discharge in latency girls. In Eissler, ed., *The Psychoanalytic Study of the Child*, 27:439–475.

Freud, Anna. 1946. *The Ego and the Mechanisms of Defense*. New York: International Universities Press.

—— 1958. Adolescence. In Eissler et al., eds., *Psychoanalytic Study of the Child*, 13:255–278.

—— 1965. *Normality and Pathology in Childhood*. New York: International Universities Press.

Freud, Elissa. 1968. *The Writings of Anna Freud*. Vol. 4, *Indications for Child Analysis and Other Papers 1945–1956*. New York: International Universities Press.

—— 1981. Private communication.

Freud, Martin. 1957. *Glory Reflected*. London: Angus & Roberts.

Freud, Sigmund. 1962. Standard Edition. James Strachey, ed. 24 vols. London: Hogarth, New York: Macmillan.

—— 1895. A reply to criticism of my paper on anxiety neurosis. Standard Edition, 3:123–239.

—— 1895. On narcissism: An introduction. Standard Edition, 14:73–102.

—— 1895. Project for a scientific psychology. Standard Edition, 1:283–397.

—— 1900. The interpretation of dreams. Standard Edition, 5:339–627.

—— 1901. Psychopathology of everyday life. Standard Edition, vols. 1–2.

—— 1905a. Fragments of an analysis of a case of hysteria. Standard Edition, 7:1–122.

—— 1905b. Jokes and their relations to the unconscious. Standard Edition, 8:120.

—— 1905c. Three essays on the theory of sexuality. Standard Edition, 5:135–243.

—— 1909. Analysis of a phobia in a five-year-old boy. Standard Edition, 10:3–149.

—— 1909. Notes upon a case of obsessional neurosis. Standard Edition, 10:151–318.

—— 1910, 1940. An outline of psychoanalysis. Standard Edition, 23:141–207.

—— 1911. Formulations on the two principles of mental functioning. Standard Edition, 12:213.

_____ 1914. On narcissism—an introduction. Standard Edition, 14:73–102.

_____ 1917. Introductory lectures on psychoanalysis, part 3. Standard Edition, 16:241.

_____ 1918. The history of an infantile neurosis. Standard Edition, 17:7–122.

_____ 1918. Wolfman, Standard Edition, 22:721–742.

_____ 1922. Tabu der Virginitat. _Sammlung Kleiner Schriften_, 4th ed. Quoted by K. Horney, _International Journal of the Psycho-Analytical Society._ (1922).

_____ 1923. The ego and the id. Standard Edition, 19:1–66.

_____ 1924. The dissolution of the oedipus complex. Standard Edition, 17:173–282.

_____ 1924. A note upon the mystic writing pad. Standard Edition, 19:227.

_____ 1925. Some psychical consequences of the anatomical distinctions between the sexes. Standard Edition, 19:243–260.

_____ 1926. The question of lay analysis, conversations with an impartial person. Standard Edition, 20:183–258.

_____ 1927–1931. Civilization and its discontents. Standard Edition, 21:57–147.

_____ 1932. Lecture 33, New introductory lectures to psychoanalysis. Standard Edition, 22:112–135.

_____ 1937. Constructions in analysis. Standard Edition, 23:255–270.

_____ 1938. Outline of psycho-analysis. Standard Edition, 23:188.

_____ 1940. An outline of psychoanalysis. Standard Edition, 23:141–207.

_____ 1960. A _General Introduction to Psychoanalysis_. New York: Washington Square Press.

_____ 1973. Freud and the discovery of childhood sexuality. _History of Childhood Quarterly_, 1:118–141.

Furman, Erna. 1982. Mothers have to be there to be left. In Solnit et al., eds., _The Psychoanalytic Study of the Child_, 37:15–29.

Gailer, L., S. Minuchin, and B. L. Rosman. 1978. _Psychosomatic Families: Anorexia Nervosa in Context_. Cambridge: Harvard University Press.

Galenson, E. 1979a. The impact of early sexual discovery on mood, defensive organization, and symbolization. In Eissler, ed., _The Psychoanalytic Study of the Child_, 26:195–216.

_____ 1979b. Psychology of women: infancy and early childhood, latency and early adolescence. _Journal of the American Psychoanalytical Association,,_ 24(1):141–160.

_____ 1983. Private communication.

Galenson, E. and H. Roiphe. 1971. Vicissitudes of female sexuality. In Kestenberg, _Children and Parents_, p. 12.

_____ 1973. Object loss and early sexual development. _Psychoanalytical Quarterly_, 42:73.

_____ 1974. The emergence of genital awareness during the second year of life. In Richard Friedman et al., eds., _Sex Differences in Behavior_, p. 224. New York: Wiley.

_____ 1976. Some suggested revisions concerning early female development. _Journal of the American Psychoanalytical Association_, 24(5):29–57. In Blum, ed., _Female Psychology_, pp. 29–58.

_____ 1977. Some suggested revisions concerning early female development. In H.

P. Blum, ed., *Female Psychology: Contemporary Psychoanalytic Views*, pp. 29–55.

—— 1979a. Development from one to two years: observations and psychosexual development. In Noshpitz et al., eds., *Basic Handbook of Child Psychology*, pp. 144–156.

—— 1979b. The development of sexual identity: discoveries and implications. In T. B. Karasu and C. W. Socarides, eds., *On Sexuality, Psychoanalytic Observations*, p. 14. New York: International Universities Press.

—— 1980a. The preoedipal development of the boy. *Journal of the American Psychoanalytical Association*, 28(4):805–827.

—— 1980b. *Sex and Gender Identity*. New York: International Universities Press.

Galenson, E., R. Miller and H. Roiphe. 1976. The choice of symbols. *Journal of the American Academy of Child Psychiatry* (Winter), 15(1):83–96.

Garai, J. 1966. Formation of the concept of "self" and the development of sex identification. In Kidd and Rivoire, *Perceptual Development in Children*, pp. 344–390.

Gardner, R. A. and B. T. Gardner. 1969. Teaching sign language to a chimpanzee. *Science* (August 15), 165:664–672.

Garner, Marilyn M. 1980. Creativity and mental health: a case study. Presented at the 23d Annual Meeting of the American Association of Children's Residential Centers.

Garner, D. M. and P. E. Garfinkel. 1979. The eating attitudes test: an index of the symptoms of anorexia nervosa. *Psychological Medicine*, 9:273–279.

Geleerd, Elizabeth R. 1958. Borderline states in childhood and adolescence. In Eissler et al., eds., *The Psychoanalytic Study of the Child*, 13:279–295.

Gershman, H. 1967. The evolution of gender identity. *Bulletin of the New York Academy of Medicine*, 42:1000–1018.

Gesell, Arnold and Frances L. Ilg (in collaboration with Louise Bates Ames and Glenna E. Bullis). 1946. *The Child from Five to Ten*. New York: Harper & Row.

Gesell, A. et al. 1940. *The First Five Years of Life: A Guide to the Study of the Preschool Child*. New York: Harper & Brothers.

Gillespie, W. H. 1969. Concepts of vaginal orgasm. *International Journal of Psychoanalysis*, 50:495–497.

—— 1976. The Psychoanalytic Dimension in Sex Differences. P. C. Lee and R. S. Stewart, eds. New York: Urizon.

Glossary of Psychiatric Terms and Concepts, A. 1984. B. Moore and B. Fine, eds. Washington, D.C.: American Psychological Association.

Glover, E. 1943. *On the Early Development of Mind*, pp. 307–323. New York: International Universities Press.

—— 1949. *Psychoanalysis*. 2d ed. New York: Staples Press.

—— 1968. *The Birth of the Ego*. New York: International Universities Press.

Goode W. J. 1970. *World Revolution and Family Patterns*. New York: Free Press.

Gould S. J. This view of life. *Natural History*. 93(8):24–27.

Grala, C. 1980. The concept of splitting and its manifestations on the Rorschach test. *Bulletin of the Menninger Clinic*, 44(3):253–271.

Green, R. 1974. *Sexual Identity Conflicts in Children and Adults*. New York: Basic Books.

Greenacre, Phyllis. 1952. *Trauma, Growth, and Personality*. New York: Norton.

—— 1958. Toward an understanding of the physical nucleus of some defense reactions. In Alfred J. Solnit et al., eds., *Psychoanalytic Study of the Child*, 34:145.

—— 1960. Considerations regarding the parent–infant relationship. *International Journal of Psychoanalysis*, 41(6):571–584.

—— 1968. Early physical determinants in the development of the sense of identity. *Journal of the American Psychoanalytical Association*, 6:612–627.

—— 1969. The fetish and the transitional object. In Eissler et al., eds., *The Psychoanalytic Study of the Child*, 24:144–164.

—— 1978. Reconstruction and the process of individuation. Solnit et al., eds., *The Psychoanalytic Study of the Child*, 34:121–144.

—— 1979. Reconstruction and the process of individuation. In Solnit et al., eds., *The Psychoanalytic Study of the Child*, 34:121–144.

Greenson, R. R. 1968. Dis-identifying from mother: Its special importance for the boy. *International Journal of Psychoanalysis*, 49:370–374. Reprinted in *The Journal of the American Academy of Psychoanalysis* (April 1983), 11(2):204–226.

Greenspan, Stanley I. 1980. Analysis of a five-and-a-half-year-old girl: indications for a dyadic-phallic phase of development. *Journal of the American Psychoanalytical Association*, 28(3):557–595.

Grotjahn, M. 1957. *Beyond Laughter*. New York: McGraw-Hill.

Guidano, V. F. and G. Liotti. 1983. *Cognitive Processes and Emotional Disorders*. New York: Guilford.

Gull, William Withey. 1868. The address in medicine delivered before the annual Meeting of the British Medical Association at Oxford. *Lancet*, 2:171. In Palazzoli, *Self-Starvation*, p. 5.

—— 1873a. Anorexia hysterica (aspepsia hysterica). In Palazzoli, *Self-Starvation*, p. 6.

—— 1873b. Meeting of the Clinical Society. *Medical Times and Gazette*, 2:534. In Palazzoli, *Self-Starvation*, p. 6.

Guntrip, H. J. S. 1971. *Psychoanalytic Theory, Therapy, and the Self*. New York: International Universities Press.

—— 1977. My experience of analysis with Fairbairn and Winnicott. In K. Frank, ed., *The Human Dimension in Psychoanalytic Practice*, pp. 49–69. New York: Grune and Stratton.

Hall, C. and G. Lindzey. 1970. *Theories of Personality*. 2d ed. New York: Wiley.

Halmi, K. A. 1978. Anorexia nervosa: recent investigations. *Annual Review of Medicine*, 29:137–138.

Hart, Henry Harper. 1947. Problems of identification. *Psychiatric Quarterly*, 21:11.

—— 1961. A review of the psychoanalytic literature on passivity. *Psychiatric Quarterly*, 35:331–352.

Hartmann, H., E. Kris, and R. Loewenstein. 1946. Comments on the formation of psychic structure. In *Papers on Psychoanalytic Psychology*. Psychological

Issues Monograph, no. 14, pp. 27–55. New York: International Universities Press, 1954.

Hartocollis, P. A. 1974. Origins of time: a reconstruction of the ontogenetic development of the sense of time based on object-relations theory. *Psychoanalytical Quarterly*, 43:243–261.

Hassan, M. K. and R. W. Tibbetts. 1977. Primary anorexia nervosa (weight phobia) in males. *Postgraduate Medical Journal*, 53:146–151.

Haugh, Robert. 1981. Private communication.

Heiman, M. 1963. Sexual response in women. *This Journal*, 24(5):285–304. In Blum, ed., *Female Psychology*, pp. 285–302.

Heller, Judith Bernays. 1956. Freud's mother and father. From a selection for *Commentary*, 21:418–421. In Ruitenbeck, *Freud as We Knew Him*, pp. 334–340.

Hendrick, Ives. 1942. Instinct and the ego during infancy. *Psychoanalytic Quarterly*, 11:33–58.

Herdt, Gilbert H. 1981. *Guardians of the Flutes: Idioms of Masculinity*. New York: McGraw Hill.

Herzog, J. M. 1980. Sleep disturbance and father hunger in 18- to 28-month-old boys. In Solnit et al., eds., *Psychoanalytic Study of the Child*, 35:223–230.

Hilgard, E. A. 1977. *Divided Consciousness*. New York: Wiley.

Hoffer, W. 1949. Oral aggressiveness and ego-development. *International Journal of Psychoanalysis*, 30:200–201.

Hoffman, M. 1976. Empathy, role taking, guilt and development of altruistic motives. In T. Lickona, ed., *Moral Development and Behavior*, pp. 124–243. New York: Holt, Rinehart and Winston.

Horney, Karen. 1924. On the genesis of the castration complex in women. Paper delivered at the Seventh International Psychoanalytical Congress, 1922, Berlin. *International Journal of Psychoanalysis*, 5:50–65.

—— 1926. The flight from womanhood: the masculinity-complex in women, as viewed by men and women. *International Journal of Psychoanalysis*, 7:324–339.

—— 1933. The denial of the vagina: a contribution to the problem of the genital anxieties specific to women. *International Journal of Psychoanalysis*, 14:57–70.

Horwitz, Leonard and Mary Jo Peebles. 1980. Success and failure in psychoanalysis: another look at research on predicting analyzability. Presentation delivered at the American Psychiatric Association Convention, Montreal.

Hudson, J. 1983. Cited in A deadly feast and famine. *Newsweek*, March 7, 1983, pp. 59–60.

Hunt, M. M. 1974 *Sexual Behavior in the 1970s*. New York: Playboy Press.

Hurvich, M. 1979. Aspects of borderline personality and psychopathology. In Saretsky, Goldman and Milman, eds., *Integrating Ego Psychology and Object Relations Theory*, pp. 199–216.

Imperato-McGinty, J., L. Guerrero, T. Gautier, and R. E. Peterson. 1974. *Science*, 186:1213.

Imperato-McGinty, J., R. E. Peterson, T. Gautier, and E. Sturla. 1979. The effects of androgen. *New England Journal of Medicine* 300:1233–1237.

Jacobson, Edith. 1950. Development of the wish for a child in boys. In Eissler, ed., *The Psychoanalytic Study of the Child: Abstract and Index, Volumes 1–25.*

—— 1954. The self and the object world: vicissitudes of their infantile cathexes and their influence on affective development. In Eissler, ed., *Psychoanalytic Study of the Child: Abstract and Index, Volumes 1–25.*

—— 1964. *The Self and the Object World.* New York: International Universities Press.

—— 1971. *Depression.* New York: International Universities Press.

Jessner, Lucie and D. W. Abse. 1960. Regressive forces in anorexia nervosa. *British Journal of Medical Psychology,* 33(4):301–312.

Jones, Ernest. 1925. The early development of female sexuality. In *Papers on Psychoanalysis,* pp. 438–451. Boston: Beacon Press, 1961.

—— 1925. Hate and anal eroticism in the obsessional neurosis. In *Papers on Psychoanalysis,* pp. 540–549. 3d ed. London: Balliere, Tindall & Cox.

—— 1948. *Papers on Psychoanalysis.* London: Balliere, Tindall & Cox.

—— 1953. *The Life and Work of Sigmund Freud.* Vol. 1. New York: Basic Books.

Josselyn, Irene. 1948. *Psychological Development of Children.* New York: Family Services.

—— 1953. Early development. In E. Rexford et al., eds., *Infant Psychiatry: A New Synthesis,* pp. 148–172. New Haven: Yale University Press, 1976.

Jung, C. J. 1910. Quoted in Hall and Lindzey, *Theories of Personality,* p. 93.

Kagan, J. 1978. The baby's elastic mind. *Human Nature,* 1:66–73.

Kagan, Jerome, Richard B. Kearsley, and Phillip R. Zelazo. 1980. *Infancy: Its Place in Human Development.* Cambridge: Harvard University Press.

Kagan, J. and M. Lewis. 1965. Sex discrimination at 6 months: studies of attention in the human infant. *Behavior and Development,* 11:95–127.

Khan, M. M. R. 1960. Clinical aspects of the schizoid personality: affects and technique. *International Journal of Psychoanalysis,* 41:430–437.

Kanzer, Mark. 1978. Current concepts of object relations theory. *Journal of the American Psychoanalytical Association,* 26(3):599–613.

Kanzer, Mark and Jules Glenn. 1979. *Freud and His Self-Analysis.* New York and London: Jason Aronson.

Kataguchi, Y. 1966. *Psychological Diagnoses of Japanese Writers with New Critical Essays.* Tokyo: Shibun-do.

Kay, D. W. K. and D. Leigh. 1954. The natural history, treatment, and prognosis of anorexia nervosa based on a study of 38 patients. *Journal of Mental Science,* (April), 100:411–419.

Kehrberg, Lawrence. 1966. A cognitive developmental analysis of children's sex role, concepts and attitudes. In E. Macoby, ed., *Development of Sex Differences,* pp. 82–173. Stanford: Stanford University Press.

Kern, Stephen. 1973. Freud and the discovery of child sexuality. *History of Childhood Quarterly* (Summer), 1:118–141.

Kernberg, O. 1966. Structural derivatives of object relationships. *International Journal of Psychoanalysis,* 47:236–251.

—— 1967. Borderline personality organization. *Journal of the American Psychoanalytical Association,* 15:641–685.

—— 1968a. *Object Relations and Clinical Psychoanalysis.* New York: Jason Aronson.

—— 1968b. The treatment of patients with borderline personality organization. *International Journal of Psychoanalysis,* 49:600–619.

—— 1971. Early ego integration and object relations. Presented at the New York Academy of Sciences, May 5. In Lichtenberg and Slap, Notes on the concept of splitting and the defense mechanism of the splitting of representations. *Journal of the American Psychoanalytical Association* (1973), 21(4):778.

—— 1975. *Borderline Conditions and Pathological Narcissism.* New York: Jason Aronson.

—— 1976. *Object Relations: Theory and Clinical Psychoanalysis.* New York: Jason Aronson.

—— 1980. Implications of psychoanalytic technique. In Blum, ed., *Psychoanalytic Explorations of Technique,* pp. 207–239.

Kestenbaum, C. 1980. Early childhood: the toddler years. In J. Bemporad, ed., *Child Development in Normality and Psychopathology,* pp. 99–120. New York: Brunner/Mazel.

Kestenberg, Judith S. 1968. Outside and inside, male and female. *Journal of the American Psychoanalytical Association,* 16:457–520.

—— 1969a. From organ-object imagery to self and object representations. In McDevitt and Settlage, eds., *Separation/Individuation,* pp. 325–355.

—— 1969b. Problems of technique of child analysis in relation to the various developmental stages of prelatency. In Eissler et al., eds., *The Psychoanalytical Study of the Child,* 24:358–383.

Kestenberg, Judith S. (in collaboration with E. Robbins, J. Berlowe, A. Buelte, and H. Marcus). 1975. *Children and Parents: Psychoanalytic Studies in Development.* New York: Jason Aronson.

Kestenberg, Judith, S. et al. 1971. Development of the young child as expressed through bodily movement. *This Journal,* 19:746–764.

Kidd, A., and J. Rivoire. 1966. *Perceptual Development in Children.* New York: International Universities Press.

Kinsey, A., W. Pomeroy, and C. Martin. 1948. *Sexual Behavior in the Human Male.* Philadelphia: Saunders.

Kleeman, J. 1966. Genital self-discovery during a boy's second year. In Eissler et al., eds., *The Psychoanalytic Study of the Child,* 21:358–392.

—— 1976. Quoted in *Journal of the American Academy of Psychoanalysis* (April 1983), 11(2):211.

Klein, Melanie. 1928. Early stages of the oedipus conflict. *International Journal of Psychoanalysis,* 9:167–180.

—— 1932. *The Psycho-Analysis of Children.* London: Hogarth Press.

—— 1937. *Love, Guilt and Reparation.* London: Hogarth.

—— 1940. Mourning and its relation to manic-depressive states. In *Contributions to Psycho-Analysis, 1921–45,* pp. 311–338. London: Hogarth Press, 1948.

—— 1945. The Oedipus complex in the light of early anxieties. *International Journal of Psychoanalysis,* 26:11–13.

—— 1946. Notes on some schizoid mechanisms. In J. Riviere, M. Klein, P.

Heimann, and S. Isaacs, eds., *Developments in Psychoanalysis*, pp. 292–320. London: Hogarth Press, 1952.

—— 1950. *Contributions to Psycho-Analysis*. London: Hogarth Press.

—— 1957. *Envy and Gratitude*. New York: Basic Books.

Koehler, O. 1954. The smile as an innate facial expression. *Zeitschrift fuer Menschliche Vererbungs und Konstitutionslehre*, 32:390–398.

Kohlberg, Lawrence. 1966. A cognitive-developmental analysis of children's sex-role concepts and attitudes. In E. E. Macoby, ed., *The Development of Sex Differences*, pp. 82–173. Stanford: Stanford University Press.

Kohut, H. 1971. *The Analysis of the Self*. New York: Basic Books.

—— 1977. *The Restoration of the Self*. New York: Basic Books.

Kolansky, H. 1967. Some psychoanalytic considerations on speech in normal development and psychopathology. In Eissler et al., eds., *The Psychoanalytic Study of the Child*, 22:274–295.

Kowalski, Anthony. 1976. Discussion of "Some Effects of the New Feminism" by Ruth Moulton. Presented to the Topeka Psychoanalytic Society Meeting, Topeka, Kansas, April 19. In Chediak, The so-called anorexia nervosa. pp. 453–474.

Kramer, Paul. 1954. Early capacity for orgastic discharge and character formation. In Eissler et al., eds., *The Psychoanalytical Study of the Child*, 9:128–141.

Kramer, Selma. 1974. A discussion of the paper by John A. Sours on the anorexia nervosa syndrome. *International Journal of Psychoanalysis*, 55:577.

—— 1980. The technical significance and application of Mahler's separation/individuation theory. In Blum, ed., *Psychoanalytic Explorations of Technique*, pp. 241–262.

Krout, M. H. 1939. Typical behavior patterns in 26 ordinal positions. *Journal of Genetic Psychology*, 55:3–30.

Kubie, L. S. 1953. The distortion of the symbolic process in neurosis and psychosis. *Journal of the American Psychoanalytical Association*, 1:64–66. In Stoller, *Sexual Excitement*, appendix B2.

Kuhn, Roland H. 1953. Zur Daseinanalyse der Anorexia mentalis II. *Studie Nervenartz*, 24:191.

Lacan, Jacques. 1957. The insistence of the letter in the unconscious. In J. D. Ehrmann, ed., *Structuralism*, pp. 101–136. New York: Anchor, 1970.

—— 1973. *The Four Fundamental Concepts of Psychoanalysis*, Jacques-Alain Millar, ed.; Alan Sheridan, tr. New York: Norton, 1978.

Lamb, Michael E. 1976a. Interactions between 8-month-old children and their fathers and mothers. In Lamb, ed., *The Role of the Father in Child Development*, pp. 307–327. New York: Wiley.

—— 1976b. Interactions between two-year-olds and their mothers and fathers. *Psychological Reports*, 38:447–450.

Lampl-de-Groot, J. 1928. Evolution of the Oedipus complex in women. *International Journal of Psychoanalysis*, 9(3):332–345.

—— 1933. Problems of femininity. *Psychoanalytical Quarterly*, 2:489–519.

Langer, J. 1969. *Theories of Development*. New York: Holt, Rinehart and Winston.

Lasègue, E. C. 1873. On hysterical anorexia. *Medical Times Gazette*, 2:265. (De l'anorexie hysterique. *Archives générales de médicine* [1873], 21:385.) In Palazzoli, *Self-Starvation*, pp. 4–6, 9, 203, 245–246.

Lebovici, Serge. 1982. The origins and development of the oedipus complex. *International Journal of Psychoanalysis*, 63:201–215.

Lee, Patrick C. and Robert Sussman Stewart, eds. 1976. *Sex Differences: Cultural and Developmental Dimensions*. New York: Urizen Books.

Lenneberg, E. H. 1964. The capacity for language acquisition. In J. J. Fodor and J. J. Katz, eds., *The Structure of Language*. Englewood Cliffs, N.J.: Prentice-Hall.

—— 1967. *Biological Foundations of Language*. New York: Wiley.

Lenneberg, E. H., F. G. Rebelsky, and I. A. Nichols. 1965. The vocalizations of infants born to deaf and to hearing parents. *Human Development*, 8:23–37.

Lerner, Harriet E. 1980. Penis envy: alternatives in conceptualization. *Bulletin of the Menninger Clinic*, 44(1):39–48.

Lester, Eva P. 1976. On the psychosexual development of the female child. *Journal of the American Academy of Psychoanalysis*, 4(4):515–527.

Levin, M. 1936. On the causation of mental symptoms. *Journal of Mental Science*, 80:1–27.

Lev-Ran, A. 1974. Gender role differentiation in hermaphrodites. *Archives of Sexual Behavior*, 3(5):391–423.

Lévi-Strauss, Claude. 1976. *The Savage Mind*. 1966. Chicago: University of Chicago Press.

Levy, David. 1953. The early development of independent and oppositional behavior. In G. Grinker, ed., *Midcentury Psychiatry*, pp. 113–122. Springfield, Ill.: Charles C. Thomas.

Lewis, Helen Block. 1940. The fifty minute hour: bulimia: the case of Laura, impregnation fantasies being at the roots. *Bulletin of the Menninger Clinic*, 43:151–152, 154, 155.

—— 1979. Gender identity: primary narcissism or primary process. *Bulletin of the Menninger Clinic*, 43(2):145–160.

—— 1980. Is Freud an enemy of women's liberation? Presented at the American Psychological Association Convention, Montreal.

Lewis, M. 1963. *Language, Thought, and Personality in Infancy and Childhood*. New York: Basic Books.

Lichtenberg, J. D. and J. W. Slap. 1971. On the defensive organization. *International Journal of Psychoanalysis*, 52:451–457.

—— 1972. On the defense mechanism: a survey and synthesis. *Journal of the American Psychoanalytical Association*, 29:4.

—— 1973. Notes on the concept of splitting and the defense mechanism of the splitting of representations. *Journal of the American Psychoanalytical Association*, 29:4.

Lichtenstein, H. 1977. *The Dilemma of Human Identity*. New York: Jason Aronson.

Lickona, T. 1976. Critical issues in the study of moral development and behavior. In Lickona, ed., *Moral Development and Behavior*, pp 3–27. New York: Holt, Rinehart and Winston.

Lidz, Theodore. 1968, 1976. *The Person: His and Her Development Throughout the*

Life Cycle. Rev. ed., 1976. New York: Basic Books.

Lindner, Robert. 1976. *The Fifty-Minute Hour.* New York: Bantam Books.

Little, Margaret I. 1981. *Transference Neurosis and Transference Psychosis.* New York: Jason Aronson.

Loewald, H. W. 1951. Ego and reality. International Journal of Psychoanalysis, 32:10–18.

—— 1970. Psychoanalytic theory and the psychoanalytic process. In Eissler et al., eds., *The Psychoanalytic Study of the Child,* 25:45–68. New York: International Universities Press.

—— 1972. The experience of time. In Eissler, ed., *Psychoanalytic Study of the Child,* 27.

—— 1980. Instinct theory, object relations, and psychic-structure formation. *This Journal,* 26:493–506.

Loewenstein, R. 1950. Conflict and autonomous ego development during the phallic phase. In Eissler et al., eds., *The Psychoanalytic Study of the Child,* 5:47–52. New York: International Universities Press.

Lopez, Thomas and Gilbert Kliman. 1980. The cornerstone treatment of a preschool boy from an extremely impoverished environment. In Solnit et al., eds., *Psychoanalytic Study of the Child,* 35:341–375.

Lorand, Sandor. 1943. Anorexia nervosa: report of a case. *Psychosomatic Medicine,* 5(3):282–292.

Ludwig, A. M., J. M. Brandson, C. B. Wilbur, F. Benfield, and D. H. Jameson. 1972. The objective study of a multiple personality. *Archives of General Psychiatry* (April), pp. 298–310.

McDevitt, John B. 1971. Preoedipal determinants of an infantile neurosis. In McDevitt and Settlage eds., *Separation/Individuation,* pp. 201–226.

McDevitt, John B. and C. Settlage, eds. 1971. *Separation/Individuation: Essays in Honor of Margaret S. Mahler,* pp. 201–226. New York: International Universities Press.

McGowan, Janet. 1981. Private communication.

McGraw, M. B. 1963. *The Neuromuscular Maturation of the Human Infant.* New York: Hafner.

McGuire, M. T. 1979. Stephen Pepper and world hypotheses: Their relevance to psychoanalysis. *Bulletin of the Menninger Clinic* (November), 43(6):525–539.

Mächtlinger, V. 1976. Psychoanalytic theory: pre-oedipal and oedipal phases with special reference to the father. In Lamb, ed., *The Role of the Father in Child Development,* pp. 277–306.

Macoby, E. and C. Jacklin. 1974. *The Psychology of Sex Differences.* Stanford: Stanford University Press.

Macoby, E., T. Newcomb, and E. Hartley, eds. 1958. *Readings in Social Psychology.* 3d ed. New York: Holt, Rinehart and Winston.

Mahler, Margaret S. 1965. On the significance of the normal separation-individuation phase: with reference to research in symbiotic child psychosis. In M. Schur, ed., *Drives, Affects, Behavior,* pp. 161–169, New York: International Universities Press.

—— 1966. Notes on the development of basic moods: the depressive affect. In R. Loewenstein, et al., eds., *Psychoanalysis: A General Psychology*, pp. 152–168. New York: International Universities Press.

—— 1971. A study of the separation-individuation process and its possible application to borderline phenomena in the psychoanalytic situation. In Solnit et al., eds., *The Psychoanalytic Study of the Child*, 26:403–424.

—— 1972. Rapprochement subphase of the separation-individuation process. *Psychoanalytic Quarterly*, 41:487–496.

—— 1973. Discussion of J. Masterson's, R. Stoller's, and C. Socarides' papers on "Early mothering: its relation to later ego and sexual disturbances." Presented to Fourth Annual Margaret S. Mahler Symposium on Child Development, Medical College of Pennsylvania and Philadelphia Psychoanalytic Institute. In Kramer, a discussion of paper by John A. Sours on the anorexia nervosa syndrome, p. 577.

—— 1975. On the current status of the infantile neurosis. In Blum, The prototype of preoedipal reconstruction, p. 578.

Mahler, Margaret S. and M. Furer. 1966. Development of symbiosis, symbiotic psychosis and the nature of separation anxiety. *International Journal of Psychoanalysis*, 47:559–560.

—— 1968. *On Human Symbiosis and the Vicissitudes of Individuation*. New York: International Universities Press.

Mahler, Margaret S. and B. Gosliner. 1955. On symbiotic child psychosis: genetic, dynamic and restitutive aspects. In Eissler et al., eds., *The Psychoanalytic Study of the Child*, 10:195–211.

Mahler, Margaret S., F. Pine, and A. Bergman. 1975. *The Psychological Birth of the Human Infant*. New York: Basic Books.

Maratos, Olga. 1973. What do babies know? *Time* (August 15), p. 55.

Martin, Carol L. and Charles S. Halverson. 1983. The effects of sex-typing schemas on young children's memories. *Childhood Development*. 54(3):563–574.

Martinez, Gilbert A. and John P. Nalezienski. 1979. The recent trend in breast-feeding. In *Pediatrics*, (November), 64(5):686–692.

Masserman, J. H. 1941. Psycho-dynamics in anorexia nervosa and neurotic vomiting. *Psychoanalytical Quarterly*, 10(2):211–242.

Masters, W. M. and V. E. Johnson. 1966. *Human Sexual Response*. Boston: Little, Brown.

Masterson, J. F. 1975. *Psychotherapy of the Borderline Adult: A Developmental Approach*. New York: Brunner/Mazel.

—— 1977. Primary anorexia in the borderline adolescent—an object relations view. In P. A. Hartocollis, ed., *Borderline Personality Disorders*, pp. 475–494. New York: International Universities Press.

—— 1980. *From Borderline Adolescent to Functioning Adult: The Test of Time (A Follow-up Report of Psychoanalytic Psychotherapy of the Borderline Adolescent and Family)*. New York: Brunner/Mazel.

Maudsley, Henry. 1867. *The Physiology and Pathology of the Mind*. New York: Appleton.

Mead, Margaret. 1949. *Male and Female*. New York: Morrow.

Meicler, Muriel and G. Gratch. 1980. Texas Children's Hospital, Houston. *Infant Behavior and Development*, (July), 3(3):265–282.

Melges. F. T. 1982. *Time and the Inner Future*. New York: Wiley.

Meltzoff, Andrew and M. Keith Moore. 1983. Cited in What do babies know. *Time*, August 15, 1983, pp. 52–59.

Metcalf, D. R. 1979. Organizers of the psyche and EEG development: birth through adolescence. In Noshpitz et al., eds., *Basic Handbook of Child Psychiatry*, 1:63–71.

Miller, Jean B., ed. 1973. *Psychoanalysis and Women*. Baltimore: Pelican.

Milner, Marion. 1944. A suicidal symptom in a child of three. *International Journal of Psychoanalysis*, 25:53–61.

Minuchin, S. 1974. *Families and Family Therapy*. Cambridge: Harvard University Press.

Minuchin, S. and B. Rosman. 1980. Cited in Anorexia nervosa studied at several centers. U.S. Department of Health and Human Services, Public Health Service, National Institute of Health. *Research Resources Reporter* (May), no. 5.

Mogul, S. Louis. 1980. Asceticism in anorexics and anorexia nervosa. In Solnit et al., eds., *The Psychoanalytic Study of the Child*, 35:155–175.

Money, John. 1970. Matched pairs of hermaphrodites: behavioral biology of sexual differentiation from chromosomes to gender identity. *Engineering Science*, 33:32–39.

—— 1975. *Hormonal Correlates of Behavior*. Basil E. Eleftherion and Richard Spratt, eds. New York: Plenum.

Money, John and Anka A. Ehrhardt. 1965. *Sex Research: New Developments*. New York: Holt, Rinehart and Winston.

—— 1972. *Man and Woman, Boy and Girl: The Differentiation and Dimorphism of Gender Identity from Conception to Maturity*. Baltimore: Johns Hopkins University Press.

Money, John and J. Hampson. 1955. Hermaphroditism: recommendations concerning assignment of sex, change of sex and psychologic management. *Bulletin of Johns Hopkins Hospital*, 97:284–300. In Thomas et al., The search for sexual identity in a case of constitutional precocity, pp. 636–662.

Money, John and Charles Ogunro. 1974. Behavioral sexology: ten cases of genetic male intersexuality with impaired prenatal and pubertal androgenization. *Archives of Sexual Behavior*, 3(3):181–208.

Morton, Richard. 1694. *Phthisiologia—or a Treatise of Consumptions*. London: Smith and Walford.

Muller, Josine. 1932. The problem of the libidinal genital phase in girls. *International Journal of Psychoanalysis*, 13:361–414.

Nagera, H. 1966. Early childhood disturbances, the infantile neurosis, and the adulthood disturbances: Problems of a developmental psychoanalytical psychology. In Eissler et al., eds., *The Psychoanalytic Study of the Child*, 21:393–447.

Newman, Leslie. 1967. Private communication.

Noshpitz, J. D., J. D. Call, R. L. Cohen, and I. N. Berlin, eds. 1979. *Basic Handbook of Child Psychiatry.* New York: Basic Books.

Novey, S. 1959. The meaning of the concept of the mental representation of objects. *Psychoanalytical Quarterly,* 27:57–79.

—— 1961. Further considerations of affect theory in psychoanalysis. *International Journal of Psychoanalysis,* 42:21–31.

Noy, Pinchas. 1979. Analytic theory of cognitive development. In Solnit et al., eds., *Psychoanalytic Study of the Child,* 34:169–216.

Nunberg, H. 1930. *Practice and Theory of Psychoanalysis,* New York: International Universities Press, 1960.

Ovesy, L. 1932. *Principles of Psychoanalysis.* New York: International Universities Press, 1955.

Palazzoli, Mara Selvini. 1974, 1978. *Self-Starvation: from Individual to Family Therapy in the Treatment of Anorexia Nervosa.* New York and London: Jason Aronson.

Palozzoli, Silvana. 1980. Quoted in J. A. Sours, *Starving to Death in a Sea of Objects,* p. 216. New York: Jason Aronson.

Parens, Henri. 1973. Discussion of R. J. Stoller's "Symbiosis anxiety and the development of masculinity." Presented at the Fourth Margaret S. Mahler Symposium, May, Philadelphia. In Blum, ed., *Female Psychology,* pp. 104–105.

—— 1979. Developmental considerations of ambivalence: Part 2 of an exploration of the relations of instinctual drives and the symbiosis-separation-individuation process. In Solnit et al., eds., *The Psychoanalytic Study of the Child,* 34:365–420.

Parens, Henri and Rachel A. Parens. 1979. *The Development of Aggression in Early Childhood.* New York: Jason Aronson.

Parens, Henri, L. Pollock, J. Stearn, and S. Kramer. 1976. On the girl's entry into the Oedipus complex. *Journal of the American Psychoanalytical Association,* 24(5)(supp.):79–107.

Parke, R. D. and D. B. Sawin. 1977. Fathers and children. *Psychology Today* (November), pp. 109–112.

Pauly, I. 1965. Male psychosexual inversion: transsexualism. *Archives of General Psychiatry,* 13:172–181.

Pedersen, Frank A., ed. 1980. *The Father–Infant Relationship: Observational Studies in the Family Setting.* New York: Praeger.

Person, Ethel and Lionel Ovesy. 1974. The transsexual syndrome in males. 1. Primary transsexualism. *American Journal of Psychotherapy,* 28(1):4–20. In *Bulletin of the Menninger Clinic,* 1980, 44(1):32–34.

—— 1983. Psychoanalytic theories of gender identity. *Journal of The American Academy of Psychoanalysis,* 11(2):203–226.

Peto. 1961. The fragmentizing function of the ego. *International Journal of Psychoanalysis,* 42:238–245.

Petrie, Asenath S. 1967. *Individuality in Pain and Suffering.* Chicago: University of Chicago Press.

Piaget, Jean. 1946. *Le développement de la notion de temps chez l'enfant.* Paris: Presses Universitaires de France. In *Child Psychology and Psychiatry* (1960),

1(3):179–190. In K. Lovell and A. Slater, "The growth of the concept of time: a comparative study."

—— 1948. *The Child's Conception of Space.* London: Routledge and Kegan Paul, 1956.

—— 1952a. *The Origins of Intelligence in Children.* New York: Norton.

—— 1952b. *Play, Dreams, and Imitation in Childhood.* New York: Norton.

—— 1954. *The Construction of Reality in the Child.* New York: Basic Books.

Pine, F. and A. Bergman. 1975. Emergence of the Oedipus complex. In Parens and Parens, *The Development of Aggression in Early Childhood*, pp. 324–326.

Porta, Simone. 1874. Quoted in Palazzoli, *Self-Starvation*, p. 5.

Powers, Joanne. 1981. Private communication.

Price, Rosalie. 1984. Private communication.

Primrose, E. J. R. 1962. Psychological illness. *Mind and Medicine.* Monograph 3. Springfield, Ill.: Charles Thomas.

Provence, S. 1966. Some aspects of early ego development: data from a longitudinal study. In R. M. Loewenstein, et al., eds., *Psychoanalysis: A General Psychology*, pp. 107–122. New York: International Universities Press.

Pruett, Kyle D. 1983. Infants of primary nurturing fathers. In Solnit and Eissler, eds., *The Psychoanalytic Study of the Child*, 38:273.

Radford, R. 1969. A case of anorexia in a three-year-old girl. *Journal of Child Psychotherapy*, 2:67–81.

Rado, W. 1933. Fear of castration in women. *Psychoanalytical Quarterly*, 2:425–475.

Rahman, L., H. B. Richardson and E. S. Ripley. 1939. Anorexia nervosa with psychiatric observations. *Psychosomatic Medicine*, 1:335. In Lorand, Anorexia nervosa, pp. 282–292.

Risen, Stephen E. 1982. Analysis of a case of anorexia nervosa. In Solnit and Eissler, eds., *The Psychoanalytic Study of the Child*, 37:433–460.

Roazen, Paul. 1973. *Sigmund Freud.* New York: Prentice-Hall.

—— 1975. *Freud and His Followers.* New York: New American Library.

Robertiello, R. Penis envy. *Psychotherapy: Theory, Research, and Practice*, 7(4):204–205.

Roiphe, H. 1968. On an early genital phase: with an addendum on genesis. In Solnit et al., eds., *The Psychoanalytic Study of the Child*, 23:348–365.

—— 1972. Early genital activity and the castration complex. *Psychoanalytical Quarterly*, 41:334–347.

—— 1979a. Outlines of pre-oedipal sexual development. In E. Kaftal, ed., *Issues in Ego Psychology*, pp. 16–21. New York: Washington Square Institute for Psychotherapy and Mental Health.

—— 1979b. Theoretical overview of preoedipal development during the first four years of life. In Noshpitz et al., eds., *Basic Handbook of Child Psychiatry*, pp. 118–127.

Rosenthal, P. 1982. Some toddlers' "accidents" are really suicidal. *Medical World News* (July 19), pp. 34–35.

Ross, Jack L. 1977. Anorexia nervosa: an overview. *Bulletin of the Menninger Clinic* (September), 41(5):418–436.

Rovee-Collier, Carolyn K. et al. 1980. Reactivation of infant memory. *Science* (June 6), 208:1159–1161.

Ruitenbeck, H. 1973. *Freud as We Knew Him*. Detroit: Wayne State University Press.

Rosenfeld, S. K. and M. P. Sprince. 1963. An attempt to formulate the meaning of the concept "borderline." In Eissler et al., eds., *The Psychoanalytic Study of the Child*, 18:603–635.

Rutter, M. 1970. Normal psychosexual development. Paper presented at the British Psychological Society Meeting, November 6, Leeds.

Sachs, L. J. 1962. A case of castration anxiety beginning at eighteen months. *Journal of the American Psychoanalytical Association*, 28(4):805–827.

—— 1977. Two cases of oedipal conflict beginning at 18 months. *International Journal of Psychoanalysis*, 58:57–66.

Sanday, Peggy Reeves. 1973. Toward a theory of the status of women. *American Anthropologist*, 75:1682–1700.

—— 1981. *Female Power and Male Dominance: On the Origins of Sexual Inequality*. Cambridge: Cambridge University Press.

Sandler, J. 1975. Sexual fantasies in childhood. *The Psychoanalytic Study of the Child*, Monograph series no. 5: *Studies in Child Psychoanalysis: Pure and Applied*. New Haven: Yale University Press.

Sandler, J. and C. Dare. 1970. The psychoanalytic concept of orality. *Journal of Psychosomatics Research*, 14:221–222.

Sandler, J., A. Holder and D. Meers. 1963. The ego ideal and the ideal self. In Eissler et al., eds., *The Psychoanalytic Study of the Child*, 18:139–158.

Sandler, J. and W. Joffe. 1969. Towards a basic psychoanalytic model. *International Journal of Psychoanalysis*, 50:79–90.

Sandler, J. and H. Nagera. 1963. Aspects of the metapsychology of fantasy. In Eissler et al., eds., *The Psychoanalytic Study of the Child*, 18:159–194.

Saretsky, L., G. D. Goldman, and D. S. Milman, eds. 1979. *Integrating Ego Psychology and Object Relations Theory*. Dubuque, Iowa: Kendall/Hunt.

Satow, Roberta. 1983. A severe case of penis envy: the convergence of cultural and individual intra-psychic factors. *Journal of the American Academy of Psychoanalysis*, 11:4.

Saul, Leon J. 1947. Some observations on a form of projection. *Psychoanalytical Quarterly*, 16:476.

Schafer, R. 1968. *Aspects of Internalization*. New York: International Universities Press.

Schaffer, H. and P. Emerson. 1964. The development of social attachments in infancy. *Monographs in Social Research on Child Development*. 29(3):94.

Schimek, J. G. 1975. The interpretation of the past; childhood trauma, psychic reality and historical truth. *Journal of the American Psychoanalytical Association*, 23(4):845–866.

Schmideberg, M. 1950. Infant memories and constructions. *Psychoanalytical Quarterly*, 19:468–481.

Seavey, Carol A., Phyllis A. Katz, and Sue Rosenberg Zalk. 1975. Baby X: the effect of gender labels on adult responses to infants. *Sex Roles*, 1(2):103–109.

Seton, P. H. 1974. The psychotemporal adaptation of late adolescence. *Journal of the American Psychoanalytical Association*, 60:243–251.

Settlage, C. F. 1972. Cultural values and the super-ego in late adolescence. In Eissler, ed. *Psychoanalytical Study of the Child*, 27:74–92.

Shainess, N. 1979. From anorexia to obesity. *American Journal of Psychoanalysis*, 39(3):225–234.

Sheridan, M. 1960. *The Developmental Progress of Infants and Young Children*. London: Her Majesty's Stationery Office.

Shneidman, Edwin S. 1976. *Suicidology*. New York: Grune.

—— 1982. The suicidal logic of Cesare Pavese. *Journal of the American Academy of Psychoanalysis*, 10:547–563.

Simmonds, M. 1914. Über embolische Prozesse in der Hypophysis. *Archives of Pathological Anatomy*, 217:226–339.

Sirota, Milton. 1969. Urine or you're in: an ambiguous word and its relation to a toilet phobia in a two-year-old. In Eissler et al., eds. *Psychoanalytic Study of the Child*, 24:252–270.

Socarides, C. W. 1959. Meaning and content of a pedophiliac perversion. *Journal of the American Psychoanalytical Association*, 7:84–94.

—— 1968. A provisional theory of etiology in male homosexuality; a case of original origin. *International Journal of Psychoanalysis*, 49:27–37.

—— 1973. Sexual perversion and the fear of engulfment. *International Journal of Psychoanalytic Psychotherapy*, 2:432–447.

Solnit, Albert and Ruth Eissler. 1983. *The Psychoanalytic Study of the Child*, vol. 38. New Haven: Yale University Press.

Solnit, Albert et al., eds. 1978–1982. *The Psychoanalytic Study of the Child*, vols. 33–37. New Haven: Yale University Press.

Solomon, R. L. 1980. The opponent-process theory of acquired motivation. *The American Psychologist*, 35:8, 691–712.

Sours, J. A. 1968. Clinical studies in anorexia nervosa syndrome. *New York Medical Journal*, 68:1963.

—— 1974. The anorexia nervosa syndrome. *International Journal of Psychoanalysis*, 35(4):567–576.

—— 1980a. Lines of maturation and development through the phallic-oedipal years of childhood. In J. Bemporad, ed., *Child Development in Normality and Psychopathology*, pp. 121–145. New York: Brunner/Mazel.

—— 1980b. *Starving to Death in a Sea of Objects*. New York: Jason Aronson.

Spence, Donald P. 1982. *Narrative Truth and Historical Truth*. New York: Norton.

Spitz, R. A. 1955. The primal cavity. In Eissler et al., eds., *The Psychoanalytic Study of the Child*, 10:215–240.

—— 1959. *A Genetic Field of Ego Formation*. New York: International Universities Press.

Stechler, G. and S. Kaplan. 1980. The development of the self: A psychoanalytic perspective. In Solnit et al., eds., *The Psychoanalytic Study of the Child*, 35:85–106.

Stekel, W. 1926. *Frigidity in Woman in Relation to Her Love Life*. New York: Liveright.

Sternschein, I. 1973. The experience of separation-individuation in infancy and its reverberations through the course of life: maturity, senescence, and sociological implications. *Journal of the American Psychoanalytical Association*, 21:633–645.

Stewart, J. M. 1981. The Second Dyad. *Smith College Studies in Social Work.* 1(3):149–161.

Stoller, R. J. 1964. Quoted by Ralph Greenson in Disidentifying from mother: its special importance for the boy. *International Journal of Psychoanalysis* (1968), 49:370.

—— 1968a. The sense of femaleness. *Psychoanalytic Quarterly*, 37:42–55.

—— 1968b. *Sex and Gender.* Vol. 1. New York: Science House.

—— 1975. Overview: The impact of new advances in sex research of psychoanalytic theory. *American Journal of Psychiatry*, 130:241–251.

—— 1976. Gender identity. In B. J. Sadock, H. I. Kaplan, and A. M. Freedman, eds., *The Sexual Experience.* Baltimore: Williams and Wilkins.

—— 1979. *Sexual Excitement: Dynamics of Erotic Life.* New York: Pantheon.

Stone, M. S. 1980. Traditional psychoanalytic characterology re-examined in the light of constitutional and cognitive differences between the sexes. *Journal of the American Academy of Psychoanalysis*, 8(3):381–402.

Storey, R. 1976. Anorexia and mimicry. *Psychiatry*, 39:176–188.

Stroufe, L. A. and E. Waters. 1977. Attachment as an organizational construct. *Child Development*, 48:1184–1199.

Sullivan, H. S. 1953. *The Interpersonal Theory of Psychiatry.* New York: Norton.

Sylvester, Emmy. 1945. Analysis of psychogenic anorexia and vomiting in a four-year-old child. In Eissler et al., eds., *Psychoanalytic Study of the Child*, 1:167–186.

Tabin, Geoffrey. 1981. Private communication.

Tennov, D. 1979. *Love and Limerence: The Experience of Being in Love.* New York: Stein and Day.

Terence. 1968. Heauton Timoroumenos (The self-torturer). Cited in *Bartlett's Book of Familiar Quotations.* Boston: Little, Brown.

Thomä, Helmut, 1961, 1967. *Anorexia Nervosa.* Stuttgart: Klett, 1961. English translation by Gillian Brundome. New York: International Universities Press, 1967.

Thomas A. and S. Chess. 1980. *The Dynamics of Psychological Development.* New York: Brunner/Mazel.

Thomas, Ruth (in collaboration with Lydia Folkart and Elizabeth Model). 1963. The search for sexual identity in a case of constitutional precocity. In Eissler et al., eds., *Psychoanalytic Study of the Child*, 18:636–662.

Tollison, C. David and Henry E. Adams. 1979. *Sexual Disorders: Treatment, Theory, Research.* New York: Gardner Press.

Tollison, C. D., Henry E. Adams and J. W. Tollison. 1977. Physiological measurement of sexual arousal in homosexual, bisexual, males. Quoted in Tollison and Adams, *Sexual Disorders*, p. 44.

Torgersen, A. M. and E. Kringlen. 1979. Genetic aspects of temperamental differences in infants. In S. Chess and A. Thomas, eds., *Annual Progress in Child*

Psychiatry and Child Development, pp. 251–263. New York: Brunner/ Mazel.

Torok, M. 1970. The significance of penis envy in women. In J. Chasseguet-Smirgel, ed., *Female Sexuality: New Psychoanalytic Views*, pp. 135–170. Ann Arbor: University of Michigan Press.

Viderman, S. 1970. *La Construction de l'espace analystique*. Paris: Denoel.

Viederman, M. 1979. Panel reports, Monica: a 25-year longitudinal study of the consequences of trauma in infancy. *Journal of the American Psychoanalytical Association*, 27:107–126.

Vigersky, R. ed. 1977. *Anorexia Nervosa*. New York: Raven Press.

Waller, J. V., M. R. Kaufman and F. Deutsch. 1940. Anorexia nervosa: a psychosomatic entity. *Psychosomatic Medicine*, 2(1):3–16.

Warner, Silas L. 1983. Can psychoanalytic treatment change dreams? *Journal of the American Academy of Psychoanalysis*, 11(2):299–316.

Waters, E. and L. A. Stroufe. 1977. Attachment as an organizational construct. *Child Development*, 48:1184–1199.

Watts, A. F. 1948. *Language and Mental Development of Children*. Washington, D.C.: Heath.

Weil, W. B., Jr. 1977. Current controversies in childhood obesity. *Journal of Pediatrics*, 91:175–187.

Weissman, P. 1967. Theoretical consideration of ego regression and ego functions in creativity. *Psychoanalytical Quarterly*, 35:37–50.

White, Burton L. 1975. *The First Three Years of Life*. Englewood Cliffs, N.J.: Prentice-Hall.

White, Robert. 1959. Motivation reconsidered—the concept of competence. *Psychological Review*, 66:297–333.

Whiting, Beatrice. 1965. Sex identity conflict and physical violence: a comparative study. *American Anthropologist*, 67(6):part 2, pp. 123–140.

Whiting, Beatrice and John W. M. Whiting. 1975. *Children of Six Cultures: A Psycho-Cultural Analysis*. Cambridge: Harvard University Press.

Whiting, John W. M., Richard Kluckhohn and Albert Anthony. 1958. The function of male initiation ceremonies at puberty. In Macoby, Newcomb, and Hartley, eds., *Readings in Social Psychology*, pp. 359–370.

Wiener, J. M. 1976. Identical male twins discordant for anorexia nervosa. *Journal of the American Academy of Child Psychiatry*, 15:523–534.

Winick, M., ed. 1975. *Childhood Obesity*. New York: Wiley.

Winnicott, D. 1958. *Collected Papers: Through Pediatrics to Psychoanalysis*. New York: Basic Books.

—— 1965. *The Maturational Process and the Facilitating Environment*. New York: International Universities Press.

Wolff, P. H. 1959. Observations on newborn infants. *Psychosomatic Medicine*, 21:110–118.

—— 1966. *The Causes, Controls, and Organization of Behavior in the Neonate*. Psychological Issues Monograph, no. 17. New York: International Universities Press.

———— 1969. The natural history of crying and other vocalizations in early infancy. In Brian M. Foss, ed., *Determinants of Infant Behavior*, 4:81–109. London: Methuen.

Yamamoto, J. and M. Igo. 1975. Japanese suicide: Yasunari Kawabata and Yukio Mishima. *Journal of the American Academy of Psychoanalysis*, 3:179–186.

Name Index

Subject Index

Language (*Continued*)
and, 33; imagistic thought and, 284–85;
secrecy and, 30; self-awareness and, 29;
sense of time and, 31; thought/feeling di-
chotomy and development of, 35
Liliana, 250–52
Lilly, 112–13
Locomotor maturation, 24
Longitudinal development, oedipal develop-
ment and, 8
Lorand's anorexic patient, 211–12, 234, 239
Lynn, 68–69, 179

Male patterns, fear of engulfment and, 302;
war and, 325
Malnutrition, anorexia and, 190
Mama's boys, 82, 301–2
Marianne, 62–63
Marie, 193, 199
Marvin, 126–27
Mary, 229
Masochism, sexual in males, 90–91, 133
Masturbation, 37, 90–91, 103–4, 114
Maternal engulfment, boy's sexuality and
fear of, 82–84
Maturational factors, primary oedipal com-
plex and, 24
Memory: contextual cueing of, 52; emotions
and, 52; evocative, 13; recognition, 13
Memory complex, xv
Mishima, 84–86
Monroe, 174–77
Multigenerational lockstep, 147

Name, ego effects of, 318
Narcissistic injury, 318
Nascent ego, 283–84, 315
Nature/nurture, 290
Negativism, self-defining use of, 90
Neonates, reaction of, 291
Nonself, self and, 14

Obesity, 230, 236
Object constancy, 14; movement patterns
and, 72
Object permanence, 13
Object recognition, movement/position by,
316
Object relations theory, 283
Obsessional behavior, language develop-
ment and, 34

Oedipal development, longitudinal development and, 8
Oedipal feelings: guilt and, 28; shame and,
28
Oedipal stage: child's perspective in, 157;
general definition of, 156
Oedipal stages: all/none dichotomy and,
170; annihilation/omnipresence dichotomy and, 169; compared, 179–80; degree
of ego organization and, 168; ego boundaries and, 169; ego development in each,
162–66; fantasy, characteristics of, 165–66;
generationality, 165; gender identity and,
168; identification patterns and, 168–69;
oral/anal elements and, 166; parental relationships and, 171–72; periodicity of occurrence, 165, 287–88; power struggle
and, 170–71; resolutions compared,
172–73; secrecy of thought and, 169; similarities between, 157–59; space-time and,
169; superego development and, 168; time
sense and, 165, 167; transition between,
176–77
Oedipus complex, significance of non-ap-
pearance of, 4
Opponent processing, 316
Oral/anal elements, oedipal stages of, 166
Oral dependency, 281
Orality, anorexia and, 191–92; fantasies and
incorporation of penis, 227
Oral/perceptual competence, 22–23
Oral phase, identification during, 73–74
Others, sense of, 14

Pam, 145–48, 155
Pars pro toto symbolization, 28
Pars pro toto thinking, 318; primary oedipal
complex and, 55
Part-object fantasy, primary oedipal complex
and, 56
Part-object identification, body image and,
98
Passivity, development of, 24; feminine,
76–76
Patty, xviii–xix, 53, 70–71, 250
Paul, 270–72
Peggy, 113, 190
Penis: active use of, 99; anorexia and oral
incorporation fantasy of, 226; an-
thropomorphizing of, 98; boy's autonomy

and possession of, 118; oral incorporation fantasies, 227; oral-incorporative impulses of girl toward, 123

Penis envy, 108–9; 114, 307, 318, 321; anal component in, 111; cultural factors in, 43; ego formation and, 43; oedipal feelings and, 41; separation-individuation and, 42

Periodicity, ego development and, 287; personality development and, 160

Personal change, 27; genderless babyhood and, 28

Personality strength, anality and, 23

Phallic mother, 307

Phallic-oedipal, 322

Phallic phase, 161–63, 288

Philip, 133–41; primary oedipal complex in, 137

Power struggle, oedipal stages and, 170–71

Prelinguistic thought, 28; fantasies and, 57

Preoedipal factors, ego organization and, 12

Pre-self, 160–61

Primal scene, 141; ego formation and, 44; fantasy of, 141, 322

Primary feminine identification, 135

Primary femininity, 3, 40

Primary masculinity, 40–41

Primary oedipal complex, 128, 281, 315; anal issues and, 23; boy of, 81; castration anxiety and, 43; components of, 52; ego fragmentation and, 54; extent of pathology and, 53–54; ego organization and 24; gender identity and, 45; girl of, 67–68; instability of, 61–62; maturational factors and, 24; memory theory and, 53; penis envy and, 43; sadomasochism and, 90–91; suicidal dynamics in males and, 83–86; suicidal impulses in human female and, 69–70; transference and, 8

Primary oedipal conflict, 280; anality and, 82; cognitive development and, 106; coquettishness in two-year-old girls, 73; discovery of genital difference and, 19; extent of pathology and, 53–54; fantasies in girl, 67–68; girl and sense of space, 72–73; girl in, 67; resolution of, 172

Primary oedipal pattern, boys, xiv

Primary oedipal phase, 280; anorexia and, 194; definition, xii; early fantasies and, 57; gender identity and, 46–47; incidence of, 132; super-ego formation and, 4

Primary process, 51, 230–31

Prostitute-madonna complex, 92

Prostitution, 92

Psychological challenges at age two, 11

Psychological cueing, parental, 283

Psychopathology, gender and incidence of, 281; hermaphroditism and incidence of, 317

Psychosocial identity, gender identity and, 44

Rachel, case of, 215–24

Reaction-formation, anality and, 26

Reactivity patterns, 290–91

Repression, 280–81; development of, 34; ego oranization and, 35; existence of ego and, 58; language development and, 34; simultaneity of oedipal feelings and self-defining activity, 111–12

Rhythmicity, order and, 23

Ritualistic behavior, language development and, 34

Romantic love, 325

Rose, 54–55

S., case of, 61–62, 162–66

Sadism, anal/sexual fusion and, 89–90

Sadomasochism, 56, 174, 176; fantasy, 257; primary oedipal complex and, 90–91

Sally, 234

Samuel, 44

Scotophilia, 100–1

Secondary process, oedipal stages and, 166

Secrecy, ego-organization and, 169

Self, 315; good/bad dichotomy and sense of, 33; language and sense of, 29; nonself and, 14; sense of, 14; sense of and ego boundaries, 26; sense of and gender identity, 17; sense of in girl, 66

Self-actualization, 27

Self-awareness: simultaneous repression of, with oedipal feelings, 111–12; boy's primary oedipal conflict in, 79; negativism and, 90

Self-concept, language and, 15

Self-definition, social, 21

Self-differentiation, 315

Self-individuation: sexual feelings and, 26; sexuality and, 26

Self-modeling, 280